CHILDREN OF ARMENIA

A Forgotten Genocide and the
Century-Long Struggle for Justice

MICHAEL BOBELIAN

SIMON & SCHUSTER
NEW YORK   LONDON   TORONTO   SYDNEY

SIMON & SCHUSTER
1230 Avenue of the Americas
New York, NY 10020

First Simon & Schuster hardcover edition September 2009

SIMON & SCHUSTER and colophon are registered trademarks of Simon & Schuster, Inc.

For information about special discounts for bulk purchases,
please contact Simon & Schuster Special Sales at
1-866-506-1949 or business@simonandschuster.com

The Simon & Schuster Speakers Bureau can bring authors to
your live event. For more information or to book an event contact the
Simon & Schuster Speakers Bureau at 1-866-248-3049 or
visit our website at www.simonspeakers.com

The author and publishers are grateful for permission to reproduce the following copyright
material: For "Nothing Gold Can Stay" from *The Poetry of Robert Frost* edited by Edward
Connery Lathem. Copyright 1923, 1969 by Henry Holt and Company. Copyright 1951 by
Robert Frost. Reprinted by arrangement with Henry Holt and Company, LLC. For the song
"Ils Sont Tombés" by Charles Aznavour, composed by Georges Garvarentz, and adapted by
Herbert Kretzmer, reprinted with permission of the author. Unless otherwise noted, translations
from the Armenian are those of the author. Every effort has been made to obtain the necessary
permissions with reference to copyright material. We apologize for any omissions in this respect
and will be pleased to make the appropriate acknowledgments in any future editions.

Designed by Kyoko Watanabe

Manufactured in the United States of America

10   9   8   7   6   5   4   3   2   1

Library of Congress Cataloging-in-Publication Data
Bobelian, Michael.
Children of Armenia: a forgotten genocide and the century-long
struggle for justice/Michael Bobelian.
p. cm.
Includes bibliographical references and index.
1. Armenian massacres, 1915–1923. 2. World War, 1914–1918—Atrocities.
3. Armenian massacres survivors. 4. War victims—Armenia.
5. Collective memory—Armenia. 6. Social justice—Armenia. I. Title.
DS195.5.B63 2009
956.6'20154—dc22   2009001217

ISBN 978-1-4165-5726-5
ISBN 978-1-4165-5835-4 (ebook)

To my grandparents Levon and Loosvart
And the nameless others whom history has forgotten
But who still await a reckoning

Contents

CHILDREN OF ARMENIA

Memories

> The struggle of man against power is the struggle of
> memory against forgetting.
>
> —MILAN KUNDERA,
> *The Book of Laughter and Forgetting*

Gourgen Mkrtich Yanikian was too focused on his mission to be concerned with his depleted finances on the morning of January 27, 1973. He owed $2,400 to creditors and was living off welfare checks and loans from friends which amounted to handouts he could never hope to repay with the $12 in his bank account. Yet he decided to forego a regular room and rent a cottage at $37.10 a night to impress his guests, diplomats from the Turkish Consulate in Los Angeles.[1]

Though rage filled his heart, he coolly followed the plan he had mapped out months earlier. After instructing a hotel maid to clean his room and ordering a buffet lunch to be served at noon, he groomed his woolly mustache and put on a white beret and brown tweed overcoat. Yanikian's vitality belied his age. At seventy-seven, he could still intimidate men half his age when standing with his barrel chest out. His hair hung back in an unkempt style, mimicking the students and hippies at the local university he had spent much of his time with since his wife of forty-eight years had slid into unconsciousness. Deeply creased cheeks sagged at the sides of his face. His pitch-black eyebrows rose steadily upward as they approached his temples, sharply contrasting with his silver mane and endowing him with a menacing countenance. His voice, thick, raspy, and muddled by accents from various tongues, could bellow belligerently when his anger rose.[2]

Satisfied with his appearance, Yanikian filled two guns with twelve bullets apiece. His hands barely trembled. Bullets loaded, he placed the blue .25-caliber Browning he had purchased from Ott's hardware store in Santa Barbara inside a dresser drawer. He fit the other semi-automatic, a 9mm Luger pistol, into a hollowed *Who's Who of the West* that he had carved out especially for this occasion—Yanikian appeared on page 880 of the work. His inexperience with the gun, which he had fired twice since purchasing it from an Army veteran twenty-six years earlier, did not concern him.[3]

Five days earlier, knowing that he was unlikely to return home, Yanikian had packed his bags with his life's work—a collection of self-published pamphlets, correspondence, and books—and checked into Cottage No. 3, Room 34 of the Biltmore Hotel. Built in 1927, the Biltmore copied the signature red-tile roofs, wrought-iron grillwork, and cream-colored stucco walls of the Spanish Colonial architecture applied throughout Santa Barbara by civic leaders after an earthquake destroyed most of the city. Carpets of well-groomed grass broken up by copses of palm trees and gardens like the one facing Yanikian's cottage covered its twenty-acre grounds. Two storms during Yanikian's stay had left the resort unseasonably cool. On this day, the temperature reverted to a tepid 64 degrees as the coastal fog that stretched down from Northern California dissipated. Oil deposits from a rig accident that had invaded nearby Butterfly Beach a year earlier were in remission, allowing observers of what locals called the "American Riviera" an unspoiled view of the Santa Ynez mountain range jutting just north of Santa Barbara.

Yanikian had little interest in the scenery, however. He had checked into the hotel for a different purpose. He wanted to avenge his family's loss—his people's loss—for a decades-old crime left unpunished and forgotten by the world.

While Yanikian finalized lunch arrangements with the hotel staff and ensured the guns were hidden in their places, the forty-nine-year-old Turkish consul, Mehmet Baydar, and his assistant, thirty-year-old vice consul Bahadir Demir, drove up to Santa Barbara. That Baydar and Demir were married with children or that neither man was alive at the time of the Genocide mattered little to Yanikian. To him, they were symbols of the enduring injustice committed against the Armenians. When the diplomats approached Room 34 of the Biltmore at 11:30 a.m., Yanikian greeted them with a bow.[4]

Yanikian's birth on March 24, 1895, came at a perilous time for his family. With pogroms taking place throughout the Ottoman Empire, Yanikian's parents took special care to placate the colicky infant in order to avoid the attention of Ottoman soldiers marauding their neighborhood. His family, based in Erzurum, a city on the eastern edge of the Ottoman Empire, managed to escape death when a friend invited them to hide in the Persian Consulate. Yanikian's maternal uncle, who remained behind, died from a gunshot wound.[5]

Eventually, his family moved east to a safer location. Snowstorms made the mountainous journey dangerous, often stranding travelers until the late spring thaw. On the way, the family lost Yanikian in a sledding accident over a mountain pass. His thirteen-year-old brother Hagop, the eldest of four children, found him a few hours later still bundled in a blanket, half frozen. Hagop cuddled his younger brother on his chest to warm him. The rescue formed a special bond between the two boys.[6]

Yanikian's family escaped the slaughter, but other Armenians were not as fortunate. The mass murders initially sparked in 1894 spread to cities inhabited by Armenians throughout the Ottoman Empire. In Urfa (the ancient city of Edessa, once occupied by European crusaders), 3,000 Armenians seeking refuge from the violence were burned alive inside a cathedral. The latest round of persecution was another episode in a long line of repression of the Armenian minority by Ottoman rulers. From the time Yanikian was conceived to his first birthday, 100,000 to 300,000 Armenians perished in a bloodbath described by the *New York Times* as ANOTHER ARMENIAN HOLOCAUST.[7]

Eight years later, Yanikian, his brother Hagop, and his mother Epraksia returned to Erzurum to retrieve gold coins and property documents that they had buried in their barn. This erstwhile wealthy family had spent much of the money that it had taken on its harried

escape, and they were now desperate to retrieve their hidden possessions. While Hagop dug for their box, two Turkish men wearing fezzes
entered the barn. Yanikian and his mother remained hidden in an unlit
portion of the building about fifteen feet away helplessly watching the
men grab hold of Hagop. Hagop looked over to Yanikian, signaling
to him with his eyes not to make a sound. Epraksia placed her hand
tightly around Yanikian's mouth to suffocate his cries. As one man
held Hagop still, the other raised his blade into the air. Before Epraksia
could move her hand to cover Yanikian's eyes, the man slashed Hagop's
throat with one swing. When his brother's body flopped to the floor,
Yanikian bit into the web of his mother's hand between the thumb and
forefinger, leaving his face covered in blood and deforming two of her
fingers. After the men left, Epraksia, still holding Yanikian in her arms,
walked over to Hagop's corpse and kissed him.[8]

As a civil engineering student at the University of Moscow after the
outbreak of World War I, Yanikian heard news of atrocities taking
place against the Armenians throughout 1915. Hundreds of articles
printed in European and American newspapers described a crime for
which mankind had no vocabulary. Almost daily, he read descriptions
of events that made the 1890s massacres of his birth seem tame by comparison: WHOLESALE MASSACRES OF ARMENIANS BY TURKS, screamed one
New York Times headline in 1915.[9]

Eager to find his family, whom he had not heard from since the
outbreak of the war, Yanikian traveled to the Caucasus during the
spring of 1915 to sign up with an Armenian volunteer regiment fighting alongside the Russian army, encamped on the eastern edge of the
Ottoman Empire. Yanikian received little training before going out to
the front. The regiment provided him with a light khaki uniform bearing red, blue, and orange stripes—the historic colors of Armenia—and
a collection of maps. With his educational background in mind, it assigned him to an engineering unit of nine men responsible for scouting
the mountainous topography ahead of the regular troops. The lightly
armed unit carried small Browning pistols and dynamite instead of the
bayonet-tipped rifles used by standard soldiers, and moved at night to
avoid detection.[10]

In May, his regiment pierced the Ottoman border. On the first day in Ottoman territory, with his unit bivouacked by a small river, Yanikian witnessed firsthand the horrors of which he had only heard. Throughout the day, a continuous stream of heads, arms, legs, torsos floated in the water like tree limbs. Famished after a day's march, and with no alternative source of fresh water, his unit had no choice but to drink from the same river. Yanikian was shaken to the core.[11]

Over the next few weeks, the men of Yanikian's unit often traveled on foot, and when they were lucky, on horseback. Everywhere they went, Yanikian saw mutilated bodies, abandoned homes, and destroyed churches. In his hometown, he found his father's business and child-hood home—like the rest of the Armenian quarter—burned down. Water fountains flowed red with blood. Decapitated bodies littered the churchyard where he had spent his Sunday afternoons as a child. Searching through the remains, Yanikian recognized a large mole on the face of a boy whose head had been hacked in two with a hatchet like a watermelon. It was his twelve-year-old nephew, who must have looked old enough to the killing squads to be grouped with the adult men for a quick death.

Next to his nephew lay his brother-in-law's severed head, the large mustache still in place but his body nowhere to be found. Yanikian searched in vain through the mangled corpses for the body so that he could bury the two in the family plot at the local cemetery. A Russian officer told the exasperated Yanikian, "What's the difference, everybody is dead, take a body." The callous remark, likely instigated by the sight of so many corpses from the carnage, did not deter Yanikian. He persisted, and offered to pay for the burial of all the bodies, numbering in the hundreds. Twenty Russian soldiers gathered the bodies onto seven trucks, with Yanikian scanning the remains for his relative's torso. They dumped the bodies in mass graves and set crosses around the site. Yanikian placed his family's remains alongside his grandmother's burial site. They were among the few Armenians to receive a formal funeral.[12]

Twenty-four other members of his extended family rotted in un-marked graves somewhere in the Ottoman Empire, perhaps killed swiftly with a blow from an ax or perhaps the victims of a slow death brought on by pestilence and malnutrition in the desert. In all, the Ot-toman Empire slaughtered 1.5 million Armenians and evicted 500,000 more from lands inhabited for 2,500 years. The tragedy would come to be known as the Armenian Genocide.

After World War I, a groundswell of support for the Armenians inspired one of the world's first ever international human rights movements. Led by the humanitarian-minded Woodrow Wilson, the United States alone sent $116 million (about $1.5 billion in today's dollars) to the "starving Armenians"—a popular term during the 1920s—in what became the nation's inaugural international aid effort. These ministrations did not end with providing food and shelter to hundreds of thousands of refugees and orphans. The war's victors—Britain, France, Italy, and the United States—vowed to prosecute the Ottoman leaders responsible for what they called "crimes against humanity." They entered into a treaty with the Ottoman Empire guaranteeing the Armenians a national state and homeland shielded from further persecution. And they labored to have the Ottomans compensate the Armenians for their losses by returning seized property and restoring destroyed assets.

Except perhaps for the Holocaust, the outpouring of support received by the Armenians surpassed anything undertaken for other victims of genocide in the twentieth century. "Armenia is to be redeemed," Wilson told a crowd in Salt Lake City, "so that at last this great people, struggling through night after night of terror . . . are now given a promise of safety, a promise of justice. . . ."[13]

Despite these noble sentiments, that promise of justice was never delivered. Instead, the world turned its back on the Armenians, allowing the perpetrators to get away with one of the greatest crimes of modern history. The world may have moved on, but the Armenians never forgot. A great crime was committed and they had nothing to show for it, not even an apology from the perpetrators. Nearly a century later, they still longed for justice.

My first encounter with the Genocide took place a few weeks shy of my twelfth birthday, in April 1985. I did not know it at the time, but it was my initiation into an old and bitter contest. Inside an Armenian cathedral in Manhattan, I followed along as everyone's eyes fixed on the procession of seventy survivors walking down the central aisle. A soloist from the choir sang the words of an Armenian prayer in an otherwise silent sanctuary. The incense used in the morning's liturgy still lingered in the air, mixing with the heavy colognes and perfumes worn by parishioners. Holding red carnations, the survivors walked slowly and deliberately toward the front of the cathedral. Our eyes moved along with every step. Left foot. Right foot. Left foot. Right foot. Alongside each of the survivors walked a young man or woman carrying a long white cross. When they reached the front of the altar, each pair planted their cross and placed a carnation at its T-section.

At my young age, the concept of "genocide" was vague. Even the idea of murder seemed difficult to comprehend. Real people were not like the digital characters I insouciantly gunned down in video games. I knew there was something significant, something grave about this occasion. Perhaps it was the seventy survivors. People looked at them with admiration and sympathy. I did not know why—I had no notion of the gravity of the horrors they had lived through—but I could sense that there was something distinctive about them.

After various speeches, I joined other children walking down the central aisle wearing blue T-shirts with a picture of the twin peaks of Mount Ararat. As we stood in front of the altar, the French-Armenian singer Charles Aznavour addressed the crowd. "Don't forget your parents and grandparents," he told me and all the other children. Aznavour, the son of two survivors, had written a song, "Ils Sont Tombés (They Fell)" in honor of the Genocide's victims.

> *They fell that year*
> *They vanished from the earth . . .*
> *And the babies they tended*
> *Left to die, left to cry*
> *All condemned by their birth . . .*
>
> *They fell like leaves*
> *A people in its prime*
> *Simple men kindly men*
> *And not one knew his crime*
> *They became in that hour*

Like the small desert flower
Soon covered by the silent wind
In sand of time . . .

They fell like tears
And never knew what for
In that summer of strife
Of massacres and war
Their only crime was life
Their only guilt was being
The children of Armenia. . . . [14]

After those baby steps in 1985, I did not think much about the Genocide. Occasionally, the gruesome photos of stick figures limping in rags, or skeletons piled atop each other during April 24, the date on which Armenians commemorated the Genocide, made me briefly wonder about the tragedy. As a student, I posted flyers about the Genocide nearly every April, but these moments were also fleeting as college life rarely allowed room for me to dwell on the topic. Yet, when rare open-ended assignments came up, I chose to write about the Genocide's continuing legacy on my generation each time. Looking back, it is clear that something was brewing inside of me.

Nearing thirty, my growing curiosity piqued an investigation into my family's past. I knew my paternal grandparents had been orphaned. And I held on to sketchy memories of my grandfather, Levon, cursing at the Turks. When I interviewed surviving family members, the fragments of information I collected started to form a terrible picture.

My grandfather Levon and his family were ordered to leave their homes in Erzurum in 1915, with little more than bags and carts to carry their essential belongings. On the city's outskirts, after the adult males were separated from the women and children, Levon's father, grandfather, and uncle were all hacked down with axes and machetes. Levon and his older brother joined his mother, aunts, cousins, and an infant brother, Ardavas, who had been born forty days earlier. The group was ordered to march through the desert, cross the Euphrates River, and settle in camps in Urfa. Every day, Levon swallowed a gold nugget to conceal it from the Ottoman soldiers overseeing the deportation. He picked it out of his excrement and repeated the process throughout his journey.

Ardavas died soon after they left Erzurum. Levon's family buried the infant in a makeshift grave. That night, Levon snuck back to find Ardavas's grave and instead found a dog chewing on his baby brother's leg. He scared the dog away and spent the night digging a deeper burial plot with his hands. His mother, aunts, and all but one older brother and one cousin died during the Genocide. In all, my grandfather lost twenty-eight members of his extended family.

Listening to these stories was challenging. Contemplating them was unendurable. While interviewing family members, I tried to soak in their words with the same dispassionate pursuit for information I utilized in every avenue of research. But on two occasions, when I found myself alone, I burst into tears. "*Inchoo?*" (why), I wondered. "*Inchoo?*"

My reaction was not unique. In fact, most descendants of the survivors—even ones several generations removed—carried with them the pain and frustration passed down from their ancestors. And my indoctrination into the heated conflict between Armenians and Turks over the characterization of the events of 1915 was also commonplace. Nearly a century after the Genocide, most Armenians refused to forget the past, and just as many wanted to right the wrong committed against their forefathers.

Uncovering my family's experience did not end my interest in the Genocide, but instead fueled new questions not so much about the tragedy as its aftermath. I had attended Genocide commemorations like the one in 1985 for nearly twenty years, and there seemed to be no end in sight. I started to wonder how this had come about. Why were the Armenians still struggling for justice nearly a century after the Genocide? What would lead a man like Gourgen Yanikian to plot a cold-blooded killing spree more than fifty years after the fact? What happened after the Genocide, and why?

As I dug further, the answer to this mystery spawned a series of new questions that revealed to me that the Armenian experience was unique among the human rights calamities of the past century. With so much widespread support for the Armenians following the Genocide, how did all the promises of justice made by the world's strongest nations fall through? Why did it take the Armenians nearly five decades to resurrect a campaign renewing the call for justice? How could an event as widely acknowledged as the Genocide—the world was better informed of the Armenian Genocide than the Holocaust while the respective crimes were taking place—eventually lapse from the world's consciousness? How could the Turkish government succeed in denying the Genocide? Its history books made no mention of the catastrophe. Its press dismissed the Armenian experience as a hoax. Its scholars accused the Armenians of treachery. It is tough to find a comparison for Turkey's posture. Only a hypothetical will suffice. Fifty years after the Holocaust, if Germany refused to apologize for Nazi crimes, denied any wrongdoing against European Jewry, and even blamed the Jews for their fate—and the rest of the world looked on indifferently as Germany spewed out these lies—then one can begin to understand the predicament Yanikian and the Armenians faced. How could the U.S. government, once the greatest champion of the Armenians after the Genocide, support Turkey's cover-up?

As I began to search for the answers to these questions, I found out that no one had the answers. The search for them confirmed for me that this incredible tale I had begun to explore deserved to be rescued from obscurity.

A note on the usage of the term "Armenia" in this book: Today, Armenia is a landlocked country about the size of Maryland, ensconced among a series of intersecting mountain ranges. To the north lies Georgia; to the east, Azerbaijan; to the south, Iran; and to the west, Turkey. The Armenia I speak of in the title of this book is not just modern-day Armenia, which gained its independence in 1991 upon the collapse of the Soviet Union. Nor is it the broader swath of territory once inhabited by the Armenians stretching from the Caspian to the Mediterranean seas. I speak of a more abstract Armenia not bound by geographic boundaries—the Armenia Charles Aznavour referred to in his song. The Armenia I speak of refers to a way of life encompassing a language with its own unique alphabet, an embrace of Christianity predating all other nations, and a heritage rooted in Anatolia (Asia Minor) and the Caucasus for 2,500 years. It is these Armenian children whom Aznavour honored in his song, and it is to their children that an accounting is owed.

The purpose of this book is neither to prove the existence nor to affirm the veracity of the Genocide. It will become apparent in later chapters that there is a significant amount of scholarship produced by Turkish and, to a smaller extent, American scholars putting forth a completely different version of events. Sometimes, these works disagree with the facts cited here, and oftentimes with my interpretations and conclusions. This book does not serve to refute these claims or argue with these findings. That has already been accomplished by dozens of scholars relying upon voluminous evidence stretching from government archives to eyewitness testimonials accumulated during the past few decades. All of this evidence convinced the International Association of Genocide Scholars in 1997 to unanimously assert that the massacres and deportations begun in 1915 of the Armenian population in the Ottoman Empire constituted genocide under international law.[15] In 2000, Elie Wiesel and 125 other notable Holocaust scholars did the same.[16] These pronouncements reflect the consensus among historians and human rights experts about the veracity of the Genocide. This book relies upon these declarations and, as evidenced by the sources cited in the Notes, often employs the very sources used to arrive at this consensus.

Rather than rehashing old debates, I hope instead to ask and answer a very different set of questions that relate to the Armenian—and the world's—response to the catastrophe in subsequent decades. No other people have suffered such a warped fate—a trivialization of their suffering and a prolonged assault on the authenticity of their experience. And few other people have participated in a global campaign for justice that has stretched across the decades. When I came to fully realize just how twisted this fate was, it led me to a final question at the center of this book: what were the consequences of this almost unprecedented delay in justice?

Though many Armenians carried the same emotional cocktail of hatred and frustration that burned inside Yanikian, most were loath to renew the violence that had already disfigured their lives. Others pursued justice through non-violent means: by building memorials, collecting archival information testifying to the Genocide's veracity, lobbying governments to support the Armenians against Turkey's campaign of denial, and through the courts. Two divergent histories run on parallel tracks in this post-Genocide story—one violent and one political-legal. Both serve as stark reminders of the consequences of justice denied, whenever and wherever it may occur.

The book is also a response to this twisted fate. As a child, I was indoctrinated into the Armenian pursuit of justice. As an adult, I questioned the origins and evolution of this multifaceted struggle. Finally, the mystery that intrigued and befuddled me for years felt closer to resolution as I completed the last pages of this work.

For many years, the fate befalling the Armenians had been referred to as the "forgotten genocide." Ten years ago, few non-Armenians were aware of the Genocide, and even fewer knew more than a handful of details about it. The ensuing decade saw a bevy of books, films, and educational materials that began to chip away at this widespread ignorance. As we approach the one hundredth anniversary of the Genocide, in 2015, even fewer people know about the nearly century-long pursuit of justice embarked upon by Armenians. Few other movements of social justice have spanned so many years and places around the globe. And even fewer have captivated a people through the generations. Yet little is known about this unique tale, packed with dramatic setbacks and advances, and more important, one that offers plenty of lessons on the consequences of failing to bring about justice in response to genocide. For the children of Armenia, neither the passing of the Genocide's survivors nor the passage of more than nine decades has diminished their passion for justice. This book tells the story of this enduring passion and unearths a historical quest for justice with few comparisons in human history.

Death of a Nation

If it should happen that we are unable to endure
This uneven struggle, and drained of our strength
Fallen down, unable to stand again
And if death prevails over the will to live . . . ,
And if this crime ends and the last vengeful Armenian
    eyes close
Without seeing the dawn of victory
Let us vow that when we find God in the afterlife
And He in exchange for our suffering offers His
    untimely sympathy,
We will refuse
And we shall say to Him
"Send us to hell, to hell again
Don't we know it well,
Didn't you make us know it well,
Bestow your heavenly kingdom to the Turk."

          —VAHAN TEKEYAN[1]

Up to now, Turks and Armenians have been living as brothers," Krikor Zohrab, a member of the Ottoman Parliament and a prominent lawyer revered for his eloquent speeches on behalf of his Armenian brethren, wrote to his Ottoman colleagues in April 1915; but the "present situation is very serious and has caused deep concern and despair. . . ." News of mass arrests among the Armenians worried the fifty-three-year-old Constantinople native, who had been a strong advocate for his people through decades of persecution. The latest crackdowns against the Armenians placed his people in danger like at no other time in their history—a danger that would threaten their very existence.

A few weeks later, Zohrab confronted the Ottoman interior minister, Mehmet Talaat. Talaat, though once friendly with the Armenians, was personally responsible for the arrest of scores of Armenian leaders, and was suspected of hatching an even darker plot to rid the empire of the ethnic minority he had now labeled an arch enemy. "Someday you will have to account" for your behavior, Zohrab told him. Talaat was unmoved by the reproach, responding, "Who, pray tell me, is going to ask for this accounting?" Within days of his confrontation with Talaat, Ottoman officials arrested Zohrab and transported him to the interior of the empire far from prying eyes.

At first, Zohrab did not feel imperiled. He was after all a wealthy man and a well-regarded member of Parliament, with connections throughout the government; surely he would soon be back with his beloved family. But as his journey away from home grew longer, and Ottoman authorities remained evasive about his future, Zohrab began to realize the gravity of the danger he was in. He sent word for his friends in the government and foreign diplomats to arrange for his release. Over the next few weeks, as none of his solicitations bore fruit, his pleas became more desperate. "I miss you and our children," Zohrab wrote to his wife when his hopes for emancipation began to fade. "I know not if I will ever see you again." In his last letter, he asked his wife to make a personal appeal to Talaat. Though Zohrab encouraged his wife to remain upbeat, resignation had set in after weeks of captivity. Along with his last letter, he enclosed a handwritten will.

A few days later, on a road not far from Urfa, Zohrab's escort ordered him out of a transport wagon and directed him to a secluded area in the woods. Zohrab grew suspicious of the detour, and when he received a gruff command from his escort, he tried to talk the man out of executing him. "I am unarmed and unable to protect myself. But listen, how will my death benefit you? You have a conscience. How can you forsake your sense of guilt . . . ?" Zohrab's words stirred the escort. For a moment, he thought about setting the acclaimed jurist free. But he had his orders and he was not going to disobey them no matter how sympathetic Zohrab appeared. After a single gunshot to the chest—an execution unaccompanied by any kind of trial—the revered writer and jurist lay dead on the forest floor. Zohrab was not alone; many other Armenian notables of his generation suffered a similar fate. And with the Armenian political leadership out of the way, there was nothing to prevent the six-hundred-year-old Ottoman Empire from eradicating an entire race.[2]

The Ottomans were one of many Turkic tribes pouring in from Central Asia (where the "Stans" stand today) into Asia Minor, starting in the eleventh century. The first Ottoman ruler, Osman, forged a dynasty in the early part of the fourteenth century. In centuries of further expansion, the empire reached its apogee, stretching from its base in Asia Minor to modern-day Algeria, much of the Middle East, and a huge swath of Southeast Europe reaching the outskirts of Vienna during the sixteenth and seventeenth centuries.[3]

The glory days of the Sultanate of Osman did not last. In the face of middling leadership, continual warfare, and growing unease among its many ethnicities clamoring for reform and autonomy, including Greeks, Bulgars, Slavs, Albanians, Armenians, Arabs, Jews, Georgians, Egyptians, and others, the twenty-five Sultans succeeding this glorious epoch of the sixteenth century allowed the empire to fall behind an ascendant Europe. Losing ground both economically and militarily starting in the late seventeenth century, the Ottomans stagnated as Europe, through the transformative progression of the Renaissance, Enlightenment, and the Industrial Revolution, soared.

The empire that had once frightened and awed Europe resented its emasculation as a second-rate power facing constant encroachment into its affairs by outsiders. European creditors, due to the debts incurred by the Ottomans, now controlled the empire's fiscal policy. Judicial and economic privileges, known as "capitulations," originally granted to foreigners on a small scale, became a thorn for the empire as its subject nationalities exploited these privileges to gain exceptions to Ottoman law unavailable to the general populace. The decline in power triggered self-doubt among the empire's Turkish rulers. Having viewed themselves as superior to the peoples they had conquered and governed for centuries, the governing Turks now found themselves at the mercy of foreign powers and pestered by subjugated nationalities demanding equality.[4] By the middle of the nineteenth century, Osman's once mighty empire had been reduced to the "sick man of Europe."

Sultan Abdul Hamid II inherited his throne under these precarious circumstances in 1876. During the next three decades, his poor leadership and despotic treatment of subjects plunged the Ottoman Empire further into turmoil, ultimately leading to his downfall. Hamid reigned in isolation from palatial grounds on the Bosporus from which he almost never left, a place *Time* magazine called the "most glamorous and sinister harem in the Ottoman Empire." The compound included more than 5 million square feet of buildings, gardens, farms, an artificial lake, stables, workshops, a menagerie, a fire brigade, and cemeteries. A gilded decor of paneled walls, Murano glass chandeliers from Venice, thick carpets, and European furnishings decorated the buildings that a French observer dubbed a *macédoine*, a salad of various fruits and vegetables. Innumerable watchtowers dotted the landscape for Hamid's 7,000 guards, who outnumbered the rest of the staff. To further satisfy his paranoia, the redoubt sat behind two high walls blocking the outside world. The Sultan wielded absolute power with insouciance, shooting at those who startled him with a gold pistol. He often called upon fortune-tellers for advice, and when one of them convinced him to drink water only from a specific well, he followed her instructions religiously.[5] Hamid oversaw a dwindling empire wracked by ethnic dissent and continual warfare. Of its few remaining minorities, none troubled the Sultan more than the Armenians.

The history of the Armenians had been one of continuous foreign dominion.

Armenians emerged on the highlands surrounding Mount Ararat during the first millennium B.C. A cycle of independence followed by conquest was repeated during the next two millennia as Armenians often thrived within the footnotes of history. The first great Armenian kingdom, carved out of the two leading empires of the day—Persia and Rome—began under Tigran II in 95 B.C. Twenty-nine years later, Rome overtook the kingdom.[6] The last independent state—known as the Armenian kingdom of Cilicia—based its capital not in the foothills of Mount Ararat but 600 miles away to the southwest near the Mediterranean coast.

Over the years, Armenians scattered throughout Anatolia, the name given by ancient Greeks to what is now Asia Minor, and the Caucasus, establishing significant communities in the Ottoman Empire, Russia, and a smaller enclave in Persia, as well as tiny outposts in other continents. "Armenia," wrote a *National Geographic* correspondent in 1915, "is not a State, not even a geographic unity, but merely a term for the region where the Armenians live."[7]

Anatolia was a diverse land topographically and demographically. Flanked by the Black Sea to the north and the Mediterranean to the west and south, its tubular shape stretched from the western edge on the precipice of Europe to its eastern border with Asia. Portions of the interior were arid yet also gave birth to the Tigris and Euphrates rivers. The eastern frontier adjacent to the Caucasus was a rugged country where mountain ranges intersected each other like city boulevards. Tallest of these was Mount Ararat, a twin-peaked behemoth at the center of an ancient civilization. Unlike most other mountains that tended to have jagged edges of peaks and valleys, Ararat was uncluttered. Instead, the foundation of the mountain existed with one purpose, to support its isolated peaks erected seven miles apart like a king and queen sitting atop their kingdom. As the resting place of Noah's Ark, the mountain attracted many travelers. "Avidly I looked at the Biblical mountain," wrote the Russian poet Alexander Pushkin, "saw the ark moored to its peak with the hope of regeneration of life, saw both the raven and dove, flying forth, the symbols of punishment and reconciliation."[8] The mountain's twin peaks—named *Sis* and *Masis* in Armenian—would come to witness a people's greatest triumphs and tragedies for more than two millennia.

Within this maze of mountain ranges stood a path that connected Asia to Europe, placing these crossroads that constituted historical Armenia at the center of international trade and a hotbed of conquest, what President Warren G. Harding came to call "the gateway between the Occident and the Orient."[9] Over the millennia, lands inhabited by Armenians in the region switched hands between countless empires, some familiar to us today: Persian, Roman, Byzantine, Arab, Russian,

Mongol, and Soviet; others more obscure: Sajid, Safavid, Ilkhanid, Parthian, and Sasanid. Rarely did one power rule over the entire Armenian population. As the conquerors battled on this bridge between eastern and western continents, the frequent invasions resembled a Ping-Pong match, with Armenian borders shifting with each attack and counterattack. From the sixteenth to the seventeenth centuries, the Ottoman and Persian empires fought countless wars on lands largely occupied by Armenians in which the current Armenian capital at the base of Mount Ararat, Yerevan, changed hands at least fourteen times. Despite answering to new rulers and dispersing throughout the region, the Armenians rarely succumbed to assimilation, and instead obdurately maintained their unique language, religion, and heritage with the biblical Ararat as the central symbol of national identity.[10]

After another series of wars climaxed in 1829, the Ottoman, Russian, and Persian empires divided up the lands historically inhabited by the Armenians, with most of them placed under Ottoman rule in the eastern portion of Anatolia. The rest of the population lived further east under Russian rule in the Caucasus and southeast in Persia.[11]

From the fifteenth to the nineteenth century, the relationship between the ruling Ottomans and their Armenian subjects had been largely free of conflict; the Armenians, in fact, were once known as the "loyal community" of the empire. But Ottoman rule turned oppressive during the 1800s when Armenian demands for an end to excessive taxation, second-class citizenship, and protection against unwarranted and oppressive violence from local officials met with increasing resistance.[12] A British diplomat described the plight of the empire's largest non-Muslim minority: "The Armenian population is everywhere oppressed by a system of government which takes from them the means of circulating freely, of earning a livelihood, and of enjoying a feeling of security to life and property. . . . Taxes are levied without mercy. . . . The prisons are filled with innocent men. . . ."[13]

As the maltreatment of the Armenians increased during Hamid's reign (1876–1909), Europe stepped in to help the persecuted minority. The Continent's fascination with the Armenians stemmed from various sources. Europeans perceived the Armenians as Christian captives in a

Muslim-dominated region. Historical and cultural ties to the Roman and Byzantine empires as well as medieval crusaders further bound the two peoples. Lord Byron, a student of Armenian monks based on a Venetian island in the 1810s, encapsulated Europe's affinity for the ancient tribe:

> It would be difficult, perhaps, to find the annals of a nation less stained with crimes than those of the Armenians, whose virtues have been those of peace and their vices those of compulsion. But whatever may have been their destiny—and it has been bitter—whatever it may be in the future their country must ever be one of the most interesting on the globe. . . . If the Scriptures are rightly understood, it was in Armenia that Paradise was placed—Armenia, which has paid as dearly as the descendants of Adam for that fleeting participation of its soil in the happiness of him who was created from its dust. It was in Armenia that the flood first abated, and the dove alighted. But with the disappearance of Paradise itself may be dated almost the unhappiness of the country; for though long a powerful kingdom, it was scarcely ever an independent one, and the satraps of Persia and the pashas of Turkey have alike desolated the region where God created man in his own image.[14]

European efforts to institute reforms on behalf of Armenians (and other non-Muslim subjects of the empire) in 1839 and 1856 and, most notably, through the 1878 Treaty of Berlin following the Russo-Ottoman War, failed as the Ottoman Empire repeatedly agreed to the reforms only to flout them. In one such instance, the Ottoman Parliament and constitution created under pressure from Europe in 1876 granted the empire's various nationalities a forum to voice their concerns. Fourteen Armenians and 125 other non-Turks held seats in the 286-member legislature. Yet Hamid disbanded the legislative body and constitution in 1878 without facing any consequences.[15] The Armenians lost what political clout they had, while the very European powers that had called for the government reorganization stood silently by.

Ultimately, despite genuine concern for the Armenians, the strategic interests of Britain and France handcuffed the implementation of effective reforms. Because both nations saw the Ottoman Empire as a buffer to Russian expansion into Anatolia and the Black Sea straits, they rarely pressed it to carry out suggested reforms. Recognizing his strategic importance to the two powers, Hamid defiantly mocked Anglo-Franco demands. When Europeans asked for the dismissal of an abusive Ottoman official, for instance, Hamid often promoted the offender to a higher office.[16]

Europe's inability to rein in Ottoman excesses against its minorities fueled Armenian frustrations. Fed up with extortionist taxes and the refusal of the government to punish those raping and abducting their women, Armenians in the remote mountain enclave of Sasun repelled local officials in 1894. The Sultan reacted to this act of defiance by sending in troops to burn down local villages and arbitrarily kill the Armenian population. His action triggered recriminations throughout Europe, which again demanded reforms from the Sultan. As in past instances, the Sultan dismissed these calls for reform. But this time, instead of sitting by passively, Armenian frustrations reached a boiling point. Two thousand Armenian demonstrators in Constantinople protested against the Sultan's brutality in October 1895. Hamid responded in an autocratic manner, ordering a massacre of the demonstrators. Within weeks, a chain reaction of massacres flared up across the empire through the end of 1896.[17]

Desperate to stop these massacres, a group of teenagers and twenty-somethings from the Armenian Revolutionary Federation (ARF), known in Armenian as the *Tashnagtsutiun*, hatched a plan in the summer of 1896 to take over the Ottoman Bank. By capturing the headquarters of Ottoman finances, and threatening to blow up its bullion and people inside, the group planned to force European governments to end the ongoing massacres. In essence, they wanted to use the bank as a hostage for political negotiations. Founded in Tiflis, Georgia (at the time, the city was under Russian rule) in 1890, the ARF was ideologically socialist and influenced by European political ideals. It pushed for reforms within the Ottoman Empire that would grant the Armenians equal rights and protection from the Sultan's persecutions.[18]

Twenty-six operatives showed up at the Ottoman Bank on a hot, clear afternoon in August 1896, armed with guns and dynamite. As they started to fight their way into the building, a bank guard shot their leader dead, compelling a twenty-four-year-old horticulture student named Armen Garo (Karekin Pastermadjian) to take over. The cloud of "smoke and white dust" permeating throughout the neoclassical building slowed down the Armenian advance but also camouflaged them from guards who could not see through the fog. One Armenian, believing he had seen a security guard in the pandemonium of gunfire and explosions, nearly shot Garo. Because few of them had any experience with dynamite, their explosives burst arbitrarily, chopping the callow group into pieces. One man, shot in the foot, dropped a bomb. The blast shredded his arm, leaving only a few tendons and muscles to connect it to his shoulder. Also suffering from chest wounds, the man asked Garo to show him mercy by taking his life. When Garo could not bring himself to kill his comrade, another Armenian had to fire into the wounded man's chest. Despite this confusion, the group took control of the building.[19]

"The time of diplomatic play is passed," the ARF declared during the takeover, referring to multiple failures to assist the Armenians. European diplomats immediately commenced negotiations, and about fourteen hours after the siege had begun, they promised to put a stop to the massacres if Garo's group agreed to end the standoff. The agreement did not hold as Ottoman mobs began to attack Armenians in the capital. The Sultan ordered a new round of reprisals across the empire, leading to the murder of tens of thousands of Armenians through the end of the year.[20]

In all, some 100,000 to 300,000 Armenians perished from 1894 to 1896. These massacres revealed a dangerous attitude emerging within the Ottoman populace toward the Armenians. Envy of Armenian economic achievements and anger at repeated European intervention on their behalf justified the mistreatment of the minority to many. At the time of the massacres, a Turkish soldier wrote a letter to his parents boasting of helping to kill "1,200 Armenians, all of them as food for the dogs." He mentioned that his battalion might soon be stationed near their home: "if so, we will kill all the Armenians there."[21] The legal imprimatur, government endorsement, and social acceptance of the persecution of Armenians encouraged this mind-set, allowing it to flourish and be used to lethal effect by the Genocide's ringleaders twenty years later when thousands of ordinary Ottoman soldiers and citizens participated in mass killings.

. . .

As the Ottoman Empire descended into corruption and ineptitude under Hamid's watch, a group of Turkish intellectuals called the Young Turks began to agitate for constitutional changes and reforms in the late nineteenth century. They were just as unsuccessful as the Armenians in extracting any reforms from the Sultan. Eventually, they marched from Macedonia toward the Ottoman capital to reinstate the constitution discarded by Hamid in the 1870s. The Sultan stepped down from his throne when troops sent to quash the coup refused to fight on his behalf.[22]

The end of Hamid's rule in 1909 ushered in a great deal of hope within the empire. The Young Turks were perceived as progressive modernizers who would reduce corruption, lift the empire from its decayed state, and repair interethnic strife. But they inherited one characteristic from the ousted Sultan that would ultimately prove deadly for the Armenians: a legacy of intolerance toward the empire's ethnic and religious minorities. Despite the veneer of interethnic amity, soon after taking power, the Young Turks did little to stop a massacre in 1909 in which 20,000 Armenians perished.[23] As in Hamid's day, those responsible for the murders went largely unpunished.

A power struggle among the Young Turks in 1913 placed Mehmet Talaat and his inner circle at the helm of the empire. Talaat, who grew up in Thrace in Southeast Europe, took a job as a letter carrier where he learned to operate a telegraph, a skill he exploited during World War I. Through his crucial posting at the central post office in Salonica (a city now in modern-day Greece), he sent information gleaned from the Sultan's confidential correspondence to the Young Turks organizing in Macedonia. His career skyrocketed when he became vice president of the Ottoman Parliament and then minister of the interior, where he established and took control over the Young Turks' political organs throughout the country. The U.S. ambassador to the empire considered the "good-natured but wily giant" smarter than most of his colleagues. Of all the leaders of the Young Turks, Talaat enjoyed the greatest camaraderie with Armenian leaders, as evidenced by Zohrab's letters. He promised to return land illegally seized during the 1890s massacres and visited cemeteries to honor Armenian victims.[24]

• • •

Since Greece's independence in 1832, the Ottoman Empire first under Sultanic and then Young Turk rule had lost nearly all of its holdings outside of Anatolia. The French occupied Algeria in 1830 and Tunisia in 1881. When Britain captured Egypt in 1882 and Italy invaded what is now Libya in 1911, the Ottoman Empire lost all of its African possessions. It also lost Crete, Cyprus, and other islands in the Mediterranean. Its European holdings either seceded or joined other empires. Austria-Hungary annexed Bosnia and Herzegovina in 1908. Bulgaria declared its independence the same year.[25]

In 1912, a coalition of Balkan states—Greece, Bulgaria, Macedonia, Serbia, Montenegro—banded together to strike at the empire, leaving the Ottoman state with a tiny fraction of its European territory. The latest thrashing in the Balkans had a profound impact on the empire. Hundreds of thousands of embittered refugees swamped Anatolia, creating a toxic mix with the local Armenian population. The Balkan debacle also saw Muslims fall victim to massacres at the hands of Christians. A Young Turk official wrote to his wife, "our anger is strengthening: revenge, revenge, revenge; there is no other word."[26]

All of these setbacks convinced the Young Turks that repeated rebellions and agitation for reform by subject nationalities were contributing to the empire's demise. The lack of an overriding ideology or common history among its nationalities posed many challenges to those governing the empire. One observer noted that "The history, customs, religion, relationships, hopes and dreams, manner of thinking, occupational patterns and levels of civilization of the peoples who were Ottoman subjects were so different from one another that it was strange even to imagine them uniting in some compatible way. . . . Is . . . coexistence at all possible?"[27] The Young Turks answered this question with a resounding no. In response to the disjointed composition of the Ottoman state, they hatched a plan relying upon Turkish nationalism to salvage the empire.[28] "'Ottoman,'" the British ambassador wrote to his foreign secretary in explaining this plan, "inevitably means 'Turk' and their present policy of 'Ottomanization' is one of pounding the non-Turkish elements in a Turkish mortar."[29]

The ruling Turks came to see the significant Armenian population in Anatolia—the largest and wealthiest of the empire's remaining minorities—as the biggest threat to their vision. They no longer viewed the Armenians simply as an irritating subgroup clamoring for equality; rather, the Armenians were now perceived as a veritable rival for the last chunks of territory at the heart of the empire. Compared to the loss of Ottoman holdings outside of Anatolia, any degree of Armenian autonomy might mean the loss of the last remnants of the empire.[30] Hamid aptly characterized this mentality: "By taking Greece and Romania [the Great Powers] cut off the feet of the Turkish state. By taking Bulgaria, Serbia and Egypt they cut off our hands. Now by stirring up trouble among the Armenians they are getting to our vital organs. . . . We must defend ourselves at all costs."[31]

As relations between the ruling Turks and the Armenians grew more distrustful, Armen Garo, the student turned ARF leader from the Ottoman Bank takeover who had gone on to serve in the Ottoman Parliament, met with Talaat on June 30, 1914. The two had established a friendship after Garo and other Armenians had initially embraced the reform-minded Young Turks, thinking that they would moderate the Sultan's persecution of the Armenians and modernize the economy. The U.S. ambassador had described the downfall of the Sultan as a "love feast" among the different ethnicities and religions of the empire. The Young Turks, however, eventually turned their backs on this interethnic brotherhood. Garo's meeting with Talaat foreshadowed what was to come. "You know, Garo," Talaat said during their conversation, "it seems to me, as time goes on, we are drifting further apart, and the day may come when we will no longer understand each other's language."[32] It was the last time the men saw each other. Two days before their meeting, an assassin had killed the archduke of Austria-Hungary, plunging the empire into a global war.

An alliance with the Central Powers of Germany and Austria-Hungary at the start of World War I in 1914 pitted the Ottoman Empire against Russia, France, and Great Britain. A few months into the war, an attempted assault into Russia ended disastrously, wiping out an army of 90,000 men. Looking for a scapegoat for the botched offensive, the Ottomans blamed the Armenians. This led to the expulsion and disarmament of Armenian soldiers from a once integrated Ottoman army. At about the same time, the empire's chief cleric declared a jihad sanctioning the murder of Christians. In the past, Britain and France would have lodged complaints against these actions. But as the empire's new enemies, they no longer had any standing. Germany, which had never advocated on behalf of the Armenians, was not about to start now and threaten its new alliance just as a cataclysmic war was underway. All of these events formed a perfect storm. Months into the war, the Armenians were unarmed, isolated from their foreign patrons, and the target of a religious death warrant. Max Erwin von Scheubner-Richter, a German diplomat based in Anatolia, who later became an early inductee of the Nazi Party, reported to his superiors that under this cover of war, the Young Turks had finally found a "solution to the Armenian question."[33]

This "solution," of course, was genocide. Along with Ismail Enver, Dr. Behaeddin Shakir, Jemal Azmi, Dr. Mehmet Nazim, Ahmed Jemal, and others, Interior Minister Talaat masterminded a plan to exterminate the Armenian people.

Dr. Khachig Boghosian, a prominent psychologist and leader of the Armenian community in Constantinople, described in his memoirs what happened on the night of April 23–24, 1915:

> After supper, I went to the house of my neighbour . . . and we passed the time playing backgammon and piano. I left and came home at 1:30 a.m. and went to bed; everything was calm. . . . I had just lain down and was on the verge of falling asleep, when the outside doorbell rang loudly three times. My sister Esther hurriedly went downstairs, opened the door and, after exchanging a few words, rushed upstairs and knocked on my door, telling me that the police wanted me.[34]

Similar scenes played out across the empire over the upcoming weeks as the Young Turks arrested and banished 2,345 Armenian leaders to desolate camps to preclude any organized resistance for the slaughter that would follow. Zohrab was among them. Armenia's leading men, the patriarchs, community leaders, intellectuals, and even artists, were lost for a generation.[35]

Within days, the head of the Armenian Church asked the United States to intervene. Acting under Secretary of State William Jennings Bryan's instructions, the American ambassador to the Ottoman Empire, Henry Morgenthau, Sr., asked the Young Turks to cease their campaign. Having declared its neutrality during the war, the United States could do nothing more than implore the Young Turks. After decades of impunity under Hamid, Ottoman leaders felt neither remorse nor fear of retribution in exterminating the Armenians and they easily dismissed Morgenthau's pleas. Talaat later told the ambassador: "our Armenian policy is absolutely fixed and . . . nothing can change it. We will not have the Armenians anywhere in Anatolia."[36]

Starting in the spring of 1915, Ottoman death squads made up of gendarmes or released prisoners assembled large groups of Armenians in Anatolia and hanged, shot, and killed the vast majority of the adult men. Talaat sent instructions to the far corners of the empire through telegrams—the use of which he had mastered during his stint at the Salonica post office—and dismissed those who disobeyed.[37] With both Armenian leaders and the adult male population neutralized, the gangs faced little resistance in evicting the women, children, and elderly from their homes over the next few months. A historian chronicled the early stages of the Genocide for the British Parliament:

> After the Armenian men had been summoned away to their death, there was usually a few days interval in whatever town it might be, and then the crier was heard again in the streets, bidding all Armenians who remained to prepare themselves for deportation, while placards to the same effect were posted on the walls. This applied . . . to the women and children, and to a poor remnant of the men who, through sickness, infirmity or age, had escaped the fate marked out for their sex.[38]

The carnage proceeded in various forms. Sometimes, the Ottomans killed with bullets. Other times, they used axes, knives, or clubs to bludgeon victims or chop off body parts. In coastal cities and rivers, they drowned Armenians by dumping them into deep waters or forcing those who could not swim into the water. At one point, the number of corpses in the Euphrates clogged the river.[39]

Gendarmes chaperoning the caravans to desert camps on the outskirts of the empire in Syria and Iraq often robbed the Armenians of their valuables and clothing, leaving them to walk barefoot and uncovered through frigid mountain passes and blistering deserts where temperatures reached triple digits.[40] An American missionary in the Ottoman Empire described the plight of the deportees:

> From all over the Turkish domains . . . from every village and town where the Armenians had lived, travelled these wretched herds of persecuted humanity, driven along by their inhuman guards. . . . And as they dragged themselves along, the throngs gradually grew less and less in numbers, and the heaps of rags and bones by the waysides—after the dogs and the vultures had finished their feasts—grew more and more numerous all over the land.[41]

Even the most resilient Armenians had no defense against the random kidnappings, rapes, and murders perpetrated by the Turks and Kurds accompanying them on the deportations. They deprived the Armenians of food, and longer routes to their final destinations allowed disease, exposure, and starvation to knock off the most vulnerable deportees. All sense of dignity vanished as deportees, their faces caked with mud and dirt, their stomachs empty of food or water, and their family members dying by the day, turned bestial, begging for help, searching through feces for food, drinking from urine-infested puddles, sometimes even partaking in cannibalism. The crippled and enfeebled, the young and old, received no mercy. A German engineer observed a woman abandon her newborn twins because she would not be able to keep up with the caravan with them. Other mothers, who could no longer feed their babies, threw them into rivers rather than allow their children to suffer any longer. An American missionary witnessed one Armenian take comfort in burying her infant rather than allowing the child to be dumped in a mass grave.[42] For some, a dignified funeral was the only solace the deportations offered.

Sadists splurged. An Ottoman officer assigned to Der Zor in the

Syrian Desert recorded how soldiers gathered 5,000 Armenians to pile up stacks of wood and thorns. The men were then tied to each other around the stack, encircled by the soldiers, and set on fire. A Swedish missionary hundreds of miles away recalled a similar scene of "heart-rending . . . cries of the people and children who were being burnt to death. . . ." A regional governor earned the title of "horseshoer" for nailing horseshoes on the feet of Armenian victims. Scenes of hacked hands and feet, noses and ears, became omnipresent as sadism ran amok. The unprecedented scale of the rape, torture, and murder left eyewitnesses without words to explain the catastrophe. "In spite of all attempts to identify the horror of murderous lust, rapaciousness, religious hate, thirst for power," wrote the interpreter for Germany's top general, stationed in the empire, "so much remains incomprehensible. . . ."[43]

Many who survived were destined to fates not much better than death. Countless women and girls were sold as concubines or forced into marriage. A provincial governor boasted of selecting the prettiest teenagers as a gift for his fourteen-year-old son. Some women covered themselves in mud to make themselves abhorrent enough to evade lascivious eyes. Others committed suicide rather than succumb to rape—the fierce currents of the Euphrates River offered solace to many. Children were pried from their mothers' arms and given to Muslim families to raise as their own. Armenian mothers often tried to give them away to missionaries or friendly Muslims in the hope that they would survive. One missionary described the scene at a camp near Kharput. "One after another," he wrote, "mothers pressed up to us, holding their little children in their hands. 'Oh take my baby! Take it and save it!' and the emaciated little ones, with their starving eyes, seconded the plea." A survivor recalled his mother's efforts to protect his sisters. She gave his twelve-year-old sister to an Arab woman who offered two loaves of bread in return. A Kurdish man took his nine-year-old sister without offering anything in return. His seventeen-year-old sister was abducted.[44]

A significant percentage of those who survived received help from altruistic Turks and Kurds—a smaller percentage bribed their way to safety. Some escaped death by converting to Islam, either voluntarily or by force. Many Armenians preferred martyrdom, however, over conversion. An American missionary recalled what two boys told their father: "You may turn if you like, but we will go on the road, and die if need be." Holding a Bible in his hand, the father abandoned the life-saving idea.[45]

With few harrowing options available to the deportees, the body count grew precipitously. A *New York Times* headline in September 1915 read: 500,000 ARMENIANS SAID TO HAVE PERISHED. A month later, another headline screamed: 800,000 ARMENIANS COUNTED DESTROYED.[46]

The Genocide's ringleaders took special care to extract as much wealth as possible. The Ottoman Parliament passed laws calling for the confiscation and liquidation of Armenian property. In some instances, Armenians sold off their valuables at a fraction of the cost before leaving. In other instances, Muslims simply moved into the homes left behind by the Armenians. Some Armenians who planned on returning naively left their valuables for safekeeping at banks or with foreigners—ultimately, few ever returned to collect. "The 1,000 Armenian houses are being emptied of furniture by the police," reported the American consul in the coastal city of Trebizond. "There is no attempt at classification and the idea of keeping the property in 'bales under the protection of the government to be returned to the owners . . . ' is simply ridiculous." The Ottomans seized bank accounts, assumed businesses, and ransacked communal properties, including 2,043 churches. One contemporaneous estimate of the looted assets totaled $3.7 billion (about $44 billion in today's dollars). The American consul in Syria described the process as "a gigantic plundering scheme." No stone was left unturned, not even the riches that could be extracted from the deaths themselves. At one point, Talaat asked the American ambassador Henry Morgenthau to hand over lists of Armenians insured by American companies so that the empire could inherit the proceeds of the dead.[47]

In the end, the Ottomans killed as many as 1.5 million Armenians and evicted 500,000 others from lands occupied by their ancestors for 2,500 years. Talaat told Morgenthau before the ambassador left the region: "we have ready disposed of three quarters of the Armenians; there are none at all left in . . . Van and Erzurum." Talaat and the Young Turks were supposed to be an improvement over the deposed Sultan, who died months before the end of World War I. Instead of reforming the rotting empire as many Ottoman subjects had hoped—perhaps none more so than the Armenians—they concocted a plan more diabolical than anything Abdul Hamid could have imagined—a plan that would make the Sultan's bloodbaths pale in comparison. The totality of the Genocide hardly left any traces of the Armenians in areas they had inhabited for millennia. In Van, the prewar Armenian population totaled 197,000; 500 remained in 1922. Erzurum's population dropped from 215,000 to 1,500 during the same time span. "The hatred between the Turks and the Armenians is now so intense," Talaat told Morgenthau, "that we have got to finish with them. If we don't, they will plan their revenge."[48]

He was right. Armen Garo had begun to work on a plan to avenge Talaat and the Young Turk leadership for their crimes.

While Garo was looking to exacting retribution, his ARF colleagues initiated a more ambitious plan of forging a nation from the ashes of the Genocide that would serve the Armenians as a modicum of recompense for so much carnage and guarantee their permanent safety from any more Ottoman butchery.

The Nine-Hundred-Day Republic

The Armenian massacre was the greatest crime of the war, and failure to act against Turkey is to condone it; because the failure to deal radically with the Turkish horror means that all talk of guaranteeing the future peace of the world is mischievous nonsense.

—THEODORE ROOSEVELT

Simon Vratsian's heart must have jumped when he heard the news on November 9, 1917: EXTREMISTS RISE TO POWER IN RUSSIA, screamed the *New York Times* in a typical headline.[1] The possibilities raced through Vratsian's mind. Few Armenians clamored for sovereignty during Ottoman times, but nationalism—a murky, undefined feeling rather than a plan of action—grew stronger as Armenians who had studied in Europe returned to the region with ideas of self-determination.[2] This newfound nationalism had swept many educated young Armenians like Vratsian into a frenzy at the end of the nineteenth century.

Like Armen Garo, Vratsian had dreamed of the day Armenians would be free of the Ottoman yoke. The latest twist in world history frightened him but also opened the window to an opportunity that might fulfill his wildest ambitions: the establishment of an independent Armenian state not seen since the fourteenth century.[3] Dozens of primary and hundreds of secondary figures labored to fulfill this dream.

Few more so than Vratsian, who from the moment of the nation's birth in May 1918 to its demise two and a half years later toiled for that new nation from within, fighting its wars and quelling outbreaks of famine and disease that threatened to destroy the callow country.

Born in Russia in 1882, Vratsian preferred to speak Russian over his mother tongue as a child, and if it was not for his mother's insistence on bringing him up in Armenian surroundings, he may never have found himself at the center of Armenia's revival decades later. "Our bread be cursed," she responded to his father's protests against giving up a profitable enterprise to return to their Armenian village. "It is better to eat the paltry dry bread of our village, to live in hunger if only our children remain Armenian. . . ."[4] Vratsian's inheritance of his mother's passion inspired a life devoted to his people.

Upon joining the ARF (Armenian Revolutionary Federation) at the age of sixteen, Vratsian's prowess as a student activist and organizer propelled him to the upper ranks of the party. The carnage of the 1890s massacres weighed heavily on party thinking at the time, making its primary aim the improvement of conditions for the Armenians within the empire. Before the start of World War I, Vratsian joined the upper echelons of the party. Fluent in four languages, he studied law and pedagogy in St. Petersburg before moving to Boston in 1911 to edit an ARF newspaper. His return to the empire landed him in an Ottoman prison. "It was so dark in the cell," he later wrote, "that you couldn't see your finger even if you stuck it in your eye." He escaped from jail and went on to organize Armenian volunteer units fighting alongside the Russian army during World War I.[5]

The wounds he suffered as a political prisoner paled in comparison to those inflicted by the Genocide. Decades later, he wrote: "Now those dark days are in the past—the distant past, but they are always near. . . . You want to . . . forget, but you do not forget. You want to understand, but you do not understand. You want to be cured, but you are not cured."[6] The massacres and deportations that started in 1915 demonstrated to Vratsian and the remaining Armenian intelligentsia that all the safeguards and reforms endorsed by Europe throughout the nineteenth century amounted to little. He arrived at the conclusion that only one thing could shelter the Armenians from further persecution: the establishment of an independent state shielded from Ottoman tyranny. Launching one required a delicate dance. Decimated, living largely as refugees, bereft of government experience, the Armenians were in no position to administer a state on their own during World War I.[7] Besides, with the empire and Russia still in control of the region, carving out an Armenian state from these imperial rulers would be no easy task. Yet even as Vratsian and his colleagues weighed the possibilities, events in Moscow forced them into action.

Reeling from years of warfare and a bruising civil war with czarist loyalists, the Communist rulers of Russia capitulated to Germany in March 1918. Their sudden departure from the war left a power vacuum in Anatolia that presented a historic opportunity for the realization of an Armenian state but also invited a host of new dangers. The Armenian population of the Ottoman Empire was largely destroyed or living in refugee camps faraway from its historic lands. Fighting starvation and disease at every turn and deprived of its leadership, this population was in no condition to form the foundation for a new state. Protected from Ottoman persecution by the Czar's armies during the war, the Armenian population in Russia fared better. Yet it lacked a functioning government and commanded a standing army of little consequence. Vratsian and other up-and-coming leaders realized that with the Russians gone, the Armenians would either have to unite with their neighbors in some form of loose federation or receive the patronage of one of the Allies to survive further Ottoman onslaughts. The Ottoman leadership recognized the same vulnerability and ordered its troops to move east toward the defenseless Armenians.[8]

With hundreds of thousands of Russian soldiers removed from the front, Ottoman forces easily reconquered areas taken by the Russian army during the war. As they made their way east, they overran the inconsequential Armenian defense forces in their path, driving them into a chaotic retreat. "Their flight, in the middle of the night, on a road covered by a thick layer of snow, was extremely arduous," one general said of the withdrawal, "and was made more difficult by the necessity of repelling the attacks of the Kurds. All along the precipitous slopes the service wagons overturned . . . or plunged into the snow. Men were frozen."⁹ The unstoppable eastward march of the Ottoman army threatened to extinguish the only significant Armenian population unmolested by the empire's genocidal scheme of the previous three years—that of the Armenians in Russia.

By May 1918, Ottoman troops captured the last defensive stronghold of Kars and poured into Russian Armenia. They quickly took the region's second largest city, and made their way south via a railway. As Ottoman forces deluged the area, Armenian troops—exhausted by months of recoiling and having nowhere else to run—decided to make a stand in Sardarapat, a parched valley surrounded by two mountain ranges seventy-five miles from the capital, Yerevan. The Armenians found themselves alone. The civil war raging in Russia kept away their century-old protector. Their neighbors in the Caucasus, Georgia and Azerbaijan, with whom they hoped to forge some sort of alliance, sent no help. British and French troops, ensnared in stalemates across the globe, were in no position to tender any soldiers. A seminary near Sardarapat instructed churches in surrounding villages to ring their bells for six days to rally the local population. About 6,000 Armenians—soldiers, peasants, poets, blacksmiths, and even clergy—answered the call to repel the Ottoman force of 10,000, with some families sending four generations of men to the front. Local villagers clogged the roads with ox-driven carts supplying food and munitions to the motley defense force.[10]

A standoff ensued until a daring Armenian surge on the fourth day. "Nobody slept that night," described one participant, "everybody knew that an unequal battle was expected. . . . In the morning, with the first rays of the sun, volleys were heard from both sides along the whole front. . . . The Turks tried to attack us several times, but without success. . . . [A]t noon, our troop formations, surrounding the enemy with cries of 'hurrah,' took the offensive. . . . Literally everyone fought selflessly—officers, soldiers, volunteers, peasants. As if it were a competition on bravery." Two more successive victories evicted the invading Ottoman army.[11] The historian Christopher Walker aptly explained the battle's significance: "Had they failed, it is perfectly possible that the word Armenia would have henceforth denoted only an antique geographical term. . . ."[12]

• • •

Armenian leaders remained undecided about the next step. The Russians were out of the picture and the Ottoman army was in retreat. If the Armenians were ever going to have a state of their own, this was the moment to seize that opportunity.

After the victory in Sardarapat, the Armenian National Council, a quasi-governmental group that administered the Armenian population in the region, met in Tiflis, Georgia, to discuss the next move. Fearing that Armenians were too weak to govern a nation on their own at the time, the council hoped to form a union with its neighbors, Georgia and Azerbaijan. But the Caucasus-wide union that Armenians tried to forge collapsed when Georgia sought an alliance with the empire's ally, Germany. Azerbaijan, home to ethnic Turks, also looked favorably on working with the empire. It seemed that the Armenians would have to proceed on their own. Yet, one camp within the council still wavered. Vratsian urged for a leap into freedom despite the odds and great unknown awaiting a new state forged from the ashes of death and despair. His side won out.

May 28, 1918, days after the victory in Sardarapat, marked the birth of the Armenian Republic. Unlike America's 1776 proclamation, Armenia's declaration of independence did not read confidently: "In view of the dissolution of the political unity of Transcaucasia . . . the Armenian National Council declares itself the supreme and only administration for the Armenian provinces." It was a bittersweet beginning—as much accidental as intentional—that Vratsian likened to a sickened child.[13] Despite this dispirited inception, the Armenians finally had a nation of their own, the first since the collapse of the Cilician kingdom in 1375. Vratsian's lifelong dream came to fruition no matter the agonizing circumstances. If this nation rose to its feet, it would offer a modicum of compensation for the Genocide and guarantee a safe haven from further Ottoman persecution. In order to fulfill these ambitions, however, the new republic would have to endure a hazardous postwar world in constant flux.

For four years, Ottoman forces fended off invasions in Mesopotamia, eastern Anatolia, and Gallipoli. In October 1918, with their allies Germany and Austria-Hungary on the verge of collapse, and the drained

Ottoman army no longer capable of defending multiple fronts, the empire's representatives met with British admiral Arthur Calthorpe on his ship, the *Agamemnon*, off the island of Mudros in the Aegean Sea to negotiate an armistice leaving the Ottoman state at the mercy of the Allies.[14] A few weeks later, President Woodrow Wilson embarked on the SS *George Washington* for France. It was the first time a sitting American president had ventured to Europe, and the humanitarian-minded internationalist planned to use the historic occasion to unveil a magnanimous plan freeing occupied peoples from the Balkans to Arabia, and establishing a worldwide organization—the League of Nations—to implement his vision. Within this grand vision, Wilson favored the fortification and expansion of the newly born Armenian state—exactly the support Vratsian could have hoped for to sustain the fledgling nation.[15]

Britain's prime minister David Lloyd George, France's Georges Clemenceau, and their junior partner, Italy's Vittorio Orlando, awaited Wilson at the table of victors in Paris. Reflecting the mood of his electorate, Lloyd George exhibited far more sympathy for the Armenians than his Continental counterparts. News of Ottoman atrocities had infuriated all strata of the British public from school halls to the chambers of Parliament throughout the war. "There was not a British statesman of any party," Lloyd George later wrote in his memoirs, "who did not have it in mind that if we succeeded in defeating this inhuman Empire, our essential condition of the peace we should impose was the redemption of the Armenian valleys for ever from the bloody misrule with which they had been stained by the infamies of the Turks."[16]

Together, these four men—and a city full of advisers and consultants meeting at the French Foreign Ministry on the Seine—would remake a world badly in need of repair.[17] The carnage of World War I had left to waste lands stretching from France to Russia to the Middle East. Fifteen million people had died. Millions more were displaced. Millions of others demanded autonomy from their imperial and colonial masters. Like Greek gods of yore, the Allies played with the lives of these millions as though they were marionettes. And like those gods, they would spend the next two years bickering and dithering: drawing and erasing borders like a painter reworking a canvas, nearly impervious to the fate of those hanging in the balance. In one form or another, all four leaders swore to help the Armenians. Their words, as noble and compassionate as any people received from the war's victors, would amount to a litany of broken pledges.

When the victorious powers convened the peace talks in 1919, a bevy of delegations presented their case for lands, autonomy from overbearing empires, or liberation from the clutches of colonial rule. Two Armenian delegations, led by Boghos Nubar and Avetis Aharonian, were among those making entreaties. The two men presented competing styles and temperaments. Nubar, who was significantly older than his colleague, was the cultured son of a three-term Egyptian prime minister and a familiar face in European social circles. A true polymath, he studied engineering and agriculture and spoke several languages. He invented an auto-powered plow while sitting on the board of more than a dozen banks. These contributions earned him the highest award available to a civilian in Egypt. Nubar represented the scattered Diaspora from the Ottoman Empire and was a personal representative of the Catholicos, the head of the Armenian Church. Since his arrival in Europe in 1912 as the pontiff's envoy, he had cultivated relationships with and garnered the support of several European leaders.[18]

Aharonian, who grew up in the foothills of Mount Ararat, was a tough-minded poet and prolific writer. He studied at the prestigious Sorbonne in Paris and also in Switzerland. After the victory at Sardarapat, he led a delegation from the new Armenian Republic to Constantinople to finalize peace terms with the Ottoman Empire. His time spent in Europe and his diplomatic experience made him an ideal candidate to represent the republic at the peace talks. He sported a thick, dark goatee; deep-set eyes cast shadows under his eyelids. Aharonian's diminutive stature and intellectual persona belied his fiery disposition, however. Like his ARF colleague Vratsian, he had spent time as a political prisoner. And like Vratsian, he expended every ounce of his energy to ensure—despite its unfortuitous birth—the survival of the Armenian Republic. Regardless of their differences in outlook, personality, and otherwise, and regular clashes over authority at the peace conference, Nubar and Aharonian put up a united front.[19]

Spurred by Wilson's calls for self-determination, a number of other subjugated groups sent representatives to Paris. Ho Chi Minh pressed for more rights for the indigenous people of French-controlled Vietnam. He was dismissed with little debate. The Kurds also made a futile request for sovereignty.

Aharonian and Nubar held more hope than others at the Paris Peace Conference—and for good reason. There was a great deal of sympathy for the Armenians at the table of victors, stretching back decades. A week after the armistice with the Ottomans, an Anglo-Franco declaration pledged "the complete and final emancipation of all those peoples so long oppressed by the Turks. . . ." Lloyd George told the Armenian community in Manchester: "Britain will not forget its responsibilities towards your martyred race." A typical *Times* of London editorial in 1918 stated that the "Armenians' moral claim to . . . independence . . . is indisputable." Clemenceau wrote to Nubar in July 1918: "I am happy to confirm to you that [France], like . . . Great Britain, has not ceased to place the Armenian nation among the peoples whose fate the Allies intend to settle according to the supreme laws of Humanity and Justice." Italy's Orlando provided similar assurances, as did Wilson in face-to-face meetings with Armenian representatives. In fact, Point XII of Wilson's Fourteen Points assured the Armenians "undoubted security of life and an absolutely unmolested opportunity of autonomous development. . . ."[20]

The guilt of having let down the Armenians over the previous decades motivated the Allies. One telling example of their failure to match their words with deeds came at the end of the Russo-Ottoman War in 1878. Britain scrapped the original treaty calling for a significant transfer of Ottoman holdings populated by Armenians to Russia and imposed in its place a new treaty that reduced the size of this transfer. "Had it not been for our sinister intervention," Lloyd George wrote, "the great majority of the Armenians would have been placed . . . under the protection of the Russian flag," outside the reach of Ottoman death gangs.[21] The establishment of an Armenian homeland would undo a half century of broken promises. It would not only serve to punish the Ottomans for their crimes but also safeguard the Armenians from future persecution.

On February 26, 1919, Aharonian and Nubar made their official plea in the inner sanctum of the Foreign Ministry where the war's victors held court. The carved-wood paneling on the walls reflected little light, leaving the room dark. Clemenceau sat by a log-burning hearth with Wilson and Lloyd George planted on either side of him. They formed the base of a U-shaped seating arrangement from which the representatives of other nations stretched out on both sides. The placement of these delegations in comparison to the triumvirate made the hierarchy in the room obvious to any observer.[22] The basis for the demands made by the Armenian delegates for territory stretching from the newly established Armenian Republic in the Caucasus to Anatolian provinces near the Mediterranean, compensation for lost property, and prosecution of the Genocide's perpetrators came as no surprise. "I think it is needless to recall the numerous promises . . . [that] were never fulfilled," Nubar told the peace conference. Through "massacre and deportation, Armenia has proportionately paid in this war a heavier tribute to death than any other . . . nation." "After these experiences," Nubar and Aharonian argued, "our cause needs no further pleading. . . . The Armenians rely implicitly on the spirit of justice. . . ." Representing a people perpetually victimized by conquest, the delegation asked for one more thing: a guardian like the League of Nations or one of the war's victors to ensure the safety of an Armenian state.[23]

After the presentation, Aharonian and Nubar lobbied countless officials in Paris. "Scarcely a day passed that mournful Armenians, bearded and black-clad, did not besiege the American delegation," noted one American adviser, "or, less frequently, the president, setting forth the really terrible conditions in their own native land." At face value, the responses they received seemed encouraging. In a twenty-minute meeting with Wilson, the president assured them of his allegiance. Winston Churchill, then the minister of war and air, made a similar guarantee. "I promise to do my best for you. I beg you to accept the assurance of my deep sympathy for your people."[24] But for a nation on life support, the Armenian Republic needed far more than reassuring words.

While Aharonian and Nubar labored in Paris, Vratsian tried to keep alive the young republic. Armenia faced innumerable challenges in its first year. Nearly one half of the population took care of the other half, providing shelter, food, and medical care to 300,000 refugees from the

Ottoman Empire. A housing shortage led to overcrowding and food supplies could not keep up with demand. The people cut down most of the nation's trees to use as firewood. Confronting such a refugee crisis just after an exhausting war would have strained any nation. Armenia faced an additional challenge born of centuries of foreign rule that had circumscribed the establishment of a governing class and impeded the formation of government institutions.[25] Vratsian, who took over as agricultural minister, recalled how his work as a teenager on a harvester in his uncle's fields resulted in "wrecked . . . machines" and decapitated animals. "[S]uch experience did not qualify me to be the Minister of Agriculture." Despite the valiant efforts of Vratsian and other capable officials, the republic, still recovering from the catastrophic circumstances under which it was born, needed years—not months—to establish itself. Vratsian had pushed hard for his nation's birth after the battle of Sardarapat. Now he realized that breathing life into the fledgling nation "seemed a hopeless task."[26]

A bitter winter combined with a food shortage made for a deadly cocktail, killing off 20 percent of the population. Typhus attacked nearly every family, spreading like wildfire through dry brush in a land populated with tens of thousands of homeless refugees. Of the seventy doctors serving a population of more than 1 million, fifty-seven contracted the disease; seventeen succumbed to it. One newspaper wrote that the "populace is feeding upon . . . cats and dogs." Some starving parents, the newspaper went on to note, ate the organs of their dead children. Eyewitnesses to the devastation would never forget the plight of the Armenians. "Thousands and thousands and thousands of dirty, lousy, half-clad sick and diseased . . . are here," noted an American aid worker. "[T]he thing that grips you is the women and little children who will haunt you with their mute appeal, and force you to think very tenderly of those who are near to you and for whom you will die a hundred deaths rather than have them ever reach this condition."[27]

Internal and external battles weakened the young republic. A pair of wars first with Georgia in late 1918 and then Azerbaijan in the summer of 1919 drained scant resources. Despite Vratsian's best efforts to maintain unity, an election in June 1919 fractured the government. When a major rival party refused to participate in the election, the ARF took seventy-two of the eighty seats in the Armenian Parliament and control of the entire cabinet. Later efforts at reconciliation floundered when the minority party insisted on a disproportionate voice in the government. Even compared to today's debt-ridden governments, Armenia spent way beyond its means. The government's coffers collected 30 million rubles in its first year while spending more than 1 billion. All of these troubles undermined the nation's ability to improve living conditions. An observer for the British government reported from Yerevan that "The aspect of the city is pitiful. The streets are ill-kept, and the wind carried clouds of infected dust. Everywhere there are wretched refugees in rags, hungry, diseased, demoralized . . . [children] were picking up refuse in the streets and eating it."[28]

Unable to stand on its own, the republic's best hopes rested on its strongest advocate—America. The "starving Armenians," a popular term in the United States at the time, attested to widespread concern for the Armenians. The United States built orphanages throughout the region, fed tens of thousands of refugees, and sent more than $100 million in aid to Armenians through a set of organizations culminating in Near East Relief. Schoolchildren across the United States collected pennies (30,000 Sunday Schools contributed $1 million in 1917); their parents dropped nickels at Rotary Clubs; while well-endowed institutions like the Guggenheim and Rockefeller foundations contributed hundreds of thousands of dollars at a time. Proceeds from the 1916 Harvard-Yale football game went to Armenian-related charities.[29]

Eventually, this outpouring of benevolence sprung a call for action in support of the Armenian Republic. Out of this movement emerged an Armenian-American, called the "Lone Crusader" by one friend, the "one man army" by another, who would develop into Armenia's greatest advocate in the United States. He earned the sobriquets for almost single-handedly working on behalf of his countrymen.[30] Born in the Ottoman Empire in 1883, Vahan Cardashian lost his father at a young age. He immigrated to the United States in 1902 after attending a school run by American missionaries, and married a New York socialite, a widow several years older. (They divorced in 1916 for what he claimed was desertion.) After graduating from Yale Law School, he opened a law practice in New York and in 1911 took a job at the Ottoman Embassy. The empire placed him at the head of its Chamber of Commerce and appointed him High Commissioner for its exhibition at the 1915 Panama-Pacific Universal Exposition in San Francisco.

During the exposition, Cardashian heard the news that would come to change his life. His mother and sister had perished in the Genocide. Practically overnight, he turned into the greatest Armenian-American advocate of his generation. He did not abandon his post. Instead, he began a secret letter-writing campaign informing American officials of the atrocities taking place within the empire. Some of these letters eventually landed at the Ottoman Embassy, which promptly fired him. Upon his dismissal, Cardashian stormed into the Otto-man ambassador's office, threw the medals bestowed upon him by the embassy at his former boss, and spewed a litany of expletives.[31] The anger he exhibited during this confrontation never seemed to fade. It generated the energy Cardashian needed to advocate passionately on behalf of his people for the rest of his life.

With the war coming to a close in 1918, Cardashian relied on his diplomatic and high society contacts to lead Armenian lobbying efforts at a time when few Armenians maintained positions of influ-ence. The scattered community of less than 100,000 included only 15 lawyers, 8 professors, and 234 college students. Most Armenians had left behind their families when immigrating to the United States. News of their relatives' deaths plunged many lonely souls into despair: "One could only see grief and sorrow on their faces," wrote one Armenian-American. Some who could not bear the heartache committed suicide. Cardashian understood that this tiny community, paralyzed by grief, could not advocate successfully: "I saw that an Armenian body would be unable to push the Armenian Case in the United States."[32]

Realizing that he would have to reach beyond the Armenian-American community, Cardashian formed the American Committee for the Independence of Armenia (ACIA) in 1918. Through his persistence and boundless energy, he recruited dozens of prominent Americans to its ranks. In trying to woo Supreme Court Justice Louis D. Brandeis, his four calls during a two-day visit to Washington, D.C., turned up empty, so he wrote a letter promising to "take a special trip" to the capital to meet with Brandeis. (The two did eventually meet.) Elihu Root, a former sena-tor and secretary of war, declined Cardashian's initial invitation, claiming that commitments to far too many committees stretched him thin. Upon further prompting, he went on to serve on the ACIA Executive Committee. After initially refusing Cardashian's invitation to support the ACIA, American Federation of Labor president Samuel Gompers also signed up. The diverse makeup of the ACIA reflected America's widespread support for the Armenians and Cardashian's tireless efforts.[33] One odd pairing, for example, included the populist Democrat William Jennings Bryan and the Brahmin senator from Massachusetts, Henry Cabot Lodge. James W. Gerard, the former American ambassador to Germany, and Charles Evans Hughes both took up leadership positions at the ACIA. Few Americans boasted a more prestigious résumé than Hughes, whose storied career included stints as a Supreme Court justice, New York governor, and Republican presidential candidate in 1916.

Coordinating with Armen Garo, the ARF leader of the 1896 Ottoman Bank takeover, who by this time had become Armenia's representative to the United States, and the Armenian delegates in Paris, Cardashian went on a tour across the nation to galvanize support. He also started a prolific letter-writing campaign. His correspondence reached the highest corridors of power, from former president Theodore Roosevelt to Lodge, and he organized a petition sent to Wilson signed by thirty-five of the nation's forty-eight governors, two hundred university presidents including the chief executives of Harvard, Columbia, and Princeton, and seventy-five prominent bishops. He flooded leading newspapers with editorials. Never one to shy away from giving advice, his memoranda to the nation's highest public officials—from secretary of state to president—often included laundry lists of recommendations. No matter how far-fetched his ideas may have seemed—in one memo, Cardashian called for the invasion of Cyprus as a base to begin amphibious landings against the Ottoman Empire—Cardashian supported his proposals with exhaustive lists of arguments.[34]

The ACIA's esteemed membership paid dividends. In December 1918, Lodge, a longtime supporter of the Armenians dating back to the 1890s massacres, proposed a resolution calling for an independent Armenia. At the senator's behest, Cardashian published a pamphlet for the Senate Foreign Relations Committee, and testified before a subcommittee deliberating aid packages to Armenia. Three months later, the ACIA and Near East Relief co-hosted a gala benefit at New York's Plaza

Hotel to raise funds for the Armenians. "An example for all peoples," Wilson wrote in a telegram sent from Paris; "we need to put to rest forever the injustices and sufferings of your nation for all humankind lest they be repeated." In all, four hundred of America's cultural, industrial, and political elite attended, including John D. Rockefeller, Andew Mellon, J. Pierpont Morgan, F. Scott Fitzgerald, William Randolph Hearst, Clarence Darrow, Rudolph Valentino, former president William H. Taft, members of the late Theodore Roosevelt's family, the first lady, and future presidents Warren Harding and Calvin Coolidge. With backing from America's elite and assurances from the table of victors in Paris, the Armenian Republic, it seemed, would thrive and perhaps expand to include more of the lands historically inhabited by Armenians. Hughes, who was the honorary chairman of the ACIA's General Committee and a member of its Executive Committee, highlighted the event with a forty-minute keynote speech: "We propose tonight to throw such influence as we have into the scale for Armenian independence," he declared to the crowd.[35]

Back in Paris, the Allies kicked around many ideas to aid Armenia. They knew that without a mandate, Armenia would not survive a future invasion from its former imperial overlords. One plan called for an American mandate over the republic. Another called for an American mandate for all of the empire. A third called for the Armenian Republic to annex portions of the empire, while yet another plan reconstituted Cilicia as the Armenian homeland. In a replay of the power politics of the nineteenth century, Anglo-Franco designs on the Ottoman Empire hampered their labors on behalf of the Armenians. As early as 1916, the British and French had divided the empire into zones of interest via the secret Sykes-Picot agreement. Italy also eyed portions of the empire.[36] These mixed motives compounded by indecisiveness and procrastination prevented the implementation of any of these schemes.

With the British and French unwilling to further strain their armies to safeguard Armenia, the Allies eventually settled on selecting the United States as its protector. Cardashian and the ACIA also urged Wilson to accept a mandate. In June 1919, eight of ACIA's nine Executive Committee members, including Hughes, sent a cable to the president: "We now believe that the prevailing insecurity of life and intense want in the major portion of Armenia make immediate action an imperative and sacred duty. . . . We believe that without regard to party or creed the American people . . . expect to see the restoration of the independence of Armenia." Others added their support. "Let us not imagine that we can wash our hands of the responsibility for Armenia's fate," announced a *New Republic* editorial reflecting the ethos of the day. "If we fail at this juncture to vindicate Armenia's right to freedom we shall never again persuade the world that our moral sentiments are anything but empty rhetoric playing over a gulf of selfishness and sloth."[37]

Wilson understood the popularity of the Armenian cause among the electorate. "The whole heart of America has been engaged for Armenia," he told fellow Democrats. "They know more about Armenia and its sufferings than they know about any other European area."[38] In September 1919, he crisscrossed the nation upon his return from Europe to campaign for his postwar vision. "Armenia is to be redeemed," he told a crowd in Salt Lake City. Two days later, he collapsed from a stroke, and so did the international order he had envisioned. In a series of votes, the Senate rejected America's entry into the League of Nations. Coming off these denunciations of Wilson's internationalism, in June 1920, it also rebuffed Wilson's appeals for a mandate over Armenia by 52 to 23 votes. The mandate's chief opponent turned out to be Lodge.[39]

Why did Lodge, a member of ACIA's Executive Committee, and others who had championed the Armenians act with forked tongues? Antagonism by a Republican-controlled Senate toward Wilson's internationalist vision that stood in conflict with America's inveterate isolationism played a role. Plus, while they held a sincere desire to help the Armenians, few wanted to involve the United States in a drawn-out troop deployment in a faraway place, especially at a time when the nation's isolationism had regained primacy after a brief respite during the war. "There is no desire to turn a completely deaf ear to their cry for help," Lodge said of the Armenians, "but that is wholly different from taking the mandate and assuming the care of that country for we can not say how many years to come."[40]

While things were turning sour for Armenia, a resurgent Ottoman Empire began to take shape under a brilliant and charismatic general.

By the middle of 1919, the Ottoman state resembled a European colony. Italian troops entrenched themselves in the southwest portion of Anatolia. British troops were stationed near Constantinople and the Black Sea straits. French forces occupied southern Anatolia. On May 15, at the encouragement of the British, a Greek invasion force joined the party. It seemed that Europe was primed to take over the last remnants of Osman's empire.[41] One man stood in its way.

The Greek invasion springboarded Mustafa Kemal from a military hero to the father of modern Turkey. His defense of Gallipoli, a drawn-out bloodbath that may have saved the empire from an early defeat in the war, had made him one of the few victorious Ottoman generals of World War I.[42] In 1919, his career took an unimaginable turn, placing him at the center of a Turkish resurgence few would have thought possible after the prostrated condition the empire found itself in at the end of the war.

Since his birth in 1880, Kemal had seen the Ottoman state get pushed around. Decades of military losses cost the once mighty empire the Balkans, North Africa, and the Arabian Peninsula, confining the Ottomans to Anatolia by the end of World War I. When his own birthplace fell to European armies just before the war, his mother fled alongside thousands of Muslims from homes they had inhabited for centuries. Kemal had seen enough. He admonished a friend for the Ottoman withdrawal from the Balkans: "How could you leave Salonica, that beautiful home-town of ours? Why did you hand it to the enemy . . . ?"[43]

For Kemal and his supporters, the Greek invasion was the final indicator of Europe's desire to divvy up the remainder of the Ottoman state and leave nothing but a sliver for the Turkish people. Traversing eastern Anatolia in a beat-up car or on horseback, Kemal recruited Turks to an emerging nationalist movement aimed at liberating the empire from European imperialism and preventing any further loss of territory.[44] At the time, Kemal did not hold an official post. But in a country reeling from defeat and destabilized by the presence of occupation troops, he grew in stature, and came to rival the new, ineffectual Sultan—the only living brother of Abdul Hamid—who had been restored to the Ottoman throne at the end of the war. The Sultan remained the titular head of the empire, but by the middle of 1920, his power did not stretch very far from Constantinople. Kemal's nationalists established an alternate parliament in central Anatolia that gradually came to wrestle the country from the centuries-old Sultanate.

While Kemal amassed power during 1919 and 1920, the Allies continued to draw up plans to partition the Ottoman Empire. Looking over color-coded maps like children playing a board game, they reconfigured potential borders: southern Anatolia to Italy or Greece, northern Anatolia to France, and so on. Armenia got lost in all this talk. An American diplomat in Paris aptly noted that "the independence and protection of Armenia became a thing men talked about, but did not work for." When Arthur Balfour, the British foreign secretary, realized what the leaders of the peace conference were up to, he became livid with anger: "I have three all-powerful, all-ignorant men sitting there and partitioning continents with only a child to take notes for them." Dithering often spilled into bickering. Italian troops stationed in the empire skirmished with the Greeks laying claim to the same booty. Italy began to secretly arm Kemal's insurgency to counter Greek and French forces. British and French designs also complicated matters. The French wanted to control Cilician Armenia—as did the Greeks and Italians—while the British looked to the Arabian Peninsula. At one point, Clemenceau blew up at Lloyd George's oversized ambitions: "You say that France mustn't be in Asia Minor because that would displease Italy. . . . France is . . . of all Europe, the country with the greatest economic and financial interests in Turkey—and here she is thrown out to please first the Mohammedans, and then Italy." With their attention largely focused on Germany during the peace talks, the Allies put off making any final decisions about the empire. "As for the way we will dispose of the territories of the Turkish Empire," Clemenceau told Lloyd George and Wilson, "after our last conversations, I must say I no longer know where we are."[45] This infighting and indecisiveness inhibited the Allies from striking a knockout blow against Kemal, allowing the commander to build grassroots support.

On the afternoon of August 10, 1920, Avetis Aharonian's two-car calvacade departed from Paris for Sèvres, a small town just across the Seine southwest of the City of Lights. Home to one of Europe's finest porcelain manufacturers that once served the French monarchy, Sèvres boasted a museum of the factory's finest china preserved since its founding in the middle of the eighteenth century. As the head of

Armenia's delegation at the postwar peace talks, Aharonian took a seat next to delegates from Romania and Czechoslovakia to sign the Treaty of Sèvres in the town palace. In 1919, the Allies had selected the Hall of Mirrors at Versailles for the signing of the peace treaty with Germany. The treaty with Hungary, Germany's junior partner in the war, also took place on Versailles's sprawling grounds. Now, inside the Sèvres palace—a far less triumphant locale than Versailles—Aharonian and delegates from several other nations gathered to sign a long-overdue agreement that would set peace terms with the Ottoman Empire.

The Treaty of Sèvres embodied nearly all of Armenia's aspirations. Articles 88–93 of the main agreement called for Ottoman recognition of the Armenian Republic and authorized Wilson to draw new borders between the nations that would likely transfer a handful of Ottoman provinces to the Armenian Republic. "This is the happiest day of my life," Aharonian wrote. "My struggle, my protest, my sufferings and hopes of thirty years were crowned with a glorious success."[46]

Aharonian's happiness was short-lived. By providing a blueprint to amputate what little remained of the empire, the treaty confirmed every suspicion held by Kemal's movement of Allied designs. Working with new urgency, nationalist forces grabbed control of the country from the weakening Sultan, who had submitted to the treaty's austere terms. Once fully entrenched in power, Kemal vowed never to allow the treaty to take effect.[47]

Short of another war, the Allies could do little to stop him. Though the Ottomans had succumbed in October 1918, the Allies had not begun to seriously deliberate the empire's fate until almost 1920 as they focused their energy on Germany, which signed the Treaty of Versailles in the summer of 1919, a full year before the Ottoman Treaty of Sèvres.[48] This delay allowed Kemal to resurrect the prostrated nation and reject terms the Ottomans would have likely accepted at an earlier date. In essence, he acted not like the leader of a losing power but a victorious one who dared the Allies to start a new war to get their way.

Indeed, Kemal's next move made the treaty moot. In September, he ordered an attack on the Armenian Republic. Armenia, a land of refugees with an air force of three airplanes, could offer little resistance against the resurrected empire. "It is impossible to depict the situation in Armenia," explained Herbert Hoover, then the head of a war relief agency, "for until the last sixty days the population has been eating the dead." Armenia needed a lifeline but it found itself alone. The victors who had granted it large swaths of land could not safeguard even a square inch. Outside of sending humanitarian aid, they had done little more than make promises and endlessly debate how much territory Armenia might accumulate. Aharonian again made entreaties on behalf of the republic. But after two years of near-continuous lobbying from him during the postwar peace talks, his pleas to secure troops and munitions fell on deaf ears. When he approached Lord George Curzon, the new British foreign minister, he was rebuffed not in person but with a letter. This was an especially painful rejection as Curzon had been perhaps Armenia's greatest advocate in the British government. Wilson's secretary described the delegate's fate: "Poor Aharonian! Unfortunate Armenians! Our promises are out the window and the reconstituted Armenian state has not a Chinaman's chance."

With the Allies failing to deliver on their promises, Aharonian turned his entreaties to Cardashian's ACIA. "Our numerous steps with the Conference have remained fruitless," he wrote in one cable. "We now ask [the ACIA] to appeal to the great and noble American people and Government. . . . Very existence and future of Armenia depend on your answer." Cardashian felt equally bleak. "To-day, the very existence of the Armenian race is threatened," he wrote in a letter to Harvard University's president, "and America and Europe are watching. . . . And while debate is going on . . . men, women, and children are dying by the thousands in Armenia."[49]

With Ottoman forces making their way to Yerevan, Soviet troops launched a simultaneous invasion from the north. Russia and the Ottomans had been enemies for more than a century, fighting in five wars since the beginning of the 1800s. It was as if the gods were out to ruin the Armenians with another stroke of bad luck. After so much bloodshed, these adversaries decided to forge an alliance opening the door for the USSR to retake its imperial holdings—including Armenia—lost during the three-year civil war against czarist loyalists. On November 17, 1920, with Turkish troops nearing Yerevan, Armenia conceded defeat: there would be no miraculous repeat of Sardarapat. Five days later, almost in a comic display of the foolish postwar peace process employed by the

Allies, Wilson released the borders he had so carefully drawn up under
the Treaty of Sèvres, granting the Armenians immense tracts of the Ottoman Empire. Like the treaty that had given birth to Wilson's boundaries,
his report was moot. Years later, Kemal aptly commented: "Poor Wilson
did not understand that a frontier which is not defended with bayonets,
force and honour cannot be secured by any other principle."[50]

Before his death in 1919, Theodore Roosevelt made a prophetic as-
sertion about the consequences of America's—and the Allies'—failure to
protect the Armenians: "The Armenian massacre was the greatest crime
of the war, and failure to act against Turkey is to condone it; because the
failure to deal radically with the Turkish horror means that all talk of
guaranteeing the future peace of the world is mischievous nonsense."[51]

In the midst of the invasion, Vratsian became Armenia's fourth prime
minister. With enemies tightening the noose around the nation's neck,
he did not covet the top job. "Under these circumstances and with
heavy heart, I was compelled to accept. . . . In all Armenia, there was
not a man who envied me at this moment." His nine-day tenure at the
helm was excruciating. He juggled negotiations with Ottoman forces in
hopes of stalling the invasion while reaching out to the Soviets for help,
knowing full well that their terms might be equally onerous. Both responded with increasingly harsher demands. Meeting inside a candlelit
Parliament chamber, Vratsian's cabinet argued for two days on the next
step. The gathering was eerily similar to the one held just before the
birth of the republic in which opposing sides argued over the creation
of the new state. Now, they deliberated over its death. One camp argued
that without agreeing to the USSR's terms, the Armenian state and its
people would cease to exist. A smaller camp insisted that the Armenians
fight on to the death. Without support from the Allies and with two
superior armies targeting his tiny state, Vratsian could not pull off the
miracle needed to keep Armenia alive. Nine hundred days earlier, he
had urged his colleagues to jump headfirst into freedom. Now, he made
a gut-wrenching decision to end the deadlock. On December 2, 1920,
Armenia acquiesced to join the Soviet Union rather than face annihilation at the hands of the Turks. Vratsian aptly announced that "Nothing
remains for the Armenians to do but choose the lesser of two evils."[52]

• • •

The long-term consequences of the Armenian Republic's demise cannot be overstated. Without a government of their own, Armenians lacked the diplomatic muscle to challenge Turkey on the global stage for the next seventy years when it came to Genocide-related matters. Without a state to speak on their behalf, they lacked a voice to keep alive the promises made to them after the war. Without a nation to memorialize their tragedy, the Armenians had no one to remind the world of their suffering. Without Armenia, the massacres so widely acknowledged across the globe that had nearly wiped out this ancient tribe would come to be known as the "forgotten genocide."

Vratsian had more immediate concerns on his mind. On the last night of the republic, his friends gathered at his home to mourn the loss of their country. "From the broad window," Vratsian recalled, "in the semi-darkness could be made out the silhouette of [Mount Ararat]. Silence enveloped the room, as it did our souls."[53]

All of the men who had worked so hard for the Armenians—all the children of Armenia—pressed on. Nubar turned his energy toward philanthropy after his departure from the postwar peace talks, helping to house and feed tens of thousands of Armenian refugees and orphans trying to recover from the Genocide. Cardashian continued his advocacy in the face of a shifting American policy forsaking the Armenians. Aharonian plunged into another international conference three years later when the Allies congregated in Switzerland to draw up a new peace treaty with Turkey. Vratsian and his ARF colleagues went into exile, keeping alive the spirit of the dead republic for decades to come. He too received one more opportunity to address the world's powers on behalf of the Armenians after World War II, when the globe's borders were again redrawn. Garo turned his attention to another broken promise made during the postwar peace conference. The murderers of 1.5 million Armenians—Talaat and others—remained free. When the Allies failed to prosecute these criminals, Garo made sure to exact a different brand of justice.

Judgment in Berlin

With the help of German officials, the ringleaders of the Genocide—Mehmet Talaat and others—boarded the German torpedo boat *Lorelei* and headed for Odessa in the Ukraine two days after the conclusion of the war in 1918. From his posting in the Interior Ministry, Talaat had ordered the execution of hundreds of Armenian leaders, including Krikor Zohrab, in 1915 as one of the opening acts of the Genocide. Those infractions paled in comparison to his oversight of the death of 1.5 million Armenians. Fearful of the consequences of his crimes, Talaat fled the empire in November 1918. In search of a safe haven, he used the 10 million deutsche marks he had appropriated during the war to move into a luxurious nine-room villa in Charlottenburg, the fashionable west end district of Berlin. The friendly confines offered by the empire's ally shielded him from the war's victors should they decide to pursue him. To throw off anyone else who might come looking for him, he decided to take on an alias.[1]

The magnitude of the loss suffered by the Armenians during the Genocide was immeasurable. Talaat and his cohorts not only massacred men, women, and children; they uprooted a people from their ancestral lands, severed them from their ancient heritage, and left them in a penurious state, robbed of their homes and possessions. Those lucky enough to survive enslavement, famine, disease, and death had to start anew largely in refugee camps and orphanages, simultaneously forced to rebuild their lives and mourn the dead. In appreciation of the scale of the crime committed against the Armenians, the war's victors looked to prosecute the Genocide's perpetrators. During the next two years, as those victors deliberated the fate of the doomed Armenian Republic in the halls of the French Foreign Ministry, they simultaneously tried to establish a mechanism for such prosecution. Both undertakings met the same fate. Like their guarantee of establishing an Armenian state, the prosecution of the Genocide's organizers also fell by the wayside, doomed once again by actions on the ground that rendered moot the endless debate in Paris. When the Allies failed to secure the most basic element of justice—punishing those responsible for the near annihilation of a people—Talaat's former colleague from the Ottoman Parliament, Armen Garo, and a network of ARF agents spread across the globe took it upon themselves to exact their own brand of rough justice.

On May 24, 1915, Russia, France, and Britain issued a warning to the Young Turks in a message hand-delivered by U.S. Ambassador Morgenthau:

> For a month, the Turkish and Kurdish populations, in agreement with the agents of the Turkish government, and often with their assistance, have been massacring Armenians. . . . In view of this new crime against humanity perpetrated by the Turks, the Allied Governments make known publicly . . . that they will hold all members of the Turkish government as well as those officials who have participated in these massacres, personally responsible.[2]

At a time when human rights law was still in its infancy, this declaration signified a seminal step in holding a state accountable for persecuting its citizenry and it laid the foundation for postwar prosecutions of the Young Turks. When British troops disembarked in Constantinople upon the signing of the armistice in November 1918, the overseer of the occupation force, British High Commissioner Admiral Calthorpe, echoed the sentiments of this declaration to the Young Turks in his message to the Ottoman foreign minister: "His Majesty's Government are resolved to have proper punishment inflicted on those responsible for Armenian massacres." General Franchet d'Espèrey of the French occupation force seconded Calthorpe's message, telling the incumbent Ottoman administrator: "If your government does not take severe measures the judgment passed on you shall be dire."[3]

It was no mystery that the victors wanted to make their vanquished foes pay dearly for the war. The Treaty of Versailles stripped Germany of more than 10 percent of its territory, imposed humiliating military restrictions, and shackled it with decades of reparation payments. The Austro-Hungarian Empire fared no better as the Allies oversaw its disintegration. The Allies planned to impose equally harsh terms against the Ottoman Empire. The release of the secret Sykes-Picot agreement between France and Britain revealed Allied designs to dismember the empire. And many saw its decapitation as just punishment for Ottoman sins. "Punishing those responsible for the Armenian atrocities means punishing all Turks," the deputy commissioner of the British occupying force noted. "That is why I propose that the punishment . . . should be the dismemberment of the last Turkish Empire. . . ."[4]

The Ottoman leadership hoped to forestall these punitive measures by mollifying the Allies through prosecutions of those guilty of the Genocide. Its foreign minister told a British commander, "with regard to the Armenian massacres, it was not merely the intention but the firm decision of the Government to punish the guilty." Grand Vizier Damat Ferid, the equivalent of a prime minister serving at the behest of the Sultan, assured the Allies that his government would establish special tribunals to punish those responsible for crimes that "make the conscience of mankind shudder with horror." "The aim which I have set myself," he told the Allies, "is that of showing to the world with proofs in my hand, who are the truly responsible authors of these terrible crimes."[5]

In January 1919, the Ottoman government arrested dozens of Young Turks for proceedings before a military tribunal that divided its investigation into geographic zones and targeted midlevel bureaucrats in building a case against the Genocide's ringleaders. Among its first targets was Kemal Bey, the former governor of Diyarbakir, a region in southern Anatolia from which the Ottomans deported more than 120,000 Armenians. His lawyer pressed an argument heard decades later at Nuremberg: his client was following orders. Employing the logic later cited at Nuremberg, the chief prosecutor rejected the defense. "It is true," he responded, "that everyone is obligated to carry out orders from the highest offices, but he must judge and weigh in balance whether the issued order does not violate justice and the law. . . ." The tribunal found Kemal Bey guilty, and he was hanged in April 1919.[6]

The verdict may have appeased the war's victors, but it stirred neither approbation nor contrition within much of the empire. Instead, Turkish nationalists, many of them former members of the Young Turk regime, placed memorial wreaths all over Constantinople honoring Kemal Bey, whom they considered an innocent victim of victors' justice imposed upon the self-flagellating empire. A British official sent word in 1919 to his superiors explaining the nationalists' impression of the tribunal: "those guilty of the deportations have become a symbol of Turkish patriotism." The Greek invasion of the empire in May 1919 added new fuel to this mounting resentment. To pacify the mass demonstrations instigated by the invasion, Ottoman officials released dozens of prisoners under investigation and the tribunal temporarily suspended its work.[7]

The Ottoman government was in a quandary. Should it continue the unpopular trials and face the wrath of the rising nationalist forces or bring them to a halt and contend with the retributive Allies? Under pressure from Britain, the tribunal continued its investigation of the Young Turk leadership. Evidence of telegrams ordering the deportations, memoranda establishing death squads, and witnesses describing the workings of the Genocide piled up. On July 5, 1919, the tribunal found Talaat and his inner circle guilty of massacring the Armenians. There was one major problem. The Ottoman government did not hold a single member of this inner circle in custody. The inability to capture many of the defendants and Germany's refusal to extradite Talaat and others forced the tribunal to enter sentences in absentia.[8]

After the verdict, the tribunal slowed to a crawl. British pressure had stirred it into action before. But with nationalist forces slowly taking control of the empire, the British found it difficult to press the Ottomans any further. "In view of the unfavorable conditions now prevailing in this country," Calthorpe's replacement, Admiral John de Robeck, wrote in a report filed on September 21, 1919, "I have decided to refrain . . . from making suggestions to the Turkish Government for the arrest of further persons implicated in the deportations and massacres."

He told a British diplomat that because of the Ottoman government's dependence on the "toleration" of nationalist forces, "I feel it would be futile to ask for the arrest of any Turk accused of offenses."[9]

Mustafa Kemal and his followers took a pragmatic approach to the tribunals. With a century of Ottoman losses on his mind, he suspected that the Allies aimed to dismember the heart of the Turkish state itself. If that meant that the empire had to hold trials to appease the Allies and thereby dissuade them from carving up his country, then he would support them. If the Allies proceeded with their plans for partition regardless of the trials, then Kemal saw no need for them. To him, the preservation of what remained of the empire trumped all other concerns. "The matter of the arrests and trials . . . is the simplest thing to resolve. The basic problem that has to be solved is the future existence of the state, which is presently in danger." He told Parliament that "these shameful acts belonging to the past" should not stand in the way of establishing a Turkish state. The Treaty of Sèvres confirmed his worse suspicions. It called for the complete dismemberment of the Ottoman state. Turkish nationalists realized that the prosecutions would not placate the Allies. As such, they had no reason to support their continuation. On August 11, 1920, they abolished the tribunal.[10]

The Allies were unwilling to exert the force necessary to countermand these developments. Had they acted quickly, before nationalist forces resurrected the enfeebled empire, the prosecutions would have likely succeeded. They missed out on that opportunity, and by 1920, the million-man British occupation force in the Ottoman Empire had dwindled to 320,000. "I never contemplated that the Allies would reduce their military forces so thoroughly before they had made peace and imposed their conditions," a British official explained. Unlike Germany and Austria-Hungary, Kemal refused to swallow the bitter terms submitted by the Allies in the Treaty of Sèvres, including provisions calling for prosecutions of the Young Turks. With their occupation forces depleted, the Allies were unwilling to expend any more lives or resources to assure the continuation of the tribunal in the face of this defiance, allowing its closure to go unanswered.[11]

Despite the tribunal's shortcomings, it did unearth vast amounts of valuable evidence secreted from later generations. Though it fell far short of what the Allies had envisioned, its final legacy may be that it was among the first bodies to prosecute a government for the persecution of its own citizens.

As the tribunal faltered, the Allies proceeded with their own plans to prosecute the Young Turks. The unprecedented prosecution of foreign leaders for yet to be defined crimes encountered a series of imposing legal obstacles. Up to that time, the concept of "crimes against humanity" had just begun to register in legal circles through a series of international human rights conventions in 1899 and 1907. Yet, no nation had ever prosecuted members of a foreign country, especially for crimes committed against its own citizens, and the undeveloped legal terrain lacked penalties for such criminals. Despite these challenges, a commission assigned to study the subject concluded that the perpetrators should face prosecution.[12] The question remained: would the war's victors be willing to work together and use force to see through such prosecutions?

The answer was simple: no. The same machinations—a cocktail of self-interest, procrastination, and indecisiveness that doomed the Armenian Republic—frustrated these efforts. Establishing tribunals to prosecute the Young Turks required diligent planning, steady determination, and a united vision to overcome considerable legal, evidentiary, and logistical obstacles. The war's victors rarely exhibited these traits in overseeing the postwar peace process. Besides, with all the issues they confronted at the peace talks, prosecuting the Young Turks never appeared at the top of their packed agenda. Their bickering over Ottoman spoils further encumbered the establishment of a tribunal. Seeking to befriend the new nationalist movement in Turkey, the Italians eventually rejected Britain's requests to establish European tribunals. The French also dropped their support.[13]

Guilt-ridden by a century of broken promises to safeguard the Armenians from Ottoman tyranny, the British decided to go it alone in hopes of making amends for the past. Lloyd George described this feeling of remorse in his memoir: "The actions of the British Government led inevitably to the terrible massacres of 1895–1897, 1909, and worst of all the holocausts of 1915. . . . Having regard to the part we had taken in making these outrages possible, we were morally bound to take the first opportunity that came our way to redress the wrong we had perpetrated."[14]

Britain transferred sixty-seven detainees accused of partaking in the Genocide to Malta for eventual prosecution, gradually adding to this number over time. But its attempt to establish a prosecutorial body of its own sputtered. Drafting a series of unprecedented laws and rules of evidence, and establishing bodies to prosecute, defend, and judge the perpetrators, required navigating through a field of legal land mines with few precedents to provide guidance. And the Ottoman tribunal declined to hand over inculpating documents to British authorities. "The Turkish government collected a considerable amount of incriminating evidence," said a British judge, "but hoping to lay our hands on it is in vain." The British were unwilling to grab that evidence by force. In 1921, Winston Churchill, then the head of the War Office, decided to exchange the Maltese prisoners for British officers held by the empire.[15] Churchill's exchange confirmed what had already been obvious: without Allied persistence and unity, there would be no trials of those who brought about the near extermination of the Armenians.

The war's victors had failed to keep their promise of establishing an Armenian homeland. Their failure to prosecute the Genocide's perpetrators was far more insulting. How could those responsible for the murder of millions go free? For some Armenians, it was simply too much to stomach. Justice would prevail, one way or another.

In 1913, seventeen-year-old Soghomon Tehlirian left his family in Erzincan, an Ottoman city near the Russian border, for a Serbian university to pursue his dream of becoming an engineer. When war erupted, Tehlirian abandoned his studies to sign up with an Armenian volunteer regiment fighting alongside the Russians. The border between the Ottoman Empire and Russia shifted back and forth during the war, like a clothesline slapping in the wind. On July 25, 1916, Russian forces, with Tehlirian's regiment at their side, captured his hometown. Having heard tales of mass deaths from stragglers along the way, he was eager to find his family.[16]

The barren Armenian enclave did not bode well for his search. He ran to his childhood home to find the doors of the house torn off. Half the building had collapsed from a fire, leaving the inner quarters exposed to the elements. Sobbing at the sight of his wrecked home,

Tehlirian pictured his mother baking in their circular fireplace that doubled as a gathering place for nighttime meals and conversation, his older brothers studying to become doctors, his father reading the Bible. A colleague urged him to return to the unit. "My family may be alive and well," Tehlirian responded in desperation, "perhaps in another house, on another street." "Soghomon," his friend replied wistfully, this "is a city of ghosts and memories."[17]

Two Armenians who had been spared by converting to Islam explained to Tehlirian how Ottoman officials eradicated the city's 20,000 Armenians. "They murdered our people in cold blood," one of them told Tehlirian. "My mother! My family," Tehlirian asked the man. "You knew them. Did they escape?"

"There were no survivors," he responded.

News of his family's demise overwhelmed Tehlirian. He returned to his house for one last time. In the garden, he suffered the first of many hallucinations of his mother's lacerated body. "Oh, God in Heaven, give me the strength and wisdom to . . . punish the slayer—the man responsible for the murder of my people," he vowed. Then black spots clouded his vision and he collapsed.[18]

After the war, Tehlirian placed ads in Armenian newspapers attempting to match separated family members. He grew more dispirited with each passing day as surviving family members failed to turn up. During his stay in Constantinople, he learned that Talaat and his cohorts had masterminded the murder of his people. Aiding them was an Armenian traitor, Harootiun Mugerditchian, who, at Talaat's request, had compiled the list of Armenian leaders to be arrested on April 24, 1915. Weeks later, Tehlirian shot the traitor in the heart.[19]

The assassination made him an ideal agent for an ARF operation code-named "Operation Nemesis"—an operation designed to track down and kill the Genocide's chief perpetrators. The ARF asked Tehlirian to come to the United States should he be willing to join this mission. Within three days, Tehlirian stepped aboard a ship headed for New York and made his way to ARF headquarters in Boston to meet up with Armen Garo.[20]

Like Tehlirian, Garo suffered through episodes of haunting visions of his dead relatives left behind in the empire. "Endless piles of corpses would come into view," he wrote in his memoir, "and among them I would discern the beautiful eyes and face of my adorable mother, my sisters and brothers." Garo explained the mission to Tehlirian. Because the perpetrators were still unpunished, the ARF sought to hunt them down.[21] With no legal recourse available, it seemed like the only option. In this regard, the Armenian position after World War I stood in sharp contrast to Israel's after World War II. Nazi criminals were prosecuted at Nuremberg. The Israeli government then tried other Nazis like Adolf Eichmann in its own courts. The stateless Armenians had no such courts to rely upon. With the Ottoman tribunal defunct and Allied efforts grounded, there were no other options for bringing the perpetrators to justice.

Garo designated Talaat as the top target and sent Tehlirian to Germany, where Operation Nemesis scouts suspected the former interior minister might be hiding. Within days of his arrival in Berlin in December 1920, Tehlirian's colleagues notified him that several prominent Young Turks were congregated in the Charlottenburg section of the city. After weeks of stakeouts in search of potential targets, Tehlirian identified a hefty, well-dressed man clutching a cane at a train station. When the man left the station with his comrades, Tehlirian followed them to the nearby Zoological Gardens and later to a villa at No. 4 Hardenburgstrasse. The man bore a striking resemblance to Talaat, but ARF intelligence reports had placed Talaat in Geneva. Tehlirian, though, remained confident that the man he had spotted—and later followed over the next few days—was the man in the photos Garo had shown him in Boston. Yet the address Tehlirian tracked down was registered to someone named Ali Salieh Bey. Tehlirian rented an apartment across from Salieh's villa for round-the-clock observation to determine the man's identity. In March 1921, ARF agents uncovered Talaat's use of the alias Ali Salieh Bey. The man under Tehlirian's reconnaissance was indeed Mehmet Talaat. The time had come for Tehlirian to fulfill the vow he had made years ago at his family's demolished home.[22]

Ever since he had left that scene, seizures, recurring bouts of typhoid, and nightmares had haunted Tehlirian. For five years, he suffered from epileptic attacks. Waiting in seclusion in a tiny apartment in Berlin months on end further aggravated his condition, allowing his mind to wander to its darkest recesses. Sleep provided little comfort: he would repeatedly see visions of his mother sliced into bloody pieces. Yet these very visions fueled his commitment to press on.[23]

On the morning of March 15, 1921—the Ides of March—a damp, cold day, Tehlirian pulled up a small table to the window, opened a German grammar book, and through a gap in the curtains kept his eyes on the residence across the road. The thoughts swirling in his mind hindered his language lessons. Would this be the day? After three months of scouting the villa, would this be the day? Talaat would normally leave home at 10 a.m. for a stroll. The breaking of the routine the day before sent Tehlirian, already sallow and fatigued after months of anticipation, into panic. Perhaps Talaat had found him out?[24]

And then, after all that angst, his target appeared right on schedule. Wearing a long gray coat and carrying a cane, Talaat stepped out to the sidewalk and insouciantly strolled toward the Zoological Gardens. Tehlirian grabbed a German army gun from a suitcase full of laundry, put on his hat and coat, and raced down the stairs. With the gun in his breast pocket, and the brim of his hat tipped over his forehead, Tehlirian followed his target from across the street to evade detection. He took quick steps to catch up to the slower Talaat, and at the music school two blocks from the villa, he pulled ahead, eventually crossing back to meet Talaat face-to-face in front of a gabled building with a metal fence.[25]

Back in 1915, Talaat had justified the complete annihilation of the Armenians to Henry Morgenthau, noting that "If we don't, they will plan their revenge."[26] On this day, Talaat demonstrated no outward signs of caution, however. He did not turn around to look for a tail, nor had he employed a bodyguard. Perhaps he felt that his alias, having helped him elude Allied dragnets, would protect him from any vengeful Armenians.

For a brief moment, the two men peered into each other's eyes before passing one another. Then Tehlirian pulled out his revolver, aimed at the back of Talaat's head, and fired. The bullet entered just below Talaat's left ear. Leaving bone splinters in its wake, it ripped through the brain, and exited from the top of the skull. A woman screamed instantly at the sound of the blast as the blood-covered body spun around and fell. Tehlirian, momentarily frozen by the shock, inexplicably dipped his foot into the blood, then dropped the gun and started to flee a crowd of pedestrians chasing after him. A woman fainted as he ran past her, but a few steps away, the mob caught up to him. One person stabbed him with a key; another kicked him in the ribs. "Me Armenian, him Turkish," the assassin said in poor German, hoping to fend off the attackers, "no harm for Germany."[27]

Inside police headquarters, Tehlirian's scraped knees, aching head, and sore ribs began to radiate; he developed a fever. Beaten, bruised, and likely to face the death sentence, Tehlirian remained in good spirits in spite of his circumstances. Through a local Armenian translator, he confessed to an interrogator:

> Under the same circumstances, I would do so again . . . and gladly offer my life for the bargain. . . . [I]t was on his orders that my mother, brother, and family were massacred. It was on his orders that my people were systematically butchered. . . . I have lived only to avenge my people with his life. . . . I took an oath on my mother's unmarked grave that if he ever fell into my hands, I would kill him without condition or hesitation.[28]

On June 2, 1921, Tehlirian entered a Berlin courtroom dressed in black. When he sat down, he took note of the crystal chandelier, the semicircular bench, and the tall ceiling. He turned to see Talaat's wife, dressed in black silk, staring at him.[29]

Several of Germany's finest lawyers, led by Dr. Adolph von Gordon and Dr. Johannes Werthauer, arranged for by Tehlirian's Nemesis associates and the German-Armenian community, presented to the jury a slew of experts and survivors describing the Genocide. Johannes Lepsius, a German scholar of the Ottoman region, was the chief witness. Because censors had blocked his efforts to inform the German public of the crimes being committed by their ally during the war, this was the first time most Germans got to hear of the atrocities. Through telegrams, government memoranda, and a host of documents compiled from government sources and interviews, Lepsius presented the twelve male jurors with a detailed chronology of the Genocide, from the April 24 gathering of leaders to the deportations of women and children. "The plan for the deportation . . . was decided upon by the Young Turk Committee," he said on the witness stand. "Talaat gave the orders." Officially, it was stated that the deportations were precautionary measures, but "authoritative individuals blatantly declared that their purpose was to annihilate the whole Armenian population." Talaat signed a decree, Lepsius testified, stating that the "'destination of the deportation is annihilation.'" Otto Liman von Sanders, a German general stationed in the Ottoman Empire during World War I, testified in the same vein, pinning the blame on the empire's use of "an auxiliary police force. . . . consist[ing] mostly of criminals" for the depredations committed against the Armenians. Armenian survivors rounded out the defense with harrowing accounts of the Genocide. One witness described how the men in her caravan, once separated from the women and children, were "thrown in the river. . . . When it grew somewhat dark," she continued, "the gendarmes came and selected the most beautiful women and girls and kept them for themselves."[30]

Evidence that should have been used to prosecute the Young Turks was instead used to defend Tehlirian, turning the proceeding into an indictment on the Ottoman Empire's—and Talaat's crimes—rather than a judgment upon the defendant. In a way, the very trial the Allies had wanted to stage against Talaat took place inside the Berlin courtroom.

The linchpin of Tehlirian's defense was his own testimony, which though translated from Armenian to German, still captured the rapt attention of those in the courtroom. Inside a chamber packed with members of the world's press and viewers overflowing to the courthouse entrance, Tehlirian told the tale of his family's plight during the massacres, grudgingly continuing only at the judge's insistence. When the bench asked him point-blank if Tehlirian was guilty of murder, the whispers in the courtroom turned silent. Tehlirian raised his head, and without a hint of self-doubt told the jury of his vision:

> I do not consider myself guilty because my conscience is clear. . . . Approximately two weeks before the incident . . . I saw my mother's corpse. The corpse just stood there before me and told me, "You know Talaat is here and yet you do not seem to be concerned. You are no longer my son. . . ."[31]

When Tehlirian returned to his cell for the night, his nightmares returned. From dunes of dead bodies, he heard his mother's cry: "Soghomon, Soghomon. . . . I knew you'd come. . . . Thank you, my son. Go. Please . . . go home, sleep."[32]

After an hour of deliberation on the second day of the trial, the jury acquitted Tehlirian under a form of temporary insanity. Unlike the crowd that burst into applause and rejoiced around him with shouts of "Bravo," Tehlirian was stunned. Having confessed to the murder to interrogators and the jury, he believed that he would surely face execution. The press echoed the crowd's glee: the *Los Angeles Times* declared from a half a world away, VENGEANCE JUSTIFIED.[33]

Nine months after Tehlirian's assassination, an associate from Operation Nemesis killed another leading figure of the Young Turks. Two associates then killed two more significant perpetrators, Dr. Behaeddin Shakir, who had identified Talaat's body to German authorities and presided over his funeral in Berlin, and Jemal Azmi, in April 1922. Two more Armenians killed Ahmed Jemal in Tiflis, Georgia, in July 1922. Ismail Enver had escaped from Berlin to Azerbaijan to lead a dissident group. An Armenian branch of the Soviet army hunted down and killed every member of his insurgency. Turkey hanged the last of the significant perpetrators, Dr. Mehmet Nazim, for his role in a plot against the Turkish government in 1926.[34]

Tehlirian's trial marked a critical turning point in how the Genocide came to be remembered. From being the subject of countless news articles, fund-raisers, and political debate during the preceding six years, the atrocity would receive little attention after the trial. No episode, no voice, no government would direct the world's consciousness to the Genocide with such intensity for more than a half century, until a new generation of Armenians would again resort to murder to exact the justice denied to them.

Seeds of Denial

Each age writes the history of the past anew.

—FREDERICK JACKSON TURNER

The Armenian Republic's last prime minister, Simon Vratsian, could simply not let go of the nation he had fought so hard for. After all, he had pushed for its birth in May 1918, only to witness its death nine hundred days later. Hoping to wrest his homeland back from Soviet hands, he led an uprising in February 1921. A month later, with fresh Soviet troops surrounding Yerevan, the capital city that Vratsian had retaken, his forces fled to the highlands to mount a guerrilla campaign. There, the Armenian Revolutionary Federation established a short-lived state known as "Mountainous Armenia." It took months before Soviet forces stamped them out, forcing Vratsian and his ARF compatriots to flee to Iran.[1]

With all dissent in Soviet Armenia extirpated by the middle of 1921, the USSR went about dismembering the subject nation, ceding lands to Turkey through treaties that shrank the Armenian holdings by two thirds. The new border—one that survives to this day—placed Mount Ararat, which is so close to the Armenian capital Yerevan that its twin peaks loom over the city, in Turkish hands. The contraction continued when at Turkey's behest, Joseph Stalin handed over various Armenian regions to another of the USSR's provinces: Soviet Azerbaijan.[2]

The Armenia of the mid-1920s barely resembled the independent republic established in 1918. It was now a fraction of its original size. Its democratic government lay prostrate at the hands of Soviet totalitarianism. What had come to symbolize the hopes and aspirations of so many Armenians following the horrors of the Genocide lay in ruins. The long-term consequences of the republic's demise were equally consequential. The death of an independent Armenian government, the most powerful entity capable of speaking on their behalf on the world stage, incapacitated the Armenians against their adversaries in diplomatic and political circles. Whether it was the League of Nations or its successor, the United Nations, or the halls of the U.S. Congress, or the House of Commons, the Armenians would lack the standing accorded to Turkey. For decades to come, they would have to press their case without the benefit of a government of their own, an almost insurmountable handicap.

All seemed lost. The promises encapsulated in the 1920 Treaty of Sèvres—the guarantee of an independent Armenian state; procedures for the return of lost or seized Armenian property; and Ottoman coop-eration in the prosecution of those responsible for the Genocide—were dashed. The republic was dead. Outside a handful of perpetrators snared by Tehlirian and his associates in an extralegal operation not endorsed by the war's victors, those guilty of organizing the Genocide went unpunished. And the Armenians had not received a penny in reparations or compensation for the loss of life and property. They had not even received an apology from the empire.[3]

The best and last chance to restore the Sèvres promises came in 1923, when international delegates once again gathered at a conference in Lausanne, Switzerland, to hammer out a new pact with Turkey. Though never enforced, the Treaty of Sèvres had at least memorialized and guaranteed Armenian hopes and aspirations. If a sliver of these guarantees remained intact at Lausanne, it would give the Armenians something tangible to hold on to after suffering through so many disappointments. But things did not look encouraging heading into the talks.

By 1923, the Ottoman state no longer represented the enfeebled loser of World War I but a resurrected nation under Kemal, who had displaced the Sultan as his nation's sole ruler and evicted European occupation troops from Turkish soil.[4] Under these circumstances, the likelihood that the Armenians would get shortchanged at the conference was predictable. What was not foreseeable at the time was that after Lausanne, the Genocide would fade from the popular consciousness—so much so that by 1965, few even remembered the tragedy.

How could one of the greatest and most widely known human rights disasters of the twentieth century simply disappear from memory? The answer begins at Lausanne, where the world's Great Powers removed the Genocide and the fate of the Armenians from their agenda. Since the mid-nineteenth century, Europe had acted as a patron for the Armenians of the Ottoman Empire. Few of its actions proved helpful to the persecuted minority in hindsight. But European—and American—sentiment for the Armenians was genuine and widespread. After Lausanne, not only did the promises made at the Treaty of Sèvres vanish, but those sentiments also withered. And the Armenians were in no position to keep alive the memory of the Genocide in the face of this neglect.

At the same time, a resurgent Turkey unshackled from the glaring eye of the war's victors established a policy of denying the Genocide. Such a posture would have seemed absurd in the 1920s when memories of the Genocide remained fresh in people's minds. But as the world turned its back on the humanitarian ideals that had filled the Armenians with anticipation, Turkey's denial began to take root; and by 1965, what would have been considered impossible—the refutation of one of the greatest crimes of modern history—became plausible as the seeds of denial took root.

The United States was also undergoing a profound shift in its stance toward Armenia, a shift from humanitarianism toward one of cold calculation. And perhaps no one in the American government embodied this reversal better than Rear Admiral Mark L. Bristol. While Vahan Cardashian, the Armenian-American advocate responsible for promoting Armenia's interests in the United States, continued to champion Woodrow Wilson's humanitarian principles, Bristol represented a divergent branch of America's foreign policy. Though the two men rarely—if ever—engaged each other face-to-face, their competing visions of America's foreign policy would pull and tug at each other throughout the 1920s. And to the detriment of the Armenians, Bristol's vision would win out.

• • •

At no time before or after Wilson's presidency has humanitarianism been such a central tenet of America's worldview and a critical element of the nation's foreign policy. Wilson led this groundswell of support for a new international order through his unprecedented ideals calling for application of his Fourteen Points and the creation of the League of Nations. The Armenians were among the largest beneficiaries of Wilson's noble philosophy. Yet this policy of humanitarian concern was about to be displaced as the U.S. Senate rejected much of Wilson's vision and the nation returned to its prewar outlook.

Admiral Bristol, the U.S. high commissioner in the Ottoman Empire since 1919 and the highest ranking American official in the region, favored a much more pragmatic worldview than Wilson. Bristol's was a realpolitik mind-set concerned with practical gains; his overarching philosophy was one that envisioned the U.S. government as an enabler of commercial ventures. Bristol himself often acted as a broker, bringing together American business executives with members of the Turkish government, and he made available the U.S. Navy's destroyers to transport American goods and businessmen. Business officials often contacted him directly for help, including Standard Oil, whose director Bristol described as his "closest friend." His biographer wrote of the admiral: "Protecting and extending business interests was undoubtedly the job Bristol enjoyed the most. . . ."[5] As Bristol's influence in the region grew, he used his position to help redirect U.S. interests toward closer relations with Turkey, which he considered a commercial ally.

Since the empire's defeat in World War I, Bristol had shunned the Armenians in favor of his commercial vision. In so doing, he disagreed with both Wilson's call for an Armenian mandate and the expansive territory granted to the Armenians by the president in accordance with the Treaty of Sèvres. The British and French, he wrote during the Paris Peace Conference, "are going to try to get a division of the spoils, and then force us into taking the mandate for the so-called Armenia. . . . To use a slang expression, 'we would be given the lemon.'" Lacking in natural resources, landlocked, and burdened by a large refugee population, Armenia did not satisfy Bristol's thirst for commercial prospects. His opposition to America's patronage over Armenia helped sway the

Senate—and particularly Henry Cabot Lodge—to reject Wilson's mandate. In comparison to impoverished Armenia, Bristol saw Turkey as "practically a virgin field for American business. . . ."[6]

Commercial interests alone did not motivate Bristol. Popular racial stereotypes of the day fueled his antipathy for the Armenians. The Armenians and Greeks "have many flaws and deficiencies of character," Bristol argued, while "the Turk has some individual traits of character that are so far superior . . . that one is led to sympathize with the Turk even though you never forget the bad traits of his character that are illustrated by the acts committed against subjugated races."[7] "Armenian merchants have been the leeches in this part of the world sucking the life blood out of the country for centuries," he went on.[8] "The Armenians are a race like the Jews," he wrote on another occasion, "they have little or no national spirit and have poor moral character."[9] His appraisal of the Armenian minority sounded eerily like the later Nazi depiction of Jews.

Bristol's former assistant, Allen W. Dulles, left his position to head the Near East (today called the Middle East) desk at the State Department. The two saw eye to eye: "It was a fine thing to have Dulles go to the Department," Bristol wrote in 1922; "we were in complete agreement. . . ."[10] Along with Secretary of State Charles Evans Hughes, the two would come to craft America's policy toward Turkey, launching the nation on a path that would eventually lead to an about-face against the Armenians for whom America had shown so much compassion.

The U.S. team headed for the conference in Lausanne set out several objectives, including among other things an "open door" economic policy prompted by the interests of American oil companies and the guarantee of an Armenian homeland. Though the two objectives were not, on the face of it, necessarily in conflict with each other, Bristol knew that he had to reverse America's antipathy toward Turkey to place his economic program at the top of the delegation's agenda. Since 1915, after all, thousands of American missionaries and relief workers had come to the aid of Armenian refugees and orphans. Appeals and fund-raisers had flooded the nation, with children and adults alike contributing tens of millions of dollars to charities aiding Armenians. Though diminished since its heyday immediately after World War I, a significant portion of America's political elite also continued to back the Armenians.[11]

Recognizing that negative public opinion of Turkey remained the biggest impediment to his plan, the admiral downplayed the severity of the Genocide in order to shine a more favorable light on Turkey. To the American press, he put forward instances of Turkish victimization— Armenian troops killed thousands of innocent Turks in reprisals for the Genocide upon invading Anatolia with the Russian army during World War I—as part of an attempt to cancel out the enormity of Ottoman crimes. In one telling instance, Bristol overrode an American diplomatic report describing Turkish brutalization, instead cabling the State Department that "Armenians are not being massacred by Turks." The message confused the department, which responded: "Do you mean massacres have now ceased?" Later on, the admiral tried to block relief workers from transporting Christian orphans out of Turkey, claiming that "he knew well that they were perfectly safe."[12]

Colby Chester, a retired rear admiral who sought the help of the State Department at Lausanne to secure rail and oil rights in the empire, employed a similar tactic. In 1922 he wrote in *Current History*, a monthly magazine associated with the *New York Times*, that "the Armenians were moved from the inhospitable regions . . . to the most delightful and fertile parts of Syria . . . where the climate is as benign as in Florida and California, whither New York millionaires journey every year for health and recreation. . . . In due course . . . the deportees . . . entirely unmassacred and fat and prosperous, returned (if they wished to do so). . . ."[13] Bristol's and Chester's revisionism made few inroads at the time with news of the massacres and deportations fresh in people's minds. "If we could state that the stories of the Turkish atrocities were unfounded or even grossly exaggerated," Bristol's likeminded former assistant lamented in a letter to the admiral, "it would make our position easier, but unfortunately the evidence, even though it be from prejudiced witnesses, has not been refuted, and I am afraid cannot be."[14]

While Bristol prepared for the Lausanne Conference, Cardashian began rallying the pro-Armenian forces in the United States to chime in. The advocacy group he had created during the Paris Peace Conference— the American Committee for the Independence of Armenia—sent a memorandum at the beginning of the talks signed by fifty prominent officials, including New York governor Alfred Smith and future president Franklin Delano Roosevelt, urging the government not to "resume relations with Turkey . . . until the Turkish government shall have recognized the right of the Armenian people to an independent national existence."[15]

This last-minute lobbying by Cardashian and his supporters did not alter the State Department's plans at the conference. But the sentiments it evoked did cause angst within the agency. The unabashed pursuit of the nation's commercial interests in the face of continuing public support for the Armenians bedeviled the department, especially its leader Hughes. The secretary could not appear to be intervening to protect American commercial interests and give no consideration to popular opinion supportive of the Armenians.[16] Further complicating matters, Hughes had once served on the ACIA Executive and General committees, and he had to balance his allegiance to the Armenians with the reality facing the State Department heading into Lausanne.

Publicly, the government vowed to support the Armenians. President Warren Harding assured the ACIA that "[e]verything which may be done will be done to protect the Armenian people and preserve to them the rights which the Sèvres Treaty undertook to bestow."[17] But with few options available short of another war, Bristol's camp won out. "I beg to state that," Hughes responded to a critic, "strong as is the sympathy of the American people for the Christians of Turkey, it is not felt that we would find substantial support for a policy of actual intervention in the Near East. . . ."[18] Hughes understood that without sending an army—a burden the American public was unwilling to bear—the time had passed to dictate terms to Turkey.[19]

When the Armenian issue came up at Lausanne, the Turkish representatives stoutly dismissed any talk of land grants or compensation of any kind. Joseph Grew, the chief of the American delegation, noted that "there is no subject upon which the Turks are more fixed in obstinacy." Turkey's posture shocked James Barton, the head of an American missionary board. "I have not heard a word or seen a sign that the Turk is repentant of anything that has been done. . . ."[20] Instead, Turkey's representatives denied any wrongdoing, blaming the Armenians for their plight and clearing the Young Turks of all guilt. The stance reflected Turkey's emerging position to remove the Genocide from the political arena in order to smother any calls for compensatory land claims. "The Turks," a British diplomatic memorandum concluded, "consider the Armenian question as settled."[21]

In return for giving in to Anglo-American claims to the oil fields in Mosul, Iraq, the Turkish delegation otherwise got its way.[22] Whereas the Treaty of Sèvres had called for the establishment of an Armenian homeland, prosecution of the Young Turks, and compensation for the victims of the Genocide, the Treaty of Lausanne, signed in July 1923, did not even mention the Armenians. "Armenia could not hope to have a fair hearing at Lausanne," Cardashian aptly noted in an editorial, "because the Turk was on trial before a tribunal whose Judges were vying with each other to secure a part of the loot."[23] Avetis Aharonian, the head of the Armenian Republic's delegation at the Paris Peace Conference, left the conference equally embittered. Three years earlier, he had triumphantly signed the original treaty with the empire at the palace in Sèvres, capping off his ardent advocacy during the postwar peace conference. Now, he helplessly watched all his dreams fall to pieces. "Lausanne," his delegation wrote to the Allies, "ignores the Armenians and passes them over in silence."[24] One British representative in attendance at the conference summed up the fate of the Armenians in the context of the geopolitical reality of a resurgent Turkey, arriving at the same conclusion as Hughes:

> We are asked at Lausanne to repair the irreparable. We are not here to impose conditions but to submit to them. The Turks will give way only before force. We have not force to oppose them. . . . We cannot go to war for the Armenians. We recognize all our promises and our engagements, but we are not able to fulfill them. There is nothing to do. . . . Obviously the Armenians are sacrificed.[25]

The talks in Lausanne also produced a separate treaty, between the United States and Turkey, designed to establish diplomatic relations and most favored trade status between the nations. The U.S. Chamber of Commerce and the American foreign policy establishment applauded the move. Bristol had gotten his way, for which he received praise from Hughes for the "skill and patience with which [he] conducted the negotiations."[26]

At the end, Cardashian and Aharonian simply lacked the power to do anything other than make moral pleas. Cardashian was a one-man machine lacking a sustainable lobbying apparatus or voting bloc to expand his considerable but still limited influence. With the republic dead, Aharonian attended the meetings as part of a government-in-exile. He had no access to funds, arms, or any real source of power to sway the negotiators at Lausanne. Turkey, on the other hand, enjoyed all the prerogatives of nationhood. It was no contest.

It was amazing that men like Cardashian and Aharonian had gotten the Armenians as far as they did. Their failure certainly did not represent a flaw in their powers of persuasion or lack of effort but the simple reality that the powerless Armenians were completely dependent on the war's victors to bring about a just result. Those victors were unwilling to commit the blood and treasure needed to do that. The first line of the Declaration of Amnesty accompanying the Lausanne Treaty epitomized their stance: "The Powers signatory of the Treaty of Peace signed this day being equally desirous to cause the events which have troubled the peace in the East to be forgotten. . . ."[27]

And forgotten it was by everyone other than the Armenians.

Lausanne was a rout. The Armenians came away completely empty-handed. It seemed that Wilson's humanitarian principles breathed their last gasp. The rejection of the Armenian mandate in 1920 and the setback at Lausanne had neither slowed down Cardashian nor diminished his passion to help his people, however. Along with ACIA chairman James Gerard and Senator William H. King of Utah, he rallied supporters for another campaign, this time to scuttle the separate commercial treaty between the United States and Turkey negotiated during the conference.[28] It would turn out to be the last crusade on behalf of the Armenians for decades to come.

Cardashian openly accused Hughes of sacrificing the Armenians for oil interests. When Hughes confronted Cardashian over the matter, Cardashian assured the secretary that the ACIA would not slander its former chairman. In private, though, Cardashian was enraged, at one point threatening to travel to Washington to shoot Hughes.[29] The growing enmity between Cardashian and the State Department led Allen Dulles to end communications with the ACIA. When that failed to slow down Cardashian, Dulles nearly reverted to a smear campaign. "We have quite a large dossier on him," he wrote to Bristol, "which we would like to supplement by anything you might obtain . . . for he is a trouble maker and . . . can cause us a certain amount of trouble."[30] Dulles could do little to hold back the "one man army," however.

Cardashian's petition drives to block the ratification of the U.S.-Turkish trade treaty continued to collect hundreds of signatures from prominent officials. One from Bishop William T. Manning to the chairman of the Senate Foreign Relations Committee typified the ghost-written petitions Cardashian produced. "We insist that in any treaty with Turkey," Manning wrote, "the Armenian rights, as defined by the arbitration of President Wilson . . . shall be preserved."[31] Cardashian helped place the Armenian issue in the Democratic Party's 1924 election platform, which condemned the Lausanne delegation for bartering "Armenia for . . . oil Concessions." Senator Pat Harrison of Mississippi, echoing Cardashian's allegations, dubbed Hughes the "Secretary of Oil."[32]

The standoff continued until the Senate voted on the U.S.-Turkish trade treaty in 1927. Though Hughes had outflanked Cardashian by splitting off many of his supporters, the votes in favor of the treaty fell six shy of the necessary two thirds needed for ratification. Cardashian's Pyrrhic victory proved to be one of the few defeats Hughes suffered as secretary: of the sixty-nine treaties proposed to the Senate during his term, only two did not earn the body's imprimatur.[33]

The negative vote did not derail the blossoming American-Turkish relationship, however. Through Bristol's personal diplomacy, the State Department circumvented the Senate's wishes by exchanging ambassadors and establishing preferential trade conditions. Long before the Senate's vote, Bristol had visited Kemal, making him the first representative of a Western power to call upon the Turkish ruler. Upon the admiral's departure from his post in Istanbul, a prominent Turkish journalist wrote that Bristol's "activities from the beginning to the end of our struggle . . . amounted, in effect, to almost an informal alliance between Turkey and the United States." Another writer cried out: "Admiral Bristol is the only pearl in our yoke of thorns!" Eventually, the Senate followed the State Department's lead, approving in piecemeal agreements that revived many of the provisions scuttled in its 1927 rejection of the trade treaty.[34] Ultimately, the Lausanne Conference marked an unalterable shift in U.S.-Turkish relations. Cardashian's victory in scuttling the U.S.-Turkey trade treaty stood like a lone peg trying to damn this tidal wave.

Further embittered, Cardashian cast off all social restraints in vilifying Hughes, who had left the government for private practice by this time. "Under his direction," Cardashian wrote of his former colleague, "the Department of State became a concession hunting agency for the Standard Oil Company."[35] (Hughes provided legal counsel to the company before and after the war.) More than seven years had passed since the demise of the Armenian Republic, yet Cardashian persisted in trying to resurrect the Sèvres treaty.[36] Realizing that the fight for Armenia was hopeless, and finding Cardashian's increasingly splenetic attacks distasteful, his closest associates abandoned him. Undeterred, Cardashian mounted another cross-country campaign. He asked the chairman of the Senate Foreign Relations Committee to investigate accusations of oil diplomacy and haul in Bristol for questioning. With no Armenian government to speak of, Cardashian, designating himself an attorney for the government-in-exile, sent an invitation to Calvin Coolidge asking for the president's participation in an international arbitration to adjudicate Armenian claims.

When entreaties to leaders of the American government failed, Cardashian resorted to other means to harass Turkey. In 1929, he lost a lawsuit against the Turkish government for unpaid legal fees dating back to 1909. The case collapsed when the U.S. government declined to serve process on Turkey, a procedural requirement needed to initiate a case against a foreign party.[37]

Despite facing a string of defeats in the wake of this new geo-political reality, Cardashian's output—turning increasingly bitter over time—never diminished. In letters addressed to the White House, he accused the administration of committing a lawless and crooked act by exchanging ambassadors with Turkey. He objected as loudly as ever to the administrations of Herbert Hoover and Roosevelt. No one was paying any attention, however. The State Department had long stopped listening to his requests. The Senate, home to his closest allies within the American government, had become deaf to his pleas.[38] Cardashian's adversaries in the U.S. government had moved on. Hughes had returned to his law firm and went on to become Chief Justice of the Supreme Court; Dulles left public service to join his brother's law firm.

In June 1934, Cardashian suffered a heart attack. Having not vacationed for seventeen years, he was tired, his body worn out, his spirit broken from Armenia's demise. He died soon thereafter of heart disease at the age of fifty, broke after spending his life's savings on behalf of his Armenian brothers and sisters. Because Cardashian left no money for a funeral, the Armenian community raised funds for his burial.[39]

Cardashian's death silenced the most influential political voice within the fledgling Armenian-American community. For a people scattered across the globe, wary of their immigration status, and focused on rebuilding their lives and communities, he was one of the few Armenians with access to the highest corridors of power. With the death of Armenian leaders like Krikor Zohrab during the Genocide, there were few people alive to take up the mantle. One of the few who were capable of such leadership, the urbane Boghos Nubar, who had represented the Armenians at the Paris Peace Conference alongside Aharonian, died in 1930. Aharonian, who had given his all for the Armenian Republic, was living in exile, as was Vratsian, the last prime minister of the republic. With their passing from the world's political scene, it would take an entire generation before a new crop of politically active Armenians again pressed for justice. Until that generation's maturity, the Genocide, which had received so much attention leading up to the Lausanne Conference, would fade from the world's memory.

While Cardashian seethed at America's abandonment of the Armenians, Mark Bristol laid the seeds for an amicable relationship between the United States and Turkey. After his stint in Turkey ended, attempts to have Bristol appointed as the second ambassador to Turkey fell through. Instead, he inspired and later became the president of the American Friends of Turkey, bringing together American Turkophiles and Turkish officials to improve U.S.-Turkish relations and broaden business cooperation. William Hoover of vacuum cleaner fame established a trust to fund the endeavor.[40]

At that point, relations between the United States and Turkey existed primarily on a government-to-government level. Bristol and his colleagues recognized that for the relationship to evolve, Turkey had to improve its tarnished image lingering from the Genocide. In that light, they urged the Turkish government to commence a public relations campaign. Bristol helped place articles written by prominent Turks in American periodicals and arranged for receptive audiences within the United States.[41] His organization also contacted a public relations firm "to combat" what it considered "ignorance, misinformation, and misunderstandings on the part of many Americans. . . ." In particular, the public relations campaign targeted "stories . . . circulated in the United States reporting Armenian 'atrocities. . . .'"[42] With Bristol's help, Turkey was beginning to discover the tools available in America to influence the media and sway public opinion. Their attempts to repaint Turkey's image stretched beyond the general populace to America's political elite. At the behest of the Turkish ambassador, one of the first tasks undertaken by Bristol's group involved lobbying the Democratic Party to drop the establishment of an independent Armenian state from its plank. "Our organization of course would oppose the adoption of any such policy," wrote the organization's day-to-day manager to Bristol. The American Friends of Turkey membership considered Armenia "a lost cause, a geographical expression."[43]

By the mid-1930s, it was patently clear that Bristol's commercial vision had triumphed over Cardashian's humanitarian viewpoint, a turnaround that spelled doom for the Armenian homeland Cardashian had struggled to sustain.

After securing Turkish territorial and economic integrity at the Lausanne Conference in 1923, Kemal began a revolutionary transformation of Ottoman society. Such a political and cultural makeover of a six-hundred-year-old society would have normally taken generations. Turkey completed this break with the past in about a decade. Kemal had proven himself a brilliant and courageous military strategist during World War I. He had used sheer will to depose the Sultan and drive out invading armies after the war. He played chicken with the Allies and won, preventing the victors from imposing their terms on his defeated nation and partitioning it as they had wished. Lausanne, which he described as a "political victory unequalled in the history of the Ottoman era," was the apotheosis of his achievements.[44]

The establishment of the Turkish Republic on October 29, 1923, encapsulated the first part of his dream. Until his death in 1938, Kemal would embark upon a new phase of his esteemed career that reshaped Turkey into a modern, secular, Western-leaning state. He so badly wanted to improve his beloved nation that he missed his mother's funeral to see to its needs (he also skipped his honeymoon).[45] Such a feat of social reengineering was nearly unprecedented in history, but came at a time in which others attempted similar feats. In the USSR, Vladimir Lenin and Stalin brushed aside centuries of religious worship, serfdom, and aristocracy in the name of communism. In Europe, fascism spread to Germany, Spain, and Italy to displace outdated monarchies and handicapped democracies. Kemal, however, did not rely on any of these conventional ideologies sweeping the world. His vision, an intertwined mixture of modernization and Turkification, was far more personal. In 1988, when Kemal's imprint on Turkey remained undiminished by the passage of decades, one writer maintained: "it is probably accurate to say that no social metamorphosis in history is so much the product of the vision of one man."[46]

The path to modernization upended centuries of Ottoman life. Kemal's first major initiative came in secularizing Turkish society. He abolished the Caliphate in 1924, for centuries the supreme religious figure of the Ottoman state, and closed down religious schools in favor of public education.[47] He broke from long-established traditions by banning women from wearing head scarves in public and outlawing men from wearing a turban or fez.[48] He abandoned the Muslim solar calendar in favor of the Christian one and implemented the twenty-four-hour clock. International numerals replaced Arabic ones. Kemal modeled the Turkish legal system on Europe, borrowing from the Italian penal, the German commercial, and the Swiss bankruptcy codes.[49] Women acquired equal treatment in the fields of inheritance and divorce, and gradually entered professions and the public sphere once the exclusive domain of men. Turkey granted female suffrage in 1930 in local elections, placing it ahead of most of the world.[50] By contrast, the United States granted women the right to vote in 1920; France in 1944; and Switzerland in 1971.

Radical transformations of the Turkish language made it unrecognizable to its Ottoman predecessor. Kemal switched the alphabet from Arabic to Latin letters. He then purged the language of foreign elements. A Turkish Language Society searched dictionaries and regional dialects to find Turkish replacements for foreign words in the name of purifying the language.[51] Cities received Turkish names: Smyrna to Izmir nad Angora (the new capital) to Ankara. For himself Kemal added a surname, Atatürk, father of the Turks, and announced that others should follow suit.[52]

While the progression to modernity broke from the Ottoman past, a move toward Turkification established the underpinnings of denial. The Ottoman Empire's multinational and multiethnic hodgepodge of peoples stretching across three continents lacked a unifying feature, an omission that contributed to its demise as independence movements among its subject nationalities splintered the empire. (The empire even lacked a national anthem.) Along with his Republican People's Party, Kemal looked to Turkish nationalism to create the unity missing in the formerly fragmented empire. Prior to Kemal, few Ottoman citizens thought of themselves as "Turks"—a term mostly used by Europeans. Kemal displaced this heterogeneous concept of Ottoman citizenship with a homogenous one rooted in Turkish identity.[53] This policy positioned ethnic Turks in a dominant position. The loss of the empire's Arab, African, and European populations along with the removal of its Armenian and Greek inhabitants eased the implementation of this policy.[54] Only the Kurds stood in the way of Turkish homogeneity. By severely restricting the teaching of Kurdish in schools and integrating formerly isolated Kurdish regions into mainstream Turkish society, Turkey hoped to assimilate the lone significant minority. The government went as far as banishing Kurdish names in favor of Turkish ones to promote homogeneity.[55]

The process of Turkification not only looked forward but backward in time as well.[56] To Kemal and his cadre, history—along with language—remained not merely a field of study but another tool in reshaping society. He established a team of scholars to rewrite Turkish history not as it was but as it should have been.[57] Working toward the same goals as the language engineers, the Turkish Historical Society took up the task in 1931, quickly forging textbooks calling the multinational composition of the Ottoman regime an aberration.[58] This image contrasted with the reality of an empire stretching from the Caspian Sea to Algeria to the Balkans in which Arabs, Assyrians, Egyptians, Kurds, Greeks, Bulgarians, Slavs, Jews, and Armenians all lived.

This aspiration to rewrite history, and in doing so completely break away from a backward Ottoman past to adopt a national narrative consistent with a modern, powerful Turkey, played a critical role in distorting the historical record when it came to the Armenians. Armenians made no appearance in these voluminous tomes covering the ancient eras up to the Middle Ages, despite having roots in Anatolia since the middle of the first millennium B.C. They barely appeared in the volumes covering more recent history. The Genocide went unspoken.[59]

Armed with a revisionist historiography, the Turkish government utilized public education as the primary tool in teaching and spreading this new ideology. Within the classroom, students learned the new dogma placing the Turkish state at the center of civic life and cementing their bond with Turkish ethnicity. Outside the classroom, regularly scheduled ceremonies, pledges, anthems, poetry readings, and commemorations of secular events and heroes confirmed their curriculum. In the years up to 1950, Turkey established 83,931 schools for adults to combat widespread illiteracy and indoctrinate adults with this new civic dogma.[60]

Kemal succeeded in implementing such far-reaching changes so quickly because of his immense popularity. Whereas America boasted several founding fathers, Turkey had one: Atatürk. Monuments and pictures in his honor popped up ubiquitously across Turkey; mobs of adorers followed him in public. He won the presidency with unanimous votes in Parliament on three occasions. Generations of students still memorize his six-day speech of 1927, a speech so famous it has a name: *Nutuk*.[61]

Throughout this process, Turkey concomitantly established a policy of denying the Armenian Genocide. Several of the Young Turk leaders, including Talaat, forged the earliest forms of denial by authoring publications defending the regime from international condemnation and absolving themselves of responsibility.[62] It is unclear when or how a campaign of denial progressed from these guilty individuals to a state policy administered by the Republic of Turkey. Looking at the totality of the changes Turkey went through, a picture begins to emerge which shows that modernization, Turkification, and effacement of the Ottoman past piloted the nation to conceal this episode from its official history. The Turkish historian Taner Akçam, who has become a pariah in Turkey for writing extensively on this subject, has pointed out that a "state that asserts itself as a new entity must provide a basis for its legitimacy and predicate that legitimacy on the historical past."[63] Because Islam and the Ottoman dynasty had dominated Turkish life for centuries, Akçam explained, modern Turkey distanced itself from these pillars of identity, instead looking to a more distant past for its roots. A new generation of Turks learned an official history that spoke little of minorities and nothing of Ottoman sins.[64] The war of independence that ended in the triumph at Lausanne spawned a narrative of the Turkish Republic born from a war against imperialist Europe. Though this narrative carried a good deal of truth, it hid the second element of this birth: the destruction of Christian minorities in Anatolia, and specifically the murder of 1.5 million Armenians.

Denial of the Genocide rested on more than a desire to cover up a shameful episode of the Turkish past, which was antagonistic to the proud, honorable image fashioned for the newly minted nation. During the postwar peace talks, Armenian territorial claims against Turkey were justified as punishment for the Genocide. Disclosure of the massacres would keep these territorial claims alive no matter how unlikely such demands may have become with the Armenian Diaspora scattered across the globe and the Armenian Republic immolated by the USSR. Further, Turks took over many of the abandoned homes left behind by the Armenians; some of Turkey's wealthiest individuals built their fortunes on abandoned Armenian enterprises.[65] The cloak placed over the Genocide smothered any claims against this wholesale theft.

Because many of the original leaders of the Turkish Republic came from the ranks of the Young Turks, they too were motivated to hide their crimes. Arif Fevzi Pirinççizade, for instance, who helped organize the Armenian massacres in Diyarbakir, became minister of public

affairs in 1922–23. Dr. Tevfik Rüştü once headed a council responsible for burying Armenian corpses during the Genocide; he served as
foreign minister from 1925 to 1938. Şükrü Kaya, who implemented
the deportation orders during the massacres, thereby earning the title
"Director General for Deportation," headed the leading political party
in the early years of the Turkish Republic. Many of the rank and file of
the nationalist movement came from the ranks of the Young Turks—
including those wanted for human rights violations.[66]

Memories of the violence remained alive in Turkish witnesses. The
state's complete disregard of the event, however, inculcated new generations with a version of history in which the Genocide had no existence.
Instead of reminding itself of the decaying Ottoman Empire ending
with a crime of grotesque proportions, Turkey chose to ignore the past.

Turkey's historical revisionism did not infect other nations. But
they began to view Turkey in a new light that reflected its progress
under Kemal. By the tenth anniversary of the republic, Kemal had
raised Turkey from a pariah state on the verge of disintegration to
membership into the world's leading institution, the League of Nations. Countries that had for decades disparaged the "sick man of
Europe" now congratulated Turkey for its secular, Western-leaning
conversion. Bristol's American Friends of Turkey arranged for a radio
program as part of a media blitz and launched a membership campaign
to accompany a celebration at the Waldorf-Astoria Hotel in New York,
where President Roosevelt sent a congratulatory note.[67]

This newfound friendship between the United States and Turkey
would face its first test in Hollywood—a test that revealed that Turkey's
policy of denial was not limited to its population but would be applied
across the world.

When the acclaimed Jewish writer Franz Werfel set out for Damascus
in 1929, the spectacle of stick-figured children among the looms of
a rug-weaving factory shocked him. "The miserable sight of some
maimed and famished-looking refugee children . . . gave me the final
impulse to snatch from Hades . . . this incomprehensible destiny of
the Armenian nation," Werfel later wrote.[68] Werfel spent two years
poring over the files of Johannes Lepsius, the chief defense witness in

the Tehlirian trial, and others in preparing a book.[69] Instead of writing about the Genocide as a whole, he turned his attention to one community of Armenians that saved itself from destruction atop a peak called the Mountain of Moses, or *Musa Dagh* in Turkish.

Werfel's novel, *The Forty Days of Musa Dagh*, retold the story by replacing the commander of the Armenian defense force with an assimilated Armenian who, upon his return home from France after twenty-three years to clear up family affairs, defended the mountainous enclave for a biblically influenced forty—rather than fifty-three—days. Werfel told reporters: "The struggle of 5,000 people on Musa Dagh had so fascinated me that I wished to aid the Armenian people by writing about it and bringing it to the world."[70]

After its release in November 1933, the novel, with its vivid details of courageous military battles and heroism, appeared in thirty-four languages. When the 824-page book hit stands in the United States a year later, it sold 34,000 copies in the first two weeks, placing it at the top of the best-seller list in 1934.[71] The *New York Times Book Review* opined that "Werfel has made of it a noble novel, and if Hollywood does not mar and mishandle it, it should make a magnificent movie." Recognizing the same potential of *Musa Dagh* as a movie, Metro-Goldwyn-Mayer had already purchased cinematic rights to the book and slated Clark Gable for the lead role.[72]

When news of the production reached the Turkish government, it sent its ambassador, Mehmet Munir Ertegun (father of the founder of Atlantic Records), to meet with Wallace Murray, who held Allen Dulles's old post at the Near East desk in the State Department. The ambassador told Murray that he "earnestly hoped that [the movie studio] would desist from presenting any such picture, which could only give a distorted version of the alleged massacres."[73] Ertegun's message revealed that Turkey's policy of denial was not limited to its own borders. It intended to project this policy across the world.

Knowing that MGM would not easily concede to dropping a project with the potential for a big payday, the State Department tried to assuage Turkey that the film would not besmirch the nation. Ertegun, however, insisted on terminating production; the policy of denial required absolute conformity in Turkish eyes. The ambassador wrote to Murray at the State Department: "I refer to your letter . . . in which you informed me that . . . there would be nothing in [the movie] which could give offense to Turkey. . . . I am sure that you will appreciate how much importance I place on preventing the misleading of public opinion in America through erroneous features concerning the history of my country."[74]

When the State Department's initial assurances failed to appease Ertegun, it offered the ambassador a copy of the finalized script prior to filming, a concession it won from MGM through the Motion Picture Producers and Distributors of America—the industry watchdog that often censored or altered movies. That too did not palliate the Turkish government, as it vetoed increasingly watered-down versions of the script. Eventually, Turkey upped the ante by threatening to ban all MGM productions—even all American movies—in Turkey should *Musa Dagh* be made into a film and asked friendly governments to institute a similar ban.[75]

With no Armenian state to counter Turkey and the Armenian-American community immobilized after Cardashian's death, only MGM could stand up to its threats. Ertegun's attempts to censor an American filmmaker appalled MGM's production chief, who declared: "To hell with the Turks, I'm going to make the picture anyway." For him and other like-minded executives at MGM, the issue rested not so much on the Armenians but on Turkey's attempts to strong-arm America's leading film studio.[76] As the studio proceeded, the Turkish government grew more vituperative, however. Ertegun told an MGM official at a meeting in Washington: "If the movie is made, Turkey will launch a worldwide campaign against it. It rekindles the Armenian question. The Armenian question is settled."[77]

Ertegun's message revealed Turkey's fear in reopening an issue the nation had buried a decade earlier in Lausanne. *Musa Dagh*, Turkey feared, might rekindle Armenian demands for a homeland carved out of Turkey.

Eventually, MGM's chief, Louis B. Mayer, the "Lion of Hollywood," caved in to Turkey's demands.

Ertegun was grateful. "I have already informed my government of the satisfactory result reached through the kind support of the State Department," he wrote to the agency.[78] The incident gave the State Department an understanding of Turkey's intense desire to efface the Genocide from its past. Murray of the Near East desk wrote in a memo that the Genocide reflects a "chapter in Turkish history which the present government is only too glad to soft-pedal."[79] Over the years, the State Department would come to appreciate Turkish sensitivity about its dark past on many occasions.

The *Musa Dagh* incident is critical in understanding the evolution of Turkey's campaign of denying the crimes committed by the Young Turks. Obfuscation of the Genocide reflected more than an internal policy intended for consumption by the Turkish populace. The standoff with MGM revealed that Turkey would pressure foreign governments to go along with its policy of denial.

The incident also exemplified how Turko-American relationship began to flourish during the 1930s. With Armenians powerless to stop the progression of this relationship, Bristol's American Friends of Turkey strengthened social, political, and economic ties between the nations, paving the way for the strategic alliance forged during the Cold War.

The Truman Doctrine

Even if we put things in the best light,—
We are tourists in our own country,
Guests in our own homes.
A river over which we rule one bank,
A mountain which appears only from a distance,
An unpeopled land,
A landless people
Who like scattered beads cannot be reassembled.

—GEVORG EMIN[1]

"The gravity of the situation which confronts the world today necessitates my appearance before a joint session of the Congress," President Harry S. Truman began at an unhurried pace on the afternoon of March, 12, 1947. After this solemn introduction, he got to the point. "One aspect of the present situation . . . concerns Greece and Turkey." He then explained that a Communist threat to these nations made it necessary for the United States to embark on a groundbreaking path to come to their aid. "I am fully aware of the broad implications involved," Truman continued in his matter-of-fact delivery. "Great responsibilities have been placed upon us. . . ."[2]

Truman delivered perhaps the biggest foreign policy speech of his presidency. In one of the opening volleys of the Cold War, he boldly announced America's intention to stand up to the USSR. In his memoirs, he called this "the turning point in America's foreign policy"—the point at which the United States forged an aggressive stance toward its rival superpower the Soviet Union.[3] A member of the White House staff went further, noting in a diary that it "may well prove to be the most important speech of his life."[4] What came to be known as the Truman Doctrine would stand as a pillar of America's Cold War policy for the next four decades.

Unbeknownst to probably anyone in the audience and the millions listening on the radio, the twenty-minute speech introducing the world to the Truman Doctrine would tie the fate of Armenian dreams and aspirations to the Cold War for nearly half a century. The Communist threat that Truman identified in his seminal speech would powerfully influence America's relations with Turkey. And the growing bond between these two Cold War allies would have, in turn, a profound impact on America's relationship with the Armenians.

Truman stepped into the presidency as America's standing in the world began to peak. The nation hardly resembled the callow country plunged into war from a sneak attack on Pearl Harbor in 1941. Its unrivaled economic resurgence vanquished the malaise of the 1930s. With a monopoly over atomic power, its military might stood unequaled. The end of the war brought with it an end to rationing, replacing the sacrificial ethos of the war years with a newfound optimism. The Americans had won the war in two theaters, the only nation to do so. GIs returned home to populate the nation's universities in unprecedented numbers. Postwar America basked in triumph and relief.

At the same time, with the prewar powers of Germany and Japan defeated, a new enemy—a more dangerous enemy—loomed: the Soviet Union. Since the end of the war, this new threat appeared more menacing at every turn. The USSR modernized its massive army. It began to experiment with atomic power. Its brutal leader Joseph Stalin placed a chokehold over Eastern Europe. The USSR armed, financed, and aided Communist factions in China and North Korea. Communist parties gained ground in Italy and France, two nations still reeling from wartime capitulation.

None of these actions pitted Soviet and U.S. armed forces directly against each other. The collision of two colossal armies coming off the massive casualties of World War II was a spectacle everyone wanted to avoid. This was a "cold" war, not a "hot" one. But it was still a war. Though the USSR fired no bullets at U.S. troops, American policy makers perceived the spread of communism and the Soviet Union's intimidation of its neighbors as aggressive tactics intended to strengthen the USSR at the expense of the United States and its allies. Nearly every nation seemed in peril of submitting to Soviet might. In particular, Soviet domination of Europe threatened America's vision of converting these formerly occupied nations into pro-American, capitalist-oriented democracies that would hold the same values as the United States. And in waging this war where direct military confrontation was an anathema, the United States looked to other means to win.

Truman's doctrinal speech was motivated by this desire to block Soviet control of Europe and contain the USSR's influence without resorting to a direct military attack. Specifically, in 1947, the United States feared that Greece would collapse. A civil war in the Hellenic state pitted a fragile pro-Western camp against foreign-backed Communists. The economy suffered a meltdown with starvation and pestilence on the rise.[5] Would Soviet-backed left-wing forces lead Greece away from its Western orientation in favor of the USSR? Greece's pending demise symbolized an emerging crisis in which every nation seemed at risk of a Communist takeover.

Just as Greece was teetering, Soviet intimidation of Turkey also entered into the American calculus. While the Soviet Union targeted Greece through proxies, it aimed directly at Turkey by looking to take control of the Black Sea straits and seize provinces on Turkey's eastern border adjacent to Soviet Armenia. The USSR's aggression would have an impact that extended far beyond the Cold War to cast a shadow over the Armenian Genocide itself.

Stalin's first overture for the straits at the conduit between the Black and Mediterranean seas came in 1940 when, allied with Germany at the early stages of World War II, he saw an opportunity to grab the strategic naval chokepoints. Hitler, though, rebuffed Stalin. The Führer did not want to add to his growing list of enemies and knew a move to snatch the straits would encourage Turkey to join the Allies. Hitler wanted to keep Turkey neutral throughout the war. In 1943, Germany sent Mehmet Talaat's remains back to his home country where the chief perpetrator of the Genocide received a second funeral—the first coming in Berlin at the hands of Soghomon Tehlirian—this time attended by representatives of Turkey's leadership who had shunned Talaat after the war. A member of the British Embassy noted that the eulogy lionized the Young Turk while ignoring his crime against the Armenians. Hitler's strategy to keep Turkey neutral largely succeeded, despite British pleas urging the Turks to enlist on its side. Turkey did not join the Allied war effort until February 1945, doing so at that point in order to meet the cutoff date to join the United Nations then under formation.[6]

The demands of World War II put Stalin's ambition for the Black Sea straits on hold. But as soon as the war's end seemed in sight, he began to make overtures for them. The straits—though his main objective—were not Stalin's only target. Two of Turkey's eastern provinces—Kars and Ardahan—at the periphery of Soviet Armenia had switched hands innumerable times between Sultans and Czars over the centuries. Despite the constant transfer of title, Armenians remained in the area until the USSR imparted the provinces to Turkey in the early 1920s during the dismemberment of the Armenian Republic. At the end of World War II, Stalin wanted the provinces returned to Soviet Armenia.[7]

Stalin recruited the head of the Armenian Church to help. In June 1945, Soviet authorities allowed the election of a new Catholicos to fill a seven-year vacancy left open when Soviet henchmen had strangled the previous pontiff. Moscow's pick for the job won easily, garnering 110 of 111 votes. The Catholicos had historically acted in a quasi-diplomatic role on his people's behalf. Once in office, he reprised this role. "We do not wish to dwell unduly on this boundless tragedy," the Catholicos wrote to a meeting of the war's victors in the autumn of 1945. "It is [your] duty to remove past injustices. . . ."[8]

Stalin masked the territorial demand as something other than a naked land grab by arguing that Armenians needed the additional lands to thrive. While his motives were impure, the Catholicos's entreaties for these lands reflected genuine Armenian sentiments. At this time, many Genocide survivors still longed to return home to re-create the life stripped from them. Their lost land remained etched in their memories, a concrete place they hoped to rehabilitate after years of separation rather than the mythical homeland it became for later generations. The magnetic pull of the homeland spurred the Catholicos, with Stalin's blessing, to accompany the call for Turkey's provinces with a repatriation campaign urging Armenians in the Diaspora to return to their mother country. The potential accretion of hundreds of thousands of new Armenians justified the argument for additional land at Turkey's expense.[9]

Most of the 100,000 to 150,000 repatriates emigrated to Soviet Armenia from the Middle East and Eastern Europe, with only a few hundred Armenian-Americans making the trip. Many emigrated despite their dislike of the Soviet Union. "[I]f a child is to be beaten," one repatriate told the British Embassy in Turkey, "it prefers to be beaten by its own father rather than a stranger."[10] The lure of a homeland was simply too attractive for some. They preferred to live in Armenia—any Armenia, no matter how disquieting—rather than remain in exile. "As a group," an American intelligence report aptly described the Armenians, "they have never felt at home in the lands to which they fled only 30 years ago, and thus respond readily to the appeal of repatriation."[11]

The repatriates found life in Soviet Armenia dreadful. Few received the homes and jobs promised by Soviet authorities, and the locals resented the addition of new mouths to feed at a time of scarcity. Many ended up living in makeshift structures similar to the refugee camps they had inhabited as survivors in the 1920s, and worked in physically demanding trades. Some endured constant surveillance from the KGB and ended up in prison camps. Repatriates established a "picture code" to signal to family members left behind whether they should join them in Soviet Armenia. In pictures sent to relatives abroad, if the head of the family was standing in the photo, it meant that the family prospered in Soviet Armenia, thus urging the rest to emigrate. If the patriarch remained seated in the photo, then it signaled to those left behind not to join the repatriates in their paltry state. Few of the photos showed the patriarchs standing.[12]

Stalin buttressed the Catholicos's pleas with increasingly belligerent tactics. Near the end of the war, the USSR terminated a twenty-year treaty of friendship with Turkey to cap off the diplomatic pressures the Soviet giant would press upon the Turks. Stalin also sent his trusted hound dog, Foreign Minister Vyacheslav Molotov, to demand the provinces back and renegotiate the terms of the Black Sea straits.

If Turkey wanted to remain friends with the USSR, then it would have to give up these territories. The warmongering increased through veiled threats in the Soviet press and the deployment of hundreds of thousands of troops fortified by several armored divisions in Bulgaria and Romania amassed around Turkey.[13]

While the Soviet Union exerted diplomatic and military pressure against Turkey, Armenians across the world initiated an ad hoc campaign urging governments to support the territorial transfer. One of the leaders of this campaign was a familiar name, the last prime minister of the Armenian Republic, Simon Vratsian.

The preceding two decades had been tough on Vratsian. After Soviet forces snuffed out his counterinsurgency in 1921, Vratsian, and other leaders of the Armenian Republic, fled to Iran. His son died during the escape. From there, his peripatetic path took him to Baghdad, Bombay, Paris, and finally to Boston, where he decamped at the ARF's headquarters.[14] Vratsian never set foot in his homeland again. Despite these setbacks and the onset of middle age, Vratsian's dreams for his country and people remained as ardent as ever. The 1923 Treaty of Lausanne signaled the death knell of the post–World War I campaign to help the Armenians. The passage of twenty years since the treaty's signing failed to reduce Vratsian's rage; he described it as "one of the most shameful pages of history."[15]

During World War II, new declarations of self-determination and just treatment of small nations by the world's Great Powers rekindled Vratsian's aspirations. In 1941, Winston Churchill and Franklin Delano Roosevelt issued the Atlantic Charter, promising "self government . . . to those who have been forcibly deprived of [it]."[16] Spurred by the Charter's idealistic language, Vratsian prepared a booklet in 1943 to remind the world that the "Armenian Question still remains unsolved, and that Armenia anxiously awaits the justice which is due her."[17] The exigency of war drowned out his advocacy until 1945.

At the talks leading up to the Charter, Roosevelt and Churchill also discussed the creation of a new international body of governments to displace the ineffectual League of Nations. Four years later—from April to June 1945—fifty nations met in San Francisco to forge this new organization that would come to be known as the United Nations.[18] Though its structure favored the world's largest nations, those powerful enough to join the Security Council club, and it was by no means perceived as a utopian creation that would forever end conflict, the United Nations espoused ideals like "universal peace," "human rights," and "self-determination."

While the Soviet Union worked through official diplomatic channels, Vratsian and others from the Diaspora labored as unofficial spokesmen on behalf of the Armenians. The United Nations' willingness to entertain representatives lacking government imprimatur made it the perfect venue for Vratsian. He attended the United Nations Conference in San Francisco alongside 1,500 advocates, lobbyists, and consultants vying for attention. Despite the glut of voices competing against it, Vratsian's delegation delivered presentations on May 7 and June 13 asking the United Nations to grant "a just and durable peace" to the Armenian people consistent with the ideals giving birth to the organization. Two days before the termination of the conference, George Mardikian, the proprietor of the famous Omar Khayyam restaurant, which had catered much of the conference with its international menu free of charge, telecast an hour-long program on NBC Radio entitled *The Voice of Armenia*, backing Vratsian's words.[19]

The endeavors made by Vratsian and others capped off two years of advocacy by Armenians from the Diaspora.[20] Though their efforts were often uncoordinated amongst each other and largely disconnected from the Soviet Union's campaign against Turkey, advocates managed to stage rallies throughout the world, placed ads and editorials in newspapers, participated in radio shows, and lobbied governments. Petitions from Armenian communities in France, Britain, Syria, Greece, Lebanon, Egypt, and even a tiny contingent in Cuba reached nearly every major international diplomatic conference from 1945 to 1947.[21] Leaders in Britain, the United States, and the Soviet Union, as well as the Secretary-General of the newly formed United Nations, received numerous letters from these advocates.[22] The Armenian issue again echoed in the halls of Congress. In a repeat of Cardashian's ACIA following World War I, a group of politicians like Senator Charles Tobey of New Hampshire, who since childhood had carried a "burning impression" of the Genocide, supported the Armenians.[23]

With the Genocide still fresh in the world's memory, these advocates spent little energy rehashing its details when arguing for the territorial transfer. "Knowing your familiarity with the record of subjugation, persecution and massacre of the Armenians by the Turks," read a typical letter addressed to Truman, "the Committee refrains from a long and detailed statement thereon. . . ."[24] No one took Turkish denial at face value in the mid-1940s, so the Armenians had no need to remind world leaders or the general population of the Genocide.

Just as the Armenian campaign hit its stride, the emergence of the Cold War came to overshadow the endeavor. Soviet aggression throughout 1945 and 1946 fueled American fears that the USSR would plow down every nation that stood in its path. Then, in August 1946, Britain announced the withdrawal of its armed forces from the Middle East. At about the same time, the Soviet Union increased its pressure on Turkey by issuing new demands for control of the straits.[25] With the region left undefended in the face of these amplified threats, Turkey seemed like the Soviet Union's next victim.

These developments spurred one of Truman's closest associates, Under Secretary of State Dean Acheson, to convene a committee selected from the State, War, and Navy departments in August 1946 to update and solidify the strategy already forming in U.S. diplomatic and military circles. With his bosses spending most of their time attending international conferences abroad after World War II, Acheson often remained the State Department's top man in Washington. His proximity to Truman helped form a trusting relationship, granting Acheson a strong degree of influence with the president: frequent phone calls compounded four to five weekly face-to-face meetings. Acheson described the relationship as "a great thing between Mr. Truman and me"; Truman called Acheson his "top brain man." "History, I am sure," he wrote in his memoirs, "will list Dean Acheson among the truly great Secretaries of State. . . ." Acheson reciprocated this mutual admiration. The budding relationship blossomed after the 1946 election in which the Republicans took control of Congress for the first time since Roosevelt's sweeping victory in 1932. When Truman returned from Missouri demoralized after the lopsided defeat for which he received much of the blame, Acheson greeted him at the train platform in Union Station. No one else did.[26]

Soviet intimidation of Turkey contributed to Acheson's—and the nation's—gradual turn from a posture of conciliation with the USSR, which only a year earlier had been locked in an apocalyptic battle against a common enemy, toward an aggressive stance that would transform the diplomat into a zealous Cold Warrior. By the time of the Acheson meeting in August 1946, Churchill had already delivered his "iron curtain" speech in Fulton, Missouri, warning of Soviet expansion, and some in the U.S. government had already embraced a tougher stance toward Stalin. After watching the Soviets bully their neighbors since the waning days of World War II, Acheson eventually came to the same conclusion. Soviet belligerence toward Turkey pushed him over the edge. This is where he drew the line. He wanted to let the Soviet Union know that war with Turkey meant war with the United States.[27]

The group overseen by Acheson met with the president on August 15. With General Dwight D. Eisenhower at his side at one end of a crescent formed around the president's table, the under secretary urged Truman to take a tougher position with the Soviets—concluding that only force could deter Stalin from obtaining control of Turkey.[28] "In our opinion," Acheson's group concluded in its report, "the time has come when we must decide that we shall resist by all means at our disposal any Soviet aggression and, in particular, because the case of Turkey would be so clear, any Soviet aggression against Turkey."[29]

Turkey's position melded neatly with America's emerging posture toward the Soviet Union. Sitting at the USSR's underbelly, Turkey could control the Black Sea, block access to the Mediterranean Sea to the Soviet navy, and shield the essential oil fields—the lifeblood of the West—of the Middle East. It could also house air bases, conveniently accessible by sea to the U.S. Navy, to strike at Soviet targets unreachable from Western Europe. Only Turkey could play this essential role in the region, Acheson told the president. In a precursor to the "domino theory" that would later underpin American policy in Vietnam, Acheson argued that if Turkey fell, then every country in the region could fall one after another to communism's octopus-like reach. At that mid-August meeting, Acheson's group designated Turkey a key player in America's global struggle with the USSR, an essential ally if the

United States and the Soviet Union locked into a global war, and a key impediment against the spread of communism. Despite the dramatic shift in U.S. policy enunciated by the report, no one in the working group objected when Acheson told the president that "our national policy should be to support Turkey."[30]

Upon finishing the presentation, Acheson uttered out loud a question whispered into his ear by Eisenhower: did the president understand that the policy recommended by Acheson's committee could lead to war? Truman did not hesitate. At the Potsdam Conference in the summer of 1945, he had stood by diffidently as Churchill resisted Stalin's moves against Turkey. By the time of this meeting, Churchill had been displaced as prime minister and Britain as a world power. Truman stepped into the void with the lessons of Neville Chamberlain's failed appeasement of Hitler before the start of World War II still fresh in his mind.[31]

The president responded to Acheson's query by unfolding a well-worn map of the Middle East before which he delivered a ten- to fifteen-minute lecture describing the importance of the region. Like Acheson, little by little, Truman had come to believe that Soviet expansion had to end, even if that meant catapulting the United States into a role it had previously shunned. The crisis in Greece and Turkey focused his inchoate ideas about Soviet intentions, propelling him to consolidate his brewing thoughts into a lucid, comprehensive doctrine. With the map in front of him, he made it clear to his advisers that he understood perfectly the dangers of this new policy. Even the risk of another catastrophic world war did not check Truman's determination to make a stand against the Soviet Union. "[W]e might as well find out whether the Russians were bent on world conquest," Truman told the group, smothering any remaining doubts.[32]

Four days later, Acheson hand-delivered a note to the Soviet Embassy confirming America's desire to have Turkey continue its exclusive administration of the straits. This was the first in a series of warnings issued by the United States. At the same time, Admiral Chester Nimitz ordered a new aircraft carrier group to the Mediterranean to show the Soviets that the United States was not bluffing.[33]

These steps were reactive, a game of push-and-pull with the Soviets often conducted outside the public's view. Truman wanted to make a bold pronouncement, publicly announcing a policy embracing this new role for America and warning the Soviets to back down in one turn. "The Russians would press wherever weakness showed," he wrote in his memoirs, "and we would have to meet that pressure wherever it occurred. . . . When Communist pressure began to endanger Greece and Turkey, I moved to make this policy clear and firm." Speechwriters worked independently of each other to reduce the risk of a security leak. Truman rejected the initial draft overloaded with statistical information and stalled by jargon—what he dubbed an "investment prospectus" ill-suited for public consumption. "The decision is to ask Congress for $250 million and say this is only the beginning," Truman told his cabinet during the preparation of his seminal speech. "It means the greatest selling job ever facing a President." Acheson took control of the process to bowdlerize woolly verbiage in massaging the final text. "I wanted no hedging . . . ," the president insisted of the speech. "It had to be clear and free of hesitation or double talk." Acheson delivered what Truman wanted. The result was a clear and pithy text dividing the world into two opposing camps: the democratic led by the United States and the totalitarian led by the USSR.[34]

As work on the speech progressed, the Soviets backed off from their demands. Their vacillation only bolstered Truman and Acheson. They saw it as proof of the effectiveness of their tough policy, the first major sign that defiance, not conciliation, would block Soviet aggression.[35]

Because the Truman Doctrine required years of vigilance to succeed, Truman and Acheson held a long-term view of Turkey's standing. If Turkey was going to deflect a Soviet invasion and—more important to American policy makers—play the role of a buffer on the USSR's southern flank as part of an American-led coalition, it needed an updated military trained in the latest techniques and armed with cutting-edge weapons. And if Turkey fell, American experts feared, the Soviet Union would sweep "across Iran and through the Persian Gulf into the Indian Ocean."[36] A onetime effort shielding the Turks from Stalin's belligerence would not suffice.

Turkey helped its cause throughout the process. Its recalcitrance impressed the American military eagerly searching for resolute allies when much of Western Europe lay prostrate. Throughout the crisis in 1945–47, despite being overmatched by the titanic Soviet army at the height of its power, Turkey refused to concede an inch. After all, Atatürk had built his legend in the early 1920s by blocking Europe from carving up what remained of the Ottoman Empire. The 1923 Treaty of Lausanne became the apotheosis of Atatürk's crusade in guaranteeing Turkish territorial integrity. Nothing had changed in Turkey's thinking.[37] Its foreign minister assured the United States in January 1946 that if the Soviet government "used any pretext to bring about the seizure of the eastern provinces or any other Turkish territory, the Turkish people would meet such a situation with firm resolution. . . ."[38] As Soviet demands grew louder, Turkey increased its military spending. General Kâzim Karabekir, a hero of the 1920s campaign for Turkish independence, proclaimed: "The world must know that the Straits form the throat of the Turkish nation and the Kars Plateau its backbone."[39] Despite these brave pronouncements, Turkey was no match for the Soviet Union. It relied upon World War I–era munitions.[40] It needed help, and with its interests aligned with the United States, it embraced the proposed aid with alacrity and reciprocated U.S. overtures.

Acheson and Truman clearly understood the long-term ramifications of America's responsibilities and the knee-jerk retraction toward the prewar isolationism inveterate in their nation. To ensure the Truman Doctrine's success, they assembled support from leading members of the legislative branch before relaying the doctrine to the world.[41] Perhaps no congressional opinion mattered more than that of Senator Arthur H. Vandenberg, the Republican chairman of the Senate Foreign Relations Committee. Acheson and the president corralled Vandenberg's support for the Doctrine during a meeting with congressional leaders a fortnight before Truman delivered his speech to the world. At that meeting, Secretary of State George Marshall, sitting alongside the president, previewed the Doctrine to a skeptical congressional delegation displaying little enthusiasm for sending abroad hundreds of millions in aid after years of profligate spending. At that point, Acheson whispered to his boss, Marshall, for permission to speak. "Only two great powers remained in the world," Acheson started anew. "For the United States to take steps to strengthen countries threatened with Soviet aggression . . . was to protect the security of the United States—it was to protect freedom itself." The loss of Turkey and Greece would "open three continents to Soviet penetration," Acheson explained. A

long silence followed his presentation. "I will support you," Vandenberg finally told the president, casting aside whatever quibbles the new
Republican majority in the Senate may have had about Truman's daring
plan, "and I believe that most of [Congress] will do the same."[42]

Wearing a dark suit and tie, Truman read the speech from a black note-
book in a clear-cut tone bereft of dramatic flourishes. The lack of verbal
histrionics embodied the growing self-confidence in Truman's voice as
he relayed the gravity of the dangers facing the United States. "If we
falter in our leadership, we may endanger the peace of the world. . . ."[43]

As the architect and chief salesman of this aggressive Cold War
doctrine, Acheson sat stoically in the front row dressed to sartorial
perfection, his hands folded in his lap. His hawklike nose, signature
mustache, and matching eyebrows combined with a stodgy pose to
form a declarative countenance.[44]

Senator Robert A. Taft, a conservative cast in his father's image—
albeit a slimmer version than the portly twenty-seventh president—and
a leading isolationist among the Republicans, sat further down the
front row from Acheson. Other than Vandenberg, no other man in
the government could thwart Truman's policy. Though he would come
to derail the president's pro-labor agenda, Taft did little to disrupt the
implementation of the Truman Doctrine.[45]

"The future of Turkey as an independent and economically sound
state is clearly no less important to the freedom-loving peoples of the
world than the future of Greece," Truman said after explaining to
Congress why Greece needed America's help. "Turkey is essential to the
preservation of order in the Middle East. . . . This is a serious course
upon which we embark. I would not recommend it except that the
alternative is much more serious," he noted in appreciation of the unprecedented step he asked of Congress. He did not pause to acknowledge the short burst of applause. Instead, he moved on to his final point
to clearly evoke the nature of the stakes should America waver: "The
free peoples of the world look to us for support in maintaining their
freedoms. If we falter in our leadership, we may endanger the peace of
the world—and we shall surely endanger the welfare of our nation."[46]

The president asked for $400 million (about $3.6 billion in today's dollars) in aid for the two nations. He also wanted to send American personnel to Greece and Turkey. And he reminded the packed house spilling into the aisles that he would ask for more.

All but one member of Congress—a left-wing representative belonging to the American Labor Party—stood up to applaud his speech. Except for a bow toward his wife and an ephemeral smile, the president absorbed the encomium solemnly.[47] It was a seminal moment for Truman, one of the first in a series of dramatic acts that eventually catapulted him out of his predecessor's giant shadow to an underdog victory in the 1948 election. It also set the tone for American foreign policy throughout the Cold War: a canon Truman came to call "doctrinal." According to his biographer David McCullough, the Truman Doctrine was one of Truman's greatest accomplishments.[48] After the speech, Truman flew down to Key West exhausted. "No one, not even me," he wrote to his daughter, "knew how very tired and worn to a frazzle the Chief Executive had become. This terrible decision I had to make had been over my head for about six weeks."[49]

His exertion paid off. The nation's premier media outlets—the *New York Times*, *Time*, and *Life*—praised Truman's speech, the first calling it a "Monroe Doctrine." America's European allies were pleasantly surprised by Truman's forcefulness; Winston Churchill's missive congratulated the president for his contribution to "world peace and freedom."[50] After Acheson met with Republican eaders to assuage lingering doubts—answering 110 questions at one hearing—the House approved funding for Greece and Turkey in May 1947 by a vote of 287–107; the Senate, with most of the Republicans in tow, passed Truman's measure 67–23.[51] Overwhelming bipartisan support for Turkey's friendship shielded the relationship from electoral capriciousness in the future.

Armenian territorial demands made by the Soviet Union and backed by Armenians from the Diaspora like Vratsian did not go unnoticed during the development of this Doctrine. A comprehensive memorandum written by the head of the Near East desk at the State Department on November 19, 1945, bluntly laid out America's policy on this issue. "[T]his Government does not now reaffirm the stand

taken by President Wilson," noted Gordon P. Merriam in response
to "a fairly steady flow of letters, telegrams and memoranda" sent by
Armenian-Americans encouraging support for the territorial transfer.
"This Government does not favor the establishment of an independent
Armenian National State at the expense of any country. . . ."[52] The
memorandum hammered a nail in the Armenian coffin. That same day,
Loy W. Henderson, also from the Near East desk, relayed Merriam's
damning assessment to Acheson. It made it plainly clear that the State
Department now rejected Wilson's vision of an Armenian homeland
and turned a deaf ear to "Armenian groups . . . in the United States."[53]
When he met with an Armenian-American delegation in May 1947,
Acheson reaffirmed the agency's stance by vowing to personally oppose
any plan to annex land from Turkey on behalf of the Armenians. Because it stood in opposition to everything he had worked for in forging
the Truman Doctrine, he told the delegation its support for a territorial
transfer was "sheer madness."[54]

This dramatic shift in American policy overturning Wilson's vision
was neither arbitrary nor capricious. The U.S. administration studied
the issue thoroughly. "The Armenians were driven from their homes and
scattered over the face of the earth as a result of the First World War,"
concluded an American military intelligence report, "and the sufferings
of the Armenians fanned the flame of their nationalism to a white heat."
Since the West failed to satisfy "Armenian desires for a homeland," the
"Soviet offer . . . appeals to these Armenians. . . ."[55] Already, decades
before it turned into a heated debate between Turks and Armenians,
the State Department rejected Turkey's denial of the Genocide. "The
argument" made by Turkey of Armenian treachery during World War I,
an agency report from the era noted, "is compatible to Nazi accusations
of Jewish subversive activities, and it is equally invalid."[56]

America's appreciation of the horrors suffered by the Armenians
during the Genocide and its understanding of their desire for a return
of their historical lands did not outweigh what it saw as a pretext for
Soviet expansion: "the Armenian problem is a part of the Russian
preparation for possible action against Turkey."[57] Besides, argued the
State Department, "[p]ractically no Armenians remain" in the coveted
lands, "thanks to Turkey's brutal policy of extermination conducted
during the period 1885–1920."[58] The Central Intelligence Agency,

then in an embryonic stage, also weighed in on the issue. It so feared legitimizing Armenian territorial demands that it issued a warning asserting that the establishment of a Jewish state carved out of Palestine might serve as a precedent to justify the Armenian land claims.[59]

America's closest ally, Britain, arrived at the same conclusions. A comprehensive British report, though confirming that "the Turkish massacres and deportations of Armenians in 1915 and 1916 . . . under barbarous conditions" might justify the territorial hand-off, found it "both wrong and inexpedient to allow a historic claim of the Armenians . . . to be exploited for the strategic advantage of the Soviet Union." Another British report simply said of Stalin's motives: "This looked phony."[60] Indeed, curing a historical injustice had little to do with motivating Stalin, who neglected to mention that he himself had overseen the negotiations of the handover of the provinces he coveted in 1945 to Turkey three decades earlier.

Perhaps due to the millions he had killed and imprisoned, Stalin neglected to emphasize the humanitarian appeal of the claim. "It would also be unwise to overlook the strength of the claim to territorial indemnification [of the Turkish provinces] which might be based on the massacres perpetrated by the Turks on the Armenians," concluded a British report issued in 1946. "These massacres were so atrocious and have left such a lasting mark on the memory of the world, that if the *Soviet Government* chose to launch a propaganda campaign recalling all this, it would be likely to arouse a lot of sympathy in humanitarian circles all over the world and it might put Turkey in a very awkward position as Black Sheep No. 1." Instead, the Soviets camouflaged their demands with false pretenses by focusing on the need to boost economic development, an argument never uttered since the USSR swallowed the Armenian Republic in 1920. The claim seemed disingenuous even to credulous and sympathetic listeners.[61]

Armenian advocates appreciated that cynics might see the land transfer as a gain for the Soviet Union rather than compensation to the Armenians. They failed to appreciate, however, that with World War II finished, the United States was slowly sliding into a new war with the USSR. Turkey represented a critical ally in this struggle, no matter the level of weight Armenians gave to the idealistic words spoken at the end of the war. The Armenians could not overcome this geopolitical reality.

Though they managed to drum up some boosters among the American public, this support was tiny in comparison to the heartfelt response to the "starving Armenians" following World War I. Many Americans had come to view the Armenians as the neediest victims of World War I. That simply was not the case after World War II.[62] "I pointed out that he continuously referred to 1920," wrote a State Department representative after meeting with an Armenian advocate, "and that it was now 1945."[63] The Armenian desire to resurrect the Treaty of Sèvres had no legs in the new postwar era. Ultimately, the passage of time and the exigency of the Cold War handicapped any effort to "turn back the clock" from the previous war and redress the "ancient wrongs." "The Armenians in the terms of practical world politics," Merriam's salient memo concluded, "are among the remnants of peoples who years ago missed, once and for all, their chance for the reestablishment of an independent homeland. . . ."[64] Merriam was devastatingly dismissive about Armenian chances. There would be no do-over.

The reality was that with no political counterweight, the Truman Doctrine precluded any reconsideration of Armenian claims arising from the Genocide. Vratsian's personal labors exemplified this futility. He tapped a Columbia law professor with connections to the State Department to arrange for face-to-face meetings with American officials.[65] Because he did not represent a politically influential group, with votes and campaign dollars at the tips of his fingers, there were no repercussions for America's leaders, who ignored his entreaties. One official wrote to Acheson that if "the Under Secretary would see him for five or ten minutes," he should "dismiss him without any comment."[66] After months of dodging by the State Department, Vratsian's connection secured a meeting with a midlevel bureaucrat. It did not proceed as Vratsian had hoped. The former prime minister repeated the arguments made at the United Nations. The world had promised the Armenians a homeland after World War I partly as compensation for the Genocide. But his interlocutor saw no merit in these arguments: "the Armenian case," a State Department representative recorded in a memorandum about the meeting, "in my opinion rested too heavily on history and massacres."[67] What the official did not write in his memorandum was the cold reality of the situation: the Armenians needed power and a more auspicious set of geopolitical circumstances to succeed.

No matter the humanitarian and historical justifications, the top brass like Acheson along with institutional policy makers at the State and Defense departments simply would not allow the Armenians to derail America's emerging alliance with Turkey. The Armenians lacked the political clout to overcome this strategic calculation. They lacked a country of their own to press their case on the world stage. And elected officials had no fear of losing elections or paying a political price for snubbing them. One congressman turned down an invitation to speak before an Armenian audience because "there were virtually no Armenians in his District."[68] An American diplomat told a colleague that Turkey should not worry about negative publicity. "The Turks," he wrote, "ought to know by now that the American Armenians don't count for much."[69] The salient memorandum drafted by the head of the Near East desk laying out America's rejection of Armenian demands summed it up best: "the Armenians in the United States are not sufficiently numerous or important to represent a genuine 'pressure group.'"[70] The same dynamic had appeared during the 1923 negotiations leading up to the Treaty of Lausanne, where the largely powerless Armenians relied on past promises and moral suasion to make their case. In both instances, it simply was not enough to surmount all the forces pitted against them. Ultimately, with the Soviet threat looming large, the claims of a small, insignificant people like the Armenians no matter how compelling paled in comparison to geopolitical urgency. And at the end, geopolitical interests and the exhibition of raw power—not justice—prevailed. Of all the lands ceded by Russia in World War I (other than Finland and Poland), the USSR recaptured everything after World War II except for Kars and Ardahan.[71]

Having come during the formative stages of the Truman Doctrine, these territorial demands had profound consequences on the U.S. government's relationship with the Armenians for decades to come. Perhaps if Stalin had only made overtures for the Black Sea straits—which did not involve the Armenians and their Genocide-related claims against Turkey—America's pro-Turkish position would not have necessarily led to a complete rejection of Wilson's principles. But the convergence of the Armenian territorial claims sponsored by the Soviet Union with the start of the Cold War meant that in developing a pro-Turkish strategy, the United States was simultaneously

compelled to explicitly side against the Armenians. Though this shift
had already begun in the 1920s under the watch of Admiral Bristol, the
U.S. government did not maintain an overt anti-Armenian policy prior
to 1945. By 1947, however, the government not only viewed Turkey
as an essential partner in the Cold War but completely overturned the
post–World War I vision embraced by Wilson and so many others in
the United States at that time. And unlike in the 1920s, economic
interests no longer steered American policy. Rather, America's strategy
depended on an alliance built on a far stronger foundation: the threat
of Soviet domination. The end result was that the Armenians, already
stateless and powerless, had one more hurdle to overcome in their
fledgling pursuit for justice—an American government devotedly loyal
to Turkey. After all, if America was prepared to risk plunging into a
global war to shield Turkey from the Soviets, there seemed little chance
that it would side with the Armenians against this new ally.

Soon after congressional endorsement of the Truman Doctrine, $175
million poured into Turkey in 1947 and 1948 to modernize Turkey's army, revamp its infrastructure, and establish bases for American
bombers. Turkey also received a small slice of the pie doled out from
the Marshall Plan. By 1970, that slice ballooned to $3 billion in mili-
tary assistance on top of $1 billion in economic aid.[72]

The relationship quickly blossomed to America's delight. In 1949,
the State Department noted that the "cornerstone of Turkish foreign
policy in recent years has been traditional and unflinching resistance
to Russia." Two years later, another report explained that the "Turks
are determined to resist Soviet expansion. . . . They consider that
alignment with the US" the "only hope of effectively resisting Soviet
pressures. . . ."[73]

Turkey's entry into the North Atlantic Treaty Organization in
1952 would cement the alliance for the long haul. Turkey wanted
to enlist in the grand alliance, but its initial overtures to join were
rejected, as the NATO founders saw the military pact as one only
between Europe and the United States. Once again, Acheson, now
promoted to secretary of state, played a key role in U.S.-Turkish relations. Turkey's participation in the Korean War, along with a threat

that continued exclusion would thrust Turkey back into a neutral stance, led the United States to change its position under Acheson's watch.[74] Fearful of the loss of Turkey's friendship, and conscious that as a member of NATO, Turkey would not just stubbornly defend itself against Soviet attack but would be willing to fight for its allies, Acheson urged NATO's reluctant members and a wary Defense Department fearful of further stretching U.S. defense commitments to extend Turkey an invitation. "A full-fledged security arrangement . . . would be an important factor in obtaining Turkey's cooperation in security measures which might only indirectly benefit its security but which would be of considerable value to the anti-Soviet coalition," wrote Acheson to his former boss, George Marshall, his peer in the Defense Department in 1951.[75]

After the Senate voted in favor of Turkey's admission 73–2, U.S.-Turkish relations flourished under NATO's auspices. Turkish and American diplomats and military personnel worked closely together in NATO deliberations and exercises. They signed several bilateral defense pacts and cooperated to bring the Middle East into NATO's camp. The nations' armed forces formed ever closer bonds as the Cold War progressed throughout the 1950s. Nuclear warheads destined to become a critical element of the Cuban missile crisis accompanied by tens of thousands of American troops stationed in Turkey fortified this relationship.[76]

The Cold War came to dominate American foreign policy after World War II for the next forty-five years. Truman, Acheson, and a few others in the executive branch largely set the policy for the entire period: containment of the Soviet Union. They viewed Turkey, the only member of NATO sharing a border with the USSR, as a critical element of this strategy.

Though dejected at these setbacks, Vratsian approached his next job as a director of an Armenian school in Beirut with alacrity. Vratsian's dreams of resurrecting an Armenian homeland had been completely dashed, but perhaps he could still play a role in fostering the future hope of his people. Soon after his arrival from the United States in 1951, he became a mentor to a young and penniless Armenian student from Iran: Vartan Gregorian. Over time, Vratsian became a "surrogate father" to Gregorian, who had lost his mother as a child and had a strained relationship with his father. Vratsian helped enroll Gregorian at Stanford University. From there, Gregorian's meteoric rise took him to presidencies of the New York Public Library, Brown University, and the Carnegie Corporation. In his memoir, which Gregorian dedicated in part to Vratsian, Gregorian said of the former prime minister of the Armenian Republic: "To the protection, benefaction, affection, and friendship of my mentor . . . I owe everything."[77]

Preparing the next generation of Armenian leaders like Gregorian was Vratsian's last and perhaps greatest legacy, for it was this generation that finally shattered decades of silence to resurrect the Genocide from dormancy. That eruption would have to wait until 1965, when, after more years of hibernation during the Cold War, Armenians across the world rose to demand the justice promised but ultimately denied to them after World War I.

Silence

O silence. . . .
Descend, descend,
And cover me
Like my mother's soul.

—Leon Surmelian (1924)[1]

President Herbert Hoover wrote in his memoirs that "Probably Armenia was known to the American school child in 1919 only a little less than England."[2] That was no longer true in 1965. One of the most well known human rights disasters of the twentieth century had practically disappeared from the world's consciousness by its fiftieth anniversary. One could not find a single museum, noteworthy monument, research center, or even comprehensive publication about the Genocide. No one held public commemorations or ceremonies to honor the victims. How could such a widely known catastrophe have been forgotten? And what role did the Armenians play?

The Nine-Hundred-Day Republic would have been best situated to keep alive the memory of the Genocide. But that republic collapsed in 1920, and its new totalitarian rulers in the USSR had no wish to publicize the Genocide. Armenians in the Diaspora were muzzled not by an authoritarian government but by their exile across the globe. The eviction of the Armenians from the Ottoman Empire during the Genocide sent 45,000 refugees to Greece. Ninety thousand deportees settled in Lebanon and Syria, a few less in the United States, and another 65,000 relocated to France, which accepted the largest number of survivors in Europe.³ This dispersion left no geographic center to incubate a politically active community that could press the Armenian case after the Genocide.

The Armenians also suffered from a dearth of leadership. The mass slaughter had wiped out the adult male population, shattering a centuries-old way of life, leaving a generation of refugees and orphans with no guidance from the very group that had always provided it. Male elders had controlled the family's finances, directed the careers and education of their sons, and picked out husbands for daughters. With their patriarchs and their greatest statesmen like Krikor Zohrab largely killed off, Armenians lacked leadership on the familial, communal, and political level. Only a rudderless generation of widows and orphans remained. Vratsian, Cardashian, Aharonian, and Nubar were among the few notable exceptions to this decimation. With no grassroots support to rely upon, however, their influence with foreign governments rested upon their personal connections and passion combined with solicitude for the Armenians, rather than on an established foundation of political power.

Armenian silence was more than a reflection of political shortcomings, however. Most survivors had no desire to publicize their anguish. Walking out of the Ottoman Empire alive did not seem the least bit heroic. There was nothing redeeming in having persevered through the humiliations of starvation and rape, in watching loved ones die before their eyes, in witnessing the dehumanization of the deportation marches where all rules of civility and morality lay at the feet of absolute brutality. Most survivors wanted to look forward, not live in the dark past. They largely shunned any conversation on the topic with outsiders, instead releasing the burdens of their memories to family members and fellow survivors. Some did not even go that far, shielding their own children from their horrific experience. Recent decades have been marked by the glorification of victims and the victim's confessional has been raised to a revered status as it is passed down to younger generations. Such sentiments did not exist for most of the twentieth century. And while the survivors received a significant amount of charity, there was no clarion call to hear their stories about the Genocide—not by their families and certainly not by anyone else in the world. Besides, the survivors had other things to worry about. They spent the decades after the Genocide rebuilding their families and communal institutions. Survival and renewal, not grand declarations of justice or retreading of dreadful memories, governed their daily lives.

Starting their lives in nations where as newcomers they had little standing provided enough challenges for the survivor generation to overcome, leaving little energy for anything else. The 40,000 survivors who arrived in Aleppo, the city in northern Syria that was home to many refugees and orphans, for instance, endured various degrees of hell. "First, there are the homeless," wrote a foreign observer of the region's refugee camps, "a stream of women and children wandering through the streets. If you stop a child toward evening and ask him where he is going, he will tell you, 'I am searching for a place to sleep. . . . ' The women clasp their wan-faced children to their breasts and their own faces wear a look of despair." Those fortunate enough to sleep in shantytowns under rows of tents or shacks, melded together from leftover boxes and empty kerosene tanks, still endured starvation. An observer saw refugee women "stripping flesh from [a] dead horse with bare hands. . . ." Those with food and shelter were not off the hook, as pestilence lurked at every corner: typhus alone killed thousands during 1916 and 1917. With relief efforts in their infancy, humanitarian workers sometimes resorted to ruthless measures to stretch their scant resources. "They tell me that they had to adopt the principle of survival of the fittest," noted one observer, "and actually required mothers to select from their children those who are to be granted the opportunity to live, while the rest of the family were inevitably condemned to death."[4] Hell indeed.

Dozens of orphanages and refugee camps dotted the region, stretching from Greece to Egypt. The American-based Near East Relief, the region's largest humanitarian organization, sent $116 million ($25 million from the American government) in aid, and assisted more than 1 million refugees and 132,000 orphans during its years of service. "Armenians would have disappeared," declared one observer, had it not been for the missionary-based relief.[5]

Despite the difficult living conditions, the orphanages provided the safety and comfort needed for the traumatized children. "There was a nice community in the orphanage," recalled one survivor decades later.

"We used to dance and sing. We would sing a lot of sad songs and cry together." Indeed, memories of the deportations never strayed far from the orphans' minds. One chime went like this: "Virgin girls holding each others' hands, threw themselves into the River Euphrates." Despondency so pervaded the children that relief workers tried to teach "every child . . . the simple art of smiling."[6]

The Armenians in the United States fared better materially but had to contend with the growing xenophobia of the 1920s, which fueled pockets of discrimination against them. The most blatant took place in Fresno, California, where a restrictive land covenant incorporated into property documents prevented sales or leases to Armenians. Both President Dwight D. Eisenhower and his second in command, Richard M. Nixon, owned property with these anti-Armenian covenants. (Similar covenants would keep African-Americans out of white communities across the country.) Fresno's establishment, who called the Armenians "Fresno Niggers," also kept these "undesirables" out of their churches and social centers.[7] The Pulitzer Prize–winning author William Saroyan wrote of his childhood in Fresno, "immigrants are quickly made aware of a number of attitudes held by others about them, mainly that they are not the equal of Americans." The humiliation mortified the Armenian children. "It was soon so undesirable," Saroyan went on, "that many boys and girls wished to God they were something else, and even tried to pretend that they were actually not Armenian. . . ."[8] Many Armenians in America changed their names in response to this maltreatment and their feeling of shame: Baghdassarian became Baxter; Jermagian White; Anoushian Sweet. Others eschewed speaking Armenian in public.[9]

Though Armenian-Americans began to prosper under these challenging circumstances, they never escaped the shadow of the Genocide. "To be an Armenian in America is to be bitterly disappointed," one immigrant wrote. "To this country, this America so beloved, so rich, free, happy, it seems impossible to import the sadness of an Armenian's life."[10]

The brutality of the Genocide even made it difficult for artists to tackle the subject. In the most extreme cases, "the pain and mortification" silenced writers like Michael Arlen (born Dikran Kouyoumdjian), an author best known for his novel *The Green Hat,* who was so overwhelmed by the tragedy he not only turned his back on the subject of the Genocide but on his Armenian identity altogether. While survivors produced a fair number of memoirs, few were written in languages other than Armenian and most lacked literary value, making them largely inaccessible to the rest of the world. Few mainstream works other than Franz Werfel's *Forty Days of Musa Dagh* touched the subject.[11] And Werfel was an Austrian Jew—not Armenian. Saroyan reflected this ethos. Although prolific—in his prime, he blasted out a short story almost daily—and regularly interweaving Armenian characters into his work, he rarely and only obliquely touched upon the Genocide. Only in the last decade of his life did he directly address the topic in a trilogy of plays written in the 1970s.[12]

The Armenian experience was not unique. Reluctant to bear its scars, the American Jewish community also largely remained silent about the Holocaust in its public discourse. In the 1940s and 1950s, leading Jewish institutions instructed their followers not to promote awareness of the atrocity outside the faith. Benjamin Meed, a Holocaust survivor living in the United States, described a fate comparable to that of Armenian survivors. " 'Forget the past,' we were told, 'it can only hurt you.' So we reached out to each other and remembered alone." There was little literature on the subject, and commemorations and monuments remained mostly for Jewish consumption. In this environment, the Holocaust remained obscure to most people outside of the Jewish community. The Adolf Eichmann trial in 1961 began the process of reminding the world of the Holocaust. It took several more decades for the Holocaust to enter the world's mainstream consciousness, becoming a term universally capable of instantly conjuring images of concentration camps.[13]

The Armenian shroud of silence lasted longer and was more absolute. It also stretched into academia. Hardly any comprehensive Genocide scholarship existed prior to 1965, especially in English. The first professional English-language work—written by a British historian—was published in 1980.[14]

One other important factor contributed to the Genocide's disappearance from public awareness. Up to 1965, it was not the Genocide that dominated Armenian political discourse, but a bitter feud centered on the demise of the Nine-Hundred-Day Republic and the Soviet state that came to replace it. This struggle within the Diaspora centered on the perception of and loyalty to Soviet Armenia. Some Armenians in the Diaspora embraced or at the least accepted Soviet Armenia as their homeland, while others vilified it as nothing but a treacherous fraud compared to the independent Nine-Hundred-Day Republic it replaced. This was no academic debate. It ripped the Diaspora into two opposing camps and helped keep the Genocide from the public arena.

As the Armenian Church's leading pontiff in the New World, Archbishop Levon Tourian entered into a frothy, internecine struggle upon his arrival in 1931 in the United States. This conflict, which had heated up during the 1920s, broke down into two factions. At one corner stood the ARF (or Tashnags). The ARF had governed the first independent Armenian state in six centuries, only to lose the prize to the Bolsheviks. Leaders of the ARF who once governed the Nine-Hundred-Day Republic lived in exile, leaving them embittered at those who had evicted them from their homeland. This group of exiles continued to lead the ARF from the Diaspora, inculcating anti-Soviet animosity through the party's ranks.[15]

In the other corner stood a loose coalition of organizations. While the ARF despised Soviet Armenia, this non-Tashnag camp adopted a far more tempered view. A minority within this group praised Soviet Armenia's turn to communism, but most came to believe that Soviet Armenia represented the only vestige of a homeland without endorsing its Communist ideology. The non-Tashnag camp saw the USSR as a caretaker against Turkish extirpation. This group wanted to establish an amicable, or at least non-hostile, relationship with Soviet Armenia without regard to its ideological standing.[16]

These opposing camps did not resemble the political parties familiar to democracies. For one thing, they were international bodies. Events taking place in one country spilled over into others. Armenians generally affiliated with either clique by the friends they socialized with, events they attended, and newspapers they read. Without a country to call their own, the camps lacked an electoral forum to fight their battles. The absence of elections made these sides behave more like rival fraternities than political parties. Their contest for the hearts and minds of the Armenian community and the right to represent that community to the outside world took place at social clubs and rallies bursting with patriotic speeches, and through party-owned newspapers spewing partisan diatribes.[17]

This division monopolized political debate from the 1920s right up to the 1970s, seeping into every element of Armenian life and dividing the Diaspora into opposing factions not just in the United States but across the world. Lost in all this turmoil was the Genocide. Certainly, Armenians never forgot the tragedy. In fact, the opposite took place as the survivors continued to mourn and their children and grandchildren inherited their scars. But the Genocide was not a topic of conversation with the outside world. It was neither a politicized issue nor a focal point of political mobilization.[18] The Diaspora's political energy concentrated on Soviet Armenia—not the Genocide.

As the leading religious—and perhaps civic—figure in the United States, Archbishop Tourian could not avoid taking sides within this debate. When he refused to address a crowd at the 1933 Century in Progress Exposition in Chicago because of the placement of the Nine-Hundred-Day Republic's flag on the stage, he became inextricably entangled in the conflict. It took fifty policemen to break up the melee between the indignant Tashnags and their adversaries. To the Tashnags, the flag represented a glorious republic won with their blood and tears. It was sacred, the secular equivalent of a religious relic. Removal of the flag dishonored that hallowed symbol. "By his undesirable conduct in Chicago, Archbishop Tourian sentenced himself to moral death," exclaimed an ARF editorial published days later.[19] Because of Tourian's perceived loyalty to Soviet Armenia and disrespect for the Armenian Republic, the ARF saw Tourian as a Soviet agent and a traitor. "It is no longer any secret that the Primate . . . is a staunch friend of the Bolsheviks," concluded another ARF editorial. "Archbishop Tourian serves the Bolsheviks with fanatic admiration."[20] When Tourian emerged the victor of a controversial and disputed clerical election over a Tashnag contingent pressing for his removal as archbishop a few months after the flag incident, it raised the level of enmity to new heights.[21]

On Christmas Eve, 1933, Armenians flocked to the Holy Cross Church on 187th Street in Washington Heights on the northern edge of Manhattan. Built in 1929, the church was narrow-bodied, with a single aisle. Two hundred parishioners filled up the pews and standing space despite the snow falling outside. Once the Christmas procession reached the aisle, Tourian's bodyguard, a diminutive-sized former rug merchant, stayed back thinking that if anyone was going to strike, they would have already done so. A procession of clergy and assistants started down the aisle. An altar boy bearing a censer led the way, spreading incense through the sanctuary. A choir of five men and five women carrying candles came next, followed by a bishop. Flanked by two deacons, Tourian walked behind them all, wearing a green and gold robe and bearing the traditional silver miter of the Armenian clergy. He carried a pastoral staff in one hand and a cross in the other. Another cross and a medallion hung from gold necklaces around his neck. The crowd stood up to honor him when he neared the pews.[22]

At 10:28 a.m., the procession reached the seventh pew when a group of men from the crowd approached. As the befuddled parishioners looked on, the men ran past the deacons to grab the archbishop, knocking off his headgear. After they surrounded Tourian, some of the men pinioned the deacons. Another man approached wielding a double-edged butcher's knife with an eight-inch blade. With his hand firmly gripping the wooden handle, he stabbed Tourian several times. The knife penetrated Tourian's abdomen, severing a major artery. The archbishop keeled over on his staff, which bent from his weight, and crashed to the floor. His eyes stared at a large picture of the Crucifixion. Bloodstains covered his priestly robes.

Parishioners attacked the assailants, holding down two of the perpetrators while the others escaped in the ensuing bedlam. Tourian's bodyguard drew out his revolver, frightening the crowd into order. Several policemen from the 34th Precinct rushed in to help. Tourian was removed to the vestry. Minutes after the attack, surrounded by his parishioners and fenced in by police, Tourian spoke his last words: "Help me, Dear God."[23]

The fallout from the murder was catastrophic, plunging the Armenian-American community into all-out war. One vendetta spawned another in an endless cycle of reprisals, with police regularly interceding to maintain order among the feuding camps. Tourian's memory became a lightning rod for the community. His supporters went to great lengths to honor him in martyrdom. Name-calling, jeers, and piercing, hateful looks menaced Tashnag sympathizers (nine members of the ARF were found guilty of participating in the murder). Tourian's detractors among the ARF vilified the archbishop, labeling the cleric a lackey who betrayed his people and disrespected the Nine-Hundred-Day Republic to appease Soviet puppet masters in Moscow.[24]

After Tourian's murder, each faction tried to wrest control of the nation's churches, the one institution that had held the Armenians together over the millennia. With the Church, the ultimate symbol of Armenian life, politicized and split, the preexisting divisions within the Armenian-American community stratified after the assassination. Both sides established parallel institutions—newspapers, social clubs, charities, and youth groups—further segregating the community. The assassination strained friends and family alike. "If I wanted to marry a Tashnag," recalled an Armenian woman of her mother's attitude years later, "either it would have killed her, or she would have killed me."[25]

Most Armenians tried to go on with their lives. But some jumped headfirst into this feud, fueling the enmity between the opposing camps for decades. And few people were as eager to fight as a young writer named Avedis Derounian.

For Derounian, the Tourian murder represented more than an ideological struggle between two factions. It was personal. The archbishop embodied not just a sacrosanct religious authority but a family friend who had baptized Derounian's younger brother.[26] "I adored him," Derounian wrote of Tourian, "and literally worshipped him as a man of God."[27] Derounian had been standing a few feet from the man he venerated when the assassin stabbed Tourian. The shock of the event overshadowed Derounian's life for decades. "I am the rebel of the household," he wrote years after Tourian's death. "I might have followed the same unruffled path"—his brother became a congressman and a judge—"except for an incident which . . . determined for me the course of my life."[28]

With the pen as his sword, Derounian put his NYU journalism degree to work, exposing Tourian's murder to detective magazines in the 1930s. Derounian was not some obscure crank. He worked for

Fortune magazine and his best-selling book, *Under Cover*, would earn him a Thomas Jefferson Award along with Frank Sinatra for promoting democracy and tolerance in 1947.[29] *Under Cover's* opening chapter, titled "A Black Christmas," introduced Americans to the Tourian murder, calling the ARF a "vicious political clique of terrorists."[30]

Derounian's smear campaign continued throughout the 1940s, reaching major press outlets and elected officials. "It's extremely urgent that I get some dope on those I've marked," Derounian wrote to a fellow journalist in October 1945. That same month, a letter to the secretary of state called the ARF "experts in deception and distortion." A fortnight later, Derounian sent a letter to Under Secretary Acheson repeating the accusations. His third book, *Cairo to Damascus*, released in 1951, continued the onslaught.[31] Derounian's colleagues in the non-Tashnag camp echoed his words, though rarely as eloquently and virulently.

The post–World War II territorial campaign did nothing to calm the hatred within the Diaspora, despite the common cause found among the warring factions. Though both Tashnags and non-Tashnags stood on the same side of the issue and lobbied for the transfer of portions of eastern Turkey to Soviet Armenia, they did not coordinate their efforts. The hatred ran so deep after Tourian's assassination that even when a unified front would have improved their chances in lobbying the world's powers, they undermined each other at every turn. And Derounian, an active participant in the territorial campaign, was among those deepening the paralyzing split through his polarizing verbal attacks.

This animosity remained white-hot, and when the Cold War hit its stride in the 1950s, it tied the Armenian intracommunal struggle to the larger global contest between the United States and the Soviet Union. The rivalry between the world's superpowers consumed the Diaspora by exacerbating preexisting divisions and providing new ammunition for Armenians to target each other. "Fifth columnists," "Marxists," "Armenian McCarthyites," and other lingo borrowed from the Cold War infiltrated and poisoned Armenian discourse. In this war of words, Derounian met his match on the other side of the aisle, a former minister from the Nine-Hundred-Day Republic who, like Derounian, was a masterful writer.

Reuben Darbinian came from the same generation of ARF leaders as Vratsian. Both were student activists and organizers during their university years in the early twentieth century. And both had served in the Armenian Republic and seen its demise. When the republic fell, the Bolsheviks imprisoned Darbinian. He may have rotted in jail if Vratsian's February 1921 uprising had not freed him.[32]

Writing came naturally to Darbinian. He wrote for a local newspaper at nineteen. A year later, he published a novel. His studies in law, economics, and philosophy took him from Berlin to Moscow, where he earned a doctorate. The multiplicity of his studies reflected his enormous intellectual capacity. With gray, frizzy hair and large spectacles, he looked the part of an intellectual. He went on to edit several newspapers, including most of the ARF publications in the United States, from 1922 until his death in 1968. He oversaw daily, weekly, and monthly periodicals in both Armenian and English. As if that were not enough, he even kept a personal diary in English to improve his adopted tongue. He also had a fine eye for talent, publishing several of Saroyan's early stories before the author achieved fame.[33]

As the editor of various ARF publications, Darbinian stuffed his editorials with venomous attacks, repeatedly calling his enemies "fifth columnists" and benighted slaves to a Communist homeland. "Formerly they operated openly," Darbinian wrote of the non-Tashnag leaders in 1954, "but today they are underhanded in their collaboration with the Communists. . . ."[34] In return, his enemies demeaned the Armenian Republic, the thing most sacred to him. Both factions hurled insults, describing each other as cheats and liars. The attacks were often personal. "Speak up, Reuben," Derounian wrote in a 1955 column, calling Darbinian the "ARF Press-and-Propaganda Chief."[35]

Things turned uglier when a New York government official cited five Armenian newspapers for harboring un-American ideals. They "tell the most horrible things about America" and pose an outright "leak in your defense system," the official told a congressional committee investigating Communist infiltration in June 1955.[36] Coming at the height of the McCarthy era, Derounian understood that the taint of being labeled a "Red" was fraught with danger. He tapped his brother Steven, a conservative Republican who became the first congressman of Armenian descent, for help. The most memorable moment in Congressman Derounian's twenty-five-year career in public service came when he castigated Charles Van Doren during the investigation of the TV game show *Twenty One* scandal. Through the congressman, Derounian set up a meeting with an Armenian archbishop belonging to the Church based in Soviet Armenia and the under secretary of state in 1955 to prove the loyalty of those Armenians under suspicion for harboring pro-Soviet sentiments. The fawning language of the scroll delivered to the State Department's offices, which promised a "loyalty . . . unreservedly bound to the best interests of the United States," reflected just how preoccupied the Armenians had become with the Cold War.[37] Other Armenian groups issued similar declarations. Perhaps to prove his personal loyalty to the United States, Derounian reported his observations of his trips abroad—including one to Soviet Armenia—to the State Department.[38]

All this built-up enmity came to a head in 1956 when the Church schism in America arising from the Tourian murder spread worldwide. At the time, two clerics held the title of Catholicos. One was based in Etchmiadzin, a city not far from the Soviet Armenian capital, Yerevan. The second, originally based in the medieval Armenian kingdom of Cilicia, had moved his headquarters to Lebanon after the Genocide. The Catholicos in Etchmiadzin had historically been accorded the status of chief cleric of the Armenian Church, while the Cilician Catholicos had presided over churches in his geographical jurisdiction in the Middle East. The two positions rarely clashed until the Cold War. In 1956, a new Cilician Catholicos won a disputed election in which the USSR and the Catholicos in Etchmiadzin tried to intervene to overturn the outcome. His election raised a new question that would come to tear apart the Diaspora even further. Which of these pontiffs was the legitimate head of the Armenian Church?

No resolution came about. Instead, months after the election, churches in America affiliated with the Tashnags asked the Cilician Catholicos to take them under his jurisdiction because "Holy Etchmiadzin remains under Soviet tyranny. . . ."[39] Churches in Greece and Iran also broke away from Etchmiadzin to join the Cilician house. The two Catholicoses saw eye to eye theologically, but the Cold War had now fueled an indivisible crack within the oldest and most venerable institution of the Armenian world. The fallout was nearly as catastrophic as the 1933 murder, plunging the Diaspora into another round of recriminations. Two years later, the tension burst into violence in Lebanon, causing the deaths of sixty Armenians.[40]

The Cold War also colored the first Armenian forays into American politics, and in doing so, contributed to the Genocide's absence from the political arena. Ethnic groups during the era molded their message to suit the day's Cold War agenda.[41] The Armenians were no different. Armenian-Americans signed on to the captive nations movement sponsored by the U.S. government that brought together people—such as the Poles and Ukrainians—living under Soviet tyranny, and throughout the 1950s, American politicians ranging from Vice President Nixon to governors and mayors participated in ceremonies honoring the Nine-Hundred-Day Armenian Republic, whose downfall fit neatly into the anti-Soviet agenda of the day.[42] Yet few spoke of the Genocide, which did not fit this agenda.[43] Likewise, when Congress held hearings on Armenia in the 1950s—the first time it had done so since the 1920s—the Genocide hardly received any attention. As a result, the exigency of the Cold War colored the entire congressional proceeding, casting nearly all blame for the downfall of the Armenian Republic on the Soviet Union. A House committee report concluded that "The external enemies of Armenia were the Bolsheviks and the Turks, and of these two the Bolsheviks must be ranked first. . . ." Buttressed by Eisenhower's endorsement, the committee recommended stronger action against Communist tyranny—pushing to the sidelines any role played by the Turks in Armenia's downfall.[44]

Within this context, the press rarely mentioned the Genocide in the more than 1,000 articles written about Armenians during the 1950s in major newspapers. Mention of the Genocide hardly occurred in Congress. Almost any political discussion of Armenians dealt with the emancipation of Soviet Armenia from its Communist bear hug. A speech by Senator Herbert H. Lehman of New York in 1955 typified the era. While speaking before eight hundred people in New York to mark the thirty-seventh anniversary of the founding of the Armenian Republic, the senator made a plea for the United States to ratify the seminal 1948 United Nations Genocide Convention. His presentation skipped over the Armenian Genocide. Instead, reflecting the pervasiveness of the Cold War, Lehman told the audience that the Soviet Union was guilty of genocide.[45] The presence of a captive audience still living with the scars of the Armenian Genocide made it an opportune occasion to mention the atrocity. If Lehman did not avail himself of that opportunity, then no one seemed likely to do so.

What started as a philosophical dispute over the role and standing of Soviet Armenia during the 1920s turned irreparably bitter after Tourian's assassination. In hindsight, this all-consuming conflict seems a bit unreal now, involving esoteric issues history later made moot. For an entire generation, however, it was a visceral and genuine struggle that stood at the center of what it meant to be Armenian.

It is difficult to pinpoint whether it was the survivors' focus on rebuilding their lives, or the political impotency generated from dispersion, or the lack of statehood, or the destruction of a generation of leaders, or a bitter struggle consuming the Diaspora that unwittingly led to decades of silence in which one of the greatest international human rights disasters faded into a distant memory. What is clear is that the Armenians lacked the resources necessary to sustain the memory of the Genocide and mobilize an enfeebled and divided population behind a political movement. By 1965, Herbert Hoover's observation no longer held true. A half century after the Genocide, few in the world remembered the "starving Armenians" or their Ottoman persecutors. It would take an unprecedented effort to shatter this silence.

Resurrection

The time has come for Armenians to stand up and be counted. . . . For too long now we have been the forgotten people of the western world. And we deserve to be forgotten if we take no action, now.

—LEON SURMELIAN (1965)

On the morning of April 24, 1965, students from Yerevan's universities skipped class. At a time and place when poets were nearly as popular and influential as celebrities are today, one of Soviet Armenia's greatest poets recited his defiant poem written for the fiftieth anniversary of the Genocide in a small theater: "We are few, but we are called Armenians." Baruyr Sevag's poem declaimed that no matter how few or weak Armenians may be in the world, no matter how "death had fallen in love" with this ancient tribe, they shall "feel proud" for being Armenians. The final line of his poem cried out defiantly that the Armenians would grow and thrive, now and forever: "We are, We shall be, and become many." Dead silence followed. Few had heard such exclamatory speeches within the rigid confines of Soviet life before. Doing so usually meant chastisement or worse, imprisonment. The students in the audience, infused with stridency after listening to the poem, then left the theater to join other students across Yerevan making their way to the city center for an unprecedented undertaking. They were about to make history by partaking in the first major public commemoration of the Genocide.[1]

Earlier in the day, the Catholicos, whose long graying beard and gentle eyes gave him a grandfatherly appearance that added to his palpable spirituality, had overseen a memorial prayer commemorating the Genocide overflowing with attendees at the church's central cathedral. He had also declared the year one of mourning throughout the world, a clear call for Armenians throughout the Diaspora to act.[2]

But the young people descending on the center of Soviet Armenia's capital wanted more than prayers to mark this occasion. They wanted political action. Carrying signs reading "A just solution to the Armenian Question" and "Our lands," along with enlarged photos of Genocide victims, the students, joined by their professors and Soviet Armenia's leading intellectuals, artists, and writers, popped in to businesses and homes to recruit others on this sunny day in which a wispy spring breeze kept the shade cool. With no previous experience in organizing demonstrations—one participant described the students' tactics as "primitive"—the procession fumbled along to Lenin Square driven as much by curiosity as militancy. Various government buildings and the city's best hotel ringed the oval-shaped public space used to hold Communist rallies. Gathering in front of a granite statue of Lenin erected during World War II—the largest of the ubiquitous iconic shrines dotting the USSR—the students saturated the square and soon spilled into adjacent streets. The demonstrators muddled their way through the city as some sang nationalistic songs while others screamed a cacophony of anti-Turkish declarations.[3]

Though free of Stalin's Terror, this was still the Soviet Union, a place where propaganda monopolized every facet of public life. Newspapers like *Pravda* published the government's credos. From kindergarten through university, young people studied and regurgitated the canonic teachings of Marx and Lenin. Government officials authorized public events staged to conform to this strict dogma. This demonstration had received no such permission from the state. The protestors understood that this one act might permanently derail their careers, placing them in shabby apartments and dreary jobs instead of the leading government ministries. They knew that many could be arrested, or worse, jailed or sent off to Siberia to suffer in isolation and exile. The KGB officers in plain sight further fueled their fears. Though nervous and worried, they pressed on. The groundswell of emotion on this day was simply too strong.[4]

Holding the largest concentration of Armenians in the world, Soviet Armenia would have been best suited to press the Armenian case against Turkey. If the Nine-Hundred-Day Republic had thrived, perhaps it could have pursued reparations and human rights trials against the Young Turks, and maintained territorial claims against Turkey. But the republic gave way to a rigid Soviet policy that reduced political activity by the population of Soviet Armenia to a standstill—even when it came to the Genocide. The USSR had prohibited Armenian scholars from studying the tragedy. The state extinguished any chance of erecting a public memorial. It censored those who brought up the topic. And it refused to sponsor Armenian claims against Turkey.[5]

Geopolitical interests in corralling Turkey away from its NATO alliance did not completely explain Soviet policy. When Lenin and his ideological brethren brought Communist revolution to Russia, they envisioned a world in which Soviet citizens would, in due time, cast off their allegiances to ethnicity and religion. This vision of the Soviet citizen had no room for nationalistic aims. As a uniquely Armenian saga, the Genocide did not accord with such ecumenical Communist ideology. Soviet authorities took every means to smother any talk of the Genocide, even among those who lived through the tragedy.

On this day, its youth refused to stand silent any longer.

All month long, Yerevan's citizenry wondered and debated what would happen on April 24. Anticipation mixed with anxiety overshadowed an event that had received no attention in the past. So when people began openly to speak of the Genocide, many of the students could not believe their ears.[6]

As the setting sun formed a silhouette behind Mount Ararat, the crowd, now swelled to 100,000, surrounded the gray-stoned opera house at the center of the city adorned with Greek columns and arches. By now, survivors of the Genocide had joined in, injecting the younger protestors with added adrenaline. To appease the growing demand for a public commemoration, authorities had decided to hold a modest ceremony for about 250 people in the opera house. Though the KGB vetted the guest list to prevent any unexpected incidents, it took immense lobbying by Soviet Armenia's leadership to their superiors in Moscow to proceed with the event.[7]

Inside the performance hall, leading representatives of the Soviet

Armenian government convened along with the Catholicos. Uproari-
ous applause interrupted the first speakers, a senior government official followed by a world-class astrophysicist.[8] Unlike the reserved
performance inside the opera house, the demonstrators listening on
loudspeakers outside had grown rowdy, choking off transportation in
Yerevan and shutting down universities and businesses. Though tame
compared to the riots of America and Europe during the 1960s—with
no looting, widespread vandalism, or violence—the demonstration
heated up as organizers delivered speeches to the crowds insisting on
Soviet sponsorship of Armenian demands against Turkey. The protestors wanted to submit a petition to those inside the opera house. When
guards refused to grant them entry, the students pushed against the
barricades placed in front of the opera house and threw stones at
the windows. After some deliberation, authorities declined to call in
the army, instead employing the municipal security force to entangle
with the protestors to avoid bloodshed. The sight of their sons and
daughters in the crowd made some officers reluctant to move against
the protestors with alacrity. Embarrassment turned others away from
facing their children. Instead, firemen blasted high-powered hoses from
the windows to keep the demonstrators at bay. These proved feeble in
the face of the energized crowd. Pumping their fists into the air, the
demonstrators repeatedly shouted "our lands, our lands" in a chorus.[9]

When the astrophysicist finished, the crowd grew more aggressive.
The opera house windows shattered amidst the continuous volley of mis-
siles. Soaked in water, the demonstrators finally overwhelmed the barriers
and barged into the main hall screaming their demands. Shocked by this
strong resolve for action, most everyone in attendance fled from a rear
exit of the building. The Catholicos remained behind. Respect for his
position temporarily silenced the boisterous crowd. "My dear children,"
he started to tell the restless listeners in his grandfatherly way. Before he
got more than a few words out, the shouts and jeers continued.[10]

The leaders of Soviet Armenia elected not to order mass arrests.
Within a year, however, the fallout from the unexpected demonstration
led to their downfall as their chieftains in Moscow installed more strin-
gent satraps to quash such nationalistic outbursts. The Soviet government's sole concession to the Armenian fervor was to erect a memorial
honoring the victims of the Genocide.[11] But it refused to do any more.

It would not change its foreign policy and sponsor Armenian claims against Turkey. As such, Soviet Armenia never again served as a staging point for the Armenian quest for justice. Instead, the demonstration's biggest impact came not in changing the policy of the USSR but in serving as an inspiration for Armenians throughout the Diaspora. And it was in the Diaspora—not Soviet Armenia—that the pursuit of justice was fought for the next few decades.[12]

On the fiftieth anniversary of the Genocide, the Armenians of the Diaspora were finally prepared to take that extraordinary step needed to reawaken a long-lost cause and remind the world of the forgotten Genocide. In Beirut, all the Armenian factions came together to speak in front of 85,000 people packed inside a stadium. Thousands marched in central Athens. In Paris, Armenians marched down the Champs-Elysées; 3,000 attended a memorial mass in Notre Dame. More than 12,000 participated in a demonstration in Buenos Aires. Armenians in Italy, Canada, Syria, Egypt, and Australia also staged events, as did Armenian-Americans. Boston's Armenians held a ceremony in a Catholic cathedral as well as a rally in John Hancock Hall. In San Francisco, three hundred mourners marched in silence to a cathedral; others held a vigil in front of City Hall. Armenians held events in Illinois, California, Connecticut, Michigan, New Jersey, Wisconsin, Massachusetts, Rhode Island, Washington, D.C., Ohio, and Virginia and in other communities throughout the world.[13]

Few people encapsulated the meaning of the Genocide to a new generation better than Charles Metjian, who organized a demonstration in New York in April 1965. The thirtysomething fire department employee was not much of a radical. Despite caring for a growing family and working two jobs, however, he took it upon himself to organize a march to the United Nations. Metjian had never met his grandfather, yet the sight of his childhood friends interacting with their own made him long for the mythical patriarch. The childhood stories Metjian had heard of how Ottoman soldiers hacked his grandfather's body to pieces outside his home, cutting off his arm and finally killing him with a blow to the head, remained etched in Metjian's mind. The bond between grandfather and grandson—between a victim and his descendant—remained strong no matter the passage of fifty years. "Time has neither changed nor lessened this crime . . . committed against you," Metjian wrote in an open letter to the grandfather he had never known. "I vow I will make every effort to make fruitful the justice that is long overdue to you."[14]

Metjian urged others to join him. "The choice is yours," he wrote to all Armenians before the April 24 march. "He who calls himself an Armenian comes to this Bridge, either he crosses it and Honors his people or he falls back and dissipates himself from his Heritage."[15] Metjian's message was clear: all Armenians, no matter how far removed in time and space from the dark days of 1915, owed it to their ancestors to fight for justice.

Numerous pamphlets rehashing old arguments about resurrecting the Treaty of Sèvres and obtaining the promises made after World War I went out to governments across the world.[16] But this time something was different. The Genocide began to take on a life of its own, detaching itself from the broader historical narrative that had defined the contours of Armenian claims against Turkey in the past. Historically—the 1945 territorial claims served as an apt example—Armenians had linked the Genocide to their desire for their ancestral lands and to a specific place, a homeland, where they would be entitled at last to self-rule and self-determination. That link remained, but starting in 1965, it began to come apart. A decade or two later, Armenians hardly mentioned the pledges of the post–World War I era in their pursuit of justice—they focused almost exclusively on the Genocide as a distinct event. No longer confined to Armenian families and community gatherings, the catastrophe became the focal point of Armenian political aspirations, a never-ending source of mobilization replenished by Turkish denial for generations to come. As other cultural markers faded or lost their appeal to a younger, assimilating population, the Genocide and the pursuit of justice associated with it gradually displaced the longing for a homeland as a central element of Armenian identity.

This new focal point for a political movement combined with heightened political awareness not seen since the post–World War I era translated into action. The Illinois, California, and Massachusetts legislatures passed resolutions marking the Genocide, as did a myriad of other U.S. cities and towns.[17] Forty-two congressman, including

Senator Edward Kennedy, honored the fiftieth anniversary in America's most hallowed legislative chamber.[18] House minority leader Gerald Ford had in 1955 delivered a speech on the Armenian Republic's fall to Soviet tyranny. That speech did not mention the Genocide. In a harbinger of what was to come, none of the Cold War rhetoric appeared in his observance of the Genocide in 1965.[19]

The Turkish response to this eruption of activity verged on the hysterical. After many years in which news of Armenians barely registered in Turkey, the flurry of activity in 1965 sent shock waves through Turkey's ruling elite. Many Turks—including the Turkish ambassador—confounded by the sudden upheaval after decades of silence, assumed that retaliatory Greeks upset at the situation in Cyprus had instigated the Armenian agitation. Turkish newspapers issued bitter denunciations; diplomats countered Armenian claims in the press.[20] The Turkish Embassy urged the State Department to quash declarations made on behalf of the Armenians by American politicians.[21] Its ambassador asked for the removal of a tiny Genocide monument erected at an Armenian senior citizens center in New Jersey because, he insisted, despite being on private property, it was "easily visible to all passersby on a busy street corner and, therefore, legally public property." Some Turkish officials, unable to appreciate that the U.S. government could not simply ban protestors, blamed the government for the demonstrations.[22]

A member of the Turkish Embassy in Washington urged readers of the *New York Times* that in dealing with the "dark days . . . the best thing to do now would be to forget them. . . ."[23] That was just the problem. Turkey wanted to forget a past Armenians could not forget. Too many survivors lived on with traumatic memories that refused to fade away. Too many of their children and grandchildren heard stories of lost relatives, tormented deaths, and a never-ending despair that fifty years had fail to heal. By obliterating their shared past, Turkey was erasing the defining event of the Armenian experience. One people could not get their way without forcing the other to overturn decades of memories. The irreconcilable positions could only result in one victor and one loser.

The Turkish reaction was monolithic. Not a single government official, public figure, or academic of any standing challenged the of-ficial position or even hinted at the need for a sincere inquiry into the past. No matter where Turks fell on the political spectrum, from leftist to conservative to nationalist, they agreed that there would be no ex-amination of the past. History—especially Armenian history—was not something one investigated in Turkey but something one designated from above.

After 1965, Turkey's denialist position collided head-on with the emerging Armenian activism demanding an accounting of the Geno-cide. Nowhere was the battle between Armenians and Turks more intense than in the United States. And the battle's first shots were fired in Southern California.

As people filled the nondescript City Hall in Montebello on the evening of January 9, 1967, thirty-five-year-old Michael Minasian, the son of Genocide survivors, finalized his speech to the town council. The government seat of the small town ten miles east of Los Angeles had rarely seen such a full house. The standing-room crowd bulged out of the two hundred or so seats, forcing many onlookers outside to lis-ten through the public speaker system.[24] After hearing a year of debate surrounding the establishment of a monument to honor the victims of the Genocide, Montebello's five council members had convened to make a decision.

Inspired by the April 1965 demonstration in Yerevan and the fifti-eth anniversary of the Genocide, eighteen Armenians, a group of pro-fessors, engineers, and businessmen—most of them second-generation immigrants—had formed a committee to build a monument to match the one being erected in Soviet Armenia. Working out of one member's office in Beverly Hills, the committee represented an unprecedented step in Armenian-American relations. Ten years earlier, warring fac-tions rarely spoke to each other. It took the enduring frustration, pain, and anger of the Genocide to bring them together. Now they were working side by side. By including a cross section of Armenians from all political backgrounds, the committee was able to garner support from every element of the fractured community.[25]

The group designated Minasian, a member of Montebello's chamber of commerce, to act as the liaison with the council. Minasian's standing with town officials, compounded with the respect local Armenians had earned from the town's chieftains, made Montebello the perfect locale in which to build the nation's first major Genocide monument.[26] But to do so, the monument's backers first had to obtain permission from the town's governing board.

Tempers flared when Myron Goldsmith, a retired Army major who doubled as an honorary consul for Turkey, spoke against the monument at the council meeting. Aside from an occasional confrontation in editorial pages, Armenians and Turks rarely confronted each other directly, making this sleepy venue their first battleground. "The council will not tolerate emotional outbursts," the mayor repeated, often slamming his gavel as Armenians hissed and yelled at Goldsmith. Fearful that the charged emotions in the room would lead to a brawl that might wreck the project, Minasian traversed the chamber trying to keep the audience calm. He received a bit of help when two policemen arrived to maintain order.[27] Goldsmith called the monument something that would "satisfy the spiteful desires . . . of a vocal few." He accused Minasian and his colleagues of concocting a Communist plot. It is a "hate-breeding memorial . . . an affront to a friendly nation and a valuable military ally."[28]

When a councilman suggested removing the reference to Turkey from the commemorative plaque, Minasian responded: "Just because July 4th may offend the British, does that mean we should eliminate that American observance? No, we can't rewrite history."[29]

Behind the scenes, Turkey pressed the State Department to "do its utmost" to block the monument. On at least two occasions, its ambassador met personally with agency officials to urge them to "make every effort" to halt construction. Turkey had unsuccessfully tried to shut down a much smaller monument on private property in New Jersey.[30] The Montebello Monument was to be built on public land, making the stakes much higher in its eyes.

The State Department contacted Montebello's city council to pressure it to shut down the project or at least tone down the language on the plaque: the wording proposed by the Armenian committee called the events of 1915 a "premeditated act of genocide."[31] It also tapped a congressman to covertly provide updates of the local scene and discuss the efficacy of pressuring city officials.[32]

The State Department did Turkey's bidding with little hesitation. Starting in 1965, it had urged American politicians to tone down their Genocide proclamations at Turkey's request.[33] And its perception of how to deal with past events mirrored that of Turkey—at least when it came to the Armenians. The State Department never denied the occurrence of the Genocide; in fact, its embassy in Ankara conducted a study in the spring of 1965 to study the effects "of the 1915 expulsions and massacres" on the Armenian population in Turkey. Yet the agency told Armenians that modern Turkey barely resembled the Ottoman regime of 1915 and it mimicked Turkey in urging Armenians to forget the past.[34]

Still, the department strained to explain to Turkish officials that in a federal system, it could not do much other than ask local officials to comply with the agency's wishes. With Turkey complaining of nearly every instance in which Armenians or American officials brought up the Genocide—including statements printed in publications ranging from the *Congressional Record* to obscure Armenian newspapers—the State Department reminded Turkish diplomats that Armenian efforts paled in comparison to muscular special interest groups.[35] A typical exchange involving the Montebello Monument illustrated Turkey's sensitivity to the unearthing of Ottoman crimes and the challenges faced by the State Department in comforting its ally. When an American official told his Turkish counterpart that the monument "was unlikely to attract even national attention," his interlocutor told him "that even modest press play on the subject would inevitably find its way back to Turkey. Moreover," the diplomat explained, "no amount of detailed official Turkish explanations of the intricacies of the American domestic scene would make the slightest difference to the average Turkish reader. He simply would not be able to understand."[36] Later on, the Turkish ambassador conveyed that his "countrymen are very sensitive about reference to any partition of Turkey, and therefore, if there is increased propaganda by the American Armenian community, he wanted to warn the U.S. Government that there would be reaction in Turkey."[37]

Attempts to address Turkish concerns over pronouncements made by American government officials about the Genocide led to the issuance of an aide-mémoire (more commonly known as a position paper) in 1968, in which the State Department assured the "Embassy of Tur-key that it will continue to do what it can to mitigate statements and proclamations . . . which might be offensive to the Turkish nation."[38] Months later, Secretary of State William P. Rogers issued a memoran-dum to President Nixon discussing U.S.-Turkish relations. Among the handful of "thoughts" mentioned by the secretary, he relayed what was commonly known in the Near East division of the department: "Turks are quite sensitive to Armenian efforts to keep alive the memory of the Armenian massacres in Turkey after the First World War. . . . We will do our best," he added, to block any congressional action on behalf of the Armenians.[39] Soon after that, a midlevel aide reminded his superior at the State Department that "[b]ecause of Turkish sensitivities," he should avoid bringing up "the Armenian experience of World War I days" during a pending meeting with the Turkish ambassador.[40]

While encouraging the State Department to act on its behalf, Tur-key also hired a local attorney to speak to Montebello council members privately. A Turkish representative asked the town to erect a memorial for Turks. The Turkish government even coaxed the Armenian patri-arch in Istanbul to ask an Armenian archbishop in Los Angeles to help tone down the language on the monument's plaque. The intensity of the Turkish opposition caught the monument's organizers off-guard. Some of them feared that with the State Department's help, Turkey might scuttle their project.[41]

Yet these were not the "starving Armenians" of the past. During the confrontation over the Montebello Monument, the infrastructure and confidence needed to mount a political fight were finally taking shape, especially in Southern California, home to one of the largest Armenian populations in the world. In the 1960s, two Armenian-Americans—George Deukmejian and Walter Karabian—won seats in the California legislature. The former went on to become governor; the latter, whose mother had been grouped with disabled children by Fresno school administrators simply because she could not speak English, the head of the state assembly.[42] In the heart of New York City, Armenians erected a mammoth cathedral, a project twenty-five years in the making. Armenian schools sprouted across the country. An Armenian research center established endowed chairs at Harvard and UCLA. Armenians began to take on prominent roles in American society. Alex Manoogian was on the way to propelling his company into the Fortune 500. Kirk Kerkorian made his first major deals as an investor. Cher—born Cherilyn Sarkissian—began her career in singing and acting, while Mike Connors—born Krikor Ohanian—reached his peak in the TV show *Mannix*, for which he won a Golden Globe. Ara Parseghian coached Notre Dame to the first of his two championships. Armenians were no longer afraid to speak their mother tongue in public. They were no longer changing their names. Spurred on by the times, they began to take pride in their ethnicity. When a change in immigration laws opened the doors to outsiders in 1965, a new wave of spirited Armenians poured in from the Middle East, infusing the Armenian-American community with renewed vigor.[43]

Montebello's Armenian community, which made up a significant voting bloc and included many campaign donors, was among the most politically advanced in the nation. Minasian and others parlayed these attributes by pooling together campaign donations from all of Montebello's Armenians, thereby forming a potent political force in the area.[44]

After three hours of debate in which a parade of witnesses—led by Minasian and Goldsmith—praised or condemned the monument, Montebello's governing body entered into a closed-door deliberation for half an hour. As the clock neared midnight, it voted 4–1 in favor of the monument, but declined to approve the language for the plaque requested by the Armenians. The Turkish diplomat Goldsmith stormed out following the tally. Minasian and the Armenians had won—with an important caveat. Two weeks later, in front of another huge crowd, the council bowed to the State Department's wishes and approved language making no mention of the Genocide or the Ottoman Empire, instead dedicating the monument "to men of all nations who have fallen victim to crimes against humanity." In doing so, it rejected four alternative versions offered by the Armenian committee. To the State Department's chagrin, even the watered-down version did not satisfy the Turkish ambassador, who explained that because the plaque mentioned Armenians, "it would be obvious" that it targeted Turkey.[45]

The setback over the plaque's wording did not deflate the euphoric Armenians. Though erected in a small town, this was the first major monument dedicated to the Genocide in the United States and it showed, in a small way, that the "starving Armenians" had finally arrived. The Montebello Monument became a symbol of ethnic pride, particularly for Armenians in California.[46]

With the legalities out of the way, the monument committee raised $105,000 for the project. Donations trickled in from all over the world, often in small increments. Designed by a local Armenian architect, it stood 75 feet tall, with eight columns strung together by arches and connected at the top to a conical dome. The heavy cement work of the 200-ton structure intended to withstand earthquakes forced the contractor to cast the columns on-site. Organizers selected Bicknell Park, an uncluttered 17-acre plot of land surrounded by a municipal golf course, for the monument. Raised on a mound, it stood at a higher elevation than its surroundings, giving drivers from the nearby highway a dramatic view of the monument.[47]

The consecration ceremony in 1968 attracted 20,000 people and various state and federal officials.[48] The erection of another mammoth Genocide monument on a hilltop in Soviet Armenia 7,000 miles from Montebello symbolized the global scope of the struggle against Turkey, and confirmed that all Armenians, no matter their location, ideology, or standing in the Cold War, were of one voice when it came to the Genocide.

Every year thereafter, Armenians would come to hold April 24 observances at the Montebello Monument. Leading Church officials as well as elected figures like Ronald W. Reagan came to visit over the years. Largely, the events went off without controversy. Like everything else involving the Genocide, however, the monument at times became a source of contention, sometimes descending into the arena of the sublimely ridiculous. At Turkey's request, the State Department asked the local Marine Color Band which had attended earlier commemorations to desist in 1971. When Congressman George Danielson inquired about the absence, the Marines lied to him. When he persisted, the unit told him that it skipped the April 24 memorial at the State Department's behest. Danielson's inquiries reached the secretary of state and the president, both of whom refused to allow the Marine Band to participate.[49]

The erection of the Montebello Monument was a harbinger of things to come. It showed that the universality of the Genocide in Armenian life could bring rivals together even if they remained far apart on other issues and deeply suspicious of each other. Within a handful of years, Armenians from all factions would come together to establish a permanent lobbying and advocacy organization in the nation's capital. The work completed by a committee rather than by an iconoclastic individual was also telling. No charismatic, larger-than-life figure like Dr. Martin Luther King, Jr., would emerge in the ongoing struggle with Turkey. There would be no repeat of the "one man army" of Vahan Cardashian. Instead, small groups, sometimes working regionally, sometimes nationally, would carry the cause. The fight over the plaque's language would also be repeated in years to come, evolving from a game of semantics to an all-out contest for history itself. Finally, the State Department's meddling in the process ensured that when Armenians clashed with the Turkish government in the future, the executive branch would always take the Turkish side, making it that much harder for the Armenians to overcome Turkish denial.

After the eruption in 1965, Armenian youth began to inject the militancy, bravura, and organizational tactics of the 1960s student movements into the Armenian scene. Few exemplified this growing radicalization better than Vartkes Yeghiayan.

Yeghiayan was born to a wealthy family in Ethiopia that sheltered him excessively, even from the family's history. His mother's close ties to the nation's imperial family—her godmother was the wife of the emperor Haile Selassie—allowed him entry to the best schools; at age eleven, he attended an American boarding school in Cyprus where he excelled in tennis far more than academics. There he befriended many Turkish students, and he was puzzled when some of his fellow Armenians called the Turks "murderers." Why they should be called murderers remained a mystery for Yeghiayan through high school and into college.[50]

In 1954, he arrived in the United States with three tennis rackets and two volumes of Gandhi. After one year at Indiana, he enrolled as a premed major at Berkeley before switching to history, a course of study that might have explained the connection between Turks and murder, but Yeghiayan's teachers never mentioned the topic. When other Armenian students told him stories of their families' hardships in Turkey, he pretended to know what they were talking about, contributing the little he could gather from his reading about Turkey at the library.

While in San Francisco, Yeghiayan met Mehmet Talaat's assassin, Soghomon Tehlirian, just before Tehlirian's death in 1960. Tehlirian's description of his trial in Berlin lit a fire under the impressionable Yeghiayan, who later wrote a book about the event. But it was not until 1961, when his father died, that Yeghiayan began to fully understand his family's—and his people's—unspeakable past. Months later, searching through two suitcases of his father's personal items, he stumbled upon a wallet. Inside, Yeghiayan found a photo of a teenager draped in shepherd's clothing. He asked his mother, "Who is this girl?" It was not a girl, his mother responded. It was his father, Boghos.

She told Yeghiayan what little she knew. Boghos had been orphaned. From where, she did not know. With the help of an archbishop in Syria, he enrolled in college and then moved to Ethiopia. Then she stopped. Where was he from? Yeghiayan asked. What happened to his family? How did he survive?

She had no answers.

Yeghiayan was overwhelmed. At twenty-five, he had learned a dreadful secret. The photo of Boghos dressed in shepherd's robes intrigued and haunted him. The mystery it incited never strayed far from his mind. What had happened to his father's family? How did he survive the deportations? Why was he dressed in shepherd's clothing? It seemed unknowable, yet Yeghiayan felt he had to learn more. Over the years, tiny morsels trickled in. The facts Yeghiayan began to uncover led him to realize why his father—like so many other survivors—preferred to stay quiet rather than overwhelm his children with sorrow.

At some point, Yeghiayan's brother found a book that included a dedication written by their father. From the paragraph-length text, Yeghiayan discerned that Boghos left his native city in the southwest portion of the Ottoman Empire with his parents and four sisters for Der Zor, the desert town on the banks of the Euphrates River where perhaps the largest number of Armenians met their end.[51]

There were no other details in the dedication, but Yeghiayan knew of the hellish conditions in Der Zor. Mass graves and unburied corpses stretched for miles. A fifteen-year-old boy wrote in his diary of a "terrible stink." "When we were advancing in the field, suddenly we felt an open hole in front of our feet. . . . [W]e could see a dead man in the bottom of the hole. Fearfully screaming, we were running back. And now in front of us . . . another dead corpse. . . . And like this . . . un-buried dead—men, women, elderly and children. All of them were bare and without clothing. . . ."[52] Two doctors were charged with treating thousands of homeless, malnourished deportees. Ottoman gangs dragged those fortunate enough to survive disease and starvation into caves and set them on fire in primitive gas chambers.[53] Up to 200,000 Armenians died in Der Zor.

Boghos's entire family perished, but Yeghiayan never learned much about how Boghos escaped their fate, even after interviewing the few remaining survivors who had heard Boghos's tales of the Genocide. Through them, Yeghiayan learned that Arab nomads found his nine-year-old father and disguised the green-eyed, flaxen-haired boy in girl's clothes so he could survive in their company. Four years later, Boghos walked out of the desert and made his way to Aleppo in northern Syria, where tens of thousands of Armenian refugees gathered after the war. Years later, he traveled to Ethiopia, where he married Yeghiayan's mother, with whom he had three sons. He worked up the ranks of an international trading firm, building sizable savings that allowed him to send his children abroad for their education.[54]

Yeghiayan wondered why his father remained silent all those years. Every survivor reacted differently to the Genocide. Some tried to repress their memories, hoping to suffocate their pain, while others talked about them incessantly. A few managed to forgive the Turks and reconcile with their loss. Many broke down in tears when retelling their experience decades later, almost as if they were reliving the horror without the shelter provided by time and distance. Post-traumatic stress paralyzed some from restarting their lives.[55]

Perhaps his father's memories were too painful to bear, Yeghiayan surmised. The arbitrary, often graphically torturous nature of the deaths left many survivors psychologically scarred. Children saw their parents killed. Parents helplessly watched their daughters being taken away. Mothers committed mercy killings of their starving infants. Few had a chance to say goodbye to their loved ones or provide for an honorable funeral for the deceased. Without their elders to comfort them, nightmares, anxiety, and depression pervaded the survivors' psyches, leaving them demoralized. "We have had no childhood," one orphan exclaimed, "because we were Armenian. . . ."[56]

On almost every April 24, Boghos commiserated with other survivors, listening to their tales and telling his own. Such conversations typified survivor gatherings in which the exchange of sad stories provided a modicum of relief. At home, though, Boghos remained silent. When his wife attempted to listen in on his confessions, Boghos pushed her away. He never told his three sons about what had happened to his family. He never described his years as a shepherd. And he never uttered a word of enmity against the Turks.[57]

Yeghiayan could only speculate as to why his father had kept his childhood hidden from his sons. Perhaps he was waiting for us to get old enough to bear the news, Yeghiayan wondered. Perhaps his premature death forestalled his plan to one day divulge his saga of survival. Or perhaps Boghos would forever keep his past a secret.

Upon graduating from Berkeley in 1959, Yeghiayan canvassed African-American neighborhoods in Oakland for John F. Kennedy's campaign while pursuing a law degree from Lincoln Law School of San Jose, a night school. After a brief stint in a small Oakland firm, he joined California Rural Legal Assistance, a non-profit group representing agricultural workers which, after Reagan became governor in 1967, gained notoriety as a thorn in the governor's side. Throughout the years, Yeghiayan took part in many antiwar and civil rights marches, but his attention never strayed far from his Armenian heritage. The Genocide stories that he had heard from his college classmates and his father's mysterious background brewed inside, turning his radicalism to the Armenian cause. He found Church memorials insufficient. Armenians, he believed, must build on the 1965 demonstrations if for no other reason than to defiantly remind the Turks of their failure to exterminate the Armenians.[58]

In 1971, Yeghiayan organized a protest in front of the newly opened Turkish Consulate in Los Angeles. Few relationships typified the stark differences between the survivor generation and its descendants better than Boghos and Vartkes Yeghiayan. Boghos internalized his pain, while his son publicized it to the world in the name of a cause. In addition to the dozens of protestors Yeghiayan brought down from San Francisco and Fresno, Gerard Libaridian, the editor of an ARF newspaper, helped organize locals, bringing the total to 2,000. Shouting into a bullhorn, Yeghiayan directed the crowd as helicopters and news vans buzzed around. Some demonstrators held signs while others handed out flyers to passing drivers. With a police escort, Yeghiayan went up to the consulate's offices on the eleventh floor. Denied entry, Yeghiayan resigned himself to attaching the petition listing Armenian grievances on the consulate door.[59]

His hesitation did not last as Armenian youth became ever more militant and brash.

A year later, Yeghiayan's collaborator Libaridian and an ARF colleague of his, Levon Kirakosian, along with a few others, again entered the Turkish Consulate's office in Los Angeles. This time, they refused to relent. One of them read out a list of grievances against Turkey and then handed it over to Consul Mehmet Baydar, who summarily tore the letter apart. When Baydar pushed aside an Armenian cameraman, the ongoing screaming match turned into a fistfight.[60]

Just as the resurrection of the Genocide began, Cold War divisions started to fade. Though Armenian factions remained deeply suspicious of each other, the détente between the United States and the Soviet Union filtered down to the Armenians. There was even talk of Church unity.

The ARF, the most politically engaged segment of the community, shifted its policy. While it remained steadfastly anti-Soviet, its Cold War agenda began to recede as the Genocide took prominence, making the quest for justice against Turkey, and not the Soviet Union, the party's primary aim. The death of leaders held over from the Armenian Republic such as Vratsian and Darbinian during the 1960s contributed to this shift as the ARF turned its significant political connections and mobilization efforts to the Genocide.[61]

Similarly, the aspirations of the survivor generation of returning to a lost homeland offered little appeal for their descendants who had never lived on Armenian soil. The generation that came of age after the Genocide had set roots in new nations. The sentimental attachment to a mythical homeland did not remain. Again, William Saroyan reflected the psyche of this generation. Born in California, in 1964 he traveled to the home of his ancestors in Bitlis, Turkey, after numerous attempts over a span of many years. Despite finding the very spot of his family's house, Saroyan realized that his family's roots had been completely torn out. No foundation remained to make possible his return. "I didn't want to leave," Saroyan said of his visit. "But it's not ours."[62]

Throughout these seminal years, the survivors remained largely on the sidelines. They attended April 24 demonstrations and relayed their experiences at communal events, but none from that generation played a leading role in the post-1965 campaign. Instead, they left it to their children and grandchildren to take up the cause.

The Armenian youth in America, swayed by the civil rights, student rights, and antiwar movements, saw the Genocide as another injustice to fight for, an injustice in which they were personally invested. Unlike the survivors, they would not cower meekly. Having inherited a sound economic and communal foundation from the survivors who spent their lives rebuilding, they had the luxury to mount a political campaign. The experience of the Genocide manifested itself differently in these younger generations. The psychological defenses used to contend with and evade the persistent strain of the tragedy had contributed to the silence of the survivors. Their offspring had not witnessed its horrors firsthand, and as such, had the necessary detachment to reawaken the forgotten episode of history. At the same time, with only a generation or two between survivors and the children of the sixties, the psychological scars of the Genocide endured. The ongoing failure to establish truth prohibited the natural healing process from taking effect.

In an era when many Americans began to search for their roots, Armenian-Americans inevitably confronted the Genocide at every turn. They came to realize that so much of who they were was begotten in the apocalyptic days of 1915. The rise of identity politics, a movement that rose to prominence during the 1960s in which groups began to come together and identify themselves by shared historical grievances, encouraged the younger Armenians' campaign for justice.[63] An overpowering sense of obligation to their ancestral legacy along with its unresolved trauma gave them the sustained emotional energy needed to carry on a decades-long struggle with Turkey. Instead of the Genocide's horrors ceasing with the death of the survivors, these horrors transplanted into subsequent generations, significantly defining Armenian identity for generations to come.

Despite their unprecedented efforts, the Armenians had hardly made a dent in attracting the world's attention after 1965. Turkey persisted in denying Ottoman sins and few others cared about a crime from a bygone era. Such disenchantment fomented a combustible environment among frustrated and radicalized youth. Into this tempest came the unlikeliest of sparks, a seventy-seven-year-old Genocide survivor.

"I will set the example"

In April 1972, Gourgen Yanikian found himself overwhelmed by memories. Again and again, he replayed his brother Hagop's death at the hands of two Turkish men. As one man held his brother down, another raised a blade into the air and slashed Hagop's throat. Apparitions from the Genocide also returned: the body parts floating down rivers he witnessed while camped out at a riverbank and the corpses of his relatives, chopped into pieces like butchered animals. This sudden flow of horrific images—scenes Yanikian had learned to live with for decades—had been triggered by the latest setback in his life, a setback that would ultimately lead to Yanikian's final act. For three days, he confined himself inside his apartment in Santa Barbara, California, trying to find a lifeline out of this abjection.[1]

Yanikian had not always been so despondent. After the Genocide, his life improved dramatically as he finished his education in Russia and married Suzanna, a gynecologist from a wealthy family. It turned rosier when the couple moved to Iran in 1930, where he established a civil engineering firm responsible for constructing a section of the railway used to transport one fourth of Lend-Lease aid shipped from the United States to the Soviet Union during World War II. Camels and donkeys were often used to carry equipment across the rugged terrain as Yanikian's crew blasted through mountain ranges and spanned hundreds of valleys and gorges with bridges in order to pave a smooth path for the railroad. Occasionally running low on basic supplies of food and water, Yanikian and his army of men, which swelled to 4,000 at the height of the construction, worked on the "roughest, toughest railroading to be found anywhere in the world." Iran's king, father of the deposed Shah, decorated Yanikian with military honors for his contribution to the railway.[2]

Upon his arrival in America in 1946, Yanikian laid down shallow roots, moving from New York to Beverly Hills to Fresno. Often dressed in dapper clothes—he once wore a top hat to the opera while his wife showed off a sable coat—he was an unusual addition to the humble agrarian community in central California. He owned a house in an upscale section of town and was not shy about exhibiting his abundant wealth. When he arrived in Santa Barbara in 1955, he developed a 30-acre parcel of a land atop a hill. With his real estate holdings bringing in a sizable income, Yanikian spent much of his time writing, producing plays, and dabbling in television shows—his last project, a courtroom drama entitled *Let the Court Decide*—and movies. Ever the Renaissance man, he organized lectures at local universities, joined scientific and literary societies, received a doctorate in divinity from the Universal Life Church, signed on to radio shows, and staged plays, occasionally even luring an audience to his short-lived Gourgen Theatre. He also wrote abstract, provocative books with raffish titles like *The Triumph of Judas Iscariot* that mixed religion, politics, and philosophy. In one of his many projects, Yanikian surveyed students from U.C. Santa Barbara about their sexual habits. Published at his own expense, none of his books attracted much of an audience, but his imagination rarely ran dry and a new project was almost always on the horizon.[3]

Yet, no matter how many new ventures he pursued, and no matter how many years had passed, memories of the Genocide never veered far from his mind. In intimate settings with close friends, the gloomy reminiscences would often return, quickly overpowering his bonhomie and replacing his cheerful disposition with anger and sadness. A chance meeting with Franz Werfel's widow in Beverly Hills in 1950 inspired an idea that would allow Yanikian to respond to the injustice endured by him and his people. Over the years, several people had unsuccessfully tried to make a film of *The Forty Days of Musa Dagh*—a project quashed by the Turkish government and the State Department in the

1930s. Yanikian joined their ranks. His lack of experience in producing movies, however, did not deflate his zeal for resurrecting the project. Though he patched together a 600-page script, the money he raised fell short of putting on a modest film. To make up the shortfall, he looked to a past debt from his glory days. The Iranian government still owed Yanikian money dating back to his construction work during World War II. If he could only get it to pay him what he was owed, he would be able to fund production of the film.

Repeated failures to enforce a $1.5 million judgment against Iran—in 1965, he tried to contact the Shah directly—led Yanikian to seek the State Department's help in collecting the money owed to him. The department had declined his various petitions over the years, but he held out hope that a law barring foreign aid to any country refusing to pay its debt to an American citizen would lead to a breakthrough. In April 1972, Yanikian received the letter he dreaded: a final refusal from the Department of State. He felt, he said, like a "second class citizen," and the unhappy memories of the Genocide began to flow unchecked. "These letters finally let me know that all my work . . . all my program . . . all my idea," Yanikian later explained in his broken English, was "dead."[4]

After reading the State Department letter, Yanikian immured himself inside his apartment full of maps, writings, and reminders of a lifetime of memories to review his situation. The empty home reaffirmed his loneliness, and sent his mind wandering: "I came crazy." His wife of nearly fifty years was lying in a convalescent hospital ever since the onset of sclerosis had left her in a coma years earlier. They had no children to comfort him. At first, he had paid her medical bills. But when abortive land deals ate away his once mighty fortune, leaving him in debt and relying on handouts from friends and welfare, the bills proved insurmountable, forcing the proud Yanikian to rely on the state to pay for her care. Constantly dodging creditors and landlords, he had found this shabby apartment, his fourth residence in three years.[5]

Isolated inside his apartment over three days, his thoughts turned to the one event that had cast a long shadow over his life: the Genocide. Turkey's denial infuriated him and the State Department's rejection convinced him that he would never be able to deliver justice to his family. "I think . . . is most important three days in my life because I saw . . . all my life is going down," he later recalled. After quickly dismissing thoughts of suicide, he arrived at a solution. Inspired by Soghomon Tehlirian, the man who assassinated Mehmet Talaat in Berlin in 1921, Yanikian meticulously concocted a plan that would redress all his wrongs in one dramatic act. Putting his engineer's mind to use, he diagrammed every step of the operation. Bankrupt and alone, Yanikian could not find one bright spot in his life to turn back his plans for retribution. "I have burned all bridges," he later wrote of his decision, with "nothing to live for."[6] For three days, he mused over how his families' murderers went unpunished. For three days, he plotted a murder that in one fell swoop would remind the world of the forgotten Genocide and spur the Armenians to cast off decades of timidity in their pursuit of justice. He longed to make himself a household name. He longed to publicize the Armenian case to the world. And he longed to redeem his brother. The memories of loss swept away every doubt intruding upon his plan. Instead, his brother's repeated apparition during these three days of solitude confirmed its righteousness.[7]

Yanikian began work on a 119-page manifesto, which he came to call his "most important work," just after his three-day self-imposed isolation. In the rambling document, he disclosed his objective to awaken an indifferent world to the Armenian fate. "I will do it in such a way that the whole world will know," Yanikian wrote of his murderous plan. "I am going to make a noise so all will hear." He typed it out in Armenian over a four-month period so that the document would remain incomprehensible if it fell into someone else's hands. He applied the same care in making copies by refusing to leave the manifesto with a store clerk overnight.[8]

Once finished with the manifesto, he launched the next stage of his plan by contacting the Turkish Consulate in Los Angeles in August 1972 with news of a rare oil painting and a valuable bank note he was prepared to hand over to the Turkish government. To avoid raising suspicions, he disguised his Armenian heritage, instead identifying himself as Persian under the pseudonym Gourg Yaniki. In October, Yanikian visited Vice Consul Bahadir Demir at the Turkish Consulate to show him a photo of the portrait depicting a harem woman thought to have been stolen from the Sultan's palace a century earlier. In December, the consulate notified Yanikian that it was eager to bequeath the work to a museum in Turkey.[9]

His ruse worked.

Insisting that the consulate head, Mehmet Baydar, collect the painting and currency in person in Santa Barbara, Yanikian declined to bring them to Los Angeles or hand them over to lower-level officials. It was agreed that they would all meet at the Biltmore Hotel on January 27, 1973.[10]

Like a man about to set off to war and not expecting to return, Yanikian spent the next few weeks getting his life in order. He gave a painting to a neighbor around Christmas. By then, he had visited Soviet Armenia to donate a painting to a museum and see his sister for the last time. He discarded most of his other belongings, sold his Buick to a used car dealer for $800, and gave away his television and furniture. Days before the designated meeting, he packed his cherished items—primarily writings, a passport, and medication cards—along with some clothes, and checked into the Biltmore.[11]

Yanikian appreciated the need for secrecy. Yet he also felt the need to unburden himself. Weeks before his scheduled meeting with the Turkish diplomats, he told a friend of the decision that would dramatically alter his life. "My brother is coming to my mind in my dreams," Yanikian said. "I'm going to send you my library because I'm going to kill the Turks." His interlocutor, an editor of an Armenian newspaper, did not take his words seriously.[12]

After the consulate confirmed their appointment, Yanikian prepared eight to nine copies of his manifesto, accompanied by a cover letter addressed to the U.S. president and a host of Armenian and American news outlets, including *Time* magazine and the *Los Angeles Times*, to maximize publicity for his impending attack. About two days before the scheduled meeting, he dropped off the packages in different drop boxes to avoid raising any suspicion at the post office. There was no turning back now.[13]

The day before his meeting, Yanikian visited his wife for the last time. He normally brought her two or three Hershey bars, a symbolic gift since she could not eat anything in her condition. During this visit, he brought an entire box of chocolates and stayed about an hour. Later, he appeared nervous and upset while preparing dinner at a friend's home. His restlessness continued throughout the night. He woke up on Saturday, January 27, tired from an anxious night of sleep on the beach, steps away from his cottage at the Biltmore. The thoughts and memories that haunted him during his three days of isolation in the apartment had returned to disturb his rest. A big breakfast reenergized him for the task ahead. He locked the windows of the cottage and latched the screens shut. Wearing his signature white beret, brown tweed overcoat, and cufflinks, he asked the front desk to clean his room and prepare lunch for three.[14]

While Yanikian finalized arrangements with the Biltmore, the forty-seven-year-old Baydar, and his assistant, thirty-year-old Vice Consul Demir, drove up to Santa Barbara. Baydar, the father of two teenage girls, had been a lifelong diplomat who had served in the Turkish Embassy in Washington and with CENTO, a NATO-like defense pact in the Middle East. He took over as the Los Angeles consul in October 1970. The younger Demir, coming off a five-year stint at the Foreign Ministry, had married twenty months earlier, just before arriving at the Los Angeles Consulate, his first posting abroad. Because Baydar's wife, who normally drove the consul, was unavailable, Demir acted as his chaperone.[15] The fact that Baydar and Demir were both married with children, and that neither man was alive at the time of the Genocide, mattered little to Yanikian. Just as Ottoman dehumanization of the Armenians a half century earlier opened the door for so many ordinary citizens to participate in the Genocide, Yanikian came to view the men not as human beings, but as symbols of decades of injustice.

The diplomats arrived at the Biltmore at 11:30 a.m. When they approached the cottage surrounded by trees and flowers, the six-foot-tall, 205-pound Yanikian, who towered over the shorter men, bowed in a courtly manner before inviting them inside. In stark contrast to Yanikian's hippielike attire, Baydar wore a gray suit, blue tie, and white shirt.[16]

Baydar was fully cognizant of Armenian antagonism toward Turkey. While serving in the Turkish Embassy in 1965, he had discussed the issuance of Genocide proclamations by American politicians with the

State Department. More recently, after having tangled with Armenian protestors at the L.A. Turkish Consulate and the Bel-Air Hotel just a few months earlier, Baydar had requested security from the Los Angeles Police Department for an event scheduled on the night of his meeting with Yanikian. A colleague at the Turkish Consulate in Chicago had asked for permission to carry a gun a few months earlier. Despite these precautions, the diplomats must not have suspected the potential for foul play at the Biltmore because they took no security precautions in meeting with Yanikian. Neither of them arrived armed or accompanied by security guards.[17]

As waiters laid out a buffet, Yanikian took off his coat and beret, releasing his unkempt hair. He brought over the bank note from the dresser and handed it to Baydar. The diplomat handed him a receipt. With his two guests sitting on yellow chairs in one corner, Yanikian placed himself on the edge of the bed so that he could see them both at a glance. As Baydar and Demir began lunch, the three men started to discuss Turkish history. Any conversation between an Armenian and a Turk inevitably led to conflicting versions of this history. This one was no different. Yanikian told the men the truth about his identity—he was not Persian but Armenian. When Baydar heard the news, he dropped the bank note. A shouting match ensued until Yanikian yelled out, "I will kill you." The diplomats stood still. When Yanikian pulled out his Luger from a hollowed-out volume of *Who's Who in the West* lying on the bed, they realized it was a trap.

Baydar clumsily swung a chair at Yanikian, who although seventy-seven years old, maintained a barrel-chested physique strong enough to fend off men half his age. The chair grazed Yanikian's left shoulder and clipped the side of his head but failed to dislodge the firearm from his right hand. Yanikian fired nine times from eight feet away, blasting bullets through the men's shoulders and chests. None of the shots was lethal. Moments later, he removed the Browning handgun from the dresser and fired twice at the back of each man's head—what he considered mercy shots—leaving the prostrate men lying in a pool of blood. Those bullets carried with them more than a half century of frustration, anger, and unmended anguish. Stepping over the bodies to reach the telephone, he saw his brother's apparition on the wall. Was it a sign? His brother had given him life by saving him as an infant. He now gave his brother two lives in return. Perhaps Yanikian would find peace at last.[18]

Baydar died almost instantly. Blood hemorrhaging from Demir's mouth could not suffocate his groans, which were heard by guests in the adjacent cottage. He died four hours later in St. Francis Hospital without regaining consciousness.[19] Neither man left this world surrounded by loved ones. Neither of them saw their families before bullets ripped through their bodies. For all of Yanikian's genuine anguish, he had done to the men what the Ottomans had done to his family. He had scarred their families as the Ottomans had scarred him. For him, the exchange of blood for blood justified one crime with another.

Yanikian did not flee. Nor did he attempt to hide the bodies. Instead, he called the front desk and instructed the operator to "call the sheriff, I have just killed two men." While police raced to the hotel, Yanikian moved to a wooden chair underneath an umbrella located on the cottage patio and waited. He appeared cool and collected. He flippantly told a passerby, "I killed the two men in my room." Just as cavalierly, he told a bellboy to send the hotel bill to his jail cell. When someone headed for his cottage, Yanikian urged the man not to enter the room and risk spoiling the crime scene. In a steady voice, he asked the manager of a nearby casino who had rushed to the scene for a glass of water. After taking a sip, he said: "I promised my brother I would kill them."[20]

A plainclothes officer approached Yanikian a few minutes later. "You may go in," Yanikian told him, still resonating calmness. "I have been waiting for you." Yanikian arrived at the county jail in the same pensive mood. His only request to the police was to remain uncuffed and that the officers should bring along his briefcase. During the ensuing interrogation with the sheriff's department and FBI, he readily admitted to killing the two diplomats. And he did not utter a word during the arraignment.[21] The calm pervading the proceedings contrasted with the chaos quickly spreading through Armenian circles.

Armenians were shocked by the crime. Many simply refused to believe it. How could one of their own end up plastered on the front pages of newspapers accused of murder? When the news sank in, many condemned Yanikian; some praised him for getting back at the

Turks, while most others disapproved but instinctively understood.[22] It almost seemed inevitable. After decades of bottled-up frustration, one survivor who relived in his mind the traumatic moments endured in 1915 would strike back.

For all his planning, Yanikian had overlooked one critical element: a lawyer. He sat through the interrogation and a psychological exam without any legal advice. He at first refused to take on counsel before finally accepting the help of a Beverly Hills attorney, Vasken Minasian.[23]

Over objections from the FBI, a group of Armenians—some of whom had worked on the Montebello Monument—hastily formed a defense committee to provide Yanikian adequate legal representation.[24] The committee saw Yanikian's trial as an opportunity to publicize the Genocide and bring attention to the Armenian case against Turkey. Like Yanikian, the defense committee recognized parallels with the Tehlirian case fifty years earlier where the trial was not so much a judgment of the assassin's guilt as of the victim's. Like that case, it hoped to turn Yanikian's trial into a political indictment of Turkey—what the committee called in its national fund-raising and media campaign an "ARMENIAN NUREMBERG." Funds arrived from across the world, often from Genocide survivors who looked upon the trial in the same light. "My wife and I live on an old age pension," wrote one donor. "This small check of $10 for Mr. Yanikian is contributed for his trial which is the trial of 1915. . . ."[25]

The committee intended to select a nationally renowned attorney to maximize media coverage. It made it clear to potential lawyers that publicity for the Genocide took precedence over Yanikian's acquittal.[26] Its first choice, Texas native Percy Foreman, was among the leading defense lawyers in the nation, with experience in more than 1,500 capital cases. Of all his notorious clients, James Earl Ray, the assassin of Dr. Martin Luther King, Jr., was the most infamous. Ever flamboyant, Foreman adopted black and white plaid sports jackets over the conservative attire preferred by his colleagues. Foreman's outsized ego—he boasted that "There is no better trial lawyer in the U.S. than me"—surpassed Yanikian's.[27] The two domineering personalities, each demanding to take center stage at the trial, would inevitably have clashed. After months of negotiations with the committee over fees and final say in running the case, Foreman dropped out by checking into a hospital for an ostensible heart problem when the committee failed to raise enough cash.[28] Yanikian rejected the committee's other choice, Charles Garry, an Armenian-American lawyer who represented the Black Panthers. Like Foreman, Garry offered solid courtroom credentials and experience in high-profile cases. From a strategic standpoint, Yanikian thought a lawyer representing African-American radicals would turn off a jury in conservative Santa Barbara. But perhaps just as important to Yanikian, he complained of Garry's name change from the Armenian original, Garabedian.[29] Yanikian finally settled on James T. Lindsey, a highly respected local attorney who had already been working on the case, along with Minasian.

After an initial honeymoon, Yanikian sparred with the committee over control. Always a loner, his temperament was ill-suited to working with a group. He wanted to have final say over the committee's communications, select his own defense counsel, oversee expenditures, and manage the case. "I am the commander-in-chief," he declared at a press conference. "It is Yanikian's case, not the committee's."[30] Arguments erupted regularly. During one spat, one committee member feared that the imposing Yanikian—though outnumbered by much younger men—might strangle all the visitors inside his jail cell. On the eve of the trial, the committee returned the more than $50,000 that it had collected on Yanikian's behalf to the original donors. Yanikian lashed out at the last-minute withdrawal of funds, threatening to sue what he labeled the "enemies of Armenian martyrs."[31]

As soon as news of the murders came out, the American government mobilized its vast resources. A team of fifty FBI agents launched an investigation that would come to produce thousands of pages of materials on a case they code-named "ARMUR." Forensic experts combed through the crime scene. Investigators interviewed anyone remotely connected to Yanikian, from his neighbors and friends to bartenders at the taverns he frequented. Thinking there might be a connection between Yanikian and protestors based in Los Angeles, agents questioned dozens of Armenian advocates. They recorded Yanikian's conversations in jail. Others delved into Yanikian's history. They found his myriad writings. They dove into tangential links to communism from decades past. No detail of his life escaped examination. They tracked down a woman they believed to be a former mistress in Paris and uncovered the existence of a child potentially born out of wedlock, which may have been a secret Yanikian had kept from his own wife.[32]

The key question for investigators was not so much whether Yanikian was guilty. There was little doubt of that. The U.S. government wanted to unearth a possible conspiracy. After all, Yanikian was a septuagenarian with a limp and a heart condition. How did he manage to kill two men half his age on his own? Did he have help? What did Yanikian discuss with Soviet authorities on his visit to the USSR just two months before the murders? Was he the front man of a Soviet plot?[33]

The assassination pricked Turkish sensitivity about its past. The Turkish government felt that Yanikian's murder was not just directed at the victims but "designed as an affront to the Turkish nation."[34] Not even the worldwide demonstrations in 1965 aroused this much suspicion of Armenian designs on Turkey.[35] It saw the potential in Yanikian's act to inspire young radicals, and it feared that the April 24 demonstrations of 1973 would lead to more "terrorist activities."[36]

While the FBI led the criminal probe, the State Department tried to safeguard America's relationship with Turkey. It wanted to avoid adding more fuel to these simmering fires. The United States and Turkey remained—at least on a government-to-government level—close allies. State was not going to permit the Armenians to spoil that alliance. The department assiduously monitored Turkish domestic reaction and made sure at every opportunity to assuage the Turkish government, whose foreign minister had sunk to "the gravest of moods" after the double murder.[37] A bevy of American officials from President Nixon and Secretary of State Rogers to lower-level diplomats conveyed personal messages of grief.[38] The FBI provided regular updates to Turkey and promised to do its utmost in prosecuting the case.[39] But it struggled to dissuade incredulous officials who were "convinced . . . that [the] deaths resulted from a well-organized plot by an Armenian gang" that Yanikian had acted alone.[40]

Knowing that Turkey would hold it responsible for anything "untoward that might occur," the State Department arranged for increased security at Turkish locales, and spoke to Armenian-American leaders to prevent further violence. Turkey wanted the State Department to go further than what the agency already considered "a most unusual step" in trying to persuade Armenian-Americans to reduce their anti-Turkish rhetoric. Its foreign minister asked the U.S. ambassador in Ankara to block all upcoming April 24 demonstrations.[41]

Jury selection began on May 29, 1973, inside one of America's most majestic courthouses. After an earthquake wiped out much of Santa Barbara's downtown in 1925, city planners had settled on an Andalusian template harking back to the area's colonial era. The courthouse completed in 1929 stood as the gem of the collection. William Mooser's design juxtaposed a mix of Spanish styles. A turret and a 114-foot clocktower offering observers a 360-degree view stood atop white walls. Scattered archways, lush gardens, and handcrafted details decorated the site's interior and exterior. Whereas most government buildings in America ranged from dingy yet pragmatic to outright hideous, Santa Barbara's courthouse could have doubled as a museum. Iron grilles covered the windows; hand-carved stones adorned the arches; mosaic tilework in geometric patterns reminiscent of Moorish architecture lined the interior hallways. Leather-padded doors decorated with raised moldings welcomed observers to the packed courtroom located in an L-shaped building, one of the compound's four structures. Windows on one side of the chamber provided a view of the palm trees outside. A blue carpet stretched across the floor. Brown leather benches behind the attorneys' tables were designated for visitors.[42]

The trial began under the tightest security ever seen in Santa Barbara. Up to ten officers hovered in the courtroom, with one of them assigned exclusively to Yanikian. Spectators passed through a metal detector and were submitted to searches. During breaks, sheriff's deputies inspected the courtroom for weapons. As an extra precaution, Yanikian wore a bulletproof vest.[43]

A motley collection of spectators added to the frenzy in an eighty-seat courtroom filled to capacity. Sketch artists, journalists, and a local celebrity, a retired actress from Australia, regularly attended the trial, as did a Turkish representative. A busload of Armenians transported from Los Angeles and Montebello also came daily. When Yanikian entered the courtroom for the first time, his supporters stood and clapped, prompting a warning from the judge. Though they obeyed his instructions thereafter, their rapt attention raised the energy inside the courtroom throughout the trial.[44]

Yanikian had trimmed his shoulder-length hair for the trial and replaced his hippie attire with a conservative blue suit. Yet he was still an unlikely icon for Armenians. Armenian institutions distanced themselves from his violent act. His craggy appearance combined with a sourpuss personality made him unlikable to many and a pariah among local Armenians. Yanikian had hardly ever participated in Armenian activities. Despite these alienating characteristics, his excruciating experience during the Genocide made many Armenians look upon him with a combination of awe and sympathy.[45]

When Yanikian devised his plan months earlier, he wanted a judicial proceeding that would allow him to publicize the Armenian story. He was right to assume that the brazen murder of two diplomats would attract media attention. Though home to a small population, Santa Barbara was only a two-hour drive away from one of the nation's media centers in Los Angeles, and close to significant Armenian populations in Fresno and Los Angeles. Indeed, news of his double murder reached the nation's largest newspapers well beyond Southern California and the Armenian community.

Like Tehlirian's trial a half century earlier, he also planned on presenting his case not so much as an indictment of himself, but of Turkey. But unlike Tehlirian, Yanikian refused to go along with some kind of insanity plea as his lawyers suggested. A psychiatrist concluded that Yanikian suffered from severe paranoia and was insane but his own freedom seemed to matter little to him. "Don't call me insane," Yanikian yelled out when a member of his defense team suggested an insanity defense, "I knew what I was doing."[46] This handicapped his lawyers throughout the trial, forcing them to argue for "diminished capacity," a legal doctrine asserting that a defendant—though not insane—lacked the necessary mental state needed for guilt. Its usual application led to the mitigation of a crime, knocking murder down to manslaughter, for example. Lindsey, a tall, slender chain smoker with salt and pepper hair and hypnotic hands, argued that Yanikian did not see his act as immoral or illegal—thus lacking the necessary mental state—but as a symbolic act of retribution for his family and the Armenian people. Yanikian repeatedly insisted that he did not "kill" the two men but instead "destroyed two evils." In order for this strategy to work, Lindsey had to convince the jury that Yanikian's lasting trauma endured during the Genocide combined with the continuing injustice suffered by the Armenians caused his client's impairment in judgment. The defense planned on introducing a great deal of testimony about the Genocide to bolster this argument: professors would provide a broad history and survivors would contribute personal accounts. This strategy would not only help Yanikian's defense but conform to his objectives.[47]

The prosecutor, on the other hand, intended to block the jury from seeing any such evidence of the Genocide to avoid raising sympathy for Yanikian among the jurors.

David D. Minier had been Santa Barbara's district attorney for five years when news of the double murder electrified the city. Overseeing an office of a dozen lawyers and a handful of investigators, his position allowed him to cherry-pick the most interesting cases. He used that prerogative to work as the prosecutor for the Yanikian case. To date, the biggest case in Minier's career involved a rig accident off the central coast of California that disfigured the pristine coastline with unsightly oil deposits. Matched against a handful of oil companies and a phalanx of lawyers, the Stanford Law School graduate went down to the federal court in Los Angeles alone with nothing more than an innovative legal theory untested in the courts.[48]

The odds were stacked in his favor in the Yanikian trial. With Yanikian's eager admission of killing the two diplomats, and a mountain of forensic evidence furnished by the FBI, Minier saw only one tactic the defense could employ to avert a guilty verdict. Cases with such overwhelming evidence rarely made it to trial. Defense lawyers avoided going to court on the losing side of such a one-sided adjudication so they encouraged their clients to plead guilty in the hopes of a lesser sentence. But this was no ordinary case. Yanikian did not want a typical trial, he wanted a bully pulpit to make his case against Turkey.

Yanikian's objectives were of little concern to Minier, however. Two men had been murdered. Their assassin needed to be punished for his crime. Nothing should get in the way of that. Minier feared that a litany of survivors brought into the courtroom to testify about the Genocide might sway the jury to sympathize with Yanikian, and nullify what would otherwise be an obvious verdict against the defendant. If he could block the inclusion of such evidence, then he could derail the defense's only strategy.[49]

Minier and Lindsey had faced each other in Santa Barbara's cozy legal scene on many occasions. Their amicable relationship infused the proceedings with an air of civility that rarely erupted into finger-pointing or strenuous objections. Only one issue caused them to lock horns: would the judge allow the defense to introduce evidence about the Genocide? This question rested at the center of the defense's strategy. For Yanikian, it was the main reason he had taken two lives. With the crux of the case at stake, both lawyers strenuously argued their positions. When Lindsey asked the U.S. government to purvey all of its archives related to the Genocide, Minier mocked his opponent by offering a library card. Judge John Westwick, a softspoken senior judge in Santa Barbara with a reputation for fairness, rejected Yanikian's request. He could not warrant a retelling of Armenian history through witnesses that would take up weeks of the jurors' time.[50] The court was a forum to determine one man's guilt or innocence, not an arena to issue edicts on the past.

Minier would come to have some misgivings about his strategy. "Looking back," he wrote in an editorial twenty-five years later while reflecting upon his decision, "I regret that I did not allow the genocide to be proven. Not because Yanikian should have gone free, but because history's darkest chapters—its genocides—should be exposed. . . ."[51]

After the jury of seven men and five women selected as its foreperson twenty-nine-year-old Patricia Montemayor, a public relations representative, the tall, wiry district attorney methodically presented his case through twenty-five witnesses. A member of the Turkish Consulate explained how Yanikian lured the diplomats to the hotel cottage. A witness described the harrowing deaths suffered by Baydar and Demir. Various people from the Biltmore and two psychiatrists testified about Yanikian's state of mind.[52]

The defense's case was simple. There was little doubt about whether Yanikian killed the two men. The key issue was: what was his state of mind? After Judge Westwick's refusal to allow historians and survivors to testify about the Genocide, the defense saw no other recourse than to convey all the historical material about the Genocide through Yanikian's weeklong testimony, starting on June 15.[53] Though they hit the highlights—describing the arrest of Armenian leaders, the backdrop of World War I, and conditions during the deportations—the overview provided by Yanikian was a clumsy performance, as if he and Lindsey stood on opposing sides of the case. Compounded by a booming, stentorian voice punctuating his verbal barrage, Yanikian's jeremiad on the witness stand often descended into a rant. He was regularly unresponsive and his poor hearing and occasional use of a translator slowed down the testimony. William Saroyan's uncle Aram, an eighty-one-year-old former attorney, acted as the interpreter. Bald, with thick dark glasses and a white beard, he had befriended Yanikian years earlier during their days in Fresno. Unlike most court interpreters, however, his role was not just to translate, but to brief Yanikian on the case so that the defendant could keep up with the proceedings. Yanikian had lived in the United States for twenty-seven years and had written many works in English. But when he took the stand, he wanted an interpreter to translate certain questions to give himself a few extra moments to come up with a response.[54]

When Lindsey finally turned to Yanikian's personal experience, the entire proceeding changed radically. Despite his choppy and bellicose delivery, the earnest recounting of the horrors he had witnessed pulled at everyone's heartstrings, turning the packed chamber lachrymose. He broke into tears while describing his brother's death. His animated and authentic description of the mutilated bodies he had seen during the Genocide, and of finding his decapitated relatives among a field of corpses, introduced to jurors a horror they had never known. Throughout this portion of the testimony, the entire chamber remained engrossed. At the most excruciating moments, some of the jurors wept. Montemayor, the jury's forewoman, did all she could to hold back the tears. At last, Yanikian got the chance to tell the world his story. And his retelling turned out to be the most dramatic part of the case.[55]

Minier did not believe Yanikian's yarn of having spent decades of his life fighting on behalf of Armenians. The district attorney did not see Yanikian as a crusader but as a beaten man with nothing to lose, desperate to recapture some lost glory at the closing stages of his life. Minier's access to hundreds of FBI interviews allowed him to draw an intimate character sketch that differed considerably from the impression that Yanikian's own testimony had left. Minier learned that Yanikian, though deep in debt and on the welfare rolls since 1967, consistently spent beyond his means, often presenting himself as a wealthy real estate developer in order to hide his poverty. Several people described Yanikian's flamboyance and his predilection for bragging. His decline into destitution broke his pride and left him bitter at the world. This profile colored Minier's perception of Yanikian's motives. To him, Yanikian was not just out to boost the Armenian cause but his own shattered ego.[56]

The unsavory biographical information on Yanikian uncovered by FBI investigators also gave Minier the opening he needed to counter the defendant's moving testimony and refocus the jury on Yanikian's cold-blooded murder of two diplomats. People interviewed by the FBI mentioned Yanikian's habit of approaching young women. Several described him as a "dirty old man" who boasted of sexual conquests. Yanikian apparently asked one woman to pose nude for him. Another told the FBI that he wanted sexual favors in return for loaning her $200. Three years earlier, Yanikian had been tried and found innocent of molesting children. Minier acknowledged that introducing this evidence was a "low blow," but he felt that he had to impeach Yanikian after his stirring testimony. Judge Westwick cut short Minier's effort to introduce sexually provocative testimony, but not before the jury heard some of the evidence involving Yanikian's sex survey of local university students.[57]

During the closing arguments, Minier reminded jurors that the proceeding was not an "Armenian Nuremberg" but a murder trial in which the victims "have become . . . forgotten. . . . The defense boils down to one thing," he said. "They are making the most blatant appeal to the emotions of this jury."[58] His reading of the case was spot-on. The jury had little sympathy for the victims, whose lives remained absent from the courtroom. They appreciated Yanikian's genuine agony and found his motives compelling. When the five-week trial ended, it was up to members of the jury to weigh all of these factors in deciding Yanikian's fate. The sequestered group deliberated for ten and a half hours, from Thursday afternoon through the middle of Saturday. The judge made everyone wait until Monday morning to hear the outcome.[59]

Several jurors were in tears as Montemayor prepared to announce their decision. She had to hold back nerves in reading the verdict out loud, finding Yanikian guilty on two counts of first-degree murder. The jury had certainly sympathized with Yanikian, but its members put aside their personal feelings in methodically processing the various crimes he was charged with. At the end, they could not nullify what was an obvious double murder.[60]

Expecting the outcome, Yanikian showed no emotion but directed a sarcastic smile at the jury.[61] "It would be interpreted as a sort of license to others to go out and kill," he told the press minutes later, flanked by his lawyers. "I am opposed to killing. What I did was to destroy two symbols of evil . . . to focus world attention upon the injustice done to the Armenian people."[62] But he remained angry that the Armenians were no closer to a resolution. Blaming Turkish machinations for the denouement of the trial, he pounded the press table furiously, arguing that others "had their Nuremberg but we have not."[63]

Almost forgotten by everyone in the commotion of Yanikian's murder and trial was his manifesto. The sprawling, sometimes incoherent document urged Armenians to unshackle themselves and follow his example. "I . . . have no time or desire to keep silent any longer," he wrote. "Armenians everywhere should pursue this tactic. This new type of war. . . . Turkish representatives should be exterminated all over the world." Yanikian ended the manuscript with a prophetic declaration: "I will set the example for many more to follow."[64]

Half a world away, a man going by the moniker of Hagop Hagopian was listening. The details of Hagopian's life remained sketchy—including his real name. Sometime in the late 1960s, he joined a Palestinian terrorist group, where he honed his organizational, operational, and recruiting skills. In 1973 came the inspiration from Yanikian's double murder.[65] Within months, a group, calling itself the Yanikian Commandos sent a letter bomb to a Turkish facility in New York. In January

1975, Hagopian orchestrated an attack against the World Council of Churches. For a while, he considered calling his creation the Gourgen Yanikian Group before settling upon the Armenian Secret Army for the Liberation of Armenia (ASALA). A month later, the Marxist-leaning ASALA bombed the Turkish Airlines office in Beirut.[66] A rival group, the Justice Commandos of the Armenian Genocide (JCAG), gunned down the Turkish ambassador to Austria in October. Two days later, the JCAG killed the Turkish ambassador to France along with his chauffeur.[67] Yanikian's prophecy had come to fruition.

Few Armenians took notice at first. The year 1975 was a watershed one in which feuding Armenian factions held joint commemorations of the Genocide throughout the world. For the first time in history, they forged a comprehensive program to work together on the defining goal of the Armenian world. Local committees filled with former adversaries popped up across the globe with each side giving in on what had always been non-negotiable terms.[68] Times had changed dramatically since the 1950s when mere civil discourse lay beyond reach. The year marked the largest demonstrations ever held for the Genocide.

The terrorists cared little for this newfound brotherhood. The attacks continued throughout the decade, with different cells named after places or heroic Armenians—one group called itself the Yanikian Commandos—targeting Turkish diplomats, airline offices, and diplomatic facilities, as well as non-Turkish targets they considered loyal to Turkey. In 1980 there were thirty-one attacks across the world. The peak came in 1981, with forty-one attacks.[69] The attacks also grew more brazen over time. In 1981, a four-man ASALA team took over the Turkish Consulate in Paris, killing a guard in the process. It held fifteen hostages—the first operation of its kind—for fifteen hours before negotiations with French authorities ended the standoff. Coverage of the takeover received among the highest television ratings in France that year.[70] Having established their credentials as crack terrorist organizations, ASALA and the JCAG utilized a public relations campaign employing magazines, press conferences, and a daily radio program broadcast from Beirut.[71] While one could have written off Yanikian's double murder as the onetime act of a madman or a survivor lusting for revenge, it became clear by the early 1980s that Armenian terrorism had turned into a regular and deadly blood sport.

These groups did not exist in a vacuum. They came of age at a time when international terrorism—from Palestinians to the Irish Republican Army—metastasized. Just as the Armenian youths who marched against the Turks a decade earlier absorbed the vibrancy and borrowed the tactics of the civil rights and antiwar movements, Armenian terrorism developed in a milieu of armed aggression. In this case, it was Beirut, where many of the terrorists, having witnessed and fought in the Lebanese civil war and trained with nearby Palestinians, became ripe targets for recruiters.[72]

Yet there was something uniquely Armenian about the wave of violence. Armenian terrorism underscored decades of frustration and rage. The world's indifference to the Armenian fate combined with Turkey's denial of the Genocide forged a perfect cocktail to fuel this hunger for revenge. The suffering that Armenians had internalized for decades now turned outward, at first against their enemy and then on to others as non-Turks increasingly became targets of terrorism. Yanikian's pain was not so unique after all. And neither was his solution.

It is difficult to gauge Armenian sentiments about terrorism. There were no polls conducted. No more than 100 to 150 people ever belonged to these organizations, but they did receive some support from a broader populace. For its supporters, terrorism's allure was its capacity for empowerment. For more than a century, Armenians had asked—often begged—foreign powers to come to their aid. Now, they struck fear in Turkey. It was this feeling of empowerment that energized terrorism's youthful adherents, who had grown weary of hearing much talk but seeing little action from established institutions.[73] Generally, most Armenians denounced the terrorists while some harbored a hint of admiration for them. Many established institutions and community leaders issued absolute condemnations. Others employed a "yes, but" stance in which they condemned the violence but understood its source. Others still did not endorse the killings but blamed Turkey's policy for the deaths.

Serving out his two concurrent life sentences, Yanikian watched all of this from his prison cell. He never showed an iota of remorse for murdering two innocent men or regret for spending his last years in confinement. Nor did he exult over his prescience. When various appeals failed to overturn his verdict, his lawyers tried to obtain early parole. His age and growing infirmity boosted his application, but the parole board turned down his request. Many Armenians believed a letter written by Kemal Arikan, the new Turkish consul in Los Angeles, led to the board's decision.[74] One day after the ninth anniversary of Yanikian's double murder, Hampig Sassounian, a recent immigrant from Beirut, and another gunman from the JCAG, killed Arikan while the diplomat was driving to work in Los Angeles.[75]

Sassounian and Yanikian could not have been further apart. The latter was a survivor who murdered Turks near the end of his life; the former, the grandson of survivors, had not even turned twenty when he murdered Arikan. Yanikian was educated and well-read while Sassounian failed to finish high school. They did have one similarity, however. Sassounian repeatedly heard his grandparents describe the Genocide. Tales of drowning relatives, the march through the desert, the extermination of an extended family, played like a broken reel inside his mind. Like much of his family, he came to despise the Turks. "My son feels like me," his father told a reporter after Sassounian's arrest, "like every Armenian . . . I have the hate. Every Armenian has the hate."[76] As a member of the JCAG, Sassounian was surrounded by like-minded young men engrossed with tales of their grandparents' stories.[77] Another terrorist about Sassounian's age told a researcher: "I think my personality was developed when my grandfather was carrying me around . . . talking to his survivor friends about the horrible times. I think my responsibility started to be conveyed to me even that early . . . he holding my hand and talking to me. . . . These conversations about the genocide were ubiquitous."[78] Another member of the JCAG acknowledged that perhaps "this is my mistake in life—actually trying to feel what my grandfather felt. . . . I almost felt like I was there, just from hearing so much about it. . . ." Yet while in prison, he displayed no regrets for his crimes: "If I had to do ten years in jail, it would be a small price to pay if it would ease [my grandfather's] tortured soul a little. . . . Right is right, whatever the price is."[79] Within this milieu, the idea of revenge leapfrogged from an ephemeral contemplation where it would have quickly sputtered in most people to a rational possibility. Sassounian did not witness the Genocide but he may as well have done so, so deep was his emotional reaction to it. He was not Yanikian's grandson by blood but his kin in spirit.

On July 15, 1983, a twenty-nine-year-old member of ASALA from Syria asked a passenger at the Turkish Airlines terminal at Paris's Orly Airport to check in a bag for him. The passenger agreed and placed the luggage on his cart. At 2:13 p.m., a bomb exploded on the baggage ramp ten feet from the checkout counter. Some people fled the scene with their clothes still burning from the initial burst of orange flames; others escaped covered in ashes. The wounded cried for help; the dead lay motionless. Emergency workers converted the airport into a first-aid station before transferring the neediest cases to local hospitals. Eight people died; sixty-three were injured. If the bomb had detonated as planned—while the plane was in midair—it would have killed 170 passengers and crewmembers.[80]

The Orly bombing represented the last major, desperate gasp of the terrorist movement as a combination of factors took their toll. Once turned on, aggression had a way of running out of control. It did just that as rival subgroups resorted to attacking each other to sort out their squabbles. Bombing accidents and other blunders allowed international authorities to find the once mysterious assassins who had largely escaped detection up to 1980. And after the indiscriminate targeting of innocent lives exhibited during the Orly bombing, and other excesses, their acts seemed merely demonic, not heroic.[81]

Yanikian's health rapidly deteriorated during his last years in jail. By 1983, doctors placed a hospital bed and medical equipment in his cell to combat his senility and a host of illnesses. Over the wishes of the Turkish government, Yanikian was released in January 1984 to a convalescent home. He did not have much time to enjoy his freedom. On February 26, he died of a heart attack, weeks after a Los Angeles jury found Sassounian guilty of murder. Just as Yanikian's act of terrorism instigated more than a decade of violence, his death oversaw its closing chapter. Suffering from eroding support, internecine conflict, and bereft of a safe staging area once Israel invaded Lebanon in 1982, the terrorists faded away. They left behind a death toll of more than forty Turkish officials and dozens of others in two hundred attacks stretching across twenty-three nations.[82]

Yanikian's prophecy had come to fruition. Many did follow his example. But what did they leave behind? What was their ultimate legacy? The Genocide broke out of its confinement as many news outlets and world leaders who had hardly given the Armenians a second thought now took a careful look at their grievances. Armenians became electrified by the terrorists even as they disparaged their violence. The toll was heavy, however, costing dozens of innocent lives. And from a standpoint of cold calculation, the attacks only strengthened Turkey's resolve to deny the Armenians the one thing they really wanted, even more than the ephemeral exhilaration of revenge some enjoyed: justice.

In hindsight, Yanikian's appalling act had a certain inevitability to it. Among the hundreds of thousands who had suffered through so much during the Genocide, it was not surprising that one of those survivors might resort to revenge. At Yanikian's eulogy, his lawyer aptly stated: "He had done the unspeakable but not the unthinkable." To Yanikian's last days, the doleful memories that tortured him and spurred him to murder induced emotional breakdowns.[83] The exacting of blood failed to bring him the solace he so desired. It remained beyond reach, not just for Yanikian but for all Armenians.

Legislating History

Maybe we can redeem ourselves a bit today by letting
the world know that we do not always support the rich
and the powerful and those with the most lobbyists.
Sometimes we judge right from wrong.

—ROBERT DOLE

E ver since a shell ripped through his right shoulder in Italy during
the waning days of World War II, Robert J. Dole was in search
of a miracle that would turn him back to the man he was before
he nearly lost his life. When he returned home in 1945 barely clinging
onto life, doctors resorted to experimentation to try to save his wrecked
body. He had shrunk to 122 pounds, lost an infected kidney, and suffered from a meteoric 108.7 degree fever at one point. His right arm
hung lifelessly. After the war, the despondency of his spirit exceeded the
physical damage suffered by his body. Two years of medical procedures
ended in frustration. Dole's body would never return to its prewar
strength. Though still a young man, he was crushed by despair. "I was
not ready to accept the fact that my life would be changed forever," he
explained in his memoir. His uncle told him about a pioneer ortho-
pedist in Chicago working with veterans; Dole jumped at the chance.
There he met Dr. Hampar Kelikian—whom Dole would come to call
"Dr. K"—an Armenian who had arrived in the United States in 1920.[1]
　At their first meeting, Kelikian sat the injured soldier down and
administered what Dole later came to call "the verbal equivalent of a slap
in the face." He would never regain his body. He would never fulfill his

ambitions of playing basketball or becoming a surgeon. There would be no miracle. As a man who had lost three sisters at Ottoman hands, Kelikian told Dole to focus not on what he had lost but on what he could do with what he had left. He told Dole to do what he himself had done in rebuilding his life after bearing the unbearable. Over the next seven years, the doctor conducted seven operations on the disabled veteran at no charge in which he managed to give Dole some movement in his right arm and shoulder. Dole never fully recovered—he never got the miracle he so desired—but the interaction became a life-changing event. "He inspired within me a new attitude, a new way of looking at my life, urging me to focus on what I had left and what I could do with it, rather than complaining about what had been lost," Dole wrote in a memoir decades later. Kelikian could not give Dole his arm back, but he taught Dole how to empathize with others and he gave the future senator a new start on life, two traits that would carry the Kansas veteran from a small town to great heights. "'Dr. K' had an impact on my life second only to my family," Dole said nearly a half century after meeting the physician.[2]

Their relationship continued long after Kelikian finished operating on Dole. When Kelikian died in 1983, Dole's voice choked up as he nearly broke down in tears delivering a eulogy on the Senate floor in which he recited a poem by Robert Frost:

> *Nature's first green is gold,*
> *Her hardest hue to hold.*
> *Her early leaf's a flower;*
> *But only so an hour.*
> *Then leaf subsides to leaf.*
> *So Eden sank to grief,*
> *So dawn goes down to day.*
> *Nothing gold can stay.*[3]

"Hampar Kelikian was pure gold," Dole continued. (The eulogy so touched Senator Jesse Helms, who was listening, that he called it "one of the most moving experiences for me since I have been a Member of the Senate.")[4]

• • •

Starting in 1965, Armenians across the world asked governments to acknowledge the crimes committed against them by the Ottomans. With no court or similar forum available for the Armenians to prove their case, these affirmations served to establish the historical truth of the Genocide in the face of Turkish denial. Local officials around the world routinely issued such proclamations. That was easy. Getting a national legislature to pass a similar declaration in the face of Turkish diplomatic pressure was a whole other matter. The Uruguay Parliament in 1965 became the first national legislative body to recognize the Armenian Genocide since the World War I era. In order to avoid offending the Turkish government, the language of the resolution excluded mention of Turkey.[5] No other nations followed suit.

The Armenian-Turkish conflict next erupted in the United Nations where in 1973 a subcommission chronicling human rights violations made a passing reference to the Genocide. It would not have received much attention, but for Turkey, any mention of the Genocide, particularly by a body holding any type of official imprimatur, instigated a severe response. The reference was later removed from the subcommission's report at Turkey's behest.

The battle then leaped from the United Nations to the U.S. Congress. If Congress passed a resolution labeling the events of 1915 a "genocide," Armenian advocates monitoring the UN proceedings strategized, it could counter Turkey's move at the United Nations. Previous congressional resolutions introduced in the late 1960s had gone nowhere in the face of the State Department's objections, and neither did one submitted in 1974 by New Jersey congressman Henry Helstoski.[6] With their small population, and inexperience in lobbying, Armenians lacked the political might needed to win such a contest. They needed a patron to champion their cause.

By the 1970s, Stephen Mugar had become a household name in Boston by transforming a humble grocery store inherited from his father into a regional powerhouse incorporating the latest in supermarket technology and know-how. He became one of New England's most prolific philanthropists, donating millions to various universities (most notably the Mugar Memorial Library at Boston University), and sitting on many civic and university boards.[7] He also became a benefactor of the Armenian Assembly from its inception. Created by two professors from George Washington University and two Boston attorneys in 1972, the Assembly represented an unprecedented evolution in Armenian-American affairs. For the first time, opposing factions that had for decades ridiculed and vilified each other joined forces under an umbrella organization—at least when it came to representing Armenian interests in Washington.[8] Mugar had someone in mind to advance the Assembly's fledgling influence in Congress.

House majority leader Thomas "Tip" O'Neill and Mugar had been friends for many years. O'Neill's district in Massachusetts included Watertown and Belmont, two towns just outside of Boston that were home to many Armenians. But their friendship was not just based on political expediency. Similar in age, and avid debaters, the two men built their relationship on mutual respect. O'Neill regularly visited Mugar at his home in Florida, where the two enjoyed playing golf together. Mugar reciprocated with frequent visits to O'Neill in Washington. He addressed the House leader, among the most powerful men in the nation, by his sobriquet, "Tip." Mugar had never asked for O'Neill's help before. This time was different. Mugar was not asking for a business or political favor. He was asking O'Neill to right the wrong committed against the Armenians. He was asking him to confirm one of the greatest crimes of the century. O'Neill, a loyal friend, vowed to help by co-sponsoring Helstoski's resolution in 1975.[9]

With the backing of the second highest ranking member of the House (O'Neill became Speaker in 1977), the resolution had a fighting chance. When the State Department failed to smother it as it had done with past resolutions, the White House and the Turkish government countered loudly by warning of "adverse consequences" should the resolution pass.[10] The administration's stance placed President Ford in an awkward position. Ten years earlier, he had delivered a speech in the House condemning the "Turkish genocide of the Armenian people."[11] When the editor of a Michigan newspaper pressed the president to reaffirm his statement, Ford had to eat his words. His contorted response allowed his statement to stand without reaffirming it. When Armenians asked to meet with Ford, Robert M. Gates (then working at the National Security Council), who later would go on to serve as director of the CIA under President George H. W. Bush and secretary of defense under George W. Bush as well as Barack Obama, advised him to shun them.[12]

During the 1960s, Turkey largely relied on the State Department to curb Armenian political activity. In 1975, it could no longer depend solely on the agency in light of O'Neill's powerful standing in Congress, so its ambassador met with the House leader face-to-face to change his mind about the congressional resolution. During the meeting, O'Neill called in Linda J. Melconian, a recent Mount Holyoke graduate who, as O'Neill's legislative aide, acted as his "eyes and ears" in Congress. As the point person on the resolution, she responded to the ambassador's arguments by telling the story of the extermination of her grandmother's family during the Genocide. O'Neill decided to proceed over the ambassador's objections.[13]

With O'Neill's blessing, Melconian and Dr. Dennis R. Papazian of the Armenian Assembly secured enough votes for passage. Yet Congress's innumerable parliamentary roadblocks still loomed. It was at this juncture that O'Neill's patronage paid dividends. To prevent any possible obstruction, O'Neill suspended the usual House rules—a procedure that bypasses most committees and limits debate and amendments but requires a super-majority vote—to propel the resolution to a direct vote on the House floor. But with O'Neill away in the Middle East as the vote neared, the House leadership began to flounder under continuing pressure from the State Department. Melconian felt that if they did not vote promptly—when the Armenians had corralled the necessary number of votes—a delay might kill the resolution. Gathered with the leadership in O'Neill's office, Melconian decided to call him. Having seen his fair share of State Department lobbying, O'Neill asked for a recommendation from his aide. Melconian, whose loyalty to the United States had been questioned by a State Department representative during the preceding months, did not hesitate to proceed after the slight and she did not hesitate when speaking with O'Neill. She wanted to pass this legislation for her grandmother—to make the matriarch who married at Ellis Island just to remain in this country far away from the carnage in the Ottoman Empire proud. She urged O'Neill to "go with it." He did, and his lieutenants followed. They made one concession by removing any reference to "Turkey" from the resolution's language. On April 9, 1975, the resolution prevailed overwhelmingly, with 332 votes.[14]

• • •

A year later, a House subcommittee held hearings on the Genocide for the first time since the 1920s. In a harbinger to the heated debate that would consume the Senate years later, two congressmen objected to the hearings for incriminating a key NATO ally. One stormed out of the proceedings while the other badgered the witnesses.[15]

The Armenians received another boost in 1981, this time from the president. As governor of California, home to the largest and most active Armenian community in the United States, President Reagan was in all likelihood more cognizant of the Genocide than any major politician in the country. On at least one occasion, he attended an April 24 Genocide commemoration at the Montebello Monument, and during the 1980 presidential campaign, he issued a "Statement on the Armenian Genocide." A 1981 presidential proclamation drafted by Kenneth Khachigian, his campaign's chief speechwriter, included a reference to the Armenian Genocide. Before releasing it, Khachigian— well aware of Turkish sentiments—asked for and received approval from the national security adviser.[16]

Turkey struck back through a State Department bulletin, which questioned the authenticity of the Genocide. The 1982 bulletin covered uncontroversial items like the number and method of Armenian terrorist attacks, but the last paragraph triggered a firestorm. It stated that because "the historical record of the 1915 events . . . is ambiguous, the Department of State does not endorse allegations that the Turkish Government committed a genocide against the Armenian people."[17] Armenian-Americans immediately reacted to the bulletin. It was no secret that the State Department sided with Turkey over them. What shocked them was the department's first foray into active denial. With congressional heavyweights O'Neill and Helms demanding an explanation, the State Department backed off, indicating that the bulletin did not reflect official U.S. policy.[18]

The Armenians pushed for another congressional resolution in response to the bulletin, turning the competition with Turkey into a game of tit-for-tat. In 1984, once more buttressed by House leaders, a resolution commemorating the "victims of the genocide perpetrated in Turkey" overcame objections from the White House and Turkey, again bypassing potentially hazardous parliamentary obstacles.[19] It was the second victory for the Armenians, and Turkey was determined to never let it happen again.

A decade of terrorism had hardened Turkey by the mid-1980s. The wave of attacks against Turkish targets moved the Genocide from an obscure issue infrequently appearing in the Turkish press to a regular item in the news. Combating Armenian terrorism became one of the chief objectives of Turkey's foreign policy. The government measured its allies by the level of cooperation they provided in this undertaking.[20] All of this made Turkey more determined than ever to block further resolutions. And after 1984, it developed a winning formula to do just that.

In the face of this unprecedented resolve by Turkey and the executive branch, resolutions submitted in 1985 and 1987 faltered. Reagan's reversal from his 1981 proclamation acknowledging the Genocide did not cost him in the polls.[21] Like the State Department bureaucrats who had deemed Armenian-Americans too few and weak to matter during the 1940s territorial dispute, Reagan's advisers concluded that the loss of the Armenian-American vote—though considerable in California and a handful of other states—was not enough to surmount the Turkish government's opposition.[22]

Most of the tactics employed by the resolutions' opponents had been seen and heard before. Only this time, they came in waves. Defense contractors like General Dynamics sprung an "extensive campaign of Hill consultations" while leading members from the executive branch were recruited to contact congressmen. It was no longer left to midlevel bureaucrats but the biggest guns in the cabinet to lobby on Turkey's behalf. Secretary of State George P. Shultz and Secretary of Defense Caspar W. Weinberger warned Congress that passage of another resolution would irreparably damage the relationship with Turkey, cause massive rioting against American targets, and could cost the United States its military bases there. Turkey's vow to close air bases and suspend intelligence collection imparted a dose of credibility to these threats.[23]

On top of its usual arsenal, Turkey unleashed a new weapon in 1985. Instead of just trumpeting its own historical accounts, the state-sponsored Assembly of Turkish-American Associations advertised an open letter in leading newspapers signed by sixty-nine scholars questioning—or at the least calling for more study of—the Genocide.[24] The advertisement ushered in the high-water mark of Turkey's campaign of historical distortion, transforming the struggle from one of unresolved justice for the Armenians to one that would place the very authenticity of the Genocide in jeopardy.

Denial was as old as the Genocide. During the massacres, the Ottoman government issued rebuttals that later served as blueprints for denial. Mehmet Talaat and his cohorts pleaded their innocence in exculpatory memoirs.[25] Few in the world believed their accounts at that time. This skepticism was evidenced in the series of trials conducted by an Ottoman tribunal after World War I along with the steps for prosecution laid out in the Treaty of Sèvres. After 1921, the abandonment of the tribunal and treaty allowed the discredited strategy of denial to slowly settle in and take root—a process aided by the eventual erosion of the Genocide from the world's consciousness.

Perhaps no one from the era contributed more to denial than Esat Uras, a top Ottoman official released by the postwar tribunal when it floundered. Like other leaders of the Young Turks, he went on to serve in the Turkish government until retiring in 1950. That same year, he published a 785-page tome borrowing from propaganda materials fabricated during World War I. This sophisticated work in defense of the Young Turk regime, updated and expanded after his death, and published in multiple editions, would come to serve as the bible for future deniers of the Genocide.[26]

Up to 1965, the Turkish government had little use for such materials. It blanketed the era in silence, so that as long as the Armenians did not make any noise, there was little need for Turkey to do more. After the Armenian resurrection of that year, however, Turkey was compelled to evolve its strategy from an unrefined campaign of outright dismissal of Armenian allegations to nuanced sophistry, and to expand its target audience beyond foreign governments to the press and public. Old texts were recycled as polished works, injecting a degree of verisimilitude into the amateur productions of the past. UCLA professor Stanford Shaw eclipsed the original revisionists in 1977 through a seminal work of denial produced by an American academic in which he blamed Armenian perfidy for the Genocide.[27] Shaw's post at a major university granted the Turkish position some credibility. Two of his disciples, Heath Lowry and Justin McCarthy, and others went further, blaming, variously, civil conflict, self-defense, disease, food shortages, and war-related casualties—anything other than state-sponsored genocide—to explain away the near annihilation of a people.

Every time a denialist claim was repudiated, a new one arose in its place or changed form. Such denial required perpetual shifting to dodge the mountain of evidence invalidating it. Ultimately, the denialists could not overcome the mounds of evidence produced by the postwar Ottoman tribunal nor the tens of thousands of pages of diplomatic reports and eyewitness accounts by American, German, Russian, British, and Austrian diplomats, missionaries, and others. The final hurdle for the denialists was the survivors. Though originating in every corner of the empire, their testimony told the same sadistic tales of Ottoman terror.

Turkey's position also tripped over internal inconsistencies and faulty logic. If the Ottomans genuinely feared an Armenian uprising in the eastern provinces bordering Russia, why then did they deport Armenians from all over the empire, far away from the war zone? Why did they target the powerless women and children, and not just adult men? If Armenians were not the target of permanent expulsion from their ancient lands—and were merely moved out of wartime necessity—why then were the survivors not allowed to return after World War I? If the deportees were safeguarded by Ottoman soldiers, why then did so many Armenians die during the trek? After all, America had interned its Japanese population during World War II. Though a stain on the nation's human rights record, it did not lead to massive casualties. And what difference did it make if several hundred thousand Armenians died rather than 1.5 million? Would the Holocaust be any less of a crime if 2 million Jews had died rather than 6 million? Germany lost millions of military and civilian lives during World War II. That fact did not mitigate the magnitude of the crimes committed against the Jews. Applying this logic, did it mean that Turkish deaths during World War I whitewashed the crimes committed against the Armenians?

To overcome these shortcomings, Turkey resorted to three Ds: distort; distract; delay. Sympathetic scholars distorted the historical facts by questioning their authenticity or accusing the sources of bias. Turkey distracted people from concentrating on the issue by bringing up Armenian terrorism and the American-Turkish alliance. And it delayed the onset of a final judgment by pointing to the lack of absolute consensus by historians.

Turkey's reasoning turned historical inquiry on its head. By posing the adage that there are two sides to every issue, Turkey discarded, ignored, and smeared overwhelming evidence. Originally intended to grant scholars the freedom to reveal unpopular truths, academic independence was instead employed to shield scholars serving as Turkish hacks. Free speech became a tool not to find the truth but to obfuscate it. Similarly, the instructive method of looking at two sides of every issue turned against the realization of truth rather than a discovery of it. "In the Orwellian world of modern governments," wrote the Holocaust survivor and scholar Terrence Des Pres in 1986, "the past is rewritten or excised as shifting policy dictates." In other words, history became a tool of the powerful rather than a field of objective inquiry. "The unpalatable fact," he continued, "in this age of disinformation, is that political order requires the subservience of knowledge."[28]

General ignorance of the facts by politicians and the press, compounded by inveterate respect for a close ally insisting on "two sides" to the story, allowed Turkey to get away with these tactics. But there was something else at work. Victims ask the world to engage in their suffering and help them attain justice. Perpetrators demand far less, asking bystanders to do nothing, a prospect far easier for the average person than to weep alongside the Armenians and absorb their pain. Anyone who closely scrutinized Turkey's assertions, however, as did the editorial board of the *Wall Street Journal*, concluded that the Armenians were indeed victims of genocide.[29]

Human rights scholars considered denial the final stage of the Genocide. It not only covered up a crime, but acted as its continuation by questioning the authenticity of the survivors' memories and the potency of their anguish. By reassigning blame from the perpetrators to the arbitrary vicissitudes of World War I, it dishonored those who perished by equating theirs with other wartime deaths. Denial impeded the process of compensation for the loss of life and property, allowing the descendants of the perpetrators to enjoy the fruits of the Genocide. More important, it blocked the passage of time from mitigating the agony of the survivors, instead aggravating their trauma through repeated dismissal of their suffering. It relegated the Armenians to perpetual victimhood pleading that one day, their perpetrators would set them free. The fallout caused by denial was inherited by later generations of Armenians, linking them to the fateful days of 1915, and compelling them to set the record straight.[30]

The open letter of 1985 granted respectability to denialist claims: Turkey's allies in the American government could use them against legislative resolutions affirming the Genocide.[31] It provided officials prone to support Turkey an easy cover. They need not confess that they were swayed merely by military and political calculations, but could, under the guise of "genuine" debate, argue that they responded to historical uncertainty. Buttressed by relentless Turkish lobbying, the letter marshaled in an era where the establishment of truth lay in peril. The Genocide, once the greatest international human rights calamity known to the world, and the inspiration for America's first major international aid effort, was in danger of being excised from history itself.

By the late 1980s, the House resolutions of 1975 and 1984 seemed like a distant memory in the face of Turkey's renewed resolve. Despite the long odds of overcoming the beefed-up Turkish lobby that had defeated Genocide resolutions in 1985 and 1987, Van Z. Krikorian, the head of legislative affairs at the Armenian Assembly, was determined to try to gain official recognition of the Genocide through another congressional resolution. Krikorian's disarming boyish looks, personified by a thick lock of hair and wide-rimmed glasses, belied both his personal intensity and his passion for this mission. In that sense, he was no different than most other Armenians, almost all of whom could point to a Genocide survivor among their ancestors. Krikorian's grandmother was eight when kidnappers snatched her from a caravan of deportees and sold her into slavery. Only one other family member escaped death by playing possum among a stack of corpses after being stabbed with a bayonet. After two years of captivity, Krikorian's grandmother escaped and landed in an orphanage in Beirut. Years later, caretakers sent her photo to the United States, where Armenian men searched for orphans to marry.[32]

The practice was widespread. Surviving relatives or orphanage administrators acting as intermediaries sent photos of eligible women to bachelors abroad. When the men identified someone they desired, the intermediaries shipped the woman over. The choice between life as a refugee in the Middle East versus the relative comfort and security of the New World motivated many women to traverse the vast ocean to betroth men they had never met. "When you are alone," recalled a picture bride, "and when you have no choice and there is someone who will look after you, what can you do?" The desperation of the times led to many strained nuptials. The age gap between the men and women typically reached twenty years. People of different socioeconomic backgrounds, who would have never crossed each other's social circles prior to 1915, found themselves flung together. Armenians from different parts of the Ottoman Empire, who rarely interacted in the past, checked their provincial inclinations. The marriages were a crapshoot, particularly for the women, who were often at the total mercy of the men. Those with overbearing in-laws or abusive husbands had no avenues for escape. Some forged loving families while others had no luck in this bizarre lottery. A reporter for the *New York Times* described one such voyage aboard a steamship that arrived in New York in August 1922. Some of the prospective husbands, unimpressed with the women they had selected once they saw them in person, reneged on their conjugal promise. As immigration workers called off the names of the women, about two hundred in all, the fifteen unclaimed by the men at the pier had to return across the Atlantic. Perhaps a hefty dowry would have convinced the unscrupulous men. Perhaps not.[33]

The photo of Krikorian's grandmother made its way across the ocean to his grandfather, who having immigrated to the United States prior to 1915, found himself stranded with no surviving relatives back home. Due to restrictive immigration laws, Krikorian's grandparents married in Cuba before moving to the outskirts of Boston.[34]

Their story, told to Krikorian during his childhood, remained etched in his identity, serving as inspiration for his advocacy. Krikorian and other descendants of survivors could not allow denial to triumph.

Doing so would insult the memories of their ancestors. "These are the kinds of things that never leave you," Krikorian remarked. "They just burn in your mind, and so no Armenian . . . will ever forget." These memories kept him going through month after month of legislative trench warfare. He was married, on his way to starting a family, and had a promising career as a lawyer. Yet he simply could not let go of the enduring injustice. No Armenian could.[35]

After a stint at a law firm, in 1988 the twenty-eight-year-old Krikorian rejoined the Armenian Assembly, where he had interned in college, in order to spearhead efforts in Congress. Ross Vartian, the longtime director of the Assembly, and a staff of about a dozen people provided additional manpower. The Armenian National Committee of America and the Armenian Rights Council of America, two other lobbying and advocacy shops, also contributed. With the entire community firmly united behind this mission, additional help came from the unlikeliest of quarters. Armenians with personal relationships to congressmen or large campaign donors provided assistance, as did youth groups, social clubs, and others otherwise uninvolved with the political process.

Entering the 1989 legislative session, two victories outside the United States gave the Armenians some hope. In 1987, the European Parliament called for Turkish acknowledgment of the Genocide. And in 1985, the UN subcommission based in Geneva that first took up the issue in 1973 included the Genocide in its final report. The twelve-year saga epitomized just how difficult it was for the stateless Armenians to match the Turkish government. Turkey employed a staff of full-time diplomats and enjoyed privileges granted to nation states. The Armenians, on the other hand, were represented by Harut Sassounian, a Procter & Gamble executive and publisher of an Armenian-American newspaper who had to corral a spot with random NGOs just to be able to speak at the subcommission's meetings. Sassounian had no vote in the subcommission, no staff, and no diplomatic equality with the Turkish representatives who could rely on allies like the United States to advance their case.[36] Despite the odds, he and the report's author, a British human rights expert, ensured that the Genocide would be listed along with other crimes against humanity in the subcommission's report.

Things appeared tougher in the United States, home to Turkey's strongest ally: the American government. Despite some hiccups over the years, military ties and trade fortified the relationship forged during the Truman Doctrine. In 1982, the nations formed a joint Armenian terrorism task force.[37] During the 1980s, Turkey was the third largest recipient of military aid and among the largest recipients of economic assistance from the United States: the two categories added up to more than $5 billion.[38]

In the face of this reality, Krikorian and his colleagues also knew that in heading into a new contest they would have to avoid all the potential pitfalls that had wrecked the 1985 and 1987 resolutions. They approached the process as if it were a series of obstacles to be overcome. The parliamentary tactics utilized by O'Neill to suspend the rules in 1975 faltered when proponents of the Armenian resolution could not garner the necessary two-thirds vote. That meant that for a resolution to prevail, it would have to surmount three lethal hazards: it would need to receive committee approval; enter the voting calendar, which could only be secured through the wishes of congressional leaders; and garner enough votes to actually pass. The resolution would also have to overcome the surge in denialist scholarship capped off by the 1985 open letter submitted by sixty-nine scholars. The Armenians needed someone just as powerful and personally attached to their cause as O'Neill to prevail.

Dr. Kelikian was the first person to tell Senator Dole the story of the Genocide. His uncle, a surgeon in the Ottoman army, rescued much of Kelikian's family before their village was wiped out. Like so many other survivors, Kelikian ended up in Aleppo before arriving in the United States with two dollars in his pocket and a rug under his arm. But the tragedy was never anything he dwelled upon or urged Dole to pursue. Dole, one of the leading human rights activists in the Senate (he oversaw the ratification of the UN Genocide Convention as majority leader of the Senate), came to that conclusion on his own. He had co-sponsored Genocide resolutions in the past, and when the Armenian Assembly and Kelikian's daughter Alice asked him to help with a new resolution under preparation in 1989, Dole signed on without hesitation.[39]

Dole made an ideal patron. Upon entering the Senate in 1969, he became a consummate insider to the legislative process, what one observer described as a "tour de force in coalition building."[40] As minority leader in 1989, he led his fellow Republicans in the Senate and carried the party's biggest voice in Congress. He would need every ounce of that experience and political capital to succeed. The resolution was a massive undertaking. Dole had to take on the Turkish government, its allies in military and diplomatic circles, companies doing business with Turkey, and the entire executive branch from the president down to department heads.

With Dole on their side, the youthfully energetic Krikorian and his more seasoned colleagues took on other potential roadblocks. They had seen Turkey's tactics in combating earlier resolutions so they tried to anticipate every move. They drafted a new resolution bowdlerizing any mention of "Turkey"—a reference that had upset some congressmen in the past. Instead, the resolution stated that the Genocide took place within the reign of the "Ottoman Empire . . . prior to the establishment of the Republic of Turkey. . . ."[41] They were also hopeful that President George H. W. Bush would not object as strenuously as past presidents. During the 1988 presidential campaign, Bush had in absolute terms pledged to acknowledge the "genocide of the Armenian people" and vowed that the "Bush administration will never allow political pressure to prevent our denunciation" of it.[42]

It helped that the taint of terrorism had begun to wear off. In previous years, Turkey's supporters in the American government had argued that the passage of a Genocide resolution would play into the terrorists' hands by acceding to their demands. In a telling example of the sullied reputation caused by Armenian terrorists, Secret Service agents accompanied an Armenian delegation led by Governor George Deukmejian of California into the Oval Office in the early 1980s. Reagan's speechwriter Khachigian was stunned to see the agents in the office—something he had never seen during his many visits there. He surmised that they must have accompanied the delegation because of the fear of terrorism attached to Armenians.[43] The absence of terrorist attacks in the preceding five years largely removed one of the arguments used against past resolutions from the table.

Finally, a devastating earthquake in Soviet Armenia in 1988 inspired a great deal of sympathy for the Armenians in the U.S. government, which sent millions in aid. The tiny province's defiance of the USSR in the late 1980s, in which tens of thousands of Soviet Armenians regularly demonstrated against Moscow's rule, also helped make the Armenians the darlings of Washington during the late stages of the Cold War.[44]

Krikorian's team reached out to senators and their staffs to sign them up as co-sponsors, a process that took months. Co-sponsorship was no guarantee of loyalty to a piece of legislation, but generally, co-sponsors stuck with the bills they signed up to support. Armenians with personal contacts and other advocacy groups helped raise the tally, as did Dole and his staff.[45]

The resolution started with fifty-four co-sponsors (eight more signed on in the ensuing months) when Dole submitted it on September 29, 1989; there were heavyweights from both parties, such as Senators Edward M. Kennedy and Jesse Helms. If this bipartisan coalition held firm, then it looked like the resolution would succeed. That was the question that would come to monopolize Van Krikorian's frenzied life for the next five months. Would the coalition hold? He soon got a taste of what to expect when a storm of lobbying rarely seen in the nation's capital overtook the Senate, what one staffer described as "[o]ne of the slimiest campaigns I've seen. . . ."[46]

It started with President Bush, who opposed the resolution in spite of his campaign promises. In 1984, when Reagan was asked to reaffirm his stance on the Genocide, then–Vice President Bush urged Reagan's advisers not to have the president "in retreat from where he was on this issue."[47] Yet, when he took over the Oval Office in 1989, Bush too retreated. If anyone in Congress had doubts about where Bush stood, he made his opposition to the resolution clear to them. In a little known 1987 agreement with Turkey, the United States had apparently promised to block such Genocide resolutions. Bush intended to honor that agreement no matter his past declarations.[48] To explain away the inconsistency of his campaign pledge and his opposition to the resolution, Bush, like past presidents, had to resort to amusing acrobatics. When a reporter asked a State Department representative how the two positions could be reconciled, she responded: "It can to my mind." "I still find it a little bit difficult to understand," the reporter persisted. "It isn't causing me any trouble," responded the agency spokeswoman.[49]

National security adviser Brent Scowcroft became the point man in the Bush administration to lead the charge against the resolution.[50] He recalled Ambassador Morton Abramowitz from Turkey in the autumn of 1989 to meet with more than forty-five senators in person. In addition to Abramowitz and Scowcroft, the State and Defense departments did much of the legwork in contacting senators. When oft-repeated geopolitical arguments proved insufficient, they resorted to the so-called scholarly debate about the authenticity of the Genocide to make their case.[51] The inroads made by Turkey to cast doubt on the Genocide's veracity now became regular fodder for the resolution's opponents.

Turkey unleashed its own forces. Its president, foreign minister, ambassador, and lower-level officials met with Bush, Dole, and various senators. Turkish institutions like the Assembly of Turkish-American Associations arranged for 70,000 telegrams and calls to Congress.[52] Turkey's strength came not just through formal pronouncements and actions of its government but through its lobbyists and allies, who were capable of exerting immense influence in the American government.

During his tenure as Turkey's ambassador to the United States in the 1980s, Şükrü Elekdağ had built and revitalized various American-Turkish institutions, gathering together prominent Turks, American diplomats and servicemen who served in Turkey, and corporations doing business there.[53] Having inherited this infrastructure, its new ambassador, Nuzhat Kandemir, put it to use. Dozens of American corporations from defense contractors to major manufacturers pitched in for Turkey. Halliburton's CEO was among those to chime in, warning the White House and various senators that passage of the resolution "risks considerable harm to an important economic relationship" of Halliburton's to the benefit of its competitors.[54]

Richard Perle, an assistant secretary of defense under Reagan, was among Turkey's biggest cheerleaders in Washington, D.C. While in the Pentagon during the 1980s, Perle helped make Turkey the third largest recipient of American aid and established a defense panel—which he co-chaired—between leading American and Turkish military officials. Perle urged Turkey's president to beef up lobbying efforts to combat the

Armenians.[55] Turkey was already well on its way, paying Washington stalwarts Hill & Knowlton and Gray & Company with contacts on both sides of the aisle close to $1 million a year in the late 1980s for round-the-clock service to polish its public image. The thoroughness of the polishing would have pleased a quality-control supervisor at the Four Seasons. It included scrubbing away "errors about . . . Turkish history contained in secondary school social science textbooks" and "standard reference encyclopedias"; and in 1988, Turkey tapped another prominent D.C. law firm just to counter a little seen Genocide documentary.[56] At Perle's urging, his former intern Douglas Feith established a lobbying shop called International Advisers, Inc., in 1989 just to serve Turkey, which as its sole client lavished the operation with $875,000 in its first year.

As Dole's resolution neared a vote, Perle personally got involved, reportedly earning $48,000 in annual consulting fees.[57] (Feith and Perle were part of the team that pushed the United States into invading Iraq in 2003.) Feith hired Morris J. Amitay, the former executive director of the American Israel Public Affairs Committee—among the most powerful lobbying groups in Washington—to help fight the resolution at $5,000 a month. A month before the resolution neared the Senate floor, Turkey piled on the Washington insiders, paying $200,000 for a three-month stint with a lobbying firm run by Terry McAuliffe, a leading Democratic fund-raiser and future Democratic National Committee chair. By the beginning of 1990, it had signed up eight lobbying and public relations firms with annual fees near $3 million—three times the Assembly's annual budget.[58]

The barrage from all of these forces overwhelmed some senators, who received countless telegrams, letters, and personal visits from pro-Turkish companies, lobbyists, and government officials.[59] The attack led several co-sponsors to drop out in what a number of senators described as one of the biggest lobbying efforts they had ever seen.

Lobbyists like Hill & Knowlton were mercenaries with few qualms about whom they represented. The role of American Jewish organizations in the battle over the resolution was far more perplexing. The relationship between Armenians and Jews was a complex one. Both ancient peoples had long lived through persecution and exile. And of course, both had suffered through cataclysmic mass murder. It was the interaction over their common fate that brought them together but also led to strains.

In 1982, the Holocaust scholar Israel Charny teamed up with Elie Wiesel, perhaps the preeminent Holocaust chronicler and activist in the world, to put together the first ever conference, to be held in Tel Aviv, covering both the Holocaust and other genocides. Though only 6 of the 150 papers scheduled for the conference covered the Armenian Genocide, their inclusion set off a firestorm. When Turkey found out about the conference, it urged Israel to exclude the Armenian participants at the cost of severing diplomatic relations. Coveting its relationship with Turkey, the only Muslim nation not in a state of antagonism with the Jewish state, the Israeli Foreign Ministry acquiesced. Israel's future president, Shimon Peres, then in the Foreign Ministry, personally called Charny to exclude the Genocide from the conference. Various compromise plans negotiated by Charny, Wiesel, and the ministry faltered, offering no easy way out of the quagmire.

As the opening day neared, the growing pressure—made more acute by veiled threats to Turkey's Jewish community—finally led the anguished Wiesel to resign as conference president. Wiesel never questioned the validity of the Genocide: he simply would not put lives at risk. His departure triggered a wave of resignations from Jewish participants. Rabbi Marc H. Tanenbaum, noted for his role in interfaith dialogue, arrived in Tel Aviv only to be told by his superiors at the American Jewish Committee to return to the United States. Telling reporters that he "must on some occasions be mindful of public constraints called for by my colleagues," Rabbi Arthur Hertzberg, vice president of the World Jewish Congress, also dropped out on the eve of the event. Funding from two Jewish organizations was withdrawn at the midnight hour, and Tel Aviv University along with Yad Vashem withdrew their sponsorship. Despite the neutering, Charny refused to budge. In June 1982 the conference went on with 250 of the original 400 members; 10 Armenian scholars participated.[60]

The same fault lines appeared during Dole's resolution. Israel discouraged American Jewish organizations from supporting the resolution, a tactic copied from the mid-1980s. While some acquiesced, others who wanted to help their homeland yet found it unpalatable to oppose the Armenians were left in a quandary.[61] Eventually, Dole contacted the Israeli Embassy to ask for an explanation. His move must have embarrassed the Israeli government. Ambassador Moshe Arad denied any interference by his staff, while the Israeli Foreign Ministry claimed its embassy acted beyond its instructions.[62] Asking how Jews could betray other people struck by such tragedy, several members of Israel's Parliament and various editorialists reprimanded Israel for its interference.[63] Because of these conflicting considerations, some Jewish organizations lobbied against the resolution while others supported it. Few backers stood out more than Fresno rabbi Kenneth I. Segel. With the help of Senator Carl Levin, Segel propelled the Union of American Hebrew Congregations, the largest such group in the United States, to pass a resolution at its conference supporting the Armenians. "If a Jew doesn't care and a Jew doesn't weep . . . and a Jew doesn't show compassion," Segel said of attempts to water down the Union's resolution, "I am prepared to leave."[64]

By the time Dole's resolution reached the Senate Judiciary Committee on October 17, 1989, it had shed fifteen co-sponsors in the face of this extensive lobbying. With the Turkish ambassador, his coterie from the embassy, Turkish lobbyists, and a small contingent of Armenians watching, Senator Howard Metzenbaum started the session by offering a substitute resolution sanctioned by Scowcroft expunging the "genocide" label. "I myself concluded that I don't think it was genocide," he said in front of the packed room. The amendment represented a complete about-face for the senator from Ohio. "I cannot imagine how anyone could find the slightest bit of ambiguity about this unspeakably cruel brutal slaughter," he had declared in 1983 while excoriating the State Department. In 1985 and 1986, he again acknowledged the Genocide on the Senate floor, dismissing the very arguments now put forward by the resolution's detractors.[65]

"I do not think this is acceptable," Senator Paul Simon from Illinois responded; ". . . no one should have any question about whether the massacre of the Armenians occurred. It occurred." Simon became familiar with the Genocide issue through a close friendship he struck with an Armenian living across the hall from him in college: "I became half Armenian," Simon explained. In his first term in the House, he voted for O'Neill's 1975 resolution. He stayed on friendly terms with the Armenian community, and they in kind supported his campaigns. Simon had been the target of intense lobbying, some of it from a friend heading a major defense manufacturer.[66] His ties to the Armenians were too deep and sincere, however, to abandon them.

Like Metzenbaum, Senator Arlen Specter had spoken in support of affirming the Genocide on the Senate floor. Though he too flip-flopped, Metzenbaum's amendment failed on a 7–7 tie. Round one for the Armenians. Senator Orrin Hatch's suggestion to reassign the resolution to the Foreign Relations Committee also failed, 8 to 6.[67] Round two for the Armenians.

After watching thirty minutes of debate, Krikorian, the legislative strategist who kept counting votes in his head, knew the final tally would be close. In September, the number of co-sponsors on the Judiciary Committee should have made it a comfortable victory. Despite several dropped sponsorships—five of which came on the day of the session—and two close votes on amendments intended to defang the resolution, Krikorian, relying on his vote count, remained confident.[68]

Even in hindsight, one can rarely discern all the reasons that go into a congressional vote. Sometimes, a senator might obey a strong personal belief. Sometimes, she may be swayed by her constituents. Sometimes, he may be returning a favor. Sometimes, loyalty to party leaders or the president may influence a vote. For issues like abortion or free trade, votes often fall along party lines. Usually, it is a combination of these factors, making it presumptive to offer a clear-cut explanation of a senator's vote. Instead, the enterprise is more like an educated guess than an exact science.

Senator Edward Kennedy, a longtime supporter of the Armenians and a friend of Stephen Mugar's, voted Yea in support of Dole's resolution without any changes in its wording. That was predictable. Metzenbaum—Nay. Senator Dennis DeConcini had signed on as a co-sponsor only six days earlier. He voted Yea. Senator Patrick Leahy had withdrawn his sponsorship on the same day but voted in support of the resolution. Senator Howell Heflin had withdrawn his sponsorship a fortnight earlier. He voted Nay. Simon was a predictable Yea. Senators

Charles Grassley and Herbert Kohl, though not co-sponsors, also voted in favor of the resolution, while Specter and Senator Gordon Humphrey voted against it. Committee chair Joseph Biden voted Yea. Objections from the administration and Turkey's ambassador convinced Hatch to vote Nay.[69] Alan Simpson was in a bind. As minority whip, he was Dole's right-hand man in the Senate and a close friend. "I became the focal point for the greatest lobbying campaign I've experienced in a long while," the senator said later. Former senator Charles Mathias, working for Hill & Knowlton, was one of many people to flood Simpson with what the senator called a "hyper-activity of lobbying efforts" to oppose the resolution. "I am truly sorry that . . . I ran a thumb in the eye of one of my finest friends in the Senate and my respected leader," Simpson wrote to Dole days later, explaining his decision to strike down the resolution.[70] That left the octogenarian Senator Strom Thurmond, who had withdrawn his sponsorship on October 2 and was poised to vote against the resolution, a move made all the more agonizing by Thurmond's close relationship to Dole, whom he had endorsed during the 1988 presidential campaign. Ultimately, his loyalty to Dole along with a nudge from an Armenian-American public relations consultant with ties to Thurmond swayed him, catapulting the resolution in the committee to an 8–6 victory.[71]

Krikorian was ecstatic, celebrating throughout the evening. Building on the momentum of the victory in the Judiciary Committee, a vote by the entire Senate may have succeeded if it had taken place directly afterwards. But discussions between Dole and Bush to find some kind of solution acceptable to both of them pushed the issue to 1990, giving Turkey time to regroup and marshal its forces. In the meantime, Turkey, in reaction to the committee's vote, raised the stakes by restricting U.S. military maneuvers and reconnaissance flights, halting visits to ports, suspending military cooperation meetings, and stopping the use of its training facilities. "Some temporary measures have been relayed to the United States to help them understand reality," its foreign minister explained to Parliament.[72] Over the next few months, dire threats popped up from every corner—to American forces in Turkey, Jewish and Armenian populations in Turkey, international trade, and defense contractors.[73]

With one hazard behind them, the resolution's backers tackled the next hurdle: convincing Senator George J. Mitchell to schedule a vote—a prerogative he held as Senate majority leader. Krikorian's first crack at Mitchell came in the fall when the senator brought a visiting Soviet delegation to an Armenian event in Maine where Krikorian happened to be speaking about the resolution. The serendipitous encounter gave Krikorian an opportunity to get face-to-face time with Mitchell in front of a crowd of sympathetic constituents. Then one of Mitchell's major campaign supporters, Armenian-American business-man Augustus "Gus" Barber, the son of immigrants who had fled Ottoman rule during the Genocide, came down to Washington, D.C., to meet with the majority leader. In January 1990, when Dole formally asked for Mitchell's support, the majority leader agreed to schedule a vote.[74] It was time for the debate to begin on February 20.

For the start of the debate, the thirty-year-old Krikorian commuted from his home on the edge of the Potomac River, not far from where he had attended law school, to the steps of the Capitol Building on an un-usually balmy winter day spoiled by a persistent drizzle. Unlike many superstitious Armenians, Krikorian did not carry a good luck charm. Despite his distinguished blue suit and white shirt, Krikorian's thick hair and oversized, glass-framed spectacles emanated a boyish look. Following a quick strategy session with colleagues, he and Dr. Rouben P. Adalian carried boxes of materials from the Assembly's headquarters a couple of blocks from the Capitol up to Dole's offices, located a few steps away from the Senate floor in the oldest section of the Capitol Building. As the Republican headquarters of the Senate, no other office in Congress matched its vista of the Mall and Washington Monu-ment. Dole called it the best view in town, second only to the Truman Balcony in the White House. A terrace—which the senator called his "beach"—adjoining the office offered an outdoor meeting space and doubled as a tanning salon. As the latest Republican leader to occupy the space stretching across several suites, Dole installed a wooden desk and hung a portrait of Abraham Lincoln on loan from the National Gallery and another of Dwight Eisenhower in his inner office. These touches, symbolic of Dole's modest midwestern roots, contrasted with the ornate rococo mirrors and frescoes trumpeting the principles of law and justice originally installed for the former occupant of the space, the Supreme Court. Inside Al Lehn's suite, Krikorian sat at a desk and Adalian set up camp on a couch in preparation for the debate.[75]

Lehn, Dole's foreign policy guru, acted as the point man in Dole's staff on the resolution. Krikorian was assigned to speak to senators and their staffs to shore up the resolution's supporters and perhaps pick up a few votes from its detractors. Success required more than straightforward lobbying, however. The Armenians needed to counter Turkey's campaign of historical distortion. Krikorian relied on Rouben Adalian, who had joined the Assembly in 1987 to head up its Genocide research program, for this task. Like so many others of his generation (he was born in 1955), Adalian was the grandchild of survivors. But it was not his own family but a survivor whose arms were tattooed by her captors who "intrigued and repulsed" him while growing up in Los Angeles. Fueled by these childhood memories, Adalian's passion for Armenian history ultimately led him to study the Genocide as a graduate student at UCLA. He heard agonizing stories while conducting more than a hundred oral histories of survivors during the early 1980s, one of which about a boy who ate his mother's corpse to survive sent Adalian fleeing from the room. Yet the interviews also showed him the determination of the human spirit. One such story involved a captive orphan who wrote her Armenian name in the sand to preserve her identity—"the Armenian language saved me," she repeated to Adalian.[76]

Rouben Adalian was the latest in a series of Armenian scholars dedicating a significant portion of their careers to fighting for affirmation of the Genocide.[77] Adalian's understanding of the field took a gigantic leap when he began to work with an obscure priest. Though not formally trained in academia, Father Krikor Guerguerian was the first to comprehensively chronicle the Genocide. At the tender age of four, Guerguerian witnessed the murder of his parents during the Genocide. In the 1940s, a chance meeting with a judge from the post–World War I Ottoman tribunal gave his life new meaning. Driven by the memories of his parents' deaths, he learned the Ottoman language, found the transcripts of the tribunal, and then began to scour other archives across the globe. In 1953, Guerguerian returned to his hometown. A few Armenians who had survived by converting to Islam turned out to be his relatives, and they took him to his family home, which lay in rubble. Eventually, a man came up to the Father and confessed to killing his family. He asked for Guerguerian's forgiveness.[78] Few Armenians ever had the opportunity for such a confrontation.

The experience taught Guerguerian the value of collecting and storing evidence of the Genocide. He knew that once the eyewitnesses died, no evidence would remain for future generations to rely upon. Working side-by-side with Guerguerian in a dingy apartment during the last two years of the Father's life, Adalian also came to realize the importance of collecting documentation. In the late 1980s, he took charge of assembling tens of thousands of documents in the American archives related to the Genocide, where he truly came to appreciate the thoroughness and continuity of the genocidal process. During his research in a separate archive, he lived through a moment almost resembling the Father's confrontation with the guilt-ridden Turk. Adalian found a document listing Armenian men to be deported from his ancestral village. On the list were three of his great-uncles.[79]

The chaotic nature of the debates suited Krikorian, who got a rush from tallying prospective votes and juggling various projects. In contrast to the frenzied Krikorian, the less animated Adalian exuded the calmness and deliberation one would expect from a scholar. His pregnant pauses during a conversation made one wonder how many times he reformulated a sentence before uttering it. Bivouacked in Dole's office on the morning of February 20, the two men were ready for the debate.

Another dropped sponsorship welcomed Dole on the first day of the debate, bringing the total to nineteen. He and his supporters monopolized most of the day trying to knock down the main pillars of the opposition. Dole's stern features made his scowl particularly menacing and his smile correspondingly placid. The tall, thin Kansan employed both during the debates. Dressed in a light blue suit with a Purple Heart pin on the lapel, Dole clutched a pen in his right hand while referring to notes from a three-ring binder. He assured Turkey in a matter-of-fact tone free of verbiage that the resolution incriminated only the Ottoman Empire. And he tried to convince his colleagues that there was no real dispute about the truth of the Genocide.[80]

All the major supporters of the resolution followed. Carl Levin was a longtime friend of the Armenian philanthropist Alex Manoogian and close to the Armenian community in Michigan. In one of his first speeches as a senator in 1979, he cemented that bond when he spoke of the need to acknowledge the Genocide. Now, speaking after Dole, he began to make the case for historical authentication of the Genocide; Paul Simon followed with affirmations of the Genocide from past American leaders; and Senator Pete Wilson of California, home to the largest contingent of Armenian-Americans, inserted a large number of American consular dispatches from 1915 into the record.[81]

Only Senator Robert C. Byrd spoke for the opposition. Ever since he had walked into the Senate chamber in 1959, his extensive knowledge of the institution's history and tactics had matured like fine wine. He was a stickler for the body's rules, and behaved like a curmudgeon when it came to their application. He wrote books on the Senate— both American and Roman—and over a period of eighteen years spent in every major leadership post from minority whip to minority and majority leader, he mastered all of its levers of power. In 1990, he chaired one of its most powerful committees, the Appropriations Committee, which controlled every discretionary dollar spent by the federal government, and sat as the Senate's president pro tempore. His chairmanship made him one of the most powerful men in the American government, allowing him to spread the government's largesse on his home state of West Virginia and cower colleagues into submission. When a fellow senator once complained of Byrd's overuse of time on the floor, Byrd reminded his colleague about a project dear to him up for review in the Appropriations Committee. The senator sat down, allowing Byrd to continue uninterrupted. His mastery was most acute over the filibuster, the parliamentary tactic that could bring any legislation to a grinding halt. At the time, stopping the endless debate that made a filibuster such an obstructive juggernaut required sixty senators. In the most infamous of his many filibusters, Byrd spoke for fourteen hours and thirteen minutes in trying to block the 1964 Civil Rights Act.[82]

As a defense hawk, Byrd had long developed a place in his heart for Turkey and its role in NATO. "I marveled at the Turks," he said of his visit in 1955, his first trip abroad as a congressman. He saw the resolution as an unnecessary affront to an integral ally, and spent a great deal of political capital to stop it. Before the start of the debate, Byrd personally visited nearly every senator to discuss his position, a rare occurrence in the Senate not seen more than once or twice a decade. If nothing else, it showed his level of commitment to stopping the resolution.[83] Once the debate began, Byrd relied on his legendary oratorical skills to carry him through.

In contrast to Dole's plainspoken midwestern style, Byrd delivered his speeches like a theatrical actor in his prime, quoting ancient and literary texts, and capping off his sentences with dramatic pauses accompanied by well-timed gesticulations. His disarming southern drawl and references to the Bible and Constitution—the latter he kept in his breast pocket—belied his incisive, sometimes astringent delivery. His slicked-back white hair, the piercing blue eyes that narrowed during speeches, and rhetorical flourishes were more reminiscent of a patrician statesman from the nineteenth century than a sound-bite politician on the cusp of a new millennium.[84]

"I am sorry to be put in this position by my own conscience and my own faith in what I believe to be the facts," Byrd began in an affected tone. "I am deeply sympathetic to the suffering endured by the Armenians." But his sympathy had its limits. "I do not know whether what happened . . . constitutes a genocide. . . . None of us—not one—is in a position to point the finger at Turkey and say Turkey is guilty of genocide." After repeating much of the historical argument put forward by Turkey, Byrd arrived at his real objection: "I am deeply concerned that . . . it will unwittingly slap the face of a very important NATO ally."[85]

Krikorian, Adalian, and their colleagues tried to prepare for every contingency. Throughout the debate, Dole sent questions over to his office, where Krikorian and Adalian were watching the proceedings on a tiny screen. Armed with key documents attesting to the Genocide collected by Adalian, Krikorian and Lehn helped the senator prepare materials for the debate.[86] Their preparation paid dividends, as when Byrd brought up pro-Turkish statements made by Rear Admiral Mark Bristol during the 1920s. Adalian quickly pulled out a correspondence from the American archives, allowing Dole to counter Byrd with a letter Allen Dulles of the State Department had sent to Bristol: "Confidentially, the State Department is in a bind," Dole read from the letter in response to Byrd when his turn came up to speak. "Our task would be simple if the reports of the atrocities could be declared untrue, or even exaggerated. But the evidence, alas, is irrefutable. . . ."[87] Without thorough preparation and fingertip access to responsive documents, such pointed rejoinders would have been impossible during the hectic and unpredictable debates.[88]

When they were not attending to Dole's needs on the Senate floor, Krikorian visited senators and their staffers for last-minute advocacy. Sometimes, when a senator wanted to hear more about the historical record, Adalian accompanied Krikorian to make a presentation. With so little known about the Genocide, Adalian had a tough hill to climb in quickly educating senators about the catastrophe and simultaneously countering Turkish denials. The constant scrambling throughout the day, in which they veered between the Assembly and Lehn's and other senators' offices, caused them to miss lunch in the process. The next day, Krikorian, frenetically typing on a computer, asked Adalian what he was doing eating a homemade meal. "The Turks starved us once," Adalian responded. "I'm not going to let them do it again."[89] It was perhaps the only moment of levity the two men enjoyed for three days.

By nightfall, when everyone but Krikorian and Adalian had cleared out, Dole invited them to his suite to discuss tactics and strategies for the next day. The senator also asked for a history lesson to help him prepare for the rest of the debate. For about two hours, with just the three of them in the room, Adalian answered his probing questions about the Genocide. It turned out to be the greatest moment in his life as an educator.[90]

The second day saw more of Byrd and other opponents of the resolution. Senator Sam Nunn, another defense hawk and chairman of the prestigious Armed Services Committee, was followed by Senator Timothy Wirth, who brought up the works of the denialist scholar Heath Lowry, and the list of sixty-nine academics introduced in 1985 to cast doubt on the veracity of the Genocide.[91]

Dole countered resolutely. Since the open letter's release, Adalian and others had been investigating its provenance. Quickly, these materials made their way to Dole on the Senate floor, arming him with the ammunition he needed to dismiss the charade of genuine scholarly debate. "I want to respond to the argument just made about the 69 scholars," Dole declared. And then he poured it on, dismantling the list brick by brick. Only four of the sixty-nine were experts on the era, while forty of the signatories had received sixty-five grants from Turkish institutions. Many of those who signed the open letter acknowledged that Turkey censored, suppressed, and falsified the historical record. Not one of the sixty-nine was an expert on the Genocide and none had written a single book or article actually showing how the claim of intercommunal warfare used to exonerate the Ottoman Empire caused the Armenian deaths.[92]

A cozy relationship between Turkey and the scholars who studied its history contributed to this condition in Turkish historiography. More than twenty years after his name appeared on the list of sixty-nine, Professor Donald Quataert was forced to resign as chairman of the Institute of Turkish Studies for writing in a book review that "what happened to the Armenians readily satisfies the U.N. definition of genocide." Quataert, another Stanford Shaw disciple, explained that the existence of strong "self-censorship" among scholars entering the field of Turkish studies, combined with fear that negative portrayals of Turkey might cut off access to its archives, left the field bereft of the "critical distance" necessary for sound scholarship. Within this restrictive ethos, the study of the "Armenian question" became "taboo."[93]

Heath Lowry also turned out to be something less than an unbiased scholar. A disciple of UCLA's Shaw, and director of the Institute of Turkish Studies—which was founded and funded by the Turkish government (along with companies like Westinghouse with business interests in Turkey)—Lowry was instrumental in obtaining the sixty-nine signatures.[94] At face value, Lowry appeared to be nothing more than a credible scholar who happened to join the minority position in the Genocide debate. But facts unearthed after the Senate debate revealed a far more insidious turn in Turkey's campaign against the Armenians.

In October 1990, the Turkish ambassador accidentally included a memorandum and draft of a letter in a correspondence he sent to Robert Jay Lifton, a scholar whose book included references to the Genocide that the ambassador found objectionable. The memorandum unintentionally included in the packet made it clear that Lowry had been working with the Turkish Embassy for several years to counter Armenian allegations. "OUR PROBLEM," Lowry bemoaned to the ambassador, "IS LESS WITH LIFTON THAN IT IS WITH THE WORKS UPON WHICH HE RELIES. . . . THOUGH THIS POINT HAS BEEN REPEATEDLY STRESSED BOTH IN WRITING AND VERBALLY TO IADA-ANKARA, WE HAVE NOT YET SEEN AS MUCH AS A SINGLE ARTICLE BY ANY SCHOLAR RESPONDING TO D A D R I A N (OR ANY OF THE OTHERS AS WELL)." Lowry, clearly frustrated at the lack of vigilance on Turkey's part, "STRONGLY RECOMMEND[ED] THAT IT BE POINTED OUT TO ANKARA THAT LIFTON'S BOOK IS SIMPLY THE END RESULT OF THE TURKISH FAILURE TO RESPOND IN A PROMPT FASHION TO THE DADRIAN ARTICLES AND THE FEIN AND KUPER BOOKS."[95] (The names refer to Genocide scholars.)

The memorandum revealed that Lowry was no objective scholar but someone in an intimate relationship—twice referring to "Our problem"—with the Turkish Embassy, in which he felt he had a personal stake in countering Armenian allegations.[96]

Dole and Byrd had two hours apiece to finish the debate before the afternoon vote on the final day, February 22, 1990. Each of the titans doled out blocks of minutes to their colleagues, who rehashed the same arguments with few new additions. When an opponent of the resolution made one claim, a supporter quickly came to the floor to denounce it. The speed and incisiveness of the last day of the debate outpaced the more leisurely pace of the first two days: after Senator John Warner of Virginia brought up three reasons to reject the resolution, for instance, Simon immediately followed him with three counterarguments.[97]

The existence of a genuine debate in the Senate indicated the degree to which the combination of the world's forgetfulness with Turkey's campaign of obfuscation had placed the veracity of the Genocide in doubt. The irony was that American representatives had done probably more than anyone to bring news of the Genocide to the world. In the U.S. archives alone, about 4,000 documents adding up to more than 37,000 pages of materials from various diplomats and others attested to the Genocide.[98]

The U.S. government had, on several occasions, authenticated the Genocide since then. In 1920, the Senate passed a resolution establishing "the truth of the reported massacres and other atrocities from which the Armenian people have suffered," after listening to testimony describing events taking place in the Ottoman Empire. In 1951, the United States noted that "the Turkish massacres of Armenians, the extermination of millions of Jews and Poles by Nazis are outstanding examples of the crime of genocide" in a report submitted to the International Court of Justice. Two congressional reports analyzing the Armenian plight at the time of the Ottoman era provided further authentication. A 1954 report issued by a House committee concluded that "the Turks decided . . . to settle the Armenian question once and forever by exterminating the entire Armenian people." The report went further in explaining that "the Turkish deportations of 1915—the attempted extermination of an entire people—was a deliberate act of the Turkish Government. . . ." A 1956 House report confirmed that the vast majority of Armenians "were expelled or massacred by their Ottoman rulers before and during World War I."[99]

If the Senate had looked at Congress's own findings, there would have been no need for a debate. But this debate was as much about politics as about history. Perhaps no senator encapsulated the dilemma facing the chamber better than Herbert Kohl of Wisconsin. He was fully cognizant of the resolution's consequences for America's relationship with Turkey. Yet his research on the issue led him to conclude that the resolution was "historically correct. . . . These conclusions create something of a quandary," he explained. "Obviously I do not wish to offend Turkey. . . . Nor do I want to commit the unpardonable sin of ignoring a crime against humanity. . . . But we cannot compromise the facts," he went on, "and the facts demonstrate that there was a planned and systematic effort to eliminate the Armenian community by the Ottoman Empire. . . . I believe that we are being asked to reject a violation of basic human rights for the sake of political expediency. That I cannot do."[100]

Throughout the debates, Dole presented archival evidence, records of the postwar Ottoman tribunal, and population statistics into the record gathered over the years by Armenians, often inserting Assembly Fact Sheets prepared for the debate into the proceedings. Senators Levin, Simon, Wilson, and Kennedy introduced similar evidence.[101] Neither Byrd nor his colleagues offered much to refute these materials. Instead, they simply relied on their fallback position by stating that a scholarly debate existed, without actually providing much evidence to counter that provided by the resolution's backers.

The historical contest seemed won, but from a vote-counting perspective, it was beginning to look bleak. The co-sponsor list stood at 43, well below the 60 votes Dole needed to end the filibuster. As several time extensions expired and the minutes winnowed down, Dole, aware that Byrd's filibuster might prevail, unveiled a new resolution he had negotiated with the Bush administration in hope of salvaging something for the Armenians.[102]

The fault lines caused by the resolution had always troubled Dole and Bush. It was the first time they had disagreed since the 1988 election, and as leaders of the Republican Party, both men had an incentive not to cross each other, especially in public. Before introducing the resolution, Dole asked Bush to override the State Department's policy on the Genocide. He also met with Scowcroft to try to avoid a brawl.[103] These attempts at diplomacy did not sway Bush.

When the administration began to lobby heavily against the resolution, both sides looked for a compromise. Scowcroft invited Dole to the White House to head off a clash before the Judiciary Committee vote, but the dispute over the use of the term "genocide" proved insurmountable.[104] The Armenians insisted upon it; Turkey insisted upon its removal. Similar negotiations between the Reagan administration and Armenian-American patrons in Congress in the 1980s had failed to overcome the same hurdle.[105] Bush was perhaps willing to be more accommodating because of his campaign pledge. Plus, he personally knew Armenian-Americans like Barry Zorthian, who chaired the Armenian-Americans for Bush-Quayle Committee in 1988, and had received their support, giving him a sincere understanding of the Armenian position. He also sent his son Jeb to Soviet Armenia in 1988 to oversee earthquake recovery efforts.[106]

With Bush's chief of staff John H. Sununu and Brent Scowcroft doing most of the legwork, negotiations commenced even before the Judiciary Committee vote in October. Dole, knowing the parameters acceptable to Armenians, conducted the negotiations with the help of two Armenian-American politicians.[107]

No one had to bend Governor George Deukmejian's arm to help. He had thrown his support to the Armenians soon after winning office in the 1960s. When he became California's first governor of Armenian descent, he ratcheted up his efforts by urging Reagan to drop opposition to a similar resolution.[108] In 1985, he traveled to Washington to make a public appeal. "Mr. President," he said during a commemoration speech, "I pray that you will reconsider your current position and take action to affirm the historical truth. . . ."[109] As the Republican governor of the nation's most populous state, Deukmejian was a key national figure. He was considered as a running mate in the 1988 presidential election before Bush settled on Dan Quayle. His standing failed to convince Bush to change his mind, however, when the two men met aboard Air Force One as Joint Chiefs Chairman Colin Powell and Scowcroft looked on unresponsively. Deukmejian left the meeting dejected at Bush's refusal to budge.[110]

Congressman Charles Pashayan, Jr., from Fresno was the second Armenian-American politician to participate in the negotiations. Like Deukmejian, he had worked on the Genocide issue before. Pashayan had never run as an "Armenian" candidate but he was glad to help when called upon. Confident that he could bring Bush and Scowcroft—both members of his own party—around to a compromise, Pashayan was stunned at their recalcitrance. When he met with Scowcroft at the White House, the national security chief urged him to remove the "genocide" tag from the resolution. Bush told him the same thing when they met on Air Force One after Pashayan showed the president his campaign pledge. But Pashayan knew that a resolution devoid of the "genocide" label was unacceptable. Like Deukmejian, Bush's stance left the congressman disheartened that the president would so blatantly backtrack on his promise.[111]

The first draft of a compromise resolution offered by Bush was worlds apart from Dole's version. Its characterization of the Genocide as a "historical tragedy" was a non-starter for the Armenians. Dozens of drafts floated back and forth during the five months leading up to the Senate debate. Their differences came down to a few critical words. One version sent by the White House characterized the death and deportation of the Armenians as a "tragic killing." "We are deeply aware," the version continued, "of the strong conviction of the survivors, scholars and indeed our own representative at the time, that those events were a genocide." A draft with the same idea in mind removed the reference to scholars and inserted the name of Raphael Lemkin—the father of human rights law—in its place. A similar version removed the reference to America's diplomatic representatives but kept much of the rest intact. Another markup added this qualification: "others in the international community who believe these events constitute a genocide." It was a clear attempt to apply the "genocide" label without ascribing the decision to do so to the American government. To make it more palatable to Turkey, the same resolution condemned terrorist attacks against Turkey and supported its territorial integrity. Another draft characterized the events of 1915 as a "Tragedy." A mid-November draft honored "victims during this tragic period." A version in December used the terms "massacres and deportations." Another version transmitted the same month included a passage reaffirming the Truman Doctrine and America's commitment to Turkey. In yet another version circulated two weeks before the scheduled debate, a member of the White House replaced the word "Genocide" with "tragic and inhumane massacres." Another called the Genocide the "systematic destruction of the Armenian people." The two sides also negotiated the number of victims, ranging from Turkey's favored "hundreds of thousands" in some versions to the "million and a half" claimed by the Armenians.[112]

The State Department objected to any use of the term "genocide"—even, as it put it, if it came from the "mouths of others" and not the American government. "The word will be unacceptable to the Turks no matter how qualified," it declared to Scowcroft. If the "genocide" label was included, the agency explained, then "we strongly urge" the inclusion of the following clause—"historians continue to dispute whether the term genocide accurately characterizes these events"—to provide "balance."[113]

To try to move things along, Pashayan sent out a comprehensive compromise package in November. Six weeks later, he sent out a second package that did not have the U.S. government declare the events of 1915 a "genocide" but instead honored the victims of the "Armenian Genocide."[114] The nuances would probably be lost on most people, but any change in the resolution's wording that might make it more palatable to Turkey yet apply the term "genocide" was taken into consideration. On the eve of the debates, Dole and Bush agreed to use the term "genocide" in return for changing the resolution from a joint to a concurrent one, thereby forgoing the need for a presidential signature. The switch took Bush off the hook, and divested the resolution of its legal standing but still affirmed the veracity of the Genocide.[115]

Byrd was not in the loop to the negotiations, and he knew the Turks would never accept any resolution with the word "genocide" no matter how watered down. When he saw victory in sight, he saw no need to go along with the deal struck by Dole and Bush near the end of the debate.[116] The filibuster vote took place without a substitution to the concurrent resolution, thereby thwarting the compromise reached by Bush and Dole. After Byrd's maneuver, Dole made one last plea to his colleagues, perhaps speaking his most moving words of the debate. "Maybe we can redeem ourselves a bit today by letting the world know that we do not always support the rich and the powerful and those with the most lobbyists," Dole declared as the last speaker. "Sometimes we judge right from wrong."[117]

As the vote neared, Armenians filled the Senate gallery. Krikorian was confident that the Armenians could win a vote on the merits, but he knew that Byrd's resolve and his chairmanship of the Appropriations Committee would make it difficult to overcome the filibuster. The resolution's support was built as an ad hoc coalition not bound by the usual glues of party, region, or ideology that piloted legislation past the Senate's many roadblocks. Any teetering might lead to its downfall. Krikorian took out an alphabetical list of senators with a column of "Yeas" and "Nays" on either side of each name to take a running tally. The resolution needed 60 Yeas to overcome the filibuster. His latest vote tally accounted for many of the senators. If most of the ones on the fence voted with Dole, then the resolution would have a chance. At 1:30 p.m., as the first senator was about to announce his vote, there was nothing left for Krikorian and Adalian to do but watch the proceedings on the small monitor in Dole's office.[118]

Senator Brockman Adams (D-WA) voted Nay.

Senator William L. Armstrong (R-CO) was an original co-sponsor. He voted Yea.

Senator Max Baucus (D-MT) was a co-sponsor but voted Nay.

Senator Lloyd M. Bentsen (D-TX) was an original co-sponsor. He voted Yea.

Senator Joseph R. Biden, Jr. (D-DE) was a major supporter of the resolution. He voted Yea.

Senator Jeff Bingaman (D-NM) was an original co-sponsor. He voted Yea.

Senator Christopher ("Kit") Bond (R-MO) withdrew his co-sponsorship in October. He voted Nay.

Senator David L. Boren (D-OK) voted Nay.

Senator Rudy Boschwitz (R-MN) was an original co-sponsor. He voted Yea.

Senator Bill Bradley (D-NJ) was an original co-sponsor. He voted Yea.

Senator John B. Breaux (D-LA) withdrew his co-sponsorship in October. He voted Nay.

Senator Richard H. Bryan (D-NV) withdrew his co-sponsorship in October. He voted Nay.

Senator Dale Bumpers (D-AR) withdrew his co-sponsorship on the first day of the debate after receiving a call from Byrd to reconsider.[119] He voted Nay.

Senator Quentin N. Burdick (D-ND) was an original co-sponsor. He voted Yea.

Senator Conrad Burns (R-MT) withdrew his co-sponsorship in November but voted Yea.

Senator Robert C. Byrd (D-WV) voted Nay.

Senator John H. Chafee (R-RI) was an original co-sponsor. He voted Yea.

Senator Daniel R. Coats (R-IN) did not vote.

Senator Thad Cochran (R-MS) voted Nay.

Senator William S. Cohen (R-ME) was an original co-sponsor. He voted Yea.

Senator Kent Conrad (D-ND) voted Nay.

Senator Alan Cranston (D-CA) represented the largest number of Armenian-Americans in the union. He voted Yea.

Senator Alfonse M. D'Amato (R-NY) was an original co-sponsor. He voted Yea.

Senator John C. Danforth (R-MO) withdrew his co-sponsorship in January. He voted Nay.

Senator Thomas A. Daschle (D-SD), Nay.

Senator Dennis DeConcini (D-AZ), Yea.

Senator Alan J. Dixon (D-IL) withdrew his co-sponsorship in October. He voted Nay.

Senator Christopher J. Dodd (D-CT) did not vote.

Senator Robert J. Dole (R-KS), Yea.

Senator Pete V. Domenici (R-NM) was an original co-sponsor. He voted Yea.

Senator David F. Durenberger (R-MN) was an original co-sponsor. He voted Yea.

Senator J. James Exon (D-NE), Nay.

Senator Wendell H. Ford (D-KY) was an original co-sponsor but voted Nay.

Senator Wyche Fowler, Jr. (D-GA) voted Nay.

Senator Edwin Jacob ("Jake") Garn (R-UT) was not a co-sponsor but voted Yea.

Senator John H. Glenn, Jr. (D-OH) was an original co-sponsor. He voted Yea.

Senator Albert A. Gore, Jr. (D-TN) asked for Adalian to meet with his chief of staff alone, so that the historian could present evidence attesting to the Genocide without interjections from lobbyists.[120] He voted Yea.

Senator Thomas Slade Gorton, Jr. (R-WA) voted Nay.

Senator Bob Graham (D-FL) withdrew his co-sponsorship in October when he realized the impact of the resolution on U.S.-Turkish relations.[121] He voted Nay.

Senator Phil Gramm (R-TX), Nay.

Senator Charles E. Grassley (R-IA) was not a co-sponsor but voted Yea.

Senator Tom Harkin (D-IA) was not a co-sponsor but voted Yea.

Senator Orrin G. Hatch (R-UT) withdrew his co-sponsorship in October days before he voted against the resolution in the Judiciary Committee. He changed his mind and voted Yea.

Senator Mark O. Hatfield (R-OR), Nay.

Senator Howell T. Heflin (D-AL) withdrew his co-sponsorship in

October but changed his mind because, Krikorian felt, of help from the Greek-American lobby.[122] He voted Yea.

Senator H. John Heinz III (R-PA) was an original co-sponsor. He voted Yea.

Senator Jesse Helms (R-NC) was an original co-sponsor. He voted Yea.

Senator Ernest F. Hollings (D-SC) had on at least two occasions acknowledged the Genocide on the Senate floor.[123] Despite these pronouncements, he voted Nay.

Senator Gordon J. Humphrey (R-NH) was not a co-sponsor but voted Yea.

Senator Daniel K. Inouye (D-HI) and Dole became lifelong friends while recovering at a military ward. Both had sustained their World War II injuries in Italy not far from each other, and Inouye's loss of his right arm was eerily similar to Dole's harrowing war injury. Inouye even credited Dole for inspiring him to enter politics.[124] Their enduring friendship did not translate into a favorable vote on Dole's behalf, however. Inouye voted Nay.

Senator James M. Jeffords (R-VT) was an original co-sponsor. He voted Yea.

Senator J. Bennett Johnston, Jr. (D-LA) voted Nay.

Senator Nancy L. Kassebaum (R-KS) was the junior senator from Dole's home state. She voted Yea.

Senator Robert W. Kasten, Jr. (R-WI) withdrew his co-sponsorship in October. Two months later, an Armenian youth group showed up at the Racine, Wisconsin, festival hall asking him to reconsider. With the support of the mayor, the local Armenian community helped sway Kasten.[125] He voted Yea.

Senator Edward M. Kennedy (D-MA) had supported the Armenian quest for justice since 1965.[126] He voted Yea.

The count looked promising at this point. Four senators who were not co-sponsors surprisingly voted Yea. Only two co-sponsors voted Nay while four who had withdrawn their support still voted in its favor. After fifty-five senators had voted, the Yeas outnumbered the Nays 30–23 (with two absentees), just off the pace needed to reach 60.

Senator J. Robert Kerrey (D-NE), Nay.

Senator John F. Kerry (D-MA) was an original co-sponsor. He voted Yea.

Senator Herbert H. Kohl (D-WI), Yea.

Senator Frank R. Lautenberg (D-NJ) signed on as a co-sponsor in mid-October. He voted Yea.

Senator Patrick J. Leahy (D-VT) withdrew his co-sponsorship in October but voted for the resolution in the Judiciary Committee. Leahy's aide acknowledged that Byrd "had drawn his line in the sand."[127] That was a line the senator would apparently not cross. He voted Nay.

Senator Carl Levin (D-MI) was a longtime supporter of the Armenians. He voted Yea.

Senator Joseph I. Lieberman (D-CT) provided a vista into all the forces at play. He told his constituents that the combination of Byrd's cajoling, pleas from Connecticut manufacturers, a visit from Ambassador Abramowitz, and materials from the denialist historian Justin McCarthy influenced his decision. To Krikorian's bitter disappointment, he voted Nay.

Senator C. Trent Lott (R-MS), Nay.

Senator Richard G. Lugar (R-IN), Nay.

Senator Connie Mack III (R-FL), Nay.

Senator Spark M. Matsunaga (D-HI), Nay.

Senator John S. McCain III (R-AZ) cited the repercussions to America's relationship with Turkey, but explained that his opposition was not "solely for reasons of realpolitik." He relied upon the so-called historical debate to vote Nay.[128]

Senator James A. McClure (R-ID) was an original co-sponsor but voted Nay.

Senator Mitch McConnell (R-KY), Nay.

Senator Howard M. Metzenbaum (D-OH) met with Armenian groups several times since his about-face at the Judiciary Committee.[129] He still voted Nay.

Senator Barbara A. Mikulski (D-MD) was an original co-sponsor. She voted Yea.

Senator George J. Mitchell (D-ME), Yea.

Senator Daniel Patrick Moynihan (D-NY) was a co-sponsor. He voted Yea.

Senator Frank H. Murkowski (R-AK) was an original co-sponsor. He voted Yea.

Senator Don Nickles (R-OK) withdrew his co-sponsorship in October. He voted Nay.

Senator Sam Nunn (D-GA), Nay.

Senator Robert W. Packwood (R-OR), Nay.

Senator Claiborne Pell (D-RI) was an original co-sponsor. He voted Yea.

Senator Larry Pressler (R-SD) became interested in the Genocide while a student at Oxford. As an original co-sponsor, he voted Yea.

Senator David H. Pryor (D-AR) withdrew his co-sponsorship in October. He voted Nay.

Senator Harry M. Reid (D-NV) was an original co-sponsor but voted Nay.

Senator Donald W. Riegle, Jr. (D-MI) was an original co-sponsor. He voted Yea.

Senator Charles S. Robb (D-VA), Nay.

Senator John D. Rockefeller IV (D-WV), Nay.

Senator William V. Roth, Jr. (R-DE) voted Nay.

Senator Warren B. Rudman (R-NH) was an original co-sponsor. He voted Yea.

Senator Terry Sanford (D-NC), Nay.

Senator Paul S. Sarbanes (D-MD), a child of Greek immigrants, had an affinity for the Armenians. He had recently grilled Ambassador Abramowitz about America's policy toward the Genocide during his nomination hearings.[130] He voted Yea.

Senator James Sasser (D-TN) withdrew his co-sponsorhip in October. He voted Nay.

Senator Richard C. Shelby (D-AL) was an original co-sponsor but voted Nay.

Senator Paul Simon (D-IL), Yea.

Senator Alan K. Simpson (R-WY), Nay.

Senator Arlen Specter (R-PA) turned out to be one of the most interesting votes. His past support of similar resolutions made his withdrawal at the Judiciary Committee in October very disappointing to Armenians. Mark Momjian, an attorney based in Philadelphia, organized a broad community effort to sway the senator. In December, girls from an Armenian day school appeared at a town hall meeting to ask Specter to reconsider. Two survivors then recounted their experience to him in person. Other Armenians did likewise, collecting 30,000 signatures for a petition.[131] The senator was conflicted. Members of the administration he spoke with, including former ambassador to Turkey Robert Strausz-Hupé, a man Specter had known and admired since his college days, urged him to oppose the resolution. Specter conducted a historical analysis of his own to settle the dispute. After reading various texts, he found the evidence overwhelming. Particularly moved by letters from survivors, which he recited on the Senate floor, Specter told his fellow senators that "the evidence does support the accepted definition of a genocide."[132] He voted Yea.

Senator Theodore F. Stevens (R-AK) was an original co-sponsor. He voted Yea.

Senator Steve Symms (R-ID), Nay.

Senator James Strom Thurmond (R-SC), Yea.

Senator Malcolm Wallop (R-WY), Nay.

Senator John W. Warner (R-VA) opposed the resolution but out of loyalty to his party leader, Dole, voted Yea.[133]

Senator Pete Wilson (R-CA) represented the largest number of Armenian-Americans in the union. He voted Yea.

Senator Timothy E. Wirth (D-CO), Nay.

Only near the end of the 49–49 tally did Krikorian accept defeat.[134]

The vote defied a straightforward explanation. Twenty-six Republicans and twenty-three Democrats voted in favor of invoking cloture to stop the filibuster, eighteen Republicans and thirty-one Democrats opposed. A look at the most powerful committees showed no clear-cut advantage to Byrd. Only ten of the twenty members of the Armed Services Committee voted against the resolution, though one would suspect more should have considering they would have the keenest insight into Turkey's military importance. Likewise, thirteen of the nineteen senators on the Foreign Relations Committee voted to end the filibuster, again surprising considering all the talk of Turkey's strategic importance. Only fifteen of the twenty-nine members in Byrd's Appropriations Committee decided to support their chairman. The Armenians even picked up 4 votes from the resolution's erstwhile opponents in the Judiciary Committee. It was largely the senators in the less influential committees from states with no Armenian political footprint that ended up supporting Byrd's filibuster.

A second vote on February 27 turned up no differently despite frantic efforts by Armenian lobbyists and Dole.[135] The Bush administration's opposition, Turkey's various lobbying apparatuses, Byrd's influence in the Appropriations Committee compounded by opposition from Senator Sam Nunn, who as chairman of the Armed Services Committee received a great deal of deference on defense matters, were simply too much to overcome.

On the fourth and last day of debate, both Byrd and Dole took time to mention Krikorian in their final speeches, the former to castigate him as the modern-day Vahan Cardashian, the latter to honor him, along with Adalian, Vartian, Pashayan, Deukmejian, and two of the governor's associates, for their efforts.[136]

The honorable mention provided Krikorian no solace. Back in the fall, he thought the Armenians had covered every base. He never thought that corporations would play such a heavy role in lobbying against the resolution.[137] Dragging their boxes on the way out of the Capitol, he and Adalian passed by the Turkish ambassador accompanied by a contingent of well-dressed men. The Turkish group did not recognize the two Armenians. The scene was emblematic of the "David and Goliath" story Dole had referred to many times during the debate: the outnumbered Armenians against the powerful Turks. Krikorian was exhausted after months of endless work and dejected from defeat. He wanted to resign. Adalian took a longer-term approach, one that Krikorian also came to appreciate over time, in which he saw the legislative effort as a watershed moment in rolling back denial.[138]

Byrd received a hero's welcome when he visited Turkey later in the year during a sort of celebration tour.[139] It was a Pyrrhic victory, however. Turkey had won the political battle but lost the historical and moral one. The mountain of archival evidence entered into the record made the debate a turning point in the Turkish-Armenian contest. The amount of time spent by the Senate on the Armenian issue—the body spent less time eleven months later deliberating whether to go to war in the Persian Gulf—alone reflected the degree to which the Armenian case had matured.[140] After the 1990 confrontation in the Senate, the tide turned against Turkey's distortions of history. Bush's April 24 statement reflected this change. Though avoiding the term "genocide," the president's statement on the anniversary of the Genocide commemorated the "terrible massacres suffered in 1915–1923 at the hands of the rulers of the Ottoman Empire. . . . On this 75th anniversary of the massacres, I wish to join with Armenians . . . in observing . . . a day of remembrance for the more than a million Armenian people who were victims."[141] In this statement free of double-talk or prevarication, it was as if the president was providing the definition of genocide without using the word. As time went on, fewer and fewer elected officials maintained their faith in Turkey's position. Hearings in 1996 rubbed out further misgivings about the Genocide's authenticity. By the start of the new millennium, few doubters remained in the U.S. government. The true legacy of the work completed by Dole, Krikorian, Adalian, and so many others was that it put in motion a process that turned the tide on Turkey's denial, helping to erase any legitimate doubt about its veracity.

The Armenian issue always placed the American government in a bind, pitting its inveterate streaks of realpolitik and humanitarianism against each other. When the Senate rejected the mandate of Armenia in 1920, it embraced an isolationist policy, the pragmatic move for the day. When the same body rejected Armenian pleas for justice seventy years later, it too sided with what it thought was pragmatic. In doing so, it lost a bit of its moral authority by aiding in the cover-up of a crime. But in each case, humanitarianism garnered significant support, keeping alive that sense of justice and compassion that has always made America's foreign policy unique among the world's strongest nations. Few symbolized that sense of justice and compassion more clearly than Robert Dole. If Dr. Kelikian was alive, he would have surely thanked the senator. Symbolically at least, Kelikian's daughter spoke on his behalf when she wrote to Dole: "I am writing to express my heartfelt thanks for all you have done. . . . Your efforts have touched me and my family so."[142]

"The past is not dead"

S ince his heady days as a young, rebellious protestor in the 1960s and 1970s, Vartkes Yeghiayan always seemed like an activist in search of a cause. By the mid-1980s, however, his youthful forays canvassing for John Kennedy and providing legal assistance to agricultural workers followed by a stint as an assistant director of the Peace Corps were well in the past as he married, and settled into a more customary life as a personal injury lawyer in Glendale, California, home to the largest concentration of Armenians in America.[1]

One thing remained constant. Throughout the years, his eagerness to uncover his father's past never waned. Ultimately, there was much that Yeghiayan would never come to know, a reality he found difficult to accept. The tidbits he did learn, however, instilled in him a personal stake in the Genocide and in the outcome of the Turkish-Armenian conflict. He had organized Genocide demonstrations in Los Angeles in 1971, and regardless of where he traveled, he joined a local Armenian community in commemorating the event every year. But as a middle-aged man with few ties to leading Armenian institutions, he was ill-suited to lead a crusade on the streets or in Washington. It was not until 1987, as he approached his fifty-first birthday, that he stumbled on the cause that would become his passion.[2]

Selected in part to safeguard the Jewish community in Palestine, Henry Morgenthau, Sr., arrived as America's ambassador in Constantinople one year before the guns of August knocked the world into war. Little did he know upon his arrival that he would instead champion the cause of another ancient people living under Ottoman rule—the Armenians.[3] Because of America's neutrality through much of World War I, he was one of the few foreign diplomats to stay in Constantinople at the time of the Genocide. The constant inflow of harrowing cables from consular officers and eyewitnesses from across the empire made his posting excruciating. After the war, he wrote a memoir that, like most accounts dating back to that era, largely collected dust over the years. He could not have suspected that one of the many exchanges he described with the Young Turk leadership would unearth a secret element of the Genocide the world had never known.

Yeghiayan's interest in Morgenthau's text stemmed from his desire as an amateur historian to better understand the Genocide. While reading the memoir in bed, Yeghiayan came across a passage recounting a conversation between Morgenthau and his frequent interlocutor, Mehmet Talaat, the Ottoman interior minister and one of the chief architects of the Genocide:

> One day Talaat made what was perhaps the most astonishing request I had ever heard. The New York Life Insurance Company and the Equitable Life of New York had for years done considerable business among the Armenians. . . . "I wish," Talaat now said, "that you would get the American life insurance companies to send us a complete list of their Armenian policy holders. They are practically all dead now and have left no heirs to collect the money. It of course all escheats to the State. The Government is the beneficiary now."[4]

Yeghiayan jumped out of bed, his mind racing with questions. What happened to these policies? Were they ever paid? The search for answers started him on a mission that would stretch over two decades.

His investigation began with a letter to the State Department. An official there referred him to the National Archives, which sent him 600 pages of documents on microfiche. Reading them at a local library alongside junior high students, Yeghiayan began to draw a picture of what had happened to the policies. The war and the disappearance of so many Armenians hopelessly complicated the efforts of the New York Life Insurance Company to run a business in the region. During World War I, a representative based in Constantinople administered 1,300 of the 3,600 policies held by Armenians. When the claims dried up, the company closed its books. As part of a corporate strategy to shutter many of its international offices, the New York–based insurer pulled out of the Ottoman Empire in 1921, assigning its policies to a French insurer.[5] Its departure did not end its interests in the policies it had issued to Armenians who perished during the Genocide, however.

On the contrary, as the American group of diplomats—including Rear Admiral Bristol—headed to Lausanne to hammer out a treaty with Turkey, New York Life, like Standard Oil, sought help from the delegation. A vice president at the insurer sent a letter to Secretary of State Charles Evans Hughes in November 1922 complaining that "[m]uch of this insurance" issued in the Ottoman Empire "was written upon the lives of subject peoples, such as the Armenians and others who have, during the years since the outbreak of the European war, been subjected to massacre and illegal killing and fatal exposure by or with the acquiescence of the Turkish authorities." Because New York Life had "incurred very heavy and extraordinary losses through the lives of its insured having been prematurely terminated by such violent death," it wanted to hold Turkey responsible. At the time, there seemed to be no legal recourse for the insurer other than to ask for assistance from the State Department. "We respectfully urge," the letter went on, "that the Department of State present and support a claim for reimbursement by the Turkish Government of these losses. . . ." Three weeks later, New York Life's outside counsel, Sullivan & Cromwell, whose partnership then included John Foster Dulles, a former U.S. legal counsel at Versailles and a future secretary of state, reiterated the plea as negotiations progressed with Turkey. Coincidentally, John Foster's brother, Allen Dulles, headed the Near East desk at the State Department. The filial connection failed to secure the insurer its wishes, however, and there the matter ended.[6]

As best Yeghiayan could determine, the death benefits totaling millions of dollars, perhaps tens of millions, on thousands of policies remained unpaid. After years of playing the dilettante, and already past his fiftieth birthday, Yeghiayan found his calling. He wanted to avenge his father's loss—his people's loss—and here was his opportunity to compensate the victims' families for the first time. Not a penny in reparations had been paid to the Armenians for Genocide-related losses. Assets were looted. Homes were destroyed or taken over by others. Communal centers like churches and schools lay fallow or were appropriated for other uses. The Armenians never received compensation for these losses, not to mention remuneration for lost lives. Insurance benefits were not reparations, but they would give the victims' heirs something of value. More important, a lawsuit could be a way of getting people to recognize that something horrible had happened in the Ottoman Empire decades earlier.[7]

As Yeghiayan began to strategize on how to a build a case, his colleagues mocked him for his fanciful aspirations. The obstacles seemed insurmountable, even to him.[8] No one had successfully filed a Genocide-related case before, and with no legal precedents allowing litigants to revive decades-old claims, courts would have granted his arguments little respect. There were no plaintiffs banging at his door, and it seemed unlikely that any records remained. Yeghiayan needed a client in possession of an unredeemed policy. His task would be difficult. The frantic and desperate nature of the mass murder and deportations made it unlikely that any survivors would have walked out of the Ottoman Empire with a policy in hand and kept it intact for more than seventy years. Indeed, a lawsuit was a fantasy. But fantasies, often begun by underdogs acting without fear of tarnishing glossy reputations, have a funny way of coming true. Ever the dreamer, Yeghiayan rested his fate on a single conversation gleaned from Morgenthau's crusty memoir. No matter the obstacles, Yeghiayan was convinced that he had to file a lawsuit, and the first thing he needed was a client.

There was nothing exceptional about Setrak Cheytanian. And little was known about him. Like many other Armenians at the dawn of the previous century, he lived with an extended family including his two children, wife, and parents in Kharput, a city in central Anatolia sitting atop a 4,000-foot plateau used as a stopping point on the Silk Road. In the only photo still in existence of his family, he appeared in the fashion of the day, sporting a thick mustache and fez.[9] Fearing the worst for himself and wanting to provide for his family, in July 1910 Cheytanian purchased a life insurance policy from a New York Life Insurance Company agent for which he owed an annual payment of 155.73 francs. Since the 1890s, New York Life's European headquarters located in Paris had managed its operations within the Ottoman Empire, selling thousands of policies to Armenians living in the region. The policy, which was written in French, would pay out a premium of 3,000 francs upon the thirty-five-year-old Cheytanian's death to his heirs. If he outlived its twenty-year term, he would receive a lump-sum payment. Cheytanian's sister-in-law, Yegsa Marootian, and her nine-year-old daughter, Alice, were heading to New York to join Cheytanian's brother, who had emigrated years earlier. Before they left, Cheytanian handed over the policy to Yegsa, figuring that should anything happen to him, it would be easier for her to collect on the policy from New York, where the insurer was headquartered.[10]

No one understood the importance of his prescience for decades to come. When the Genocide began, the Armenians of Kharput were among those targeted for the brutal deportations. The U.S. Consulate stationed there wrote to Morgenthau, "I do not believe it possible for one in a hundred to survive, perhaps one in a thousand." As a middle-aged man, the odds were against Cheytanian. He was not among the one in a thousand to survive, and neither were his wife and children.[11]

By the time of Cheytanian's death, his sister-in-law Yegsa was living in Staten Island, New York, and her family had grown to include three children in addition to Alice. Yegsa was largely cut off from her Armenian relatives, but somehow she got word by 1925 that Cheytanian was dead. She had kept the life insurance policy he had given her, and, with her family financially strapped, Yegsa was desperate to collect the death benefit. Following Cheytanian's instructions, Yegsa contacted New York Life about redeeming the policy, and a company agent told her to obtain a certificate of inheritance—essentially a death certificate—to prove that Cheytanian had indeed died. The agent instructed her to contact the Armenian Church for the certificate. There is no record of Yegsa's response to the agent, but by 1956 she had moved to Los Angeles and obtained the certificate of inheritance, which she sent to the insurer. In June of that year, the insurer instructed Yegsa to come to its Pasadena office to "discuss the matter," probably to explain that the policy may have been transferred to a French insurer years earlier. It is not known whether Yegsa went to the insurer's office or what happened next. When she died in 1982, the policy remained unpaid.[12]

Upon Yegsa's death, her oldest daughter, Alice, took possession of the materials. As the only one of Yegsa's children born in the Ottoman Empire, Alice was aware of her mother's efforts to collect the benefits, but she thought little about it until 1989, when she noticed an advertisement in a local newspaper seeking "insurance papers." The ad had been placed by Yeghiayan, who expected that at best he would find a person who had memories of a policy. He did not suspect that anyone might actually have one intact. The ad prompted dozens of Armenians to send him photos of deceased relatives but no insurance policies. His frustration turned to despair when it seemed that no one had a policy, let alone remembered if ancestors were insured, threatening to quash his lawsuit before it got off the ground. His fortunes changed when Alice called months later. When he visited her home in Irvine, California, she brought out a shoebox containing the original life insurance policy of her uncle Cheytanian, payment stubs, and correspondence between her mother and New York Life dating back to the 1920s. For Alice, it was redemption for her mother. "I've been wondering why God has kept me alive all these years," she told Yeghiayan at their meeting, "go ahead and file. . . ."[13] After years of searching, Yeghiayan, it seemed, had a client.

But the reality was not so simple. In 1994, as Yeghiayan prepared the lawsuit, Alice died, and the identity of the policy's beneficiary changed again. This time, it was Alice's younger brother, Martin Marootian.

Fifty years of marriage between Martin and Seda Marootian bound not only their lives but also their words. They preferred to use "We" instead of "I" and regularly finished each other's sentences from their home in a flowery development near Los Angeles. A retired pharmacist, Martin was a gentle-speaking octogenarian grandfather who, at a late age, inherited a decades-old family saga. Seda, a few years younger, stepped in when his memory faltered and almost never left his side. She pursued a career in radio journalism, a progressive move for an Armenian woman coming of age in the 1940s. The late Susan Sontag was one of her first journalism students at North Hollywood High School, and like her star pupil, Seda showcased an opinionated streak.[14]

Because neither his mother nor sister had told Marootian about the policy, its existence came as a shock. All of a sudden, with news of an uncle he was barely cognizant of and an insurance policy he had never known about thrust upon him, Marootian found himself the final custodian of a decades-long family legacy. Much like Yeghiayan after he had found his father's photo, Marootian began to explore his family's past. He preserved the insurance policy and the only remaining photo of his uncle dating back to about 1910 in polyurethane envelopes for safekeeping. Of the family members in the photo, only Marootian's mother, Yegsa, and his sister, Alice, survived the Genocide. The Marootians clung onto these items like holy relics because they represented the only small fragments of their family's existence prior to the Genocide. With so few connections left of Armenian life in the ancient homeland, the time before 1915 took on an antediluvian character—vague, largely unknowable, and chronicled in sweeping terms. The family legacies—the idiosyncratic traditions and tales normally passed from generation to generation—were wiped away. The enduring family stories, the ones passed down to today's Armenians, originated in 1915 in the killing fields of Anatolia. With ties to the pre–Genocide era severed, the massacres became the Armenian Genesis story. For Marootian, the unearthing of his uncle's policy exhumed a small fraction of that lost life.

Much like Yeghiayan, Marootian saw the lawsuit as a chance to honor his family. During the Depression, his mother had raised her family on a single paycheck. That money could have been useful to her, Marootian thought. Yet he also appreciated the broader historic opportunity the policy offered in helping the Armenian cause. When his sister died, Marootian came to inherit not only the policy but also the role of a lifetime—a role he came to relish.[15]

Even with a client and an insurance policy in hand, Yeghiayan seemed like an unlikely choice to bring the first ever class action suit originating from the Genocide. Prominent class action lawyers like Melvyn Weiss backed by influential institutions like the World Jewish Congress brought the Holocaust lawsuits of the 1990s. Yeghiayan operated without institutional support out of a cramped office. In 1999, he underwent emergency heart surgery.[16] Now past his sixtieth birthday, his health unstable, and lacking heavyweight legal credentials, he was far from an ideal candidate for the task.

A class action—especially one relying on moldy facts—is not like any other case. It requires immense manpower and organization to review the thousands of documents traded between the litigants and prepare the innumerable motions each side launches at the other like boxers in a fifteen-round match. Lawyers bringing the suit need a huge treasure chest because they receive no payments until the end—and then only after a victory or settlement. Yeghiayan appreciated the power of a class action back from his days at the Rural Assistance Program, but had missed the tidal wave of private class actions of the 1970s and 1980s that revolutionized the field. He operated his four-lawyer firm far from the epicenters of the local legal community in Century City and downtown Los Angeles. His wife, who co-headed the firm, was an immigration lawyer, and Yeghiayan himself worked mostly on slip-and-fall cases. Operating with no institutional support, Yeghiayan knew that to bring a suit of this magnitude, he needed to find a partner with class action experience and enough manpower to contend with New York Life, a Fortune 100 company with millions in its coffers to finance a formidable legal team.[17]

Yeghiayan first contacted Eugene R. Anderson, a founding partner of a prominent law firm in New York. Coincidentally, Anderson's wife was Ambassador Morgenthau's great-granddaughter. Her father, New York district attorney Robert Morgenthau, and her uncle, Henry Morgenthau III, advocated for Genocide recognition and were venerated figures among Armenian-Americans. Having worked extensively on Holocaust insurance recovery cases and eager to please his wife by working for an Armenian cause, Anderson seemed like a perfect candidate.[18] Yeghiayan instead settled on Roman M. Silberfeld, another big-firm lawyer experienced in litigating Holocaust cases because of his proximity to Yeghiayan in Los Angeles. When Silberfeld approached New York Life, the company offered to settle with the Marootians alone. Wanting a broader resolution and hoping to generate publicity for the Genocide, the Marootians turned down the proffered settlement, at which stage Silberfeld dropped out.

Though Yeghiayan lacked a big-name partner, the wave of Holocaust cases in the 1990s involving bank deposits, looted assets, and slave labor gave him a boost. The cases did not generate significant new laws or drastically change the legal landscape, but the numerous multibillion-dollar settlements provided Yeghiayan with a blueprint on how to proceed. In an untested field with few precedents to rely upon, Yeghiayan received free legal advice by these pioneering lawsuits. He got to see what tactics worked and failed and witnessed the path to a winning formula paved by the Holocaust litigants—a cocktail of legal pressure, public relations ploys, and political persuasion. Yeghiayan would have to rely upon all three forces to have a shot against New York Life.

Yeghiayan filed the suit alone in 1999 but eventually found two partners. The first, Brian Kabateck, joined him in May 2000. The two embodied contrasting temperaments and backgrounds. With white hair and heavy eyelids redolent of a man weighed down by contemplation, Yeghiayan's appreciation of Armenian history colored his view of the lawsuit. On the other hand, Kabateck's maternal grandparents were survivors yet he knew little about the Genocide prior to the case. Unlike Yeghiayan, who could not dine at a restaurant in Glendale without an Armenian stopping to greet him, Kabateck grew up largely outside the Armenian community. As such, he came to view the case as a unique opportunity to make his Armenian mother proud.

The two men's personalities also differed. While Yeghiayan displayed a rebellious streak developed during the 1960s, at twenty-five years his junior, Kabateck's guarded tone displayed the calculating pragmatism he brought to the team. Kabateck's office on the thirty-ninth floor of a corporate tower steps away from Frank Gehry's Walt Disney Concert Hall in downtown Los Angeles stood in sharp contrast to Yeghiayan's workplace in the hinterlands. With a penchant for what he called the "controllable risks of litigation"—the high-stakes game of trial lawyers—Kabateck cut his teeth on insurance cases arising from the 1994 Northridge earthquake.[19]

Kabateck recommended that they add William Shernoff, who had already locked horns with insurers in Holocaust-related litigation. Shernoff's main job was to begin negotiations with New York Life and its chief outside lawyers, people Shernoff was familiar with. The team divided their responsibilities according to individual strengths:

Yeghiayan acted as a liaison with plaintiffs and supplied historical ammunition; Kabateck carried the heavy load of producing the court briefs; and Shernoff coordinated negotiations with the defendant.[20]

The formation of the team did not change the hostile legal landscape Yeghiayan confronted. On August 31, 2000, Judge Sterling Johnson, Jr., handed Holocaust class action claimants their first victory in an American court.[21] It would also be their last. Though evocative, cases based on historical crimes rested on thin legal ground. Other lawsuits brought by prisoners of war, apartheid victims, and descendants of American slaves, to name a few, also ended in dismissal, often withering from lack of tangible evidence or collapsing from overstretched legal claims.[22]

The Marootian suit faced similar handicaps. The dearth of Armenians with records of policies underscored the first difficulty. The chaos of the Genocide followed by a long interval of time destroyed many of the evidentiary connections to that period. Of the twelve named plaintiffs in the class action, only Marootian possessed a policy. New York Life handed the plaintiffs a gift by passing over lists of policy holders early in the litigation process, a move sharply contrasting with the path taken by several non-German insurers in refusing to divulge Holocaust-related policies. Serendipity struck again for Yeghiayan as these records, which would have been otherwise destroyed in accordance with New York Life's document retention program, had been tagged by previous executives for safekeeping. An appraisal counted the number of policies that may not have been paid at 2,300, serving as a basis for negotiations.[23]

A review of these policies turned up new challenges. Like Cheytanian's policy, they required all disputes to be resolved in France or England, not a federal court in California. In other words, the heirs of the policy holders should have brought their cases in Europe, a toxic legal environment for class actions. If American courts provided a challenging forum for cases emanating from historical crimes, European courts were outright antagonistic to such lawsuits. The two sides also clashed in calculating the value of the policies. Yeghiayan placed their value at hundreds of millions of dollars, while the insurer responded that interest accrued only after a claim was filed, reducing the value of the policies dramatically. Class certification was another thorny issue. Normally, members of a class action were limited to parties living in the United States, and needed to provide solid proof of their injuries. Yeghiayan's team argued that the lawsuit should have global coverage and include those who were not in possession of policies. Any case reaching that far back in time inevitably faced lethal obstacles. But the biggest problem, which hung like the sword of Damocles over Yeghiayan's case, was still to come. In March 2000, New York Life filed a motion to dismiss the case, a standard move in any lawsuit—especially one endangered by so many legal hurdles—arguing that the statute of limitations voided the case.[24] The legal doctrine limited the number of years in which a claimant could bring a suit—and it did not stretch far enough to keep alive the Armenian claims.

Yeghiayan considered making a heartfelt plea to the court arguing that the doctrine should not apply in extreme cases like the Genocide. Yet he knew this was flimsy. Courts needed sound legal justifications—not righteous sentiments—on which to base their decisions. With the likelihood of a dismissal hobbling the plaintiffs at the negotiating table, Yeghiayan tapped the politically connected Armenian community for help.

The Armenian presence in California originated at the dawn of the last century as immigrants flocked to Fresno before spreading throughout the state. By the 1980s, Armenians had reached the highest corridors of power, placing George Deukmejian in the governor's seat and regularly winning favorable legislation. Two decades later, the Armenian population had ballooned to several hundred thousand and there were five legislators of Armenian descent in California's Armenian-friendly government. The retired governor referred Yeghiayan to a former aide—and one of those legislators, Senator Charles Poochigian. Poochigian, also a descendant of survivors who had heard his own share of horror stories growing up, eagerly accepted Yeghiayan's request.[25]

An existing bill extending the statute of limitations for Holocaust-era insurance cases served as a model, paving the way for Yeghiayan and Poochigian to urge the legislature to enact a similar law for the Armenians. In May 2000, a couple of months after New York Life filed its dismissal motion, Poochigian spoke before the state's Senate Judiciary Committee inside a wood-paneled room in California's

capitol building. "For decades, families have sought to resolve insurance claims related to the Armenian Genocide. However, because of
the total destruction suffered by the Armenian community at that
time, it was very difficult and remains very difficult," said Poochigian,
pausing to wait for a cell phone to stop ringing, "for heirs of victims of
the Genocide to document that their family members were insured."
Yeghiayan and Marootian followed with a one-two punch. Yeghiayan
provided the historical context, and the bearded Marootian, flanked,
as always, by Seda, spoke without notes, syncopating his testimony
with pauses, as if taking a mental note of the punctuation. "My name
is Martin Marootian and I almost feel like a survivor of the Genocide,"
he started. "When war clouds gathered . . . my grandfather said to my
mother . . . 'trouble is brewing, I think you ought to go to America.
. . . ' My uncle had an insurance policy and he gave it to my mother.
. . . He thought that the insurance policy would be safe and honored.
Well, it was safe, it was in our family for the past 85 years," he said,
holding up the policy for emphasis, "but it was not honored. . . . And
to this date we're still waiting for justice."[26]

Marootian's delivery scored a knockout. Committee chair Adam
Schiff from Burbank, who co-sponsored the bill with Poochigian,
oversaw a 7–0 vote in favor of passage. The gains made in the political
arena by generations past in Montebello and elsewhere throughout
California now paid dividends: Armenian clout in the state smoothed
the way for the bill to fly through a typically cumbersome legislative
process within months without a single dissenting vote.[27]

Armed with this legislation, in the beginning of 2001 the plaintiffs'
team entered into settlement talks with the insurance company with
a boost of confidence. The legislation did little to pull the sides closer
on the remaining outstanding issues, however. Class certification still
loomed as a problem, and the issue of interest—the issue used to
calculate the value of the policies—remained a sticking point. Shernoff
offered a compromise borrowed from a model employed in Holocaust
cases from the 1990s calculating the policies at ten times their face
value.[28] The two sides continued to negotiate and finally reached a
deal—or so they thought.

On April 11, 2001, Kabateck, Shernoff, and New York Life issued
press releases announcing a $10 million settlement.[29] The next day, a

New York Times article included quotes from the insurer, Shernoff, and Kabateck.[30] Yeghiayan was conspicuously absent.

The deal fell through and it remains unclear exactly what happened.

Yeghiayan claimed that they had never agreed to a settlement during what he considered were preliminary talks. When he saw the insurer's press release, he said to himself, "Are you out of your fucking mind?" Kabateck, Shernoff, and New York Life all believed that Yeghiayan was on board after the meeting ended with the signing of a letter of intent, and issued the press releases accordingly. The Marootians rejected the deal, however, scuttling the lawyers' work. Believing his team tried to force the Marootians to sign off on a deal, Yeghiayan felt betrayed. The Marootians were equally angry at what they perceived were pressure tactics to force them to settle. In a *Los Angeles Times* article, Yeghiayan's fury spilled over in public. He scolded New York Life for offering a pittance, claiming that the interest accrued on the policies would total hundreds of millions, and confirmed that none of the twelve named plaintiffs supported the deal. At the end of a tumultuous few weeks in which the plaintiffs' team barely spoke to each other, Yeghiayan fired Kabateck and Shernoff.[31]

Yeghiayan's fourteen-year crusade was on the verge of collapse. His legal team was in shambles and he desperately needed new partners to push the case forward. His apparent retraction poisoned the relationship with New York Life, displacing the goodwill exhibited by both sides with bad blood.[32] And plenty of legal obstacles still hung over his head.

Regardless of who was at fault, the breakup of Yeghiayan's team drove him to invite Mark Geragos to replace Shernoff and Kabateck. Geragos (whose notoriety increased after representing Scott Peterson) was both an experienced litigator and media-savvy, the very factors Yeghiayan thought he needed to exert pressure on New York Life. Of Armenian descent, Geragos was no stranger to Genocide-related lawsuits. Alongside his father, he defended Hampig Sassounian, the man found guilty of murdering the Turkish consul Kemal Arikan back in 1982. He also had personal ties to the Marootians, who were close friends with Geragos's parents, and to Yeghiayan, who had once sublet office space from him.[33]

Things did not turn out as Yeghiayan had planned. Geragos realized that they needed Shernoff's and Kabateck's expertise in trying class actions and dealing with insurance suits, so he brought about a reconciliation. It also turned out that Kabateck's grandfather had officiated at the wedding of Geragos's parents. Building on this common background, the two hit it off. Kabateck moved his office to a space adjacent to Geragos's firm (they later moved into a building they purchased together in downtown Los Angeles) and teamed up on civil matters for Michael Jackson. "We have a door between our offices," Kabateck said of the relationship.[34]

No sooner was the legal team back together, though, than they had to face New York Life's motion to dismiss the case. The insurer argued that Poochigian's bill was unconstitutional and that the policies required the Marootians and others to file their cases in Europe. A hearing on the motion, which the judge had initially delayed in the hope that the parties would settle, was set for November 28, 2001. Yeghiayan stood isolated among his team and the motion to dismiss loomed large. The legislation, which was not binding on a federal court, could not guarantee victory.

On November 28, Yeghiayan made his way past four Doric columns to the entrance of the federal courthouse in downtown Los Angeles accompanied by an assistant. Built close to City Hall during the New Deal by an architect best known for constructing visitor facilities in national parks as well as a few federal courthouses, the fifteen-story tower rested atop a larger base. The post office once residing on the first floor had given way to additional courtrooms. The courthouse had seen its fair share of memorable cases, most notably paternity suits against Charlie Chaplin and Clark Gable, and another involving the Pentagon Papers.[35]

More nervous than on any other day of his career, Yeghiayan wore the fraying navy suit that had seen him through many victories in the slip-and-fall cases he typically handled. An Art Deco chandelier hanging above the entrance greeted him once he got past security. Above it stood a mural of four California condors. One wall depicted a Spanish map of Los Angeles. A medley of images—including a saber-tooth tiger, a Spanish monk, an American Indian, and a pack of conquistadors— from the area's history covered a second wall. Opposite stood a painting depicting the historic settlers of Los Angeles. Yeghiayan walked past the murals to an escalator to the second floor, where a large contingent of attorneys overflowed a tiny conference room located in the lawyers' lounge for one last round of talks. The judge granted them forty-five minutes to finalize a deal. Top lieutenants from the state attorney general's office tried to bridge the gap between the rival camps. (At the behest of the plaintiffs' team, both the state attorney general and the insurance commissioner had filed supporting amicus briefs.) When the attorneys arrived at a tentative agreement, they pushed a term sheet outlining the material elements of the proposed settlement over to Yeghiayan. After arguing with his team over what to do next, Yeghiayan rejected the deal. He knew the Marootians would never approve of the terms. "I'm not going to sign," Yeghiayan told the negotiators. "Let's go to court."[36]

Yeghiayan knew it was a gamble. It was unlikely that this suit would survive a challenge in court. His finances were depleted. At one point during the case, he had to hawk his wife's jewelry to pay the bills. Despite the risks, Yeghiayan felt he had to press on—for his father and for the Marootians, who had stuck with him through years of ups and downs. He knew a victory would not provide a complete resolution for the wrongs suffered by the Armenians; he knew that nothing could bring back the lost lives and mend the scars of shattered families; but having worked for underdog causes for thirty years, he appreciated the power of the law. It was a power he could wield to bring about the first ever accounting for the long-ignored tragedy.

As Yeghiayan walked to the courtroom a few steps away from the conference room, an attorney from the California Attorney General's office involved in the negotiations pulled Yeghiayan aside. "What if we lose?" he asked. "So we lose," Yeghiayan responded. "I have to get up every morning . . . and I can't look at myself in the mirror and say we were shortchanged." It was clear that if they lost now, Yeghiayan would receive all the blame. He never felt so alone in his life.

After entering Judge Christina A. Snyder's courtroom through a set of red doors with long handles, like the levers found in a bank vault, he placed his heavy litigation bag on the long wooden table facing the judge's bench and sat down. The granite floors and dark walls gave the spacious room a gloomy appearance. Yeghiayan waited impatiently, as did his wife sitting nearby. The Marootians sat in the audience behind him, and around them were dozens of Armenians whom Yeghiayan had invited. They too had placed their hopes on this case. As the people waited for the judge to take the bench, her clerk appeared from a side door and announced a startling development. In place of the scheduled preliminary hearing, the judge would instead issue a ruling. All of a sudden, Yeghiayan's heart raced faster. Hope and doubt flooded his thoughts. Was this the end, or would he snatch victory against the odds? The clerk passed out several copies of the decision. As if they had rehearsed the performance, the lawyers uniformly turned to the back of the thick decision, skipping to the outcome. Yeghiayan only wanted to see the last sentence. Isolated among his team and carrying the burden of defeat, he stretched over a colleague's shoulder to scan the opinion and read the magic words: "NYLIC's motion to dismiss . . . is hereby DENIED." Judge Snyder had rejected the insurer's strategy to move the lawsuit to European courts, and upheld the constitutionality of Poochigian's bill extending the statute of limitations. Yeghiayan did not need to see the judge's reasoning just yet. The emotions surging through him made it irrelevant at the moment. Instead, he leaned back in his chair and wept.[37]

The victory forced the insurer back to the negotiating table, but Shernoff believed that New York Life did not trust Yeghiayan after the 2001 debacle, and embittered by the collapse of the settlement, refused to alter its position. Plaintiffs' attorneys commonly used the press to incriminate opponents in the public eye. Framed articles blanketing the walls of Yeghiayan's office reflected the attacks he lodged at the insurer, undermining the company's public relations effort to uphold a positive image through the agonizing process. He had censured New York Life at public appearances, as when he appeared in Times Square for the April 24 commemoration of the Genocide in 2002, even leading a protest in front of the insurer's headquarters. Yeghiayan's public statements compounded the insurer's bitterness. To those questioning its negotiating position, New York Life defended its "generous settlement," which it claimed was "disaffirmed" after "earlier acceptance." Because New York Life budged only incrementally, Yeghiayan's team tried to move him closer to the insurer's offer.[38]

• • •

During the 1990s, Holocaust plaintiffs had forced entrenched Swiss banks into a settlement with the help of American regulators. Senate hearings on the banks' behavior publicly embarrassed the Swiss. New York's regulators threatened to divest the banks' shares from their hefty pension plans, terminate lucrative bond-underwriting relationships, and considered boycotting other Swiss companies. Other states contemplated similar measures. The regulators went further, threatening to derail a banking megamerger with billions hanging in the balance. Their efforts proved to be crucial; without them the lawyers could not have extracted a bountiful settlement.[39] Holocaust claimants also received assistance from Stuart Eizenstat, a White House envoy assigned to mediate the disputes.

When neither mediation efforts from two retired judges nor dozens of settlement talks budged the parties during 2002 and 2003, Yeghiayan's team could not muster the same political leverage against New York Life. Armenians simply lacked the clout to pull it off. The standoff compelled Geragos and Kabateck to turn for help from the only political force accessible to them. They asked California insurance commissioner John Garamendi to intervene. Garamendi had helped negotiate settlements arising from the Holocaust, and he agreed to personally oversee negotiations in this case rather than sending aides. Eventually, he flew to New York to meet with New York Life's chairman and CEO, Seymour Sternberg, to move discussions forward, and after two more rounds of talks among all the parties, they managed to break the deadlock. On January 28, 2004, the parties announced a settlement of $20 million, twice the face value of the 2001 deal.[40]

Some Armenians were disappointed by the amount of the settlement, but the lawsuit represented an unprecedented step in their decades-long pursuit of justice. This pursuit had seen little in material gains over the years. The establishment of the Genocide's authenticity was well underway but the Armenians had never received an iota of compensation, whether in land, reparations for lost lives, or return of property. Certainly, insurance payments were not reparations. And they did not come from Turkey. But they did represent the first ever compensation for Genocide-related losses. The significance of these payments cannot be underestimated. Fifty years earlier, when the Genocide had disappeared from the world's consciousness, such payments would have been impossible. The eruption of 1965 and the efforts that followed, from the baby steps taken at Montebello to the big-stakes battle in the nation's capital, paved the way for Yeghiayan, culminating in the first concrete recompense for the losses suffered by the Armenians.

Just as important, the lawsuit also uncovered a fountain of information on an era largely chronicled with broad strokes that left out individual voices and family histories. The list of policy holders—which included names, occupations, and residences—provided a record that could one day serve as a foundation to bring proper recognition to otherwise nameless victims lost to history. For so many Armenians who knew so little about their deceased ancestors, an occupational description—as insignificant as it may seem—shed some new light on those who perished. And for others, the discovery of an unknown relative came as a pleasant surprise, uncovering another layer of the past that for so long remained buried. It was this unanticipated glimpse into the past that so enraptured the Marootians about the lawsuit. Most of all, the case against New York Life symbolized the Armenian resolve to achieve justice against difficult odds even after nearly a century—a resolve best reflected by Vartkes Yeghiayan, who had been a foot soldier of the struggle since its resurrection in the 1960s.

Though vindicated, Yeghiayan remained unsatisfied. The settlement did not bring closure. Instead, it served as an opening step in that process. Age had not diminished the electricity Yeghiayan felt when he first read the passage in Morgenthau's book. The Berkeley-bred activist had finally found the underdog cause to dedicate his life to. With so much left to uncover from the Genocide era, he never celebrated the outcome, instead launching new suits against other insurers and banks with Kabateck and Geragos. At the end of this seventeen-year struggle, he realized that the Armenians were little closer to reconciliation with their tragic history. The ghosts of the past were still not at peace. Yeghiayan understood this perhaps better than anyone when he summed up the significance of the case: "This lawsuit proves anew that the past is not dead."[41]

Epilogue

History, despite its wrenching pain, cannot be un-
lived, but if faced with courage, need not be lived
again . . .

—Maya Angelou[1]

Senator Dole never got a rematch with Byrd before leaving the
Senate to run for president in 1996. Likewise, Van Krikorian
stayed on as a lobbyist but to no avail. Similar resolutions put
forth by Krikorian and others lost year after year, often never making
it out of Congress's Byzantine committees. Of all Krikorian's legislative
setbacks, Speaker Dennis Hastert's last-minute about-face in 2000 left
the largest wound. Moments before a Genocide resolution reached the
House floor, Hastert—influenced by a chilling warning from President
Bill Clinton that any harm to Americans in Turkey would fall on
Republican shoulders—scuttled the vote.[2]

An intriguing proposal from the American government followed the bitter defeat. Would Krikorian be willing to join track-two
discussions—the kind Palestinians and Israelis successfully deployed
in the 1990s—with Turkish representatives? Initially, Krikorian was
apprehensive about reconciliation talks proposed by the United States,
especially with a group led by Gündüz S. Aktan, a Turkish diplomat who had helped defeat Armenian legislative efforts in 2000. For
Krikorian—as for most Armenians—amicable relations could only
begin with Turkish contrition. After months of reflection, he began
to reconsider. Krikorian had dedicated so much of his life to bringing

about justice for the Armenians, efforts that had drained him emotionally and financially. Perhaps the time was ripe for a new approach. He told an American diplomat in charge of the endeavor:

> I found myself thinking of my kids. For a long time we have been doing this lobbying work. . . . When my kids grow up, are they going to be doing the same things, using the same strategies, and hitting the same brick walls? Or will something arise that changes the path they take . . . ? Armenians and Turks continue to be divided, whatever the divisions, they are clearly compounded by the lack of dialogue and direct contact.[3]

Under the auspices of a U.S. mediator, a handful of Turkish and Armenian officials convened the Turkish Armenian Reconciliation Commission (TARC) in 2001. Although the parties had agreed to discuss various issues, no conversation between Turks and Armenians could get very far without the Genocide taking center stage. With such diametrically opposed depictions of history compounded by years of distrust and name-calling, the parties' diplomatic demeanor sometimes spilled into anger.[4]

When a series of meetings ended in an impasse, both sides accepted the mediator's suggestion of asking the International Center for Transitional Justice (ICTJ) to judge whether the events of 1915 constituted genocide.[5] After holding evidentiary hearings in which the noted human rights expert Samantha Power testified on behalf of the Armenian position, the ICTJ classified the slaughter as genocide under international law.[6] Its ruling—the closest the two sides have ever come to a courtlike proceeding—confirmed the near-absolute consensus of the Genocide's authenticity.[7] Soon thereafter, the *Boston Globe* and the *New York Times* discarded the "on-the-one-hand, on-the-other-hand" approach they had long used and instituted a policy of declaratively using the term "genocide" to characterize what happened to the Armenians.[8] Turkey's machinery still chugged along, but denial had been rolled back. Few in academia, the media, or the American government took Turkey's position seriously anymore, a far cry from 1990, when the Genocide's veracity seemed in peril.

Despite the gains made in establishing the truth of the Genocide, maintenance of that truth required constant vigilance. Turkey created museums honoring the victims it claimed had died at the hands of Armenian-led massacres. Turkish-Americans staged their own April 24 protests in the United States, turning the annual Armenian commemorations into shouting matches of divergent viewpoints. Turkish-Americans also supported a lawsuit against educators in Massachusetts for removing Turkey's viewpoint from the state's curriculum on the Genocide. The moves represented new wrinkles on old tactics; but to neutral observers who knew little about the controversy, they succeeded in obfuscating the truth.

The American government also continued to adhere to Turkey's wishes. The State Department fired the ambassador to Armenia for uttering the "g-word" in 2006. A year later, another legislative effort acknowledging the Genocide faltered in the U.S. Congress.[9] Its outcome proceeded like a passion play. None of its opponents cast doubt on the historical record, but everyone from President George W. Bush—in a last-minute plea on the White House lawn—to eight former secretaries of state decried the resolution's impact on U.S.-Turkish relations.[10] Though not nearly as eloquent, it was as if they were borrowing words right out of Senator Byrd's mouth. Like other politicians in the past, former House majority leader Richard Gephardt, once an avid supporter of Armenian resolutions, made an about-face as a lobbyist for Turkey. As in 1990, the American Jewish community also struggled with the issue. The Anti-Defamation League fired its New England regional director for disagreeing with the institution's failure to acknowledge the Genocide. Two board members resigned, and after much hand-wringing and internal debate, the League's national director admitted that the events of 1915 were "tantamount to genocide."[11]

Notwithstanding Bush's avoidance of the "g-word," the semantic gymnastics used to characterize what happened to the Armenians described the catastrophe as a genocide in all but name. In June 2008, for example, Bush's appointee to become the next ambassador to Armenia acknowledged the "mass killings and forced exile of as many as 1.5 million Armenians at the end of the Ottoman Empire" in response to questions from the Senate.[12] Again, the U.S. ambassador-designate to Turkey, James Jeffrey, affirmed a few months later that there was "an

attempt to exterminate the Armenian population" during the Ottoman era.[13]

Turkey's attempts to block similar legislative efforts abroad were
not as successful as in the United States. In the past ten years, nations
as politically and geographically diverse as France, Poland, Argentina,
and Canada passed some sort of legislative acknowledgment of the
Genocide, sometimes in the face of dire threats from the Turkish
government.

These resolutions isolated Turkey politically and were intended to
pressure it to acknowledge the Genocide. Ultimately, however, for the
Armenians to receive the justice they so desire, Turkey will have to take
an honest look at its past, no matter how unnerving. Turkish admission
of Ottoman crimes, if extracted through political leverage—an unlikely
scenario at this point—would be insincere, and might leave the Turkish
population thinking that power, not justice, prevailed. Only a sincere apology, perhaps combined with reparations, changes to Turkey's
educational curriculum, and other measures, will give the Armenians
peace. In some sense, however, waiting for Turkish contrition empow-
ers Turkey and reaffirms the perpetrator-victim relationship of the past.

Certainly, Turkey is not the foremost nation to have difficulty own-
ing up to its past. Japan struggles to acknowledge its stained human
rights record in World War II. A majority of Serbians reject any accusations of ethnic cleansing in the Balkans during the 1990s. The list goes
on and on. Turkey is not alone. But it is the foremost nation mounting
such a comprehensive campaign of historical distortion, and in so
doing, trying to cover up a crime of apocalyptic dimensions.

Turkey's policy continues for much the same reasons as it began.
First, there are the material reasons. There is a fear that admission of
the Genocide will reawaken the frightening territorial claims Turkey
tried to put to rest at the 1923 Treaty of Lausanne. Many Turks are still
convinced that the world is out to get them—to cut their country into
pieces just as the World War I victors tried to undertake in the 1920
Treaty of Sèvres. Armenian accusations feed into this fear. Avowal of
the Genocide might open the door to reparations and invite individuals
to make claims for confiscated property. The sociological reasons also
remain. Turkey has maintained a noble narrative of a nation born from
a defense against European imperialism. Its selective memory excludes

episodes that might tarnish this image. The Genocide threatens to undermine the narrative by thrusting an ugly and bloody reality into the country's creation story. If one pillar of that creation story crumbles, then all the others might topple, and with them the Turkish state. This is a real and genuine fear among Turkey's governing class.

Turkey's selective memory lies at the root of the problem for Armenians, however. Turkey wants to forget an event that resides at the center of the Armenian spirit. Its stance not only covers up a crime but dismisses Armenian memories of suffering as false, trivial, and misplaced. Only a position consistent with these memories will satisfy Armenians.

There is also a modern element to Turkey's stance that was not present in earlier decades. The systematic dismissal of Armenian charges since 1965 has made it much harder for Turkey to fess up to the truth. Its lie, uttered repeatedly and backed by dubious scholarship and a public relations campaign, has grown into a monster. To go back now and admit that not only were the Armenians correct but Turkey was lying to the world and its people all this time makes it that much harder to swallow the bitter pill of truth. Such a sudden about-face by Turkey will shock its population, undoing years of dogmatic teachings. It is the equivalent of an adult child learning that her father had led a double life. The man who had nurtured, provided for, and loved that child turned out to be a fraud. In this case, he turns out not only to be a cheat and liar but a murderer. The prospect of an entire nation simultaneously undergoing the same experience is fraught with danger. The Turkish government may believe that it needs to gradually inure its population to the harsh reality of the Genocide before full acknowledgment.

In that light, due to domestic liberalization and pressure from the European Union, which Turkey hopes to join, the once monolithic response to the Genocide has begun to crumble in recent years, albeit in tiny increments. Though the Turkish government has stuck to its position, notable contemporary intellectuals like the Nobel Prize winner Orhan Pamuk and various scholars have questioned Turkish orthodoxy on the issue. Turks are producing memoirs of Armenian grandparents who were kidnapped during the Genocide. In doing so, they are revealing what had long been a secret in Turkey: that many Armenians were forcibly kidnapped or taken away from their families and brought up as Turks. An academic conference in 2005 included open discussion of the

Genocide on Turkish soil for the first time. In 2008, two hundred Turkish intellectuals launched an online petition apologizing to the Armenians that was signed by thousands of Turks. None of these unprecedented steps came easily. Pamuk and others were prosecuted and harassed for questioning the official line; the proposed conference was twice canceled. The petition's authors became the target of recriminations from the government. And Hrant Dink, a Turkish journalist of Armenian descent who wrote about the Genocide, was murdered in 2007.

Even if Turkey is willing to offer an apology and negotiate some type of reparations, many roadblocks remain. Who will represent the Armenians in any negotiation? What these measures will look like, and how satisfied Armenians will be with any negotiated resolution, is a quagmire with no easy solution.

The Turkish Armenian Reconciliation Commission ran into this problem from its inception. Some Armenians argued that no single entity or self-selected group should speak on behalf of the Armenians spanning the globe. Some critics claimed the commission was a ruse to reduce international pressure on Turkey, allowing Turkey to tell the United States and the European Union that it was finally engaging the Armenians after years of stonewalling. Others still considered the idea of speaking to the Turks without first receiving an acknowledgment an anathema.

The same issues erupted when Turkey's president visited Armenia for the first time in 2008, initiating new bilateral talks of better relations. Armenians wondered whether this was a Turkish ploy to relieve the international pressure that the Armenians had struggled so hard to mount since 1965 or a sincere step forward in Turkish-Armenian relations. Often, this tension divides Armenia and the Diaspora. Armenia, a fledgling, landlocked post-Communist state freed from the Soviet Union in 1991, struggles with a disastrous economy and a declining population of less than 3 million. It desires open borders, economic trade, and diplomatic ties with Turkey. It certainly wants Turkey to acknowledge the Genocide, but it places no preconditions on establishing normal relations with Turkey. And Armenia does not aid Diasporan groups pushing for legislative resolutions. As a nation hobbled by many problems, the Genocide does not monopolize its foreign policy.

For those in the Diaspora, however, the Genocide remains the leading political issue. Many want to see Turkish acknowledgment and perhaps even reparations before establishing relations. Just how this dynamic will work out is difficult to predict. For any resolution to work, however, it must be satisfactory to the vast majority of the world's Armenians.

Few survivors remain, but their descendants carry an anguish that has lodged itself at the center of the Armenian soul. The story of the Genocide has now become deeply entrenched in Armenian collective memory. The nearly century-long battle with Turkey has focused Armenian attention on the Genocide more than any other aspect of their long history. The intense embrace of this event has manifested itself in countless ways. In many parts of the Diaspora, legislative bills similar to the ones championed by Senator Dole have become focal points of political mobilization. The Genocide has also begun to overshadow art and culture. For too long, Armenian artists failed to tackle the Genocide in their work—the one major exception being Michael J. Arlen's memoir in 1975. More than two decades passed before Peter Balakian produced *Black Dog of Fate,* his ground-breaking memoir exploring the aftermath of the Genocide. Since then, writers, artists, and filmmakers have used the catastrophe as the backdrop of their work, even in the unlikeliest of places. System of a Down, a heavy metal group established by Armenian-Americans, for instance, regularly advocates on behalf of Genocide recognition.

It is fair to ask whether the Genocide's omnipresence in Armenian life has turned into an unhealthy obsession. Certainly, Armenians do not need the Genocide to establish their identity. But they rarely engage the outside world otherwise, especially with anything close to the intensity attached to the Genocide. They are right to demand a reckoning of the crimes committed against them. But is this what they want to be identified with so closely: a people clinging to a tragic past?

Part of this process is natural, as groups—including Jews, African-Americans, and others—tend to seize onto heartbreaking episodes from the past. And younger generations, in an attempt to identify with a group, often rely on their communal victimization as a means to secure membership in a heritage from which they have been cut off through assimilation. As other outlets of cultural identity lose their appeal, the darkest, saddest episodes of the past often come to define membership in a group.

Building such a cultural identity has consequences, however. Descendants of survivors live with the overbearing guilt of having to perpetuate the race. It is as if an Armenian must marry within the tribe and propagate out of an obligation to defeat the monsters of a bygone age.[14] The Ottomans failed to exterminate the Armenians; let not their ghosts claim victory through assimilation. But in following this imperative to keep the race alive, Armenians define themselves not on their own terms but by the decades-old brutality of their persecutors.

Otherwise divided by geography and assimilation, Armenians have too often relied upon their common, tragic past, rather than their future, to bring them together. Sadly, in clinging to this catastrophe, taking pride in their victimization, and glorifying their survival, Armenians perpetually carry the suffering of their ancestors. They spend a great deal of time and energy trying to preserve the pre-Genocide past rather than redefining themselves for the modern world. It would be both harmful and impossible for Armenians to exorcise the memory of the Genocide. Collective amnesia is certainly not the answer. Nonetheless, they must be careful not to grant the Genocide an overwhelming place in their culture.

This is, of course, easier said than done. As long as Armenians are denied justice, it will be impossible for them to begin the healing process and confine the Genocide to its rightful place in a history dating back to the first millennium B.C. Truth has to win out for this to take place. In this light, Krikorian teamed up with Dr. Rouben Adalian and others to develop the Armenian Genocide Museum of America. Located two blocks from the White House, it is scheduled to open no earlier than 2010, and will serve as a beacon of education and warning against the cost of impunity.

After the New York Life settlement, Yeghiayan rejoined Kabateck and Geragos on additional lawsuits. French insurer AXA settled with Yeghiayan, et al., for $17.5 million in 2005. But Deutsche Bank, sued for the alleged use of slave labor, looted assets, and uncollected deposits related to the Genocide, was not so willing to negotiate. Unlike New York Life, it declined to hand over any documents, leading to an entrenched legal battle. The judge presiding over the case removed the bank's attorneys, among the most prominent law firms in the nation, for violating legal procedures. In another twist, the Turkish ambassador wrote a letter to the judge criticizing her for employing the term "Armenian Genocide." The same judge issued a ruling dismissing a significant portion of the plaintiffs' claims.[15]

Other cases also moved at a snail's pace typical to litigation. For Yeghiayan, it was never fast enough. He kept searching for plaintiffs holding on to long-forgotten documents. And he continued to explore new legal avenues to exhume a past that stubbornly wanted to stay buried. Past his seventieth birthday, it was as if he was in a hurry to uncover as much as possible before retirement—voluntary or otherwise—kicked in.

His love of history led him to another pursuit. He began publishing several Genocide-related books, basically compendiums of documents, transcripts, and other primary materials. One covered Soghomon Tehlirian's trial. Another dealt with Raphael Lemkin, the father of human rights law whose inspiration for the field arose from the Armenian Genocide. A third unveiled a host of previously unpublished documents relating to Vahan Cardashian.

Meanwhile, his quest to learn more about his father's past proceeded in fits and starts. With the passing of Boghos's fellow survivors, Yeghiayan's main source of information had dried up. Yet, tidbits still trickled in. A long-lost second cousin from Belgium who found Yeghiayan after seeing his name in the press revealed that Boghos changed his last name from Kevorkian to Yeghiayan in memory of his father—whose name was Yeghia.[16] The change must have been more than a sentimental nod to his father. It initiated a complete transformation in Boghos—a chance to completely start over with a new identity—that led to the concealment of his past from all but his fellow survivors.

In an office suite that he calls the "Asset Recovery Center," Yeghiayan's twin passions of history and law converge. A map of Anatolia on the wall lists major Armenian population centers and the estimated value of their assets (schools, churches, etc.) designated in tiny symbols.

Each of the dots on the map points to a potential lawsuit. But without documents like Marootian's insurance policy, additional legal acrobatics, and financing, these cases will never be filed.

When I visited Yeghiayan in 2007, he pointed to his father's hometown on the map. Compared to cities with large Armenian populations, it only has a few dots. Why would anyone want to harm this little town? he asked. Then he began to weep. Still crying, he took out his parents' wedding invitation. Yeghiayan's niece recently turned up the document from family boxes no one had looked at for years. It revealed to Yeghiayan once again the totality of the loss suffered by the Armenians. As is typical in invitations, his maternal grandparents were listed as invitees. His father, though, had no parents. "These orphans—who was giving away the survivors? They had no one," Yeghiayan said, barely getting the words out between sobs. Ten minutes elapsed and still the sobbing did not stop. Yeghiayan's father had kept so much inside to shield his sons from suffering as he did. When they were children, it worked, and for this Yeghiayan was grateful. But it seemed that no matter how hard Boghos tried, circumstances would not allow his children to live beyond the shadow of the Genocide.

Nearly a century after Boghos and hundreds of thousands of others watched their families perish, nearly a century after the survivors spent so much energy rebuilding their lives that they hardly had time to mourn, their children—the children of Armenia—are still waiting for justice to prevail.

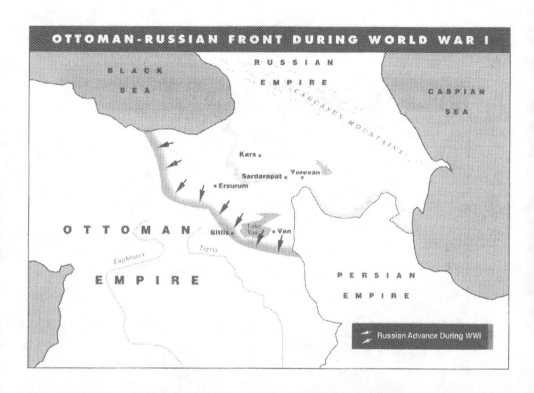

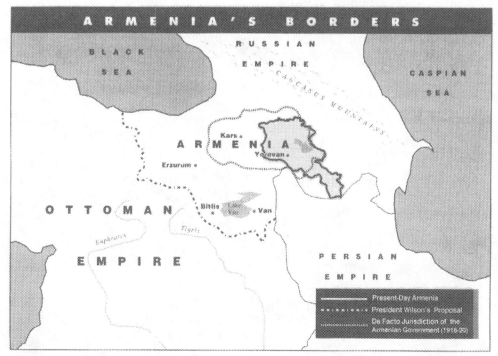

PRESENT-DAY ARMENIA

RUSSIA

GEORGIA

○ Tiflis

AZERBAIJAN

ARMENIA

Lake Sevan

○ Yerevan

TURKEY

AZERBAIJAN

IRAN

List of Characters

Genocide and Post–World War I Eras

Avetis Aharonian—Represented the Armenian Republic at the post–World War I peace talks. Signed Treaty of Sèvres in 1920 memorializing promises made to the Armenian Republic by war's victors.

Mark L. Bristol—As an U.S. admiral stationed in the Ottoman Empire, he rejected calls for the establishment of an independent Armenian state. In the 1920s and 1930s, he strengthened ties between the United States and Turkey.

Vahan Cardashian—Leading Armenian-American activist advocating for the Armenians in the 1910s and 1920s.

Allen W. Dulles—As head of the Near East desk at the State Department during the 1920s, worked with Bristol to establish a pro-Turkish foreign policy.

Armen Garo—Led the 1896 takeover of the Ottoman Bank. After World War I, he coordinated agents of Operation Nemesis assigned to eliminate the perpetrators of the Genocide.

Sultan Abdul Hamid—Leader of the Ottoman Empire responsible for massacring the Armenian population in the 1890s.

Charles Evans Hughes—Once a leading supporter of Armenians in the United States after World War I. As secretary of state in the 1920s, he could not uphold the promises of assistance made to them.

Henry Morgenthau, Sr.—As U.S. ambassador to the Ottoman Empire during the Genocide, made repeated pleas to the Genocide's ringleaders to stop the slaughter. The account of his experience recorded in a memoir became an important Genocide testimonial for later generations.

Boghos Nubar—Represented Armenians at the post–World War I peace talks as the envoy of the Catholicos (chief cleric of the Armenian Church).

Mehmet Talaat—A member of the ruling elite of the Ottoman Empire during World War I and one of the chief architects of the Genocide.

Soghomon Tehlirian—Assassinated Mehmet Talaat in 1921 as part of Operation Nemesis.

Simon Vratsian—Last prime minister of the Armenian Republic.

Woodrow Wilson—During his presidency, supported the establishment of a mandate by the United States over the Armenian Republic.

Krikor Zohrab—An Armenian member of the Ottoman Parliament murdered during the opening stages of the Genocide.

Truman Doctrine

Dean Acheson—As under secretary and secretary of state, developed close ties between the United States and Turkey in the 1940s and 1950s. He also rejected calls for transfer of portions of eastern Turkey to Soviet Armenia after World War II.

Harry S. Truman—Along with Dean Acheson, established the Truman Doctrine that led to a close alliance between the United States and Turkey.

Montebello Monument

Michael Minasian—Led efforts to build a Genocide monument in Montebello, California, in the 1960s. He later helped raised money for Gourgen Yanikian's legal defense fund.

Gourgen Yanikian Trial

James T. Lindsey—Gourgen Yanikian's chief defense lawyer.

David D. Minier—Prosecutor of Gourgen Yanikian.

Gourgen Mkrtich Yanikian—Murdered two Turkish diplomats in Santa Barbara in 1973, triggering more than a decade of Armenian terrorism.

Legislative Resolutions

Rouben P. Adalian—A scholar at an Armenian-American lobbying and advocacy group who worked with Senator Robert J. Dole to try to pass a congressional resolution affirming the Genocide in 1989–90.

Robert C. Byrd—Chief opponent in the Senate to Senator Dole's resolution.

George Deukmejian—Armenian-American governor of California who advocated for passage of Dole's resolution.

Robert J. Dole—Senator who championed congressional resolution affirming the Genocide in 1989–90.

Hampar Kelikian—Doctor who conducted several operations on Dole's war-torn arm after World War II that led to a lifelong friendship with the senator. He was the first person to tell Dole about the Genocide.

Van Z. Krikorian—Armenian-American lobbyist advocating for passage of Dole's resolution.

Linda Melconian—Armenian-American congressional aide of Thomas "Tip" P. O'Neill, Jr., who helped pass 1975 House resolution affirming the Genocide.

Thomas P. "Tip" O'Neill, Jr.—Sponsored House resolution affirming the Genocide in 1975.

Charles Pashayan—Armenian-American congressman from California advocating for passage of Dole's resolution.

Brent Scowcroft—As national security adviser serving under President George H. W. Bush, he was the point man in the administration opposing Dole's resolution.

New York Life Insurance Case

Mark J. Geragos—Represented plaintiffs in first class action lawsuit arising from the Genocide.

Brian Kabateck—Represented plaintiffs in first class action lawsuit arising from the Genocide.

Martin Marootian—Inherited New York Life insurance policy later used to file first ever class action lawsuit arising from the Genocide.

William Shernoff—Represented plaintiffs in first class action lawsuit arising from the Genocide.

Boghos Yeghiayan—Father of Vartkes Yeghiayan, he kept his experience of survival during the Genocide a secret from his son.

Vartkes Yeghiayan—Among the first activists to lead Genocide-related protests in California. In the 1990s, he filed the first ever class action lawsuit arising from the Genocide against the New York Life Insurance Company.

Abbreviations and
Bibliographical Notes

....

ABBREVIATIONS

Archives

GHWB	President George H. W. Bush Library
GRF	President Gerald R. Ford Library
RWR	President Ronald W. Reagan Library
RJD	Robert J. Dole Archive, University of Kansas
CH	Chester E. Holifield Papers, Regional History Collection 220, Special Collections, University of Southern California, Los Angeles
TPO	Thomas "Tip" P. O'Neill, Jr., Archive, John J. Burns Library, Boston College
MLB	Mark L. Bristol Papers, Library of Congress
AD	Avedis Derounian Papers, National Association for Armenian Scholars and Research
SD-RG 59	U.S. State Department, Records Group 59, National Archives
SD-63/73 POL	U.S. State Department, Subject Numeric Files, February 1963–June 1973, Political Affairs and Relations, National Archives
SD-63/73 CUL	U.S. State Department, Subject Numeric Files, February 1963–June 1973, Cultural Activities, National Archives
SD-ER	U.S. State Department, State Archiving System, July 1973–December 1975, Electronic Records, National Archives
DOJ-FARU	Department of Justice, Foreign Agents Registration Unit

AFOAM   American Friends of Armenian Martyrs (Gourgen Yanikian Legal Defense Fund) Papers

Court Records

GY-T   *California v. Gourgen Yanikian* (Trial Transcript)

GY-CM   *California v. Gourgen Yanikian* (Case Materials)

GY-I   Federal Bureau of Investigation—investigation of Gourgen Yanikian

MM-CM   *Marootian, et al., v. New York Life Insurance Company* (Case Materials)

Interviews

RPA   Dr. Rouben P. Adalian

JMH   Dr. J. Michael Hagopian

RGH   Dr. Richard G. Hovannisian

RAK   Robert A. Kaloosdian

LK   Levon Kirakosian

OK   Osheen Keshishian

VZK   Van Z. Krikorian

SMM   Seda and Martin Marootian

LJM   Hon. Linda J. Melconian

MM   Michael Minasian

DDM   Hon. David D. Minier

DRP   Dr. Dennis R. Papazian

RV   Ross Vartian

VY   Vartkes Yeghiayan

Newspapers

AMS   *Armenian Mirror-Spectator*

AR   *Armenian Reporter*

AW   *Armenian Weekly*

CC   *California Courier*

HW   *Hairenik Weekly*

BIBLIOGRAPHICAL NOTES

Unless otherwise noted, government records were retrieved from the National Archives, College Park, Maryland, branch, and the Department of Justice. All other archival records from the U.S. government originated from Freedom of Information Act (FOIA) requests. The transcript of Gourgen Yanikian's trial was provided by Judge David D. Minier. Materials related to the case originating from an FBI investigation as well as State Department records unavailable at the National Archives were obtained through an FOIA request. Sarkis Keochekian provided materials from Yanikian's defense committee. I interviewed several people on multiple occasions, sometimes in person, sometimes over the phone. I also sent and received correspondence from these same sources. In all instances, I have grouped all of these communications as "Interview with——." All *Congressional Record* citations after 1988 come from the Library of Congress THOMAS Web site: http://thomas.loc.gov/. As a result, I have excluded the volume number in the citation to these references. The pagination from THOMAS differs slightly from the printed volumes of the *Congressional Record*. I have tried to keep my citations as brief as possible, removing all titles—"Secretary of State," "President," etc.—from the citations: Gordon P. Merriam to John Foster Dulles instead of Gordon P. Merriam to Secretary of State John Foster Dulles.

In citing Armenian-American periodicals, I have included only the name of the publication and the date. I also omitted citations for well-known or uncontroversial facts. For names with variations—Girair or Jirair or Gerard—I have selected one version throughout the book to avoid confusion. For names of cities, I have used the names corresponding to the time in which I refer to them—Constantinople in the 1800s, Istanbul after the 1920s (see below). For cities with Turkish, Armenian, English, and other variations—i.e., Erzerum, Erzeroum, Erzurum, Karin—I have selected the version found in the World Atlas edition of MSN Encarta unless used in a citation or a quote.

An additional note about city names:

Aleppo is known as Halab in Arabic

Der Zor is known as Dayr az Zawr in Arabic

Erzingan is presently Erzincan

Kharput is presently Elazığ

Salonica is commonly known as Thessaloniki

Sasun is presently Sason

Smyrna is presently İzmir

Tiflis is presently Tbilisi

Trebizond is presently Trabzon

Urfa is presently Şanlrurfa

Notes

Prologue: Memories

1. GY-I.
2. Ibid.
3. Ibid; GY-T.
4. Ibid.
5. Appellant's Opening Brief, California Court of Appeal, Second Appellate District, January 17, 1974, GY-CM (hereafter cited as Appellant's Opening Brief, GY-CM); GY-T.
6. Ibid.
7. Christopher J. Walker, *Armenia: The survival of a nation*, 2nd ed. (New York: St. Martin's Press, 1990), 151–64; Razmik Panossian, *The Armenians: From kings and priests to merchants and commissars* (New York: Columbia University Press, 2006), 219; Lord Kinross, *The Ottoman centuries: The rise and fall of the Turkish Empire* (New York: William Morrow, 1977), 560; "Another Armenian Holocaust," *New York Times*, September 10, 1895.
8. Appellant's Opening Brief, GY-CM; GY-T.
9. Ibid.; "Wholesale massacres of Armenians by Turks," *New York Times*, July 29, 1915.
10. Richard G. Hovannisian, "Armenia's road to independence," in *The Armenian people from ancient to modern times: Foreign dominion to statehood: The fifteenth century to the twentieth century*, ed. Richard G. Hovannisian (New York: St. Martin's Press, 1997), 2:281; Sarkis Atamian, *The Armenian Community: The historical development of a social and ideological conflict* (New York: Philosophical Library, 1955), 199–201; Appellant's Opening Brief, GY-CM; GY-T. One hundred fifty thousand Russian-Armenians fighting in the Russian army and a few thousand Ottoman-Armenians organized in volunteer units fought in World War I; see Panossian, *Armenians*, 223; Taner Akçam, *A Shameful act: The Armenian Genocide and the question of Turkish responsibility*, trans. Paul Bessemer (New York: Metropolitan Books, 2006), 139.
11. Appellant's Opening Brief, GY-CM; GY-T.
12. Ibid.
13. Peter Balakian, *The Burning Tigris: The Armenian Genocide and America's response* (New York: HarperCollins, 2003), 303.

14. Charles Aznavour (author), Georges Garvarentz (composer), and Herbert Kretzmer (adapter), "Ils Sont Tombés," trans. provided by Charles Aznavour.

15. The document can be found at the International Association of Genocide Scholars Web site, http://www.genocidescholars.org/.

16. The document can be found at the Armenian National Institute Web site, http://www.armenian-genocide.org/.

Death of a Nation

1. Vahan Tekeyan, *Ges-Kisheren Minchev Arshaloys* (Paris: Veradsnunt, 1919), 19.

2. Haigazn K. Kazarian, "The murder of 6 Armenian members of the Ottoman parliament," *Armenian Review* 22, no. 4 (1970): 26–31; "The case of deputy Krikor Zohrab: His letters from exile, his odyssey, and circumstances of his death," *Armenian Review* 35, no. 1 (1982): 4–6, 11–17, 22, 26–29. The details of Zohrab's death remain murky but there is no doubt that Ottoman authorities arranged for his murder just outside of Urfa.

3. Caroline Finkel, *Osman's dream: The story of the Ottoman Empire, 1300–1923* (New York: Basic Books, 2006), 2; Colin Imber, *The Ottoman Empire, 1300–1650: The structure of power* (New York: Palgrave Macmillan, 2002), ix.

4. Walker, *Armenia*, 89; Bernard Lewis, *The Emergence of modern Turkey* (London: Oxford University Press, 1962), 23–29; Kinross, *Ottoman centuries*, 255, 260, 616; Donald Bloxham, "Determinants of the Armenian Genocide," in *Looking backward, moving forward: Confronting the Armenian Genocide*, ed. Richard G. Hovannisian (New Brunswick, NJ: Transaction Publishers, 2003), 24–25; Taner Akçam, *From Empire to Republic: Turkish nationalism and the Armenian Genocide* (London: Zed Books, 2004), 67–92.

5. Edwin Pears, *Life of Abdul Hamid* (London: Constable & Co., 1917), 107–10; Finkel, *Osman's dream*, 489; Balakian, *Burning Tigris*, 47–48; "Peace in the Harem," *Time*, April 29, 1935.

6. Walker, *Armenia*, 19–25.

7. Hester D. Jenkins, "Armenia and the Armenians," *The National Geographic Magazine* (October 1915): 329.

8. Ibid., 328; Ara Baliozian, ed., *Armenia observed* (New York: Ararat Press, 1979), 6.

9. Benjamin F. Alexander, "Armenian and American: The changing face of ethnic identity and Diasporic nationalism, 1915–1955," PhD diss., City University of New York, 2005, 19.

10. Walker, *Armenia*, 19–45; Panossian, *Armenians*, 35, 51, 67.

11. Walker, *Armenia*, 52–54.

12. Panossian, *Armenians*, 153–59; Lewis, *Modern Turkey*, 350; Robert Mirak, *Torn between two lands: Armenians in America, 1890 to World War I* (Cambridge, MA: Harvard University Press, 1983), 8, 17; Fatma Müge Göçek, "Turkish historiography and the unbearable weight of 1915," in *The Armenian Genocide: Cultural and ethical legacies*, ed. Richard G. Hovannisian (New Brunswick, NJ: Transaction Publishers, 2007), 345.

13. Balakian, *Burning Tigris*, 42.

14. Christopher J. Walker, *Visions of Ararat: Writings on Armenia* (London: I. B. Tauris & Co., 1997), 33.

15. Henry A. Kissinger, *Diplomacy* (New York: Touchstone, 1995), 152–53; Göçek, "Turkish historiography," 347–49; Walker, *Armenia*, 64–67, 90–91, 94–96, 108–17, 123–25; Panossian, *Armenians*, 169–71; Nicole Pope and Hugh Pope, *Turkey*

unveiled: A history of modern Turkey (Woodstock, NY: Overlook Press, 1998), 32–33; Richard G. Hovannisian, "Etiology and sequelae of the Armenian Genocide," in *Genocide: Conceptual and historical dimensions,* ed. George J. Andreopoulos (Philadelphia: University of Pennsylvania Press, 1994), 119; Şefika Akile Zorlu-Durukan, "The Ideological pillars of Turkish education: Emergent Kemalism and the zenith of single-party rule," PhD diss., University of Wisconsin–Madison, 2006, 26.

16. Kinross, *Ottoman centuries,* 555–56.
17. Walker, *Armenia,* 85–173; Balakian, *Burning Tigris,* 54–60, 110–11; Kinross, *Ottoman centuries,* 555–56.
18. Armen Garo, *Bank Ottoman: Memoirs of Armen Garo,* trans. Haig T. Partizian (Detroit: Armen Topouzian, 1990), 104; Panossian, *Armenians,* 205, 208; Louise Nalbandian, *The Armenian revolutionary movement: The development of Armenian political parties through the nineteenth century* (Berkeley: University of California Press, 1975), 170; Hovannisian, "Etiology and sequelae," 119; Balakian, *Burning Tigris,* 104.
19. Garo, *Bank Ottoman,* 108–21, 125, 132–36; Balakian, *Burning Tigris,* 103–6.
20. Balakian, *Burning Tigris,* 105–11; Nalbandian, *Armenian revolutionary movement,* 178; Kinross, *Ottoman centuries,* 562; Chalmers Roberts, "A mother of martyrs," *Atlantic Monthly* (January 1899): 90–96. The negotiation included safe passage for Garo's group to Marseilles.
21. Göçek, "Turkish historiography," 342–44; Balakian, *Burning Tigris,* 113; Hovannisian, "Etiology and sequelae," 120–21.
22. Balakian, *Burning Tigris,* 135–37, 143–44; Pope and Pope, *Turkey unveiled,* 39.
23. Balakian, *Burning Tigris,* 153–54.
24. Ibid., 159; Jacques Derogy, *Resistance and revenge: The Armenian assassination of the Turkish leaders responsible for the 1915 massacres and deportations,* trans. A. M. Berrett (New Brunswick, NJ: Transaction Publishers, 1990), 5–7; Kinross, *Ottoman centuries,* 596; Henry Morgenthau, *Ambassador Morgenthau's story,* memorial ed. (Plandome, NY: New Age Publishers, n.d.), 21, 282; "Mr. Morgenthau's Reminiscences," *New York Times,* April 28, 1918.
25. Finkel, *Osman's dream,* xxiv. Bulgaria had largely been autonomous since 1878 but gained its complete independence from the Ottoman Empire in 1908.
26. Vahakn N. Dadrian, *The history of the Armenian Genocide: Ethnic conflict from the Balkans to Anatolia to the Caucasus,* 2nd ed. (Providence: Berghahn Books, 1997), 193; Akçam, *Shameful act,* 84–87, 115; Akçam, *Empire to Republic,* 76–100; Lewis, *Modern Turkey,* 38; Bedross Der Matossian, "Venturing into the minefield: Turkish liberal historiography and the Armenian Genocide," in *The Armenian Genocide,* ed. Hovannisian, 373, 375.
27. Akçam, *Shameful act,* 71–72.
28. Kinross, *Ottoman centuries,* 584; Morgenthau, *Ambassador Morgenthau's story,* 284; Hovannisian, "Etiology and sequelae," 122–23.
29. Kinross, *Ottoman centuries,* 584.
30. Morgenthau, *Ambassador Morgenthau's story,* 274–92; Hovannisian, "Etiology and sequelae," 123; Akçam, *Shameful act,* 54–55, 101; Akçam, *Empire to Republic,* 85; Robert Melson, "Revolutionary genocide: On the causes of the Armenian Genocide of 1915 and the Holocaust," *Holocaust and Genocide Studies* 4, no. 2 (1989): 168.
31. Pope and Pope, *Turkey unveiled,* 40.
32. Dikran M. Kaligian, *Armenian organization and ideology under Ottoman rule, 1908–1914* (New Brunswick, NJ: Transaction Publishers, 2009), 2, 7–8, 121; Garo, *Bank Ottoman,* 10–13, 15, 182–92; Panossian, *Armenians,* 209, 223–24, 234–36; Morgenthau, *Ambassador Morgenthau's story,* 282; Akçam, *Shameful act,* 67; Hovannisian, "Etiology and sequelae," 121.

33. Morgenthau, *Ambassador Morgenthau's story*, 302; Ronald G. Suny, *Looking toward Ararat: Armenia in modern history* (Bloomington, IN: Indiana University Press, 1993), 109; Akçam, *Shameful act*, 121, 125, 143–44; Balakian, *Burning Tigris*, 167–70, 178, 184–85.
34. *AR*, April 21, 2001.
35. Balakian, *Burning Tigris*, 211–16; Pope and Pope, *Turkey unveiled*, 42; Edward Alexander, *A Crime of vengeance: An Armenian struggle for justice* (New York: The Free Press, 1991), 43–45.
36. "Appeal to Turkey to stop massacres," *New York Times*, April 28, 1915; "Morgenthau intercedes," *New York Times*, April 29, 1915; Morgenthau, *Ambassador Morgenthau's story*, 338; Vahakn N. Dadrian, "Children as victims of genocide: the Armenian case," Paper presented at the International Association of Genocide Scholars, Galway, Ireland, June 6–10, 2003.
37. Marjorie Housepian, "The Unremembered genocide," *Commentary* 42, no. 3 (1966), 57; Akçam, *Shameful act*, 160–61, 164, 168, 172; Heinrich Vierbücher, *Armenia 1915: What the German Imperial Government concealed from its subjects: The slaughter of a civilized people at the hands of the Turks* (Arlington, MA: Armenian Cultural Foundation, 2006), 52; Morgenthau, *Ambassador Morgenthau's story*, 332; Walker, *Armenia*, 197–237; Balakian, *Burning Tigris*, 175–298; Dadrian, "Children as victims."
38. Arnold J. Toynbee, *The Treatment of Armenians in the Ottoman Empire 1915–16: Documents presented to Viscount Grey of Fallodon, Secretary of State for Foreign Affairs, by Viscount Bryce* (London: H.M. Stationery Office, Sir Joseph Causton & Sons, 1916), 641.
39. Walker, *Armenia*, 197–237; Balakian, *Burning Tigris*, 175–298; Richard G. Hovannisian, "Bitter-sweet memories: The last generation of Ottoman Armenians," in *Looking backward, moving forward: Confronting the Armenian Genocide*, ed. Hovannisian, 120; Henry H. Riggs, *Days of tragedy in Armenia: Personal experiences in Harpoot, 1915–1917* (Ann Arbor, MI: Gomidas Institute, 1997), 136; Morgenthau, *Ambassador Morgenthau's story*, 313; Dadrian, "Children as victims."
40. Ara Sarafian, comp., *United States Official Documents on the Armenian Genocide. Vol. I: The lower Euphrates* (Watertown, MA: Armenian Review, 1993), 145; Dadrian, "Children as victims."
41. Riggs, *Days of tragedy*, 145.
42. Tessa Hofmann, "German eyewitness reports of the Genocide of the Armenians, 1915–16," in *A Crime of silence: The Armenian Genocide: The Permanent Peoples' Tribunal*, ed. Gerard Libaridian (London: Zed Books, 1985), 74–75; Guerini E Associati, *Armin T. Wegner and the Armenians in Anatolia, 1915: Images and testimonies* (Milan: Guerini E Associati, 2007), 140; Donald E. Miller and Lorna Touryan Miller, *Survivors: An oral history of the Armenian Genocide* (Berkeley: University of California Press, 1999), 85; Riggs, *Days of tragedy*, 143, 149; Dadrian, "Children as victims."
43. Morgenthau, *Ambassador Morgenthau's story*, 301–25; Donald Bloxham, *The great game of Genocide: Imperialism, nationalism, and the destruction of the Ottoman Armenians* (Oxford: Oxford University Press, 2005), 87; Vierbücher, *Armenia 1915*, 51; Dadrian, "Children as victims."
44. Riggs, *Days of tragedy*, 147; Ara Sarafian, comp., *United States Official Documents on the Armenian Genocide. Vol. III: The central lands* (Watertown, MA: Armenian Review, 1995), 13; Balakian, *Burning Tigris*, 175–298; Walker, *Armenia*, 197–237; Morgenthau, *Ambassador Morgenthau's story*, 313, 316; Miller and Miller, *Survivors*, 96, 101; Donald E. Miller and Lorna Touryan Miller, "Women

and children of the Armenian Genocide," in *The Armenian Genocide: History, politics, ethics,* ed. Hovannisian, 167; Dadrian, "Children as victims."

45. Hofmann, "German eyewitness reports," 81–82; Richard G. Hovannisian, "Intervention and shades of altruism during the Armenian Genocide," in *The Armenian Genocide,* ed. Hovannisian, 173–207; Suzanne E. Moranian, "Bearing witness: The missionary archives as evidence of the Armenian Genocide," in ibid., 115.

46. "500,000 Armenians said to have perished," *New York Times,* September 23, 1915; "800,000 Armenians Counted Destroyed," *New York Times,* October 7, 1915.

47. Levon Marashlian, "The Armenian question from Sèvres to Lausanne: Economics and morality in American and British policies, 1920–1923," PhD diss., University of California–Los Angeles, 1992, 522; Levon Marashlian, "Finishing the Genocide: Cleansing Turkey of Armenian survivors, 1920–1923," in *Remembrance and denial: The case of the Armenian Genocide,* ed. Richard G. Hovannisian (Detroit: Wayne State University Press, 1999), 116; Sarafian, *Central lands,* 62–63, 65; Ara Sarafian, comp., *United States Official Documents on the Armenian Genocide. Vol. II: The peripheries* (Watertown, MA: Armenian Review, 1994), 45; Akçam, *Shameful act,* 182, 187–88; Morgenthau, *Ambassador Morgenthau's story,* 311, 339; Balakian, *Burning Tigris,* 256; George B. Kooshian, Jr., "The Armenian immigrant community of California, 1880–1935," PhD diss., University of California–Los Angeles, 2002, 247.

48. Armenian Genocide Museum (Yerevan, Armenia), http://www.armenocide.am/ genocide_museum.htm; Morgenthau, *Ambassador Morgenthau's story,* 337–38.

The Nine-Hundred-Day Republic

1. "'Extremists' rise to power in Russia," *New York Times,* November 9, 1917.

2. Walker, *Armenia,* 85–196; Panossian, *Armenians,* 124–228, 233; Nalbandian, *Armenian revolutionary movement,* 169; Richard G. Hovannisian, *Armenia on the road to independence* (Berkeley: University of California Press, 1967), 16; Hovannisian, "Etiology and sequelae," 119; Vincent Lima, "The evolving goals and strategies of the Armenian Revolutionary Federation, 1890–1925," *Armenian Review* 44, no. 2 (1991): ix.

3. Hovannisian, *Road to independence,* 97; Richard G. Hovannisian, "Simon Vratsian and Armenian nationalism," *Armenian Review* 23, no. 1 (1970): 21–22.

4. Hovannisian, "Simon Vratsian and Armenian nationalism," 5–8.

5. Ibid., 5, 8–17; Walker, *Armenia,* 454.

6. Hovannisian, "Simon Vratsian and Armenian nationalism," 18.

7. Ibid., 18; Richard G. Hovannisian, "The role of the Armenian Revolutionary Federation in the Republic of Armenia," *Armenian Review* 44, no. 2 (1991): 16.

8. Hovannisian, *Road to independence,* 93; "Unpublished materials of Simon Vratsian and Reuben Darbinian," *Armenian Review* 33, no. 3 (1980): 236.

9. Hovannisian, *Road to independence,* 121–23, 134–37; Walker, *Armenia,* 247.

10. Armenia State Museum of Ethnography, *Sardarapat;* Hovannisian, *Road to independence,* 192–93; Balakian, *Burning Tigris,* 321; Walker, *Armenia,* 255.

11. Armenia State Museum of Ethnography, *Sardarapat;* Balakian, *Burning Tigris,* 321; Walker, *Armenia,* 254–56.

12. Walker, *Armenia,* 254–55.

13. Balakian, *Burning Tigris,* 321–22; Ara Caprielian, "The Armenian Revolutionary Federation: The politics of a party in exile," PhD diss., New York University, 1975, 106–7; Walker, *Armenia,* 255–57; Hovannisian, *Road to independence,* 190–91; Hovannisian, "Role of the Armenian Revolutionary Federation," 16.

The declaration of independence was actually made on May 30 and backdated to May 28.

14. Margaret MacMillan, *Paris 1919: Six months that changed the world* (New York: Random House, 2003), 367–69; Gregory L. Aftandilian, *Armenia, vision of a Republic: The independence lobby in America, 1918–1927* (Boston: Charles River Books, 1981), 18.

15. Balakian, *Burning Tigris*, 299–300.

16. MacMillan, *Paris 1919*, 378.

17. Ibid., 53.

18. Jenny Phillips, "Symbol, myth, and rhetoric: The politics of culture in an Armenian-American population," PhD diss., Boston University, 1978, 85; Vatche Ghazarian, trans. and ed., *Boghos Nubar's papers and the Armenian Question, 1915–1918: Documents* (Waltham, MA: Mayreni Publishing, 1996), 37, 64, 292, 342; Richard G. Hovannisian, *The Republic of Armenia: From London to Sèvres, February–August, 1920* (Berkeley: University of California Press, 1996), 107; Mirak, *Torn between two lands*, 176.

19. V. Masissian, "Avetis Aharonian," *Armenian Review* 1, no. 3 (1948): 47–51; Mac-Millan, *Paris 1919*, 377; Walker, *Armenia*, 265; Richard G. Hovannisian, *The Republic of Armenia: The first year, 1918–1919* (cited hereafter as *First year*, Berkeley: University of California Press, 1974), 251–52, 257–60.

20. Hovannisian, *Road to independence*, 248–51; Hovannisian, *First year*, 282; Mac-Millan, *Paris 1919*, 378; Mary M. Tarzian, *The Armenian minority problem, 1914–1934: A nation's struggle for security* (Atlanta: Scholars Press, 1992), 133; http://avalon.law.yale.edu/20th_century/wilson14.asp.

21. Hovannisian, *First year*, 313; Walker, *Armenia*, 111–17. The original San Stefano treaty signed between the empire and Russia also contained other provisions heavily favorable to Russia. The Treaty of Berlin that came to replace it took back many of Russia's gains, including the size of the land transfer in eastern Anatolia.

22. MacMillan, *Paris 1919*, 53–54.

23. Representatives of Armenia to the Peace Conference at Versailles, *The Armenian question before the peace conference: A memorandum*, 1919; U.S. Department of State, "The council of ten: Minutes of meetings, February 15 to June 17, 1919," *Papers relating to the foreign relations of the United States, the Paris Peace Conference, 1919* (Washington, DC: U.S. Government Printing Office, 1919), 4:151–52.

24. MacMillan, *Paris 1919*, 377; Avetis Aharonian, "From Sardarapat to Sèvres and Lausanne: A political diary, Part I," *Armenian Review* 15, no. 3 (1962): 11–12; Avetis Aharonian, "From Sardarapat to Sèvres and Lausanne: A political diary, Part II," *Armenian Review* 15, no. 4 (1962): 65–66.

25. James L. Barton, *Story of Near East Relief (1915–1930): An interpretation* (New York: Macmillan, 1930), 82–83; Hovannisian, "Simon Vratsian and Armenian nationalism," 26; "Unpublished materials," *Armenian Review*, 234.

26. Hovannisian, "Role of the Armenian Revolutionary Federation," 20; Hovannisian, *London to Sèvres*, 155; Hovannisian, "Simon Vratsian and Armenian nationalism," 26; Simon Vratsian, *Armenia and the Armenian question*, trans. James G. Mandalian (Boston: Hairenik, 1943), 49. Other Armenian political parties participated to a smaller degree in the republic's government.

27. Walker, *Armenia*, 268; Richard G. Hovannisian, *The Republic of Armenia: From Versailles to London, 1919–1920* (cited hereafter as *Versailles to London*; Berkeley: University of California Press, 1982), 6–7; Hovannisian, *First year*, 126–28.

28. Walker, *Armenia*, 267–68, 277–78; Hovannisian, *First year*, 472–73; Hovan-

nisian, *Versailles to London*, 7, 272–79; Hovannisian, "Role of the Armenian Revolutionary Federation," 29–30.

29. Suzanne E. Moranian, "The American missionaries and the Armenian question: 1915–1927," PhD diss., University of Wisconsin–Madison, 1994, 213–15; Balakian, *Burning Tigris*, 280–82, 289; Aftandilian, *Vision of a Republic*, 14–15; Mark Malkasian, "The Disintegration of the Armenian cause in the United States, 1918–1927," *International Journal of Middle East Studies* 16, no. 3 (1984): 350.

30. Aftandilian, *Vision of a Republic*, 24; Balakian, *Burning Tigris*, 309–10; James H. Tashjian, "Life and Papers of Vahan Cardashian, Part I," *Armenian Review* 10, no. 1 (1957): 4. A handful of other Armenian-Americans advocated on behalf of their brethren abroad, but none had the standing and influence of Cardashian.

31. John R. Mardick, "Life and times of Vahan Cardashian," *Armenian Review* 10, no. 1 (1957): 6–8; James H. Tashjian, "Life and papers of Vahan Cardashian, Part II," *Armenian Review* 10, no. 2 (1957): 55, 57; James H. Tashjian, "Life and papers of Vahan Cardashian, Part IV," *Armenian Review* 10, no. 4 (1957): 101–12; Aftandilian, *Vision of a Republic*, 23–24; Vartkes Yeghiayan, comp., *Vahan Cardashian: Advocate extraordinaire for the Armenian cause* (n.p.: Center for Armenian Remembrance, 2008), 278–80; "Cardashian seeks divorce," *New York Times*, January 16, 1916.

32. Aftandilian, *Vision of a Republic*, 21–26; M. Vartan Malcom, *The Armenians in America* (Boston: Pilgrim Press, 1919), 96, 110–12, 125–26; Balakian, *Burning Tigris*, 309–10.

33. James H. Tashjian, "Life and papers of Vahan Cardashian, Part V," *Armenian Review* 11, no. 1 (1958): 68; James H. Tashjian, "Life and papers of Vahan Cardashian, Part VII," *Armenian Review* 11, no. 3 (1958): 137, 141; Aftandilian, *Vision of a Republic*, 28.

34. Aftandilian, *Vision of a Republic*, 24; Marashlian, "Armenian question," 86; Hovannisian, *London to Sèvres*, 434; Vahan Cardashian, "A 1921 memorandum to the President on Armenia," *Armenian Review* 26, no. 2 (1973): 60–62; The American Committee for the Independence of Armenia, *A petition to his Excellency Woodrow Wilson*, March 1919; James H. Tashjian, "Life and papers of Vahan Cardashian," *Armenian Review* 11, no. 1 (1958): 62–63.

35. "Free Armenia is plea of Hughes," *World* (New York), February 9, 1919; "Hughes and Bryan to join in plea for Armenian nation," *New York Herald*, February 9, 1919; "New amendments forecast by Bryan," *Sun* (New York), February 9, 1919; Robert George Koolakian, *Struggle for justice: A story of the American Committee for the Independence of Armenia, 1915–1920* (Dearborn, MI: Armenian Research Center, 2008), 17, 115–16; Balakian, *Burning Tigris*, 310–11; Donald A. Ritchie, "Congress confronts the Armenian Genocide," in *America and the Armenian Genocide of 1915*, ed. Jay Winter (Cambridge, UK: Cambridge University Press, 2003), 279–80; Aftandilian, *Vision of a Republic*, 27–28; Malkasian, "Disintegration," 358; Senate Subcommittee of the Committee on Foreign Relations, *A joint resolution for the maintenance of peace in Armenia: Hearings on S.J.R. 106*, 66th Cong., 1st sess., October 10, 1919, 114–25.

36. Hovannisian, *First year*, 312; MacMillan, *Paris 1919*, 379; A. E. Montgomery, "The making of the Treaty of Sèvres of 10 August 1920," *The Historical Journal* 15, no. 4 (1972): 776.

37. Balakian, *Burning Tigris*, 349; MacMillan, *Paris 1919*, 375; The American Committee for the Independence of Armenia, *The joint mandate scheme: A Turkish empire under American protection* (New York: J. C. & A. L. Fawcett, 1990); Suzanne E. Moranian, "A legacy of paradox: U.S. foreign policy and the Armenian Genocide," in *The Armenian Genocide: Cultural and ethical legacies*, ed. Hovannisian, 312.

38. Hovannisian, *First year*, 316.
39. Balakian, *Burning Tigris*, 303, 361–62.
40. Lloyd E. Ambrosius, "Wilsonian diplomacy and Armenia: the limits of power and ideology," in *America and the Armenian Genocide of 1915*, ed. Winter, 138, 141; Richard G. Hovannisian, "The Armenian Genocide and US post-war commissions," in ibid., 259; Richard G. Hovannisian, *The Republic of Armenia: Between crescent and sickle: Partition and Sovietization* (Berkeley: University of California Press, 1996), 17.
41. MacMillan, *Paris 1919*, 427–32.
42. Andrew Mango, *Atatürk: The biography of the founder of modern Turkey* (Woodstock, NY: Overlook Press, 2002), 148–56.
43. Mark Mazower, *Salonica, city of ghosts: Christians, Muslims and Jews, 1430–1950* (New York: Alfred A. Knopf, 2005), 278, 318; MacMillan, *Paris 1919*, 370; Lewis, *Modern Turkey*, 238.
44. MacMillan, *Paris 1919*, 433–34; Hovannisian, *First year*, 432.
45. MacMillan, *Paris 1919*, 435–37, 441–42; Marashlian, "Armenian question," 22; Gary J. Bass, *Freedom's battle: The origins of humanitarian intervention* (New York: Alfred A. Knopf, 2008), 336.
46. Avetis Aharonian, "From Sardarapat to Sèvres and Lausanne: A political diary, Part VI," *Armenian Review* 17, no. 1 (1964): 64; Hovannisian, *London to Sèvres*, 107. Because Nubar represented the scattered Armenian Diaspora and not the Armenian Republic, he was not a signatory to the treaty.
47. Hovannisian, *London to Sèvres*, 107; H. C. Armstrong, *Gray wolf: Mustafa Kemal, an intimate study of a dictator* (New York: Minton, Balch & Co., 1933), 124–27.
48. Montgomery, "Making of the treaty," 775, 780.
49. Bass, *Freedom's battle*, 337; Walker, *Armenia*, 314; Montgomery, "Making of the treaty," 777, 784; MacMillan, *Paris 1919*, 449; Balakian, *Burning Tigris*, 328; Hovannisian, *First year*, 305; Hovannisian, *Partition and Sovietization*, 194, 211, 298–300, 305, 317; Aftandilian, *Vision of a Republic*, 35–36.
50. Walker, *Armenia*, 279–80, 283; Balakian, *Burning Tigris*, 329; Mango, *Atatürk*, 294.
51. Balakian, *Burning Tigris*, 308.
52. "Unpublished materials," *Armenian Review*, 243; Hovannisian, "Simon Vratsian and Armenian nationalism," 28; Hovannisian, *Partition and Sovietization*, 355, 359; Hovannisian, "Role of the Armenian Revolutionary Federation," 46–47; Walker, *Armenia*, 315.
53. Hovannisian, *Partition and Sovietization*, 388.

Judgment in Berlin

1. Derogy, *Resistance and revenge*, 1; Akçam, *Shameful act*, 243; Alexander, *Crime of vengeance*, 129–33; "Talaat's career," *New York Times*, March 16, 1921; "Talaat is mourned as Germany's friend," *New York Times*, March, 18, 1921.
2. Alexander, *Crime of vengeance*, 121; Derogy, *Resistance and revenge*, 1–2; Akçam, *Shameful act*, 214.
3. Dadrian, *Armenian Genocide*, 306; Akçam, *Shameful act*, 215.
4. Akçam, *Shameful act*, 213, 216–17, 228.
5. Balakian, *Burning Tigris*, 333; Alexander, *Crime of vengeance*, 123; Akçam, *Shameful act*, 246–47; David Lloyd George, *Memoirs of the Peace Conference* (New Haven: Yale University Press, 1939), 2:650–56; Gary J. Bass, *Stay the hand of vengeance: The politics of war crimes tribunals* (Princeton, NJ: Princeton University Press, 2000), 118.

6. Dadrian, *Armenian Genocide*, 307; Alexander, *Crime of vengeance*, 123–25; Derogy, *Resistance and revenge*, 29–31, 34; Balakian, *Burning Tigris*, 334, 337; Akçam, *Shameful act*, 293.

7. Derogy, *Resistance and revenge*, 29–31, 34; Akçam, *Shameful act*, 280, 293–95; Balakian, *Burning Tigris*, 337, 341.

8. Derogy, *Resistance and revenge*, 34–35, 37; "Talaat Pasha slain in Berlin suburb," *New York Times*, March 16, 1921; Vahakn N. Dadrian, *German responsibility in the Armenian Genocide: A review of the historical evidence of German complicity* (Watertown, MA: Blue Crane Books, 1996), 200.

9. Akçam, *Shameful act*, 297; Dadrian, *Armenian Genocide*, 309.

10. Akçam, *Shameful act*, 217, 319–20, 332–33, 345–52.

11. Dadrian, *Armenian Genocide*, 335; Balakian, *Burning Tigris*, 344.

12. Dadrian, *Armenian Genocide*, 304–5; Akçam, *Shameful act*, 222–24.

13. Dadrian, *Armenian Genocide*, 309, 336.

14. Akçam, *Shameful act*, 234.

15. Dadrian, *Armenian Genocide*, 308–10; Akçam, *Shameful act*, 238–39, 358; Balakian, *Burning Tigris*, 344.

16. Sarkis Atamian, "Soghomon Tehlirian: A portrait of immortality—Part I," *Armenian Review* 13, no. 3 (1960): 40; Alexander, *Crime of vengeance*, 40–41; Derogy, *Resistance and revenge*, 63; Walker, *Armenia*, 243.

17. Vartkes Yeghiayan, comp. and ed., *The Case of Soghomon Tehlirian*, 2nd ed. (n.p.: Center for Armenian Remembrance, 2006), 13; Alexander, *Crime of vengeance*, 71; Lindy V. Avakian, *The cross and the crescent* (Los Angeles: DeVorss & Co., 1965), 37; Atamian, "Tehlirian—Part I," 41.

18. Atamian, "Tehlirian—Part I," 41; Derogy, *Resistance and revenge*, 64; Avakian, *Cross and the crescent*, 37–39.

19. Alexander, *Crime of vengeance*, 40–44.

20. Atamian, "Tehlirian—Part I," 49–50.

21. Garo, *Bank Ottoman*, 20–21; Atamian, "Tehlirian—Part I," 42, 50; Alexander, *Crime of vengeance*, 47, 51. Shahan Natalie masterminded the operation.

22. Sarkis Atamian, "Soghomon Tehlirian: A portrait of immortality—Part II," *Armenian Review* 13, no. 4 (1961): 15–20; Alexander, *Crime of vengeance*, 56–60.

23. Derogy, *Resistance and revenge*, 78–79.

24. Atamian, "Tehlirian—Part II," 19; Alexander, *Crime of vengeance*, 9–10.

25. Atamian, "Tehlirian—Part II," 21; Alexander, *Crime of vengeance*, 9–11.

26. Morgenthau, *Ambassador Morgenthau's Story*, 338.

27. Alexander, *Crime of vengeance*, 10, 12, 22; Derogy, *Resistance and revenge*, xix, 84–85; Atamian, "Tehlirian—Part II," 21; Sarkis Atamian, "Soghomon Tehlirian: A portrait of immortality—Part III," *Armenian Review* 14, no. 1 (1961): 22; Setrak Pakhtikian, "I knew Soghomon Tehlirian," *Armenian Review* 15, no. 2 (1962): 23.

28. Atamian, "Tehlirian—Part III," 18–19; Alexander, *Crime of vengeance*, 16–19.

29. Alexander, *Crime of vengeance*, 65–66; Atamian, "Tehlirian—Part III," 24; "Says mother's ghost ordered him to kill," *New York Times*, June 3, 1921.

30. Atamian, "Tehlirian—Part III," 22–23; Alexander, *Crime of vengeance*, 117; Derogy, *Resistance and revenge*, 92–93; Morgenthau, *Ambassador Morgenthau's Story*, 343–44; Yeghiayan, *Soghomon Tehlirian*, 1, 83, 86–93.

31. Yeghiayan, *Soghomon Tehlirian*, 18; Atamian, "Tehlirian—Part III," 24; "Says mother's ghost ordered him to kill," *New York Times*, June 3, 1921; "The avenger of blood," *New York Times*, June 3, 1921.

32. Atamian, "Tehlirian—Part III," 30; Alexander, *Crime of vengeance*, 158.

33. Atamian, "Tehlirian—Part III," 35; "Talaat's assailant acquitted," *New York Times*, June 4, 1921; "Vengeance justified," *Los Angeles Times*, June 4, 1921.
34. Derogy, *Resistance and revenge*, xxvii–xxviii; Mango, *Atatürk*, 451.

Seeds of Denial

1. Walker, *Armenia*, 324–25, 327; Hovannisian, "Simon Vratsian and Armenian nationalism," 31–32; Vartan Gregorian, *The road to home: My life and times* (New York: Simon & Schuster, 2003), 78.
2. Walker, *Armenia*, 394–96; Tarzian, *Armenian minority problem*, 157–58.
3. Articles 88–93 guaranteed an independent Armenian state safeguarded from further Ottoman persecution. Article 144 laid out procedures for the return of Armenian property lost or seized during the Genocide. Articles 226–230 required the Ottoman Empire to cooperate in the prosecution of those responsible for the Genocide.
4. Mango, *Atatürk*, 364–65, 558–59.
5. Roger R. Trask, *The United States response to Turkish nationalism and reform, 1914–1939* (Minneapolis: University of Minnesota Press, 1971), 29, 31; Thomas A. Bryson, "Admiral Mark L. Bristol, an open-door diplomat in Turkey," *International Journal of Middle East Studies* 5, no. 4 (1974): 452–53, 455, 460, 464; Marashlian, "Armenian question," 100, 283–84.
6. Marjorie Housepian, *Smyrna 1922: The destruction of a city* (London: Faber & Faber, 1972), 74; Bryson, "Admiral Mark L. Bristol," 454–55; Thomas A. Bryson, "Mark Lambert Bristol, U.S. Navy, admiral-diplomat: his influence on the Armenian mandate question," *Armenian Review* 21, no. 4 (1968): 13.
7. Marashlian, "Armenian question," 107–8; Housepian, *Smyrna 1922*, 76. For more on Bristol's view of the Armenians, see Marjorie Housepian Dobkin, "What Genocide? What Holocaust? News from Turkey, 1915–1923: A case study," in *The Armenian Genocide in perspective*, ed. Hovannisian, 105.
8. Bloxham, *Great game*, 196.
9. Balakian, *Burning Tigris*, 366–67.
10. Housepian, *Smyrna 1922*, 97.
11. Aftandilian, *Vision of a Republic*, 56; Moranian, "American missionaries," 186, 229.
12. Bloxham, *Great game*, 195, 198–99, 201; Marashlian, "Finishing the Genocide," 122; Marashlian, "Armenian question," 93–94; Walker, *Armenia*, 247; Fatma Müge Göçek, "Reconstructing the Turkish historiography on the Armenian massacres and deaths of 1915," in *Looking backward, moving forward: Confronting the Armenian Genocide*, ed. Hovannisian, 218; Akçam, *Shameful act*, 322, 327–28.
13. Aftandilian, *Vision of a Republic*, 57; Moranian, "American missionaries," 189–90.
14. Allen Dulles to Mark L. Bristol, July 25, 1922, Armenian Genocide, 1990–1995, 329–96–336, Box 127, Folder 5, RJD.
15. Aftandilian, *Vision of a Republic*, 56; Moranian, "American missionaries," 186, 229.
16. American Committee for the Independence of Armenia, *In Favor of Armenia*, Charles Evans Hughes Papers, 1914–1930, 308 Z, Box 135, Columbia University; "Wants Cilicia given to the Armenians," *New York Times*, January 7, 1923; Malkasian, "Disintegration," 358. "Confidentially the State Department is in a bind," Dulles wrote to Bristol, describing the secretary's predicament. Hughes "wants to avoid giving the impression that while the US is willing to intervene actively to protect its commercial interests, it is not willing to move on behalf of the Christian minorities"—Balakian, *Burning Tigris*, 368.
17. Aftandilian, *Vision of a Republic*, 55.

18. "Deprecates threats unless backed up," *Boston Daily Globe*, September 24, 1922; Charles Evans Hughes "Recent questions and negotiations," *American Journal of International Law* 18, no. 2 (1924): 238.

19. Moranian, "American missionaries," 320–22; Marashlian, "Armenian question," 762. Hughes had always held reservations about an American mandate over Armenia, even while serving on the ACIA—see "Free Armenia is plea of Hughes," *World* (New York), February 9, 1919; "Hughes and Bryan to join in plea for Armenian nation," *New York Herald*, February 9, 1919; "New amendments forecast by Bryan," *Sun* (New York), February 9, 1919.

20. Balakian, *Burning Tigris*, 370; Moranian, "Legacy of paradox," 319.

21. Yves Ternon, *The Armenian cause*, trans. Anahid A. Mangouni (Delmar, NY: Caravan Books, 1985), 153–54; Anita L. P. Burdett, ed., *Armenia: Political and ethnic boundaries, 1878–1948* (Slough, UK: Archive Editions, 1998), 869; Moranian, "Legacy of paradox," 320.

22. Mango, *Atatürk*, 366–67; Balakian, *Burning Tigris*, 363–72; Merlo J. Pusey, *Charles Evans Hughes* (New York: Macmillan, 1951), 2:572. Admiral Chester also received concessions but never had the chance to enjoy his booty as Turkey annulled his dispensation a few months later when he failed to secure the capital needed to fund the project—Aftandilian, *Vision of a Republic*, 57; Simon Payaslian, *United States policy toward the Armenian Question and the Armenian Genocide* (New York: Palgrave Macmillan, 2005), 178; Mango, *Atatürk*, 380, 388; Roger R. Trask "The United States and Turkish nationalism: Investments and technical aid during the Ataturk era," *Business History Review* 38, no. 1 (1964): 61–62.

23. Vahan Cardashian, letter to the editor, *New York Times*, June 28, 1925.

24. Tarzian, *Armenian minority problem*, 181.

25. Ibid., 177–78.

26. Pusey, *Charles Evans Hughes*, 2: 574; Robert L. Daniel "The Armenian question and American-Turkish Relations, 1914–1917," *Mississippi Valley Historical Review* 46, no. 2 (1959): 267; Mango, *Atatürk*, 367, 391; Trask, *United States response*, 41–42; "Bristol is praised for aid in Turkey," *New York Times*, November 10, 1925; "Bristol is assigned to head Asiatic fleet," *New York Times*, March 22, 1927.

27. Declaration of Amnesty, http://www.austlii.edu.au/au/other/dfat/treaties/1924/13.html.

28. Balakian, *Burning Tigris*, 371.

29. Yeghiayan, *Vahan Cardashian*, 90–93; Malkasian, "Disintegration," 359–60; Aftandilian, *Vision of a Republic*, 51.

30. Malkasian, "Disintegration," 359; Marashlian, "Armenian question," 969.

31. Aftandilian, *Vision of a Republic*, 60.

32. Balakian, *Burning Tigris*, 371–72; Pat Harrison, "Hughes a failure as seen by Pat Harrison," *New York Times*, February 4, 1923.

33. Yeghiayan, *Vahan Cardashian*, 169–204, 300–35; Malkasian, "Disintegration," 360; Marashlian, "Armenian question," 920–22; Pusey, *Charles Evans Hughes*, 2: 611.

34. Malkasian, "Disintegration," 360–61; Aftandilian, *Vision of a Republic*, 62; Trask, "Turkish nationalism," 59, 70–74; Bryson, "Admiral Mark L. Bristol," 458; Daniel, "American-Turkish relations," 274; Tarzian, *Armenian minority problem*, 180; "Tells of treaty failure," *New York Times*, January 26, 1927; "Extends trade agreement," *New York Times*, February 6, 1927; "Turkey prolongs treaty with America," *New York Times*, February 18, 1927; "Turks will welcome Grew's appointment," *New York Times*, May 20, 1927; "Paladin Departs," *Time*, June 6, 1927; "Turkish relations upheld," *New York Times*, November 29, 1927.

35. Vahan Cardashian, "In support of an application for a hearing by the U.S. Senate upon the Lausanne Treaty: Mosul oil and Armenia," *Armenian Review* 26, no. 4 (1973): 9.

36. Housepian, *Smyrna 1922*, 225; Cardashian, "In support of an application," 46.

37. Malkasian, "Disintegration," 361; "Attacks Kellogg on Turkish policy," *New York Times*, April 11, 1928; "Cardashian details his accusations," *New York Times*, April 13, 1928; "Armenians appeal to US," *New York Times*, May 3, 1928; "Sues Turkish government," *New York Times*, July 10, 1929; "Restricts law suits against governments," *New York Times*, August 11, 1929; "Refuses to sanction suit against Turkey," *New York Times*, November 2, 1929.

38. Vahan Cardashian, "A memorandum to the Secretary of State on a proposed statement on Armenia's international rights," *Armenian Review* 25, no. 2 (1972): 3–21; Trask, *United States response*, 52–53, 56–57, 60–62, 77.

39. "Cardashian dead; Armenian leader," *New York Times*, June 13, 1934; Yeghiayan, *Vahan Cardashian*, 10–11; Aftandilian, *Vision of a Republic*, 63.

40. "Bristol is assigned to head Asiatic fleet," *New York Times*, March 22, 1927; "Turks will welcome Grew's appointment," *New York Times*, May 20, 1927; "Paladin Departs," *Time*, June 6, 1927; Clair Price, "Another big job for Admiral Bristol," *New York Times*, August 28, 1927; "Named Navy Board head," *New York Times*, March 27, 1930; "Organize to foster amity with Turkey," *New York Times*, July 14, 1930; "Head Friends of Turkey," *New York Times*, May 28, 1932; Trask, *United States response*, 76, 87–89; Marashlian, "Armenian question," 999–1000; Report of controller, American Friends of Turkey, December 31, 1930, Box 64, MLB.

41. Trask, *United States response*, 84–87.

42. Harold F. Strong Corp. to American Friends of Turkey, Outline of tentative public relations program, May 9, 1935, Box 64, MLB.

43. Marashlian, "Armenian question," 1001; Asa W. Jennings to Mark L. Bristol, June 28, 1932, Box 64, MLB.

44. Mango, *Atatürk*, 388.

45. Ibid., 370, 373.

46. Milton Viorst, "Crossing the straits," *New Yorker*, June 5, 1989, 56.

47. Mango, *Atatürk*, 374, 396–414, 469; Lewis, *Modern Turkey*, 410; Zorlu-Durukan, "Ideological pillars," 107–9; Frank Tachau, "The search for national identity among the Turks," *Die Welt des Islams* 8, no. 3 (1963): 166.

48. Erik J. Zürcher, "The Ottoman legacy of the Turkish Republic: An attempt at a new periodization," *Die Welt des Islams* 32, no. 2 (1992): 238; Mango, *Atatürk*, 433, 435; Lewis, *Modern Turkey*, 263.

49. Mango, *Atatürk*, 437–38, 464, 468.

50. Ibid., 437, 473; Pope and Pope, *Turkey unveiled*, 64.

51. Zorlu-Durukan, "Ideological pillars," 90–91, 95; Lord Kinross, *Ataturk: A biography of Mustafa Kemal, father of modern Turkey* (New York: William Morrow, 1965), 529; Mango, *Atatürk*, 464–65, 494–95; Frank Tachau, "Language and politics: Turkish language reform," *Review of Politics* 26, no. 2, (1964): 193, 196–97.

52. Meltem F. Türköz, "The social life of the state's fantasy: memories and documents on Turkey's 1934 surname law," PhD diss., University of Pennsylvania, 2004, 86; Mango, *Atatürk*, 495–98, 503; Lewis, *Modern Turkey*, 427–29; Zorlu-Durukan, "Ideological pillars," 96–97. Eventually, this process evolved into the Sun-Language Theory, which claimed that all languages derived from Turkish, making the act of borrowing words from them a simple matter of reclaiming the original Turkish.

53. Akçam, *Empire to Republic*, 62; Zorlu-Durukan, "Ideological pillars," 29, 68, 89–91; Panossian, *Armenians*, 234–35; Mango, *Atatürk*, 405–7; Mazower, *Salonica*, 263.

54. The Young Turks had already killed off and evicted the Armenians. At Lausanne, the Turks and Greeks agreed to a population exchange in which 1.1 million Greeks left Turkey while 380,000 Muslims entered from Macedonia and Crete. By the mid-1920s, cities that had once housed large minorities now contained only ghostly reminders of their former inhabitants. Non-Muslims had constituted 32 percent of Erzurum in 1900, for instance. By 1927, that number dropped to one tenth of 1 percent—Mango, *Atatürk*, 390; Finkel, *Osman's dream*, 547.

55. Mango, *Atatürk*, 403, 421–29; Robert W. Olson and William F. Tucker, "The Sheikh Sait rebellion in Turkey (1925)," *Die Welt des Islams* 18, nos. 3–4 (1978): 197.

56. Mango, *Atatürk*, 405–7; Mazower, *Salonica*, 263.

57. Zorlu-Durukan, "Ideological pillars," 90–95.

58. Mango, *Atatürk*, 493–94.

59. Clive Foss, "The Turkish view of Armenian history: A vanishing nation," in *The Armenian Genocide: History, politics, ethics*, ed. Hovannisian, 255–57; Tachau, "Search for national identity," 176.

60. Zorlu-Durukan, "Ideological pillars," 14–15, 104, 116.

61. Lewis, *Modern Turkey*, 364; Pope and Pope, *Turkey unveiled*, 50–51; Mango, *Atatürk*, 457–63.

62. Hilmar Kaiser, "From empire to republic: The continuities of Turkish denial," *Armenian Review* 48, nos. 3–4 (2003): 3–6, 12–14.

63. Taner Akçam, *Dialogue across an international divide: Essays towards a Turkish-Armenian dialogue* (Toronto: Zoryan Institute, 2001), 87.

64. Ibid., 87–88; Tachau, "Language and politics," 195; Zürcher, "Ottoman legacy," 239; Mango, *Atatürk*, 462, 496–97.

65. Mango, *Atatürk*, 391; Akçam, *Shameful act*, 341.

66. Akçam, *Dialogue*, 94–96; Akçam, *Empire to Republic*, 238–39; Akçam, *Shameful act*, 306–12; Zorlu-Durukan, "Ideological pillars," 68–69.

67. Mango, *Atatürk*, 486; Zürcher, "Ottoman legacy," 238; Asa K. Jennings to Mark L. Bristol, August 16, 1932, Box 64, MLB; Asa W. Jennings to Mark L. Bristol, October 6, 1932, Box 64, MLB; Lowell Thomas program, Box 64, MLB; "Kemal's Regime Praised," *New York Times*, October 30, 1933.

68. Edward Minasian, *Musa Dagh* (Nashville, TN: Cold Tree Press, 2007), 45–50.

69. Ibid., 53–55.

70. Hans Wagener, *Understanding Franz Werfel* (Columbia, SC: University of South Carolina Press, 1993), 121; Minasian, *Musa Dagh*, 72.

71. Minasian, *Musa Dagh*, 62, 66, 73, 96.

72. Louis Kronenberger, review of *The Forty Days of Musa Dagh* by Franz Werfel, in the *New York Times*, December 2, 1934; Minasian, *Musa Dagh*, 93, 95.

73. Minasian, *Musa Dagh*, 97.

74. Ibid., 98–100.

75. Ibid., 104, 106, 112, 117, 121, 128; "Turkey Resents 'Musa Dagh,'" *New York Times*, July 7, 1935.

76. Minasian, *Musa Dagh*, 107, 131; "Revolt in the West," *New York Times*, November 24, 1935.

77. Minasian, *Musa Dagh*, 124.

78. Ibid., 138.

79. Ibid., 139. Turkey's demands left the American government in an awkward position, however, in which the United States promoted censorship and betrayed the history of its own magnanimous efforts to save the Armenians, a predicament it

wished to hide from the public. A member of the Motion Picture Producers and Distributors of America informed Murray after MGM's cancellation of *Musa Dagh*, "I think, of course, the less said . . . the better . . . I am going to bury the matter right where it stands"—Minasian, *Musa Dagh*, 142.

The Truman Doctrine

1. Gevorg Emin, *Akh, ays Masise* (Yerevan, Armenia: "Sovetakan Grogh," 1980), 33–34.
2. Harry S. Truman, "Truman Doctrine," Speech, Joint Session of Congress, March 12, 1947. The text of the speech can be found at http://www.trumanlibrary.org/index.php.
3. Harry S. Truman, *Memoirs: Years of trial and hope* (Garden City, NY: Doubleday & Co., 1956), 106.
4. Deborah W. Larson, *Origins of containment: A psychological explanation* (Princeton: Princeton University Press, 1985), 316.
5. Kissinger, *Diplomacy*, 451; Dean Acheson, *Present at the creation: My years in the State Department* (New York: W. W. Norton & Co., 1969), 198.
6. Kissinger, *Diplomacy*, 451; Robert W. Olson, "The remains of Talaat: A dialectic between republic and empire," *Die Welt des Islams* 26, no. 1 (1986): 46–49; Ternon, *Armenian cause*, 157; George S. Harris, *Troubled alliance: Turkish-American problems in historical perspective, 1945–1971* (Washington, DC: American Enterprise Institute for Public Policy Research, 1972), 14; Zaven Messerlian, "The question of Kars and Ardahan," *Armenian Studies* (1973): 60.
7. Burdett, *Armenia*, 1025.
8. Catholicos of All Armenians, Kevork VI, *Memorandum to the Council of Foreign Ministers at London*, November 27, 1945; Felix Corley, "The Armenian Church under the Soviet Regime, Part 1: The leadership of Kevork," *Religion, State and Society* 24, no. 1 (1996): 16–20; Ternon, *Armenian cause*, 122–23; Julia Hakobyan, "At odds with God: Communist repressions were a setback, but not a defeat," *AGBU News* (April 2007): 18; Burdett, *Armenia*, 1028.
9. Constitution (Draft) of the American Committee for Armenian Rights, [1945?], AD; Armenian National Council of America, *The Case of the Armenian people: Memorandum to the United Nations Conference on International Organization in San Francisco*, [1945?], AD; Algernon D. Black, *Ethical issues of the Armenian Question* (New York: Armenian National Council of America, n.d.); Armenian National Council of America, *Proposed announcement for the World Armenian Congress*, [1947?], AD; Armen Alichanian to Harry S. Truman, September 6, 1945, SD-RG 59, 860J.01/9–645; Armen Mirjanian, et al., to Trygve Lie, May 3, 1946, AD; Bedros G. Terzian, letter to the editor, *Washington Post*, September 4, 1947; Corley, "Leadership of Kevork," 19; Vahakn N. Dadrian "Nationalism in Soviet Armenia—A case study of ethnocentrism," in *Nationalism in the USSR and Eastern Europe in the era of Brezhnev and Kosygin*, ed. George W. Simmonds (Detroit: University of Detroit Press, 1977), 248; U.S. Department of State, *Foreign relations of the United States: Diplomatic papers, 1945: The Near East and Africa* (Washington DC: U.S. Government Printing Office, 1945), 8:1284–85; Nikola B. Schahgaldian, "The political integration of an immigrant community into a composite society: The Armenians in Lebanon, 1920–1974," PhD diss., Columbia University, 1979, 102; Ronald G. Suny, "Soviet Armenia," in *The Armenian People from ancient to modern times*, ed. Hovannisian, 2:367; Richard H. Dekmejian, "The Armenian Diaspora," in ibid., 2:416; "Seeks to aid Armenians," *New York Times*, December 22, 1945.

10. Burdett, *Armenia*, 1038.
11. Military Intelligence Service, Research Unit, *Armenian nationalism and the U.S.S.R. (Project 2943)*, February 15, 1946, National Archives; Felix Cole to George C. Marshall, June 4, 1947, SD-RG 59, 860J.5584/6–447; Memorandum of conversation, June 6, 1947, SD-RG 59, 860J.01/6–1147; House Committee on Un-American Activities, *Soviet Total War: "Historic mission" of violence and deceit. Vol. 2*, 84th Cong., 2d sess., 1956, 714.
12. Suny, *Looking toward Ararat*, 159; Suny, "Soviet Armenia," 368; Mary Kilbourne Matossian, *The impact of Soviet policies in Armenia* (Westport, CT: Hyperion Press, 1981), 175; William O. Douglas, *Strange lands and friendly people* (New York: Harper & Bros., 1951), 35–37; C. L. Sulzberger, "Armenians find native land a disappointment on return," *New York Times*, March 14, 1948; Report on industries of Armenian SSR and certain Soviet objectives in the Middle East, May 13, 1949, SD-RG 59, 860J.60/5–1349.
13. Jonathan Knight, "American statecraft and the 1946 Black Sea straits controversy," *Political Science Quarterly* 90, no. 3 (1975): 459–60; Eduard Mark, "The war scare of 1946 and its consequences," *Diplomatic History* 21, no. 3 (1997): 390; Burdett, *Armenia*, 1026; Larson, *Origins of containment*, 240–41; Suny, "Soviet Armenia," 368; Messerlian, "Kars and Ardahan," 89; A. C. Sedgwick, "Future status of straits is Turkey's chief concern," *New York Times*, April 7, 1946; U.S. Department of State, *Foreign relations of the United States: Diplomatic papers: The conference of Berlin (the Potsdam Conference), 1945* (Washington, DC: U.S. Government Printing Office, 1945), 2:266–67; U.S. Department of State, *Near East and Africa, 1945*, 8:1234–35; U.S. Department of State, *Foreign relations of the United States, 1946: The Near East and Africa* (Washington, DC: U.S. Government Printing Office, 1946), 7:813–14.
14. "Unpublished materials," *Armenian Review*, 229–30; Gregorian, *Road to home*, 78.
15. Vratsian, *Armenia*, 58; JMH.
16. Atlantic Charter, http://avalon.law.yale.edu/wwii/atlantic.asp.
17. Vratsian, *Armenia*, foreword.
18. Robert Dallek, *Franklin D. Roosevelt and American foreign policy, 1932–1945* (Oxford: Oxford University Press, 1981), 283–84; Stephen C. Schlesinger, *Act of creation: The founding of the United Nations: A story of superpowers, secret agents, wartime allies and enemies, and their quest for a peaceful world* (Boulder, CO: Westview Press, 2003), 111, 121.
19. Schlesinger, *Act of creation*, 122–23; Armenian National Committee, *A memorandum relating to the Armenian Question*, April 1945; "Unpublished materials," *Armenian Review*, 230; Armenian National Committee, *Armenian Bulletin, No. 1*, August 1945; Schlesinger, *Act of creation*, 116.
20. Rival groups holding less antipathy toward the USSR than Vratsian implemented a similar campaign.
21. Burdett, *Armenia*, 1008; Messerlian, "Kars and Ardahan," 67–68, 79, 87; Black, *Ethical issues*; Armenian National Committee, *Armenian Bulletin, Nos. 1–7*, August 1945–August 1946; Finance Committee for Armenian Rights, *Donation Request*, AD; Leon Z. Surmelian, letter to the editor, *New York Times*, July 11, 1945; American Committee for Justice to the Armenians to Avedis Derounian, November 1, 1945, AD; Armenian National Council of America to John Roy Carlson, November 2, 1945, AD; American Committee for Armenian Rights to *New York Herald Tribune*, March 19, 1946, AD; American Committee for Armenian Rights and Armenian National Council of America, *Support the Armenian appeal to the United Nations, Carnegie Hall (Program)*, April 28, 1946, AD; Edwin S. Smith to Harry S. Truman, June 12, 1946, SD-RG 59, 860J.00/6–1246;

Arthur Calpakian to Harry S. Truman, May 10, 1947, AD; Armenian National Council of America, *Circular #26*, AD; Armenian National Council of America, *Circular #29*, AD; Vahan H. Kalenderian and James G. Mitchell, letter to the editor, *New York Times*, December 24, 1945; "Armenian 'National Council' asks Turks to 'return' land to Russia," *New York Times*, December 24, 1945; Edwin S. Smith, letter to the editor, *New York Times*, May 4, 1946; Vahan H. Kalenderian, letter to the editor, *New York Times*, July 29, 1946; H. M. Dadourian, letter to the editor, *New York Times*, May 25, 1947.

22. Armenian National Council of America to Harry S. Truman, Joseph Stalin, and Winston Churchill, July 16, 1945, AD; Armen Alichanian to Harry S. Truman, September 6, 1945, SD-RG 59, 860J.01/9–645; Armenian National Council of America, press release of letter addressed to James F. Byrnes, et al., September 15, 1945, AD; Armen Mirjanian, et al., to Trygve Lie, May 3, 1946, AD; Messerlian, "Kars and Ardahan," 67, 87.

23. Charles W. Tobey, "Responsibility of the United Nations towards Armenia," speech, Carnegie Hall, April 28, 1946, AD; Messerlian, "Kars and Ardahan," 86; "Armenian claims on Turkey pushed," *New York Times*, May 5, 1947.

24. Armenian National Committee, *Armenian Bulletin, No. 1*, August 1945.

25. Knight, "American statecraft," 459–60; Mark, "War scare," 390.

26. Joseph M. Jones, *The fifteen weeks: February 21—June 5, 1947* (San Diego: Harcourt Brace Jovanovich, 1955), 112; Acheson, *Present at the creation*, 200, 729–34; Truman, *Years of trial*, 429; Robert L. Beisner, *Dean Acheson: A life in the Cold War* (Oxford: Oxford University Press, 2006), 27; David McCullough, *Truman* (New York: Simon & Schuster, 1992), 752.

27. Acheson, *Present at the creation*, 195; Mark, "War scare," 399; Beisner, *Dean Acheson*, 39, 43–45; Larson, *Origins of containment*, 280, 284–85.

28. Acheson, *Present at the creation*, 195; Mark, "War scare," 383; Knight, "American statecraft," 464.

29. U.S. Department of State, *Near East and Africa, 1946*, 7:841.

30. Larson, *Origins of containment*, 282; Melvyn P. Leffler, "Strategy, diplomacy, and the Cold War: the United States, Turkey, and NATO, 1945–1952," *Journal of American History* 71, no. 4 (1985): 813–16; Mark, "War scare," 400; Jones, *Fifteen weeks*, 148.

31. Acheson, *Present at the creation*, 195–96; U.S. Department of State, *Potsdam Conference, 1945*, 2:271–321; U.S. Department of State, *Near East and Africa, 1945*, 8:1239–40; Harris, *Troubled alliance*, 18; Knight, "American statecraft," 475.

32. Acheson, *Present at the creation*, 195–96; Truman, *Years of trial*, 97; Jones, *Fifteen weeks*, 63–64; Larson, *Origins of containment*, 320; Mark, "War scare," 383.

33. Acheson, *Present at the creation*, 194–96; Knight, "American statecraft," 454, 467.

34. Truman, *Years of trial*, 96, 104–5; Jones, *Fifteen weeks*, 148, 153–54; Acheson, *Present at the creation*, 220–21; Larson, *Origins of containment*, 309–11; McCullough, *Truman*, 545–46; Clark M. Clifford, interview by Jerry N. Hess, April 19, 1971, Oral History Interviews, Harry S. Truman Library and Museum.

35. U.S. Department of State, *Near East and Africa, 1946*, 7:860; Larson, *Origins of containment*, 306; Mark, "War scare," 411.

36. Mark, "War scare," 405; Knight, "American statecraft," 461, 463.

37. U.S. Department of State, *Potsdam Conference, 1945*, 1:1045; U.S. Department of State, *Near East and Africa, 1945*, 8:1224; C. L. Sulzberger, "Russo-Turkish straits talk halted as Ankara rejects three demands," *New York Times*, August 4, 1945; Sam Pope Brewer, "Turks talk war if Russia presses; prefer vain battle to surrender," *New York Times*, August 7, 1945; Polyzoides, "Turkish anti-Russian outbreaks stir fears," *Los Angeles Times*, December 6, 1945; C. L. Sulzberger,

"Turks' refusal to cede land affirmed by foreign chief," *New York Times*, December 22, 1945; Polyzoides, "Display of ships emphasizes Truman policy," *Los Angeles Times*, March 19, 1947.

38. U.S. Department of State, *Near East and Africa, 1946*, 7:809–10.

39. C. L. Sulzberger, "Turks' refusal to cede land affirmed by foreign chief," *New York Times*, December 22, 1945; "Another Stathmos?" *Time*, December 31, 1945.

40. Harris, *Troubled alliance*, 29.

41. Larson, *Origins of containment*, 310–11; Felix Belair, Jr., "Truman Mid-East plea today is assured of bipartisan aid," *New York Times*, March 12, 1947.

42. Acheson, *Present at the creation*, 219; Larson, *Origins of containment*, 306; Kissinger, *Diplomacy*, 452.

43. Jones, *Fifteen weeks*, 18; McCullough, *Truman*, 547; Truman, "Truman Doctrine."

44. McCullough, *Truman*, 547; Beisner, *Dean Acheson*, 52.

45. McCullough, *Truman*, 547.

46. Truman, *Years of trial*, 106; Truman, "Truman Doctrine."

47. Truman, *Years of trial*, 106; Jones, *Fifteen weeks*, 23.

48. Jones, *Fifteen weeks*, 19; Beisner, *Dean Acheson*, 62; McCullough, *Truman*, 555, 990.

49. Larson, *Origins of containment*, 312.

50. McCullough, *Truman*, 548–49; Harold Callender, "Europe is amazed by blunt warning," *New York Times*, March 13, 1947; G. W. Sand, ed., *Defending the West: The Truman-Churchill correspondence, 1945–1960* (Westport, CT: Praeger Publishers, 2004), 164.

51. Beisner, *Dean Acheson*, 61, 63; Harris, *Troubled alliance*, 26; Acheson, *Present at the creation*, 225.

52. Memorandum from Gordon P. Merriam to Loy W. Henderson, November 19, 1945, SD-RG 59, 860J.00/11–1945.

53. Memorandum from Loy W. Henderson to Dean Acheson, November 19, 1945, SD-RG 59, 860J.00/11–1945.

54. Memorandum from E. M. Wright to Robert McClintock, June 23, 1947, SD-RG 59, 860J.01/6–2347. Acheson was personally involved in Armenian territorial claims from their outset; see Dean Acheson to Eleanor Roosevelt, September 8, 1945, SD-RG 59, 860J.00/8–2945.

55. Elgin Groseclose to James F. Byrnes, September 17, 1945, SD-RG 59, 860J.01/9–1745; Military Intelligence Service, Research Unit, *Armenian nationalism and the U.S.S.R. (Project 2943)*, February 15, 1946, National Archives; Memorandum of conversation, January 10, 1947, SD-RG 59, 860J.01/1–1047.

56. Suny, *Looking toward Ararat*, 173–75.

57. Elgin Groseclose to James F. Byrnes, September 17, 1945, SD-RG 59, 860J.01/9–1745; Military Intelligence Service, Research Unit, *Armenian nationalism and the U.S.S.R. (Project 2943)*, February 15, 1946, National Archives; Memorandum of conversation, January 10, 1947, SD-RG 59, 860J.01/1–1047.

58. Memorandum from Gordon P. Merriam to Loy W. Henderson, November 19, 1945, SD-RG 59, 860J.00/11–1945; Memorandum from E. M. Wright to Robert McClintock, June 23, 1947, SD-RG 59, 860J.01/6–2347; Suny, *Looking toward Ararat*, 172–75.

59. Ricky-Dale Calhoun "The art of strategic counterintelligence: The Musketeer's cloak: Strategic deception during the Suez crisis of 1956," https://www.cia.gov/library/center-for-the-study-of-intelligence/csi-publications/csi-studies/studies/vol51no2/the-art-of-strategic-counterintelligence.html.

60. Burdett, *Armenia*, 1025–30; Messerlian, "Kars and Ardahan," 69.

61. Burdett, *Armenia*, 1005, 1030; Vernon V. Aspaturian, *The Union Republics in*

Soviet diplomacy: A study of Soviet federalism in the service of Soviet foreign policy (Westport, CT: Greenwood Press, 1984), 71.

62. Armenian National Committee, *Armenian Bulletin, No. 5* (March 1946); Armenian National Committee, *Armenian Bulletin, No. 6* (July 1946); American Committee for Armenian Rights, *The Aspirations of the Armenian people appeal to the conscience of the world*, 1946, AD; Office memorandum, April 8, 1948, SD-RG 59, 867.4016/4–848; Hovannisian, "Etiology and sequelae," 128.

63. Memorandum of conversation, November 9, 1945, SD-RG 59, 860J.00/11–945.

64. Memorandum from Loy W. Henderson to Dean Acheson, November 19, 1945, SD-RG 59, 860J.00/11–1945; Memorandum from Gordon P. Merriam to Loy W. Henderson, November 19, 1945, SD-RG 59, 860J.00/11–1945; Memorandum of conversation, January 10, 1947, SD-RG 59, 860J.01/1–1047.

65. Memorandum of conversation, September 6, 1945, SD-RG 59, 860J.00/9–645; Memorandum of conversation, September 6, 1945, SD-RG 59, 860J.014/9–645; James G. Mitchell to James F. Byrnes, October 30, 1945, SD-RG 59, 860J.00/10–3045; Perry A. Hull to James F. Byrnes, November 5, 1945, SD-RG 59, 860J.00/11–545; Memorandum from Gordon P. Merriam to James F. Byrnes, November 6, 1945, SD-RG 59, 860J.00/11–645; H. E. Rhodes to James F. Byrnes, December 17, 1946, SD-RG 59, 111.11 Byrnes, James F./12–1746; Gordon P. Merriam to H. E. Rhodes, December 31, 1946, SD-RG 59, 111.11 Byrnes, James F./12–1746.

66. Memorandum of conversation, November 9, 1945, SD-RG 59, 860J.00/11–1945; Memorandum from Loy W. Henderson to Dean Acheson, November 19, 1945, SD-RG 59, 860J.00/11–1945.

67. Memorandum of conversation, September 6, 1945, SD-RG 59, 860J.00/9–645.

68. Memorandum of conversation, May 29, 1946, SD-RG 59, 860J.00/5–2946.

69. Memorandum from Mr. Moore to Mr. Jernegan, November 9, 1949, SD-RG 59, 860J.403/11–949.

70. Memorandum from Gordon P. Merriam to Loy W. Henderson, November 19, 1945, SD-RG 59, 860J.00/11–1945.

71. Aspaturian, *Union Republics*, 75–76.

72. Leffler, "Strategy," 817; Richard C. Campany, Jr., *Turkey and the United States: The arms embargo period* (New York: Praeger, 1986), 22.

73. U.S. Department of State, *Foreign relations of the United States, 1949: The Near East, South Asia, and Africa* (Washington, DC: U.S. Government Printing Office, 1949), 6:1660; U.S. Department of State, *Foreign relations of the United States, 1951: The Near East and Africa* (Washington, DC: U.S. Government Printing Office, 1951), 5:1121.

74. Beisner, *Dean Acheson*, 253; Harris, *Troubled alliance*, 35–42; Leffler, "Strategy," 819–22; Acheson, *Present at the creation*, 563–64, 570.

75. Leffler, "Strategy," 820–24; U.S. Department of State, *Near East and Africa, 1951*, 5: 4–10, 21–42, 117; Beisner, *Dean Acheson*, 133, 460; U.S. Department of State, *Foreign relations of the United States, 1951: European security and the German question, Part 1* (Washington, DC: U.S. Government Printing Office, 1951), 3:502.

76. Beisner, *Dean Acheson*, 460; Harris, *Troubled alliance*, 49–95.

77. Gregorian, *Road to home*, 76–77, 91–92, 103, 144, 334.

Silence

1. Leon Z. Surmelian, *Louys Zvart and Vahan Tekeyan's letters to Leon Zaven Surmelian* (Beirut: Atlas, 1972), 43.

2. Herbert Hoover, *Memoirs: Years of adventure, 1874–1920* (New York: Macmillan, 1951), 385.

3. Walker, *Armenia*, 349; Maud S. Mandel, *In the aftermath of genocide: Armenians and Jews in twentieth-century France* (Durham, NC: Duke University Press, 2003), 4, 25.

4. Raymond Kévorkian, Lévon Nordiguian, and Vahé Tachjian, eds., *Les Arméniens, 1917–1939: La quête d'un refuge* (Beirut: Saint Joseph University Press, 2006), 103; George Y. Gracey, "Armenian settlement in Syria," *Contemporary Review* 140 (1931): 86; Moranian, "American missionaries," 206; Ellen Marie Lust-Okar, "Failure of collaboration: Armenian refugees in Syria," *Middle Eastern Studies* 32, no. 1 (1996): 57; Barton, *Near East Relief*, 66, 75.

5. Moranian, "American missionaries," 133–34; Moranian, "Legacy of paradox," 312.

6. Miller and Miller, *Survivors*, 103, 125, 128; Barton, *Near East Relief*, 221.

7. Alexander, "Armenian and American," 119–20, 280; Mirak, *Torn between two lands*, 144–45; Bella Stumbo, "L.A. Armenians: The trauma of finding a self-image," *Los Angeles Times*, June 8, 1980.

8. Mirak, *Torn between two lands*, 273.

9. Interview with Walter Karabian; Interview with Shakeh Kadehjian; JMH.

10. Alexander, "Armenian and American," 86.

11. Rubina Peroomian, "Problematic aspects of reading Genocide literature: A search for a guideline or a canon," in *Remembrance and denial: The case of the Armenian Genocide*, ed. Hovannisian, 180; Rubina Peroomian, "New directions in literary responses to the Armenian Genocide," in *Looking backward, moving forward: Confronting the Armenian Genocide*, ed. Hovannisian, 159; Vahé Oshagan, "The impact of the Genocide on West Armenian letters," in *The Armenian Genocide in perspective*, ed. Hovannisian, 173–74; Leo Hamalian, "The Armenian Genocide and the literary imagination," in ibid., 165; RPA. One of the few Genocide-related works to reach the mainstream public in the United States was Leon Z. Surmelian's 1945 novel, *I Ask You Ladies and Gentlemen*.

12. William Saroyan, *An Armenian trilogy*, ed. Dickran Kouymjian (Fresno, CA: California State University Press, 1986), 6–7; Walter Shear, "Saroyan's study of ethnicity," *MELUS* 13, nos. 1–2 (1986): 45; David Stephen Calonne, *William Saroyan: My real work is being* (Chapel Hill: University of North Carolina Press, 1983), 47–57.

13. David B. MacDonald, *Identity politics in the age of genocide: The Holocaust and historical representation* (London: Routledge, 2008), 18; Edward T. Linenthal, *Preserving memory: The struggle to create America's Holocaust museum* (New York: Columbia University Press, 2001), 6; Peter Novick, *The Holocaust in American life* (New York: Mariner Books, 2000), 19–20, 83, 98, 100, 104–5, 123, 133, 144, 209–14.

14. A portion of Christopher J. Walker's book—*Armenia: The survival of a nation*—covers the Genocide.

15. Interview with Dikran Kaligian; Panossian, *Armenians*, 259.

16. Khachig Tololyan, "Exile governments in the Armenian polity," in *Governments-in-exile in contemporary world politics*, ed. Yossi Shain (New York: Routledge, 1991), 182; Interview with Jirayr Haroutunian (courtesy of Robert A. Kaloosdian). The primary political force in this non-Tashnag camp was the Ramgavar Party. This camp also included the Hunchakian Party, which had little prominence in the United States, as well as a smaller subgroup of Communists and Soviet sympathizers. The non-Tashnag camp also included civic, religious, and social organizations.

17. Mirak, *Torn between two lands*, 244, 252; Benjamin Alexander, "Contested

memories, divided Diaspora: Armenian Americans, the thousand-day Republic, and the polarized response to an Archbishop's murder," *Journal of American Ethnic History* 27, no. 1 (2007): 34.

18. Interview with Hagop Sarkissian; RAK; Interview with Jirayr Haroutunian.

19. "Soviet issue stirs Church delegates," *New York Times*, September 4, 1933; "Slain in 187th St. church," *New York Times*, December 25, 1933; Phillips, "Symbol, myth, and rhetoric," 123; Oshagan Minassian, "A History of the Armenian Holy Apostolic Orthodox Church in the United States (1888–1944)," PhD diss., Boston University, 1974, 453–56.

20. Alexander, "Contested memories," 32–33; Minassian, "Armenian Holy Apostolic Orthodox Church," 441.

21. "Soviet issue stirs Church delegates," *New York Times*, September 4, 1933; Minassian, "Armenian Holy Apostolic Orthodox Church," 465–75; Atamian, *The Armenian community*, 365–66. The Catholicos in Soviet Armenia broke the logjam by declaring Tourian the winner of the disputed contest.

22. "Slain in 187th St. church," *New York Times*, December 25, 1933; Minassian, "Armenian Holy Apostolic Orthodox Church," 479–80.

23. "Slain in 187th St. church," *New York Times*, December 25, 1933; "Killing of Prelate laid to 5 rebels," *New York Times*, December 26, 1933; "Prelate's murder laid to 2 at trial," *New York Times*, June 12, 1934; Minassian, "Armenian Holy Apostolic Orthodox Church," 480–81.

24. "2 more arrested in church slaying," *New York Times*, December 29, 1933; "25 policemen guard archbishop's body," *New York Times*, January 1, 1934; "Thousands honor slain archbishop," *New York Times*, January 2, 1934; "Archbishop's body is placed in vault," *New York Times*, January 3, 1934; "Slain Archbishop mourned by 3,000," *New York Times*, January 29, 1934; "Five hurt in clash of Armenians here," *New York Times*, February 26, 1934; "Marchers clash in Chicago," *New York Times*, April 9, 1934; "Armenian rivals riot in two cities," *New York Times*, April 9, 1934; "Plan tomb for slain Prelate," *New York Times*, November 8, 1934; "Armenian priest shot at funeral," *New York Times*, March 18, 1935; Alexander, "Armenian and American," 159–60; Alexander, "Contested memories," 32; Kooshian, "Armenian immigrant community," 380–81, 397. Terry Phillips, who has studied the Tourian murder and ensuing trial probably more closely than anyone else, pointed out that the judge overseeing the trial often made biased decisions against the interests of the defendants.

25. Gregory Doudoukjian, "Oral history: An intergenerational study of the effects of the assassination of Archbishop Leon Tourian in 1933 on Armenian-Americans," Master's thesis, St. Vladimir's Orthodox Theological Seminary, 1993, 76–85; RGH.

26. Avedis Derounian, "My Father's Legacy," AD; John Roy Carlson, *Under cover: My four years in the Nazi underworld of America* (New York: E. P. Dutton & Co., 1943), 16.

27. Carlson, *Under cover*, 16.

28. John Roy Carlson, *Cairo to Damascus* (New York: Alfred A. Knopf, 1951), 8–9.

29. *Real Detective* to Avedis Derounian, June 11, 1935, AD; "'Jefferson' awards presented to 10 here," *New York Times*, April 14, 1947; Glenn Fowler, "Arthur Derounian, 82, an author of books on fascists and bigots," *New York Times*, April 25, 1991; James Russell, "This land was your land, this land was my land," *Zeek*, November 2004; Ternon, *Armenian cause*, 110; Alexander, "Contested memories," 54;

30. Carlson, *Under cover*, 20.

31. "Armenian Fascists launch campaign in U.S.," *The Hour*, May 31, 1941; John Roy Carlson to Robert W. Kenney, July 20, 1944, AD; John Roy Carlson to Harry S. Truman, October 16, 1945, SD-RG 59, 860J.00/10–1645; John Roy Carlson to James F. Byrnes, October 18, 1945, AD; John Roy Carlson to Albert E. Kahn, October 23, 1945, AD; John Roy Carlson to *New York Herald Tribune*, October 31, 1945, AD; John Roy Carlson to Dean Acheson, November 8, 1945, AD; American Friends of the Armenians, "The case for and against the Armenian Revolutionary Federation," AD; Carlson, *Cairo to Damascus*, 8–9, 436–41.
32. James H. Tashjian, "Two newly-discovered English-language journals, or workbooks, of Reuben Darbinian, late editor-in-chief, Hairenik publications," *Armenian Review* 33, no. 3 (1980): 246–65.
33. Ibid., "Reuben Darbinian: an appreciation," *Armenian Review* 21, no. 3 (1968): 4–9; John Leggett, *A daring young man: A biography of William Saroyan* (New York: Alfred A. Knopf, 2002), 20–21; RAK.
34. Reuben Darbinian, "Our neutrals," *Armenian Review* 7, no. 4 (1954): 17–23.
35. *The Armenian Reporter* 2, no. 3–4 (1955): 2.
36. "34 foreign-language journals in U.S. said to follow Red line," *New York Times*, June 25, 1955.
37. Steven B. Derounian to Avedis Derounian, March 21, 1955, AD; American Committee for liberation from Bolshevism, Inc., to John Roy Carlson, April 20, 1955, AD; John Roy Carlson to Herbert Brownell, Jr., July 8, 1955, AD; Avedis Derounian to Hratch Yervant, July 11, 1955, AD; Memorandum from Mr. Barbour to Herbert Hoover, Jr., July 19, 1955, SD-RG 59, 861.413/7–1955; Memorandum of Conversation, July 19, 1955, SD-RG 59, 861.313/7–1955; Memorandum from Mr. Barbour to Herbert Hoover, Jr., July 21, 1955, SD-RG 59, 861.413/7–1955; Herbert Hoover, Jr., to Steven B. Derounian, July 26, 1955, AD; John Roy Carlson to Yaroslav Chyz, July 28, 1955, AD; Memorandum of Conversation, August 31, 1955, SD-RG 59, 861.413/8–3155; Photo of Archbishop Mampre Calfayan with Steven B. Derounian and Herbert Hoover, Jr., AD; Irving Long, "An end to a career on the right," *Newsday*, August 7, 1981; David Zenian, "Steve Derounian: The first Armenian in Congress," *AGBU News*, March 1996; Wolfgang Saxon, "Steven B. Derounian, 89, Judge and Nassau Ex-Congressman, dies," *New York Times*, April 20, 2007.
38. Dean Acheson to American Embassy (Ankara), et al., July 28, 1952, SD-RG 59, 032 Carlson, John Roy/7–2852; John Foster Dulles to State Department, February 2, 1953, SD-RG 59, 032 Carlson, John Roy/2–253; Memorandum of conversation, April 27, 1954, SD-RG 59, 032 Carlson, John Roy/4–2754; American Embassy (Moscow) to State Department, October 24, 1955, SD-RG 59, 861.413/10–2455.
39. Archbishop Mesrob Ashjian, *The Armenian Church in America* (New York: Armenian Prelacy, 1995), 33.
40. Felix Corley, "The Armenian Church under the Soviet Regime, Part 2: The leadership of Vazgen," *Religion, State and Society* 24, no. 4 (1996): 295; Suny, *Looking toward Ararat*, 227.
41. Tony Smith, *Foreign attachments: The power of ethnic groups in the making of American foreign policy* (Cambridge, MA: Harvard University Press, 2000), 76; Thomas Ambrosio, "Ethnic identity groups and U.S. foreign policy," in *Ethnic identity groups and U.S. foreign policy*, ed. Thomas Ambrosio (Westport, CT: Greenwood Publishing Group, 2002), 5–7; Interview with Aram Hamparian; RV.
42. Statement of Thomas E. Dewey, February 18, 1953, AD; American Committee for the Independence of Armenia, *Armenian revolt against Soviet rule*, 1953;

"Mayor proclaims today Armenian Independence Day," *Hartford Courant*, May 28, 1953; "Armenians mark Independence Day anniversary," *Hartford Courant*, May 28, 1954; "Armenians to hold celebration Sunday," *Hartford Courant*, June 4, 1955; "Author to speak at Armenian day dinner today," *Hartford Courant*, June 5, 1955; "Armenian day marked here," *New York Times*, June 4, 1956; "Rep. May gives address at Armenian observance," *Hartford Courant*, June 3, 1957; "Boston Armenians hear Sen. Dodd," *Hartford Courant*, February 23, 1959; "Memorial to Wilson," *New York Times*, May 25, 1959. For examples of statements regarding the Armenian Republic made in Congress before 1965, see 83rd Cong., 1st sess., *Cong. Rec.* 99 (February 18, 1953): H 1193; 83rd Cong., 2d sess., *Cong. Rec.* 100 (February 8, 1954): H 2027; 83rd Cong., 2d sess., *Cong. Rec.* 100 (March 5, 1954): H 2769; 83rd Cong., 2d sess., *Cong. Rec.* 100 (May 4, 1954): H 5977; 86th Cong., 2d sess., *Cong. Rec.* 106 (May 11, 1960): S 9967; 88th Cong., 1st sess., *Cong. Rec.* 109 (May 8, 1963): S 8017. Armenian groups routinely sent correspondence to American officials regarding Soviet conquest of the republic; see American Committee for the Independence of Armenia to John Foster Dulles, February 2, 1953, SD-RG 59, 761.00/2–253; Armenian Committee for the Independence of Armenia to Dwight D. Eisenhower, April 18, 1955, SD-RG 59, 861.424/4–1855; A. Proudian and A. Yacoubian to Dwight D. Eisenhower, July 4, 1955, SD-RG 59, 761.00/7–455; and Armenian Committee for the Independence of Armenia to Dwight D. Eisenhower, May 9, 1958, SD-RG 59, 861.424/5–958.

43. On rare occasions, when the subject of Turkey and the Genocide did come up, the State Department frowned upon such conversations; see Beglar Navassardian to John Foster Dulles, October 8, 1955, SD-RG 59, 782.00/10–855; Memorandum of conversation, November 28, 1955, SD-RG 59, 861.413/11–2855.

44. House Select Committee on Communist Aggression and the Forced Incorporation of the Baltic States into the U.S.S.R., *Communist takeover and occupation of Armenia*, 83rd Cong., 2d sess., 1954, Special Report 5, 3, 7; House Select Committee on Communist Aggression and the Forced Incorporation of the Baltic States into the U.S.S.R., *Investigation of communist takeover and occupation of the non-Russian nations of the U.S.S.R.: Hearings on H.R. 346 and 438*, 83rd Cong., 2d sess., 1954, 153–78; V. Stanley Vardys, "Select committees of the House of Representatives," *Midwest Journal of Political Science* 6, no. 3 (1962): 250, 254; John Fisher, "Demand action to stamp Reds as aggressors," *Chicago Tribune*, March 23, 1955. Reuben Darbinian testified at the committee's hearings.

45. "Genocide pact plea pressed by Lehman," *New York Times*, May 23, 1955; Gerard Chaliand and Yves Ternon, *The Armenians: From Genocide to resistance*, trans. Tony Berrett (London: Zed Press, 1983), 1.

Resurrection

1. Ludmilla Alexeyeva, *Soviet dissent: Contemporary movements for national, religious, and human rights*, trans. Carol Pearce and John Glad (Middletown, CT: Wesleyan University Press, 1985), 123; Panossian, *Armenians*, 320–21; Stepan Alajajian, *Vatsunakank* (Los Angeles: "Nor Keank," 2002), 69–74. In 1964, 10,000 Armenians in Uruguay conducted a silent march in Montevideo. The march never received much attention and did not serve as a seminal event in the resurrection of the Genocide. For details, see *HW*, July 2, 1964; Vartan Matiossian, "Haykakan Tseghaspanutian janachume Uruguayi mech (patmakan aknark)," *Haratch*, April 23–25, 2004.

2. *AMS*, February 6, 1965; *AMS*, May 22, 1965; *HW*, May 27, 1965; Dadrian, "Nationalism in Soviet Armenia," 247; Alajajian, *Vatsunakank*, 63; Haig Sarkis-

sian, "50th anniversary of the Turkish Genocide as observed in Erevan," *Armenian Review* 19, no. 4 (1966): 24–25; R. H. Dekmejian, "Soviet-Turkish relations and politics in the Armenian SSR," *Soviet Studies* 19, no. 4 (1968): 513.

3. Sarkissian, "50th anniversary," 23–24; Alajajian, *Vatsunakank*, 69–90; Gregorian, *Road to home*, 178; Alexeyeva, *Soviet dissent*, 123; Interview with Arto Vorperian.

4. Gregorian, *Road to home*, 185; Alajajian, *Vatsunakank*, 69–82.

5. Hovannisian, "Etiology and sequelae," 128; Hamalian, "Armenian Genocide," 154; Interview with Arto Vorperian.

6. Panossian, *Armenians*, 321.

7. Alexeyeva, *Soviet dissent*, 123; Alajajian, *Vatsunakank*, 83–90; Dekmejian, "Soviet-Turkish relations," 514; Dadrian, "Nationalism in Soviet Armenia," 247; Panossian, *Armenians*, 320; *AMS*, May 22, 1965; Vincent J. Burke, "Armenia irks Moscow with anti-Turkey rally," *Los Angeles Times*, May 30, 1966; Peter Osnos, "Armenians battle shift to Soviet ways," *Los Angeles Times*, November 21, 1975.

8. *AMS*, February 6, 1965; *AMS*, May 22, 1965; *HW*, May 27, 1965; Dadrian, "Nationalism in Soviet Armenia," 247; Alajajian, *Vatsunakank*, 63; Sarkissian, "50th anniversary," 24–25; Dekmejian, "Soviet-Turkish relations," 513.

9. Alajajian, *Vatsunakank*, 75–97; Alexeyeva, *Soviet dissent*, 123; Gregorian, *Road to home*, 185; Sarkissian, "50th anniversary," 23–27; *HW*, May 27, 1965; Freeman J. Dyson, "Letter from Armenia," *New Yorker*, November 6, 1971, 128.

10. Sarkissian, "50th anniversary," 26; Panossian, *Armenians*, 320; Gregorian, *Road to home*, 185; Dadrian, "Nationalism in Soviet Armenia," 247; Alajajian, *Vatsunakank*, 83–90.

11. Gregorian, *Road to home*, 185; Dekmejian, "Soviet-Turkish relations," 514–15; Vincent J. Burke, "Armenia irks Moscow with anti-Turkey rally," *Los Angeles Times*, May 30, 1966.

12. According to Razmik Panossian, the 1965 demonstration in Yerevan also gave birth to a nationalistic dissident movement in Soviet Armenia that by the late 1980s served as one of the most rebellious elements of the crumbling USSR.

13. "Armenians slate memorial service," *Hartford Courant*, March 11, 1965; *HW*, March 18, 1965; Linda Case, "Armenians to recount tragic history of 1915," *Hartford Courant*, March 27, 1965; "More Armenian groups to hold commemoration," *Hartford Courant*, April 4, 1965; *HW*, April 8, 1965; *HW*, April 15, 1965; *AMS*, April 17, 1965; "Photo standalone 23—no title," *Hartford Courant*, April 18, 1965; *CC*, April 22, 1965; *HW*, April 22, 1965; "Armenians plan memorial rites," *Los Angeles Times*, April 23, 1965; *AMS*, April 24, 1965; "Rites will memorialize massacre of Armenians," *Los Angeles Times*, April 24, 1965; "Armenians to mark massacres of 1915," *New York Times*, April 24, 1965; "Armenian mass," *Washington Post*, April 24, 1965; "Armenians mark a tragic 1915 day," *New York Times*, April 25, 1965; "Soviet article accuses Turks," *New York Times*, April 25, 1965; "500 Armenians attend rites to note massacre," *Los Angeles Times*, April 25, 1965; David Lancashire, "Armenians haunted by massacre 50 years ago," *Los Angeles Times*, April 25, 1965; "Event to mark 1915 massacres of Armenians," *Chicago Tribune*, April 26, 1965; David Rhinelander, "400 state Armenians commemorate anniversary of Turkish 'Genocide,'" *Hartford Courant*, April 26, 1965; "1915 massacre commemorated by Armenians," *Washington Post*, April 26, 1965; "Concert honors Armenians massacred by Turks," *New York Times*, April 26, 1965; *HW*, May 6, 1965; *AMS*, May 22, 1965; *HW*, May 27, 1965; *AMS*, June 26, 1965; *AMS*, July 17, 1965; *AMS*, September 18, 1965; *HW*, October 14, 1965; James H. Tashjian, "The truth about the Turkish act of genocide," *Armenian Review* 18, no. 3 (1965): 41; Vahakn N. Dadrian, "The events of April 24 in

Moscow—how they happened and under what circumstances," *Armenian Review* 20, no. 2 (1967): 9–26; Dadrian, "Nationalism in Soviet Armenia," 246–47; Ternon, *Armenian cause*, 164.

14. Interview with Charles Metjian, Jr.; *AMS*, April 8, 1967; Obituary of Charles Metjian, Sr., *Jersey Journal*, December 22–26, 2007.

15. *AMS*, April 17, 1965.

16. James H. Tashjian, *Turkey: Author of genocide* (Boston: Commemorative Committee on the 50th anniversary of the Turkish massacres of the Armenians, 1965); *Is the U.S. interested . . . in human rights . . . in justice?* (Boston: Commemorative Committee on the 50th anniversary of the Turkish massacres of the Armenians, 1965); *These were the children . . .* (Boston: Commemorative Committee on the 50th anniversary of the Turkish Genocide of the Armenians, 1965); Ignatius Peter XVI Batanian, *The Armenian tragedy (50th anniversary of the massacres), 1915–1965*, 1965; *Armenian Martyrs day: April 24, 1965* (San Francisco: Northern California Committee, 1965); *AMS*, January 29, 1966; *AMS*, October 14, 1967; *AMS*, October 21, 1967; "Lest we forget," *Armenian Review* 18, no. 2 (1965): 3–4; Delegation of the Armenian Republic, "Memorandum on the Armenian question," *Armenian Review* 19, no. 3 (1966): 3–16.

17. *AMS*, April 10, 1965; *CC*, April 22, 1965; *HW*, April 22, 1965; *AMS*, May 1, 1965; *HW*, May 13, 1965; *AMS*, May 22, 1965; *HW*, June 24, 1965.

18. Garen Yegparian, "Armenian issues in *The Congressional Record*, 1965–1983," *Armenian Review* 40, no. 1 (1987): 63; 89th Cong., 1st sess., *Cong. Rec.* 111 (April 5, 1965): S 7043; 89th Cong., 1st sess., *Cong. Rec.* 111 (April 22, 1965): H 8224; 89th Cong., 1st sess., *Cong. Rec.* 111 (April 23, 1965): S 8347–48, 8353–54; 89th Cong., 1st sess., *Cong. Rec.* 111 (April 26, 1965): H 8372, 8386–91, S 8420, 8503–04; 89th Cong., 1st sess., *Cong. Rec.* 111 (April 27, 1965): S 8510; 89th Cong., 1st sess., *Cong. Rec.* 111 (April 29, 1965): H 8885, 8888–98, S 8955, 8964.

19. Gerald R. Ford, "Armenian Independence," speech, May 27, 1955, Gerald R. Ford Congressional Papers, 1949–1973, Press Secretary and Speech File, Box D14, GRF; 89th Cong., 1st sess., *Cong. Rec.* 111 (April 29, 1965): H 8890.

20. Memorandum from American Embassy (Ankara) to State Department, April 20, 1965, SD-63/73 POL 13–6, TUR; American Consulate (Istanbul) to State Department, May 3, 1965, SD-63/73 POL 13–3, TUR; Memorandum of conversation, July 13, 1965, SD-63/73 POL, TUR-US; Memorandum of conversation, February 23, 1967, SD-63/73 CUL 10–2, US; Housepian, "Unremembered genocide," 61; James G. Mandalian, "An exposure of Turkish falsifications," *Armenian Review* 18, no. 4 (1965): 12; *HW*, May 20, 1965.

21. Memorandum of conversation, May 17, 1965, SD-63/73 POL, TUR-US; Memorandum of conversation, June 17, 1965, SD-63/73 POL, TUR-US; Memorandum of conversation, July 13, 1965, SD-63/73 POL, TUR-US.

22. William P. Rogers to American Embassy (Ankara), February 15, 1973, State 028699.

23. Altemur Kilic, letter to the editor, *New York Times*, May 4, 1965.

24. OK; LK; MM; Interview with George K. Mandossian; Irene H. Grimes, "City accepts plans of Armenian shaft," *Montebello Messenger*, January 12, 1967; *Asbarez*, January 20, 1967.

25. OK; RGH; Interview with George K. Mandossian; LK; MM; *CC*, February 29, 1968; "Announce April 21st date for monument unveiling," *Montebello News*, March 17, 1968; *AR*, April 12, 2008.

26. LK; Interview with George K. Mandossian; Interview with Missak Haigentz; OK;

CC, February 29, 1968; Steven C. Smith, "Tower leans to controversy," *Los Angeles Times*, June 3, 1971.

27. RGH; OK; MM; Irene H. Grimes, "City accepts plans of Armenian shaft," *Montebello Messenger*, January 12, 1967; *Asbarez*, January 20, 1967; *CC*, January 26, 1967.

28. *CC*, January 26, 1967; RGH; Interview with George K. Mandossian.

29. *Asbarez*, January 20, 1967; *CC*, January 26, 1967.

30. Memorandum of conversation, June 17, 1965, SD-63/73 POL, TUR-US; Memorandum of conversation, July 13, 1965, SD-63/73 POL, TUR-US; Memorandum of conversation, January 19, 1967, SD-63/73 CUL 10–2, US; Memorandum of conversation, February 23, 1967, SD-63/73 CUL 10–2, US; State Department document (untitled), February 24, 1967, SD-63/73 CUL 10–2, US.

31. Memorandum of conversation, January 5, 1967, SD-63/73 CUL 10–2, US; Memorandum of conversation, January 19, 1967, SD-63/73 CUL 10–2, US; Memorandum to files, January 19, 1967, CH, Box 82; Memorandum to files (Part II), January 19, 1967, CH, Box 82; "'Monument' gets final OK," *Montebello News*, January 26, 1967; OK.

32. Memorandum from John M. Howison to Mr. Constable, July 20, 1966, SD-63/73 CUL 12–2, US; Memorandum from John M. Howison to Mr. Constable, September 20, 1966, SD-63/73 CUL 12–2, US; Memorandum to files, January 19, 1967, CH, Box 82; Memorandum to files (Part II), January 19, 1967, CH, Box 82; Memorandum from Eliot Stanley to files, January 30, 1967, CH, Box 82.

33. Memorandum of conversation, May 17, 1965, SD-63/73 POL, TUR-US; Telegram from State Department to American Embassy (Ankara), June 18, 1968, SD-63/73 POL, TUR-US; Memorandum of conversation, May 14, 1969, SD-63/73 POL, TUR-US.

34. Memorandum from American Embassy (Ankara) to State Department, April 20, 1965, SD-63/73 POL 13–6, TUR; Douglas MacArthur II to Charles S. Joelson, February 15, 1967, SD-63/73 POL 7, TUR; DeWitt L. Stora to D. Dadourian, March 9, 1967, SD-63/73 POL 7, TUR; Dixon Donnelley to Leon Sahagian, April 28, 1967, SD-63/73 POL 7, TUR.

35. Memorandum of conversation, June 17, 1965, SD-63/73 POL, TUR-US; Memorandum of conversation, July 13, 1965, SD-63/73 POL, TUR-US; Memorandum of conversation, January 5, 1967, SD-63/73 CUL 10–2, US; Memorandum of conversation, January 19, 1967, SD-63/73 CUL 10–2, US; Memorandum of conversation, January 27, 1967, SD-63/73 POL, TUR-US; Memorandum of conversation, February 23, 1967, SD-63/73 CUL 10–2, US; Memorandum of conversation, March 16, 1967, SD-63/73 POL 7, TUR; Aide-mémoire, June 17, 1968, SD-63/73 POL, TUR-US; State Department to American Embassy (Ankara), June 18, 1968, SD-63/73 POL, TUR-US; State Department response to Turkish Aide-mémoire, August 20, 1968, SD-63/73 POL, TUR-US; Memorandum of conversation, May 14, 1969, SD-63/73 POL, TUR-US.

36. Memorandum of conversation, March 19, 1968, SD-63/73 CUL 10–2, US.

37. Memorandum of conversation, May 14, 1969, SD-63/73 POL, TUR-US.

38. State Department response to Turkish Aide-mémoire, August 20, 1968, SD-63/73 POL, TUR-US.

39. Memorandum from William P. Rogers to Richard M. Nixon, February 11, 1969, SD-63/73 POL, TUR-US.

40. Memorandum from Joseph S. Sisco to Elliot L. Richardson, April 29, 1970, SD-63/73 POL 17, TUR-US.

41. Memorandum of conversation, January 19, 1967, SD-63/73 CUL 10–2, US;

Memorandum of conversation, January 27, 1967, SD-63/73 POL, TUR-US; Douglas MacArthur II to Charles S. Joelson, February 15, 1967, SD-63/73 POL 7, TUR; "'Monument' gets final OK," *Montebello News*, January 26, 1967; "Turks want memorial, too," *Montebello News*, May 25, 1967; Steven C. Smith, "Montebello tower leans to controversy," *Los Angeles Times*, June 6, 1971; OK; LK.

42. Interview with Walter Karabian.

43. Ibid.; RPA; Denise Aghanian, *The Armenian Diaspora: Cohesion and fracture* (Lanham, MD: University Press of America, 2007), 91–92; Anny Bakalian, *Armenian-Americans: From being to feeling Armenian* (New Brunswick, NJ: Transaction Publishers, 1994), 11, 428.

44. MM.

45. Irene H. Grimes, "City accepts plans of Armenian shaft," *Montebello Messenger*, January 12, 1967; *Asbarez*, January 20, 1967; *CC*, January 26, 1967; "'Monument' gets final OK," *Montebello News*, January 26, 1967; Steven C. Smith, "Montebello tower leans to controversy," *Los Angeles Times*, June 6, 1971; Memorandum of conversation, February 23, 1967, SD-63/73 CUL 10–2, US.

46. RPA; DRP; Interview with Missak Haigentz; *Armenian Oral Histories: Walter Karabian, J. Michael Hagopian, Levon Kirakosian*, June 28, 2007.

47. *CC*, April 13, 1967; *CC*, May 2, 1968; *AR*, November 2, 1967; Interview with George K. Mandossian; OK; MM. Masco founder Alex Manoogian made the largest donation of $2,000.

48. *CC*, May 2, 1968; MM.

49. Memorandum of conversation, April 20, 1971, SD-63/73 CUL 10–2, US; 92d Cong., 1st sess., *Cong. Rec.* 117 (April 28, 1971): H 12338; *AR*, May 6, 1971; Steven C. Smith, "Montebello tower leans to controversy," *Los Angeles Times*, June 6, 1971.

50. The account that follows is based on an Interview with VY.

51. Ibid.

52. Hilmar Kaiser, *At the crossroads of Der Zor: Death, survival, and humanitarian resistance in Aleppo, 1915–1917*, in collaboration with Luther Eskijian and Nancy Eskijian (Reading, UK: Taderon Press, 2001), 13, 20–21.

53. Hofmann, "German eyewitness reports," 79–80; Balakian, *Burning Tigris*, 176.

54. VY.

55. Richard J. McNally, *Remembering trauma* (Cambridge, MA: Harvard University Press, 2003), 105, 125; Miller and Miller, *Survivors*, 157–60. Armenia's greatest musician, Komitas, was among those paralyzed by post-traumatic stress. Unable to function after the Genocide, he spent the last years of his life in mental asylums; see Rita S. Kuyumjian, *Archeology of madness: Komitas, portrait of an Armenian icon*, 2nd ed. (Princeton, NJ: Gomidas Institute, 2001).

56. Ternon, *Armenian cause*, 76.

57. VY; Miller and Miller, *Survivors*, 156, 163–64; Levon Boyajian and Haigaz Grigorian, "Psychosocial sequelae of the Armenian Genocide," in *The Armenian Genocide in perspective*, ed. Hovannisian, 180.

58. VY; *AR*, February 12, 1976.

59. *Asbarez*, April 30, 1971; VY; Interview with Gerard Libaridian.

60. Interview with Gerard Libaridian; LK; Memorandum of conversation, April 25, 1972, SD-63/73 POL 17, TUR-US; Memorandum of conversation, May 2, 1972, SD-63/73 POL 17, TUR-US; Memorandum of conversation, June 6, 1972, SD-63/73 POL 23–8, US; *Armenian Observer*, April 26, 1972; *AR*, April 27, 1972; *Asbarez*, April 28, 1972. In November 1972, dozens of young Armenians barged in on an event at the Bel-Air Hotel honoring the founding

of the Turkish Republic. After the two busloads of students entered the hotel's grand ballroom, Kirakosian took over the stage and read a proclamation. When the audience of Turkish and American military and government officials decried Kirakosian's speech, his colleagues formed a shield around him to prevent his removal from the stage. About twenty minutes passed in what Kirakosian described as "guerrilla theatre" at the black-tie event before police arrived to arrest them— LK; *Armenian Observer*, November 8, 1972; *Asbarez*, November 10, 1972; *AR*, November 16, 1972; *AW*, November 23, 1972; GY-I.

61. Phillips, "Symbol, myth, and rhetoric," 171; Bloxham, *Great game*, 214–16; Ternon, *Armenian cause*, 140, 194; Interview with Dikran Kaligian; Interview with Gerard Libaridian.

62. Leggett, *A daring young man*, 323, 347–48; Saroyan, *Armenian trilogy*, 6, 14, 29.

63. Interview with Gerard Libaridian; Interview with Dikran Kaligian; DRP; JMH; RAK; Interview with Kenneth Khachigian; Armenian Youth Federation, *The AYF legacy: portrait of a movement in historical review, 1933–1993* (Watertown, MA: Armenian Youth Federation, 1994), 42–43; Ervin Staub, "Healing and reconciliation," in *Looking backward, moving forward: Confronting the Armenian Genocide*, ed. Hovannisian, 267–70; Miller and Miller, "An oral history perspective on responses to the Armenian Genocide," in *The Armenian Genocide in perspective*, ed. Hovannisian, 198; MacDonald, *Identity politics*, 10.

"I will set the example"

1. Appellant's Opening Brief, GY-CM; GY-T.
2. GY-T; GY-I; Clyde Farnsworth, "War's Casey Jones gets aid to Soviet," *New York Times*, April 29, 1943; Keith Dalton, "2 Turk diplomats slain in hotel here," *Santa Barbara News-Press*, January 28, 1973; Roger Munting, "Lend-lease and the Soviet war effort," *Journal of Contemporary History*, 19, no. 3 (1984): 497.
3. Appellant's Opening Brief, GY-CM; GY-I; GY-T; "Man shot fatally, another wounded," *Santa Barbara News-Press*, January 27, 1973; Dalton, "2 Turk diplomats slain in hotel here," *Santa Barbara News-Press*, January 28, 1973.
4. GY-I; GY-T; Interview with Haig Nishkian; Interview with Velma Chadwick.
5. Appellant's Opening Brief, GY-CM; GY-T; GY-I; "Yanikian pleads innocent; bail hearing due Thursday," *Santa Barbara News-Press*, January 30, 1973; John Dell, "Yanikian's behavior called 'delusional' by psychiatrist," *Santa Barbara News-Press*, June 26, 1973.
6. Keith Dalton, "'Perhaps my act will awaken many,'" *Santa Barbara News-Press*, January 29, 1973.
7. Appellant's Opening Brief, GY-CM; GY-T; GY-I.
8. GY-I; GY-T; Dalton, "'Perhaps my act will awaken many,'" *Santa Barbara News-Press*, January 29, 1973.
9. GY-I; Respondent's Opening Brief, California Court of Appeal, Second Appellate District, March 15, 1974, GY-CM (hereafter cited as Respondent's Opening Brief, GY-CM); American Embassy (Ankara) to William P. Rogers, January 28, 1973, Ankara 00646 281645Z.
10. GY-T; Dalton, "2 Turk diplomats slain in hotel here," *Santa Barbara News-Press*, January 28, 1973; Dalton, "'Perhaps my act will awaken many,'" *Santa Barbara News-Press*, January 29, 1973.
11. Interview with Velma Chadwick; GY-I; GY-T.
12. OK.
13. GY-I; GY-T.

14. GY-I; GY-T.
15. Memorandum of conversation, May 17, 1965, SD-63/73 POL, TUR-US; Report on Mehmet Baydar and Bahadir Demir, n.d., WFO 185–15; "Return of painting used as lure in Consuls' slayings, police say," *Los Angeles Times*, January 29, 1973; GY-T.
16. GY-I; GY-T.
17. Memorandum of conversation, May 17, 1965, SD-63/73 POL, TUR-US; Memorandum of conversation, June 6, 1972, SD-63/73 POL 17, TUR-US; Memorandum regarding Turkish-American Club security request, January 19, 1973, SD-63/73 POL, TUR-US; Mehmet Baydar to Daryl F. Gates, January 19, 1973, SD-63/73 POL, TUR-US.
18. Respondent's Opening Brief, GY-CM; GY-I; GY-T; Dalton, "2 Turk diplomats slain in hotel here," *Santa Barbara News-Press*, January 28, 1973.
19. GY-I; GY-T; Respondent's Opening Brief, GY-CM.
20. GY-I; Interview with James T. Lindsey (courtesy of Mark Arax); Respondent's Opening Brief, GY-CM; Dalton, "2 Turk diplomats slain in hotel here," *Santa Barbara News-Press*, January 28, 1973; "Vengeance against Turks believed motive in killings," *Washington Post*, February 11, 1973.
21. Appellant's Opening Brief, GY-CM; GY-I; GY-T.
22. GY-I; *AR*, February 1, 1973; JMH.
23. GY-I; "Arraignment of Yanikian due sometime tomorrow," *Santa Barbara News-Press*, January 29, 1973.
24. JMH.
25. Ibid.; MM; OK; AFOAM.
26. JMH; AFOAM.
27. James Barron, "Percy Foreman, Texas lawyer, 86; defended the assassin of Dr. King," *New York Times*, August 26, 1988.
28. AFOAM; Interview with James T. Lindsey. A similar disagreement led to Foreman's withdrawal from Jack Ruby's defense years earlier; see "Foreman resigns as Ruby counsel," *New York Times*, March 24, 1964.
29. "The Panthers' honky lawyer," *Time*, January 12, 1970; Interview with James T. Lindsey; OK.
30. GY-I; AFOAM; JMH; OK; John Dell, "Yanikian jury picked; trial resumes Monday," *Santa Barbara News-Press*, June 1, 1973; *AR*, June 21, 1973.
31. JMH; Interview with Bruce Janigian; OK; AFOAM; John Dell, "Yanikian attorney blasts 'harassment' of Foreman," *Santa Barbara News-Press*, May 31, 1973; Dell, "Yanikian jury picked; trial resumes Monday," *Santa Barbara News-Press*, June 1, 1973; *AR*, June 21, 1973.
32. William P. Rogers to American Embassy (Ankara), February 15, 1973, State 028699; *Asbarez*, February 9, 1973; Interview with James T. Lindsey; OK; LK; GY-I.
33. William P. Rogers to American Embassy (Ankara), January 28, 1973, State 016410; William P. Rogers to American Embassy (Ankara), January 28, 1973, State 016444; Memorandum of conversation, March 6, 1973, SD-63/73 POL, TUR-US; GY-I; *AR*, March 22, 1973.
34. William P. Rogers to American Embassy (Ankara), February 15, 1973, State 028699.
35. American Embassy (Ankara) to William P. Rogers, January 31, 1973, Ankara 00757 311416Z; American Embassy (Ankara) to William P. Rogers, January 31, 1973, SD-63/73 POL 23–8, TUR; American Embassy (Ankara) to William P. Rogers, February 13, 1973, SD-63/73 POL 17, TUR-FR; Briefing memorandum

from Rodger P. Davies to Under Secretary for Political Affairs, April 23, 1973, SD-63/73 POL 17, TUR-US; American Embassy (Ankara) to William P. Rogers, April 23, 1973, SD-63/73 POL 17, TUR-US.

36. Memorandum of conversation, April 6, 1973, SD-63/73 POL 17, TUR-US; William P. Rogers to American Embassy (Ankara), April 12, 1973, SD-63/73 POL 23–8, US; William P. Rogers to American Embassy (Ankara), April 13, 1973, SD-63/73 POL 23–8, US; Briefing memorandum from Rodger P. Davies to under secretary for political affairs, April 23, 1973, SD-63/73 POL 17, TUR-US; American Embassy (Ankara) to William P. Rogers, April 23, 1973, SD-63/73 POL 17, TUR-US; William P. Rogers to American Embassy (Paris), April 26, 1973, SD-63/73 POL 17, TUR-US; Document regarding "Armenian demonstrations," April 26, 1973, SD-63/73 POL 17, TUR-US; Document regarding "Protection of Turkish diplomats in the U.S.," SD-63/73 POL 17, TUR-US.

37. William P. Rogers to American Embassy (Ankara), January 28, 1973, State 016410; American Embassy (Ankara) to William P. Rogers, January 28, 1973, Ankara 00645 281606Z; American Embassy (Ankara) to William P. Rogers, January 28, 1973, Ankara 00646 281645Z; William P. Rogers to American Embassy (Ankara), January 29, 1973, State 016576; American Embassy (Ankara) to William P. Rogers, January 29, 1973, Ankara 00662 2912517; William P. Rogers to American Embassy (Ankara), January 29, 1973, State 017122; American Embassy (Ankara) to William P. Rogers, January 31, 1973, Ankara 00757 311416Z; American Embassy (Ankara) to William P. Rogers, January 31, 1973, SD-63/73 POL 23–8, US; American Embassy (Ankara) to William P. Rogers, February 2, 1973, SD-63/73 POL 23–8, US; William P. Rogers to American Embassy (Ankara), February 14, 1973, State 027853; American Embassy (Ankara) to William P. Rogers, March 13, 1973, SD-63/73 POL, TUR-US; American Embassy (Ankara) to William P. Rogers, April 25, 1973, SD-63/73 POL 17, TUR-US; American Consul (Izmir) to American Embassy (Ankara), June 11, 1973, SD-63/73 POL 17, TUR-US.

38. American Embassy (Ankara) to William P. Rogers, January 28, 1973, Ankara 00645 281606Z; William P. Rogers to Mrs. Mehmet Baydar, January 28, 1973, SD-63/73 POL 6–2, TUR; William P. Rogers to Mrs. Bahadir Demir, January 28, 1973, SD-63/73 POL 6–2, TUR; William P. Rogers to American Embassy (Ankara), January 29, 1973, State 016617; American Embassy (Ankara) to William P. Rogers, January 31, 1973, SD-63/73 POL 23–8, US.

39. American Embassy (Ankara) to William P. Rogers, January 28, 1973, Ankara 00646 281645Z; William P. Rogers to American Embassy (Ankara), January 29, 1973, State 016617; William P. Rogers to American Embassy (Ankara), January 29, 1973, State 017122; Document regarding letter from Cevdet Sunay to Richard M. Nixon, February 8, 1973, SD-63/73 POL 23–8, US; William P. Rogers to American Embassy (Ankara), February 14, 1973, State 027853; American Embassy (Ankara) to William P. Rogers, February 15, 1973, Ankara 01171 151527Z; William P. Rogers to American Embassy (Ankara), February 15, 1973, State 028699; William P. Rogers to American Embassy (Ankara), March 9, 1973, SD-63/73 POL 23–8, US; Telegram regarding "Yanikian trial," May 25, 1973, SD-63/73 POL 17, TUR-US; American Embassy (Ankara) to William P. Rogers, May 29, 1973, SD-63/73 POL 17, TUR-US; Telegram regarding "Yanikian case," May 29, 1973, SD-63/73 POL 23–8, US; William P. Rogers to American Embassy (Ankara), May 29, 1973, State 102631, SD-ER.

40. Telegram regarding "Assassination of Turkish officials," January 28, 1973, SD-63/73 POL 23–8, US; William P. Rogers to American Embassy (Ankara), January

28, 1973, State 016410; William P. Rogers to American Embassy (Ankara), January 28, 1973, State 016444; William P. Rogers to American Embassy (Ankara), January 29, 1973, State 016576; William P. Rogers to American Embassy (Ankara), January 29, 1973, State 017122; William P. Rogers to American Embassy (Tunis), February 2, 1973, State 020625; William P. Rogers to American Embassy (Ankara), February 15, 1973, State 028699; American Embassy (Ankara) to William P. Rogers, February 15, 1973, Ankara 01171 151527Z; William P. Rogers to American Embassy (Ankara), February 16, 1973, State 030142; Document regarding "Murder of Turk diplomats," February 16, 1973, SD-63/73 POL 23–8, US; Memorandum of conversation, March 6, 1973, SD-63/73 POL, TUR-US; William P. Rogers to American Embassy (Ankara), March 9, 1973, SD-63/73 POL 23–8, US; William P. Rogers to American Embassy (Ankara), June 18, 1973, State 118342, SD-ER; Henry A. Kissinger to American Embassy (Ankara), December 28, 1973, State 251402, SD-ER; GY-I.

41. William P. Rogers to American Embassy (Ankara), January 29, 1973, State 017122; Memorandum regarding Turks in Massachusetts, January 30, 1973, SD-63/73 POL 17–7, TUR-US; Memorandum of conversation, March 6, 1973, SD-63/73 POL, TUR-US; William P. Rogers to Ronald W. Reagan, March 7, 1973, SD-63/73 POL 23–8, US; William P. Rogers to Richard J. Daley, March 7, 1973, SD-63/73 POL 23–8, US; William P. Rogers to John V. Lindsay, March 7, 1973, SD-63/73 POL 23–8, US; William P. Rogers to American Embassy (Ankara), March 9, 1973, SD-63/73 POL 23–8, US; American Embassy (Ankara) to William P. Rogers, March 13, 1973, SD-63/73 POL, TUR-US; Memorandum of conversation, April 6, 1973, SD-63/73 POL 17, TUR-US; Briefing memorandum from Rodger P. Davies to under secretary for political affairs, April 23, 1973, SD-63/73 POL 17, TUR-US; American Embassy (Ankara) to Secretary of State, April 23, 1973, SD-63/73 POL 17, TUR-US; William P. Rogers to American Embassy (Paris), April 26, 1973, SD-63/73 POL 17, TUR-US.

42. John Dell, "Yanikian trial opens with heavy security," *Santa Barbara News-Press*, May 29, 1973; Patricia Gebhard and Kathryn Masson, *The Santa Barbara county courthouse* (Santa Barbara, CA: Daniel & Daniel, 2001), 11, 13, 29, 30, 38, 83, 85.

43. Dell, "Yanikian trial opens with heavy security," *Santa Barbara News-Press*, May 29, 1973; "Trial begins in slaying of two diplomats," *Los Angeles Times*, May 30, 1973; DDM; William P. Rogers to American Embassy (Ankara), June 27, 1973, State 12464, SD-ER.

44. Dell, "Yanikian trial opens with heavy security," *Santa Barbara News-Press*, May 29, 1973; OK; DDM; Interview with Patricia Montemayor.

45. AFOAM; GY-I; GY-T; JMH; OK; *AR*, February 22, 1973.

46. *California v. Yanikian*, 39 Cal.App.3d 366, 369, 372–73 (1974); GY-T; OK.

47. Appellant's Opening Brief, GY-CM; GY-T; Interview with Bruce Janigian; DDM.

48. DDM; "Oil on troubled waters," *Time*, February 9, 1970; "Costs of an oil spill," *Time*, January 31, 1972; *Union Oil Company v. Minier*, 437 F.2d 408 (9th Cir. 1970).

49. Respondent's Opening Brief, GY-CM; DDM.

50. DDM; Interview with Bruce Janigian; *AR*, March 22, 1973; *Armenian Observer*, April 4, 1973; GY-T.

51. DDM; David D. Minier, "District Attorney regrets not allowing Genocide testimony at murder trial," *Santa Barbara Independent*, April 2, 1998.

52. Dell, "Yanikian jury picked; trial resumes Monday," *Santa Barbara News-Press*, June 1, 1973; GY-T; Appellant's Opening Brief, GY-CM.

53. GY-I.
54. Dalton, "'Perhaps my act will awaken many,'" *Santa Barbara News-Press*, January 29, 1973; AFOAM; OK.
55. *Asbarez*, June 26, 1973; *Armenian Observer*, June 27, 1973; Interview with Patricia Montemayor; DDM; Interview with Bruce Janigian.
56. William P. Rogers to American Embassy (Ankara), June 18, 1973, State 118342, SD-ER; GY-I; DDM.
57. GY-T; GY-I; DDM; John Dell, "Judge rules out testimony on Yanikian manuscript," *Santa Barbara News-Press*, June 27, 1973; "New trial sought in Yanikian case," *Santa Barbara News-Press*, July 13, 1973.
58. John Dell, "Jury ready to get Yanikian trial," *Santa Barbara News-Press*, June 28, 1973.
59. Interview with Patricia Montemayor; "Yanikian verdict due tomorrow," *Santa Barbara News-Press*, July 1, 1973; "Jury reaches verdict in envoy slaying," *Los Angeles Times*, July 1, 1973; John Dell, "Jury finds Yanikian guilty of 2 murders in first degree," *Santa Barbara News-Press*, July 2, 1973; "Armenian guilty in slaying of two Turkish diplomats," *Los Angeles Times*, July 3, 1973. Authorities never figured out who made threatening phone calls to three jurors.
60. Interview with Patricia Montemayor; "Armenian guilty of killing Turks," *New York Times*, July 3, 1973; "Armenian guilty in slaying of two Turkish diplomats," *Los Angeles Times*, July 3, 1973.
61. Dell, "Jury finds Yanikian guilty of 2 murders in first degree," *Santa Barbara News-Press*, July 2, 1973; "Armenian guilty in slaying of two Turkish diplomats," *Los Angeles Times*, July 3, 1973; *AR*, July 5, 1973; *AW*, August 9, 1973; Interview with Bruce Janigian.
62. AFOAM.
63. "Armenian guilty of killing Turks," *New York Times*, July 3, 1973; *AR*, July 5, 1973; *AW*, August 9, 1973; *AR*, December 4, 1975.
64. GY-T; GY-I; Dalton, "'Perhaps my act will awaken many,'" *Santa Barbara News-Press*, January 29, 1973.
65. Francis P. Hyland, *Armenian terrorism: The past, the present, the prospects* (Boulder, CO: Westview Press, 1991), 23–26, 57.
66. Ibid., 26; Markar Melkonian, *My brother's road: An American's fateful journey to Armenia* (London: I. B. Tauris, 2005), 78; Henry A. Kissinger to American Embassy (Ankara), October 26, 1973, State 212031, SD-ER; Henry A. Kissinger to American Embassy (Ankara), October 27, 1973, State 212574, SD-ER. It is not clear whether the 1973 incident orchestrated by the "Yanikian Commandos" is directly linked to Hagopian.
67. The JCAG was said to be affiliated with the ARF; see Alexander M. Haig, Jr., to American Consul (Cape Town), March 11, 1982, State 064897; Alexander M. Haig, Jr., to all diplomatic and consular posts, April 22, 1982, State 108630; George P. Shultz to American Embassy (Tel Aviv), January 4, 1983, State 358302; American Embassy (Ankara) to George P. Shultz, March 30, 1984, Ankara 03158 300826Z; Ternon, *Armenian cause*, 194–96; Hyland, *Armenian terrorism*, 61–68; Khachig Tololyan, "Terrorism in modern Armenian political culture," *Terrorism and political violence* 4, no. 2 (1992): 19–20; *AR*, February 4, 1982; James Ring Adams, "Lessons and links of anti-Turk terrorism," *Wall Street Journal*, August 16, 1983.
68. *AW*, September 26, 1974; *AMS*, September 28, 1974; *AW*, December 12, 1974; *CC*, December 25, 1974; Interview with Dikran Kaligian; Interview with Hagop Sarkissian.

69. Ternon, *Armenian cause*, 196–97; Hyland, *Armenian terrorism*, 235, 238.

70. Ternon, *Armenian cause*, 221.

71. Hyland, *Armenian terrorism*, 35–37; Ternon, *Armenian cause*, 206.

72. Ternon, *Armenian cause*, 168–69, 203, 216–17.

73. Khachig Tololyan, "Martyrdom as legitimacy: terrorism, religion and symbolic appropriation in the Armenian Diaspora," in *Contemporary research on terrorism*, ed. Paul Wilkinson and Alasdair M. Stewart (Aberdeen: Aberdeen University Press, 1987), 92–93; Melkonian, *My brother's road*, 111; DRP; *AR*, February 4, 1982.

74. "Armenian gets life for killing Turkish envoys," *Los Angeles Times*, July 21, 1973; *AR*, March 18, 1976; *AR*, October 28, 1976; *AR*, August 23, 1979; *AR*, July 24, 1980; *AR*, August 14, 1980; Bruce Keppel, "Turkish envoys in L.A. terrorist targets," *Los Angeles Times*, January 25, 1981; Interview with Barlow Der Mugrdechian; OK.

75. *People v. Sassounian*, 182 Cal.App.3d 361 (1986).

76. Eric Malnic and Patt Morrison, "Family offers alibi for consul murder suspect," *Los Angeles Times*, January 30, 1982; CC, February 4, 1982. Perhaps harboring many of the same feelings, his older brother had bombed Arikan's house two years earlier in response to the letter Arikan sent to Yanikian's parole board. See George P. Shultz to American Embassy (Paris), July 19, 1983, State 201778.

77. Donald E. Miller and Lorna Touryan Miller, "Memory and identity across the generations: A case study of Armenian survivors and their progeny," *Qualitative Sociology* 14, no. 1 (1991): 19–37.

78. Ibid., 26.

79. Ibid., 20, 25.

80. E.J. Dionne, Jr., "Death toll climbs to 6 in Orly bombing," *New York Times*, July 17, 1983; E. J. Dionne, Jr., "Paris says suspect confesses attack," *New York Times*, July 21, 1983; *AR*, July 21, 1983; *AR*, March 7, 1985.

81. Edmund S. Muskie to all European diplomatic posts, January 8, 1981, State 005031; Alexander M. Haig, Jr., to all diplomatic and consular posts, December 19, 1981, State 335837; Hyland, *Armenian terrorism*, 41–42; Melkonian, *My brother's road*, 159; Ternon, *Armenian cause*, 231–32; DRP.

82. Ian Black, "Terrorist groups baffle experts in Armenian tactics," *Washington Post*, July 26, 1983; "Parole date advanced for aged killer of 2 diplomats," *Los Angeles Times*, October 21, 1983; Robert W. Stewart, "Armenian found guilty of Turk's murder," *Los Angeles Times*, January 5, 1984; "Paroled assassin of two Turkish diplomats dies," *Los Angeles Times*, February 29, 1984; American Embassy (Ankara) to George P. Shultz, November 10, 1983, Ankara 10050; American Embassy (Ankara) to George P. Shultz, February 28, 1984, Ankara 01983; Hyland, *Armenian terrorism*, 29, 234–37.

83. *AR*, August 14, 1980; *AR*, September 4, 1980; David Wharton, "Armenians mourn man who killed two Turks," *Los Angeles Times*, March 11, 1984; Interview with Barlow Der Mugrdechian.

Legislating History

1. Robert J. Dole and Elizabeth Dole with Richard Norton Smith, *The Doles: Unlimited partners* (New York: Simon & Schuster, 1988), 52–53; Robert J. Dole, *One soldier's story: A memoir* (New York: HarperCollins, 2005), 161, 231–33; Willard Edwards, "Rep. Dole triumphs over his war ordeal," *Chicago Tribune*, March 22, 1964; Martin Tolchin and Jeff Gerth, "The contradictions of Bob Dole," *New York Times*, November 8, 1987; Laura Blumenfeld, "Dropping stoicism about his

war wounds, Dole reveals their strains on daily living," *Washington Post*, May 12, 1996; Michael Duffy and Nancy Gibbs, "The soul of Dole," *Time*, August 19, 1996.

2. Dole and Dole, *The Doles*, 53–55, 58; Dole, *One soldier's story*, 237, 244; *AIM*, "A friend indeed," September–October 1996, 43.

3. Edward Connery Lathem, ed., *The Poetry of Robert Frost* (New York: Holt, Rinehart & Winston, 1969), 222–23.

4. 98th Cong., 1st sess., *Cong. Rec.* 129 (July 27, 1983): S 21104–05; Dorothy Collin, "Dole has the tools to tackle Senate's breakdowns," *Chicago Tribune*, December 2, 1984.

5. Harut Sassounian, comp., *The Armenian Genocide: The world speaks out, 1915–2005* (n.p.: 90th Anniversary of the Armenian Genocide Commemorative Committee of California, 2005), 52; Matiossian, "Haykakan Tseghaspanutian."

6. Memorandum from William P. Rogers to Richard M. Nixon, February 11, 1969, SD-63/73 POL, TUR-US; Memorandum of conversation, May 14, 1969, SD-63/73 POL, TUR-US; 90th Cong., 2d sess. *Cong. Rec.* 114 (March 6, 1968): H 5458; 93rd Cong., 2d sess. *Cong. Rec.* 120 (June 7, 1974): H 18353; *AW*, November 14, 1974; *AMS*, March 15, 1975; *AW*, March 24, 1979; Richard G. Hovannisian, "The Armenian Genocide and patterns of denial," in *The Armenian Genocide in perspective*, ed. Hovannisian, 127.

7. *AW*, October 23, 1982.

8. VZK; Armenian Assembly of America Web site, http://www.armenianheritage.com/asaindex.htm. During the 1980s, the coalition that brought together the Assembly broke down as various groups split off from the umbrella organization.

9. LJM; Stephen Mugar to Thomas P. O'Neill, Jr., November 25, 1974, TPO; Stephen Mugar to Thomas P. O'Neill, Jr., February 7, 1975, TPO.

10. LJM; Henry A. Kissinger to American Embassy (Ankara), June 21, 1974, State 133347, SD-ER; Henry A. Kissinger to American Embassy (Tel Aviv), April 3, 1975, State 075891, SD-ER; American Embassy (Ankara) to Henry A. Kissinger, April 7, 1975, Ankara 02732 070858Z, SD-ER; Robert J. McCloskey to David N. Henderson, April 7, 1975, TPO; American Embassy (Ankara) to Henry A. Kissinger, April 12, 1975, Ankara 02922 121236Z, SD-ER.

11. 89th Cong., 1st sess., *Cong. Rec.* 111 (April 29, 1965): H 8890.

12. Memorandum from George S. Springsteen to Brent Scowcroft, October 25, 1974, White House Central Files: Subject Files, Box IT 10, Folder IT 64–13 United Nations Commission on Human Rights, GRF; Memorandum from A. Denis Clift to Brent Scowcroft, November 1, 1974, White House Central Files: Subject Files, Box IT 10, Folder IT 64–13 United Nations Commission on Human Rights, GRF; Memorandum from Brent Scowcroft to Ron Nessen, November 11, 1974, White House Central Files: Subject Files, Box IT 10, Folder IT 64–13 United Nations Commission on Human Rights, GRF; Memorandum from Jeanne W. Davis to John W. Hushen, December 12, 1974, White House Central Files: Subject Files, Box IT 10, Folder IT 64–13 United Nations Commission on Human Rights, GRF; Memorandum from Robert M. Gates to Jeanne W. Davis, May 29, 1975, White House Central Files: Subject Files, Box HU-12, Folder HU 4 Genocide, GRF.

13. LJM.

14. LJM; DRP; Henry A. Kissinger to American Embassy (Tel Aviv), April 3, 1975, State 075891, SD-ER; *Designating April 24, 1975, as "National day of remembrance of man's inhumanity to man,"* HJR 148, 94th Cong., 1st sess., *Cong. Rec.* 121 (April 8, 1975): H 9246, 9252; *AR*, May 8, 1975; *AR*, April 24, 1975. An

arms embargo arising out of Turkey's invasion of Cyprus strained American-Turk-ish relations, handing the Armenians a more favorable environment in Congress at the time of the vote.

15. House subcommittee on future foreign policy research and development, *Investigation into certain past instances of genocide and exploration of policy options for the future: Hearings on Armenian Massacre, 1915–1918,* 94th Cong., 2d sess., May 11, 1976, 3, 63–65, 68; *AR,* May 20, 1976.

16. Ronald W. Reagan, Proclamation 4838, April 22, 1981, "Days of remembrance of victims of the Holocaust," RWR; "Statement on the Armenian Genocide," April 15, 1980, Armenian Genocide Files, HO 213428, RWR; Interview with Kenneth Khachigian; *CC,* April 17, 1969; *Asbarez,* April 28, 1971; *CC,* November 25, 1982.

17. Andrew Corsun, "Armenian terrorism: a profile," *Department of State Bulletin* 82 (August 1982): 34.

18. Hovannisian, "Etiology and sequelae," 130; Dennis R. Papazian, "'Misplaced credulity,' contemporary Turkish attempts to refute the Armenian Genocide," *Armenian Review* 45, nos. 1–2 (1992): 203; *AR,* April 28, 1983; *AW,* April 30, 1983. Years later, a FOIA request initiated by Van Z. Krikorian revealed that it was not the author—as the department had told Congress—but the agency itself that introduced uncertainty into the characterization of the events of 1915.

19. VZK; *CC,* June 30, 1983; *AW,* April 14, 1984; *AW,* April 17, 1984; *AW,* April 21, 1984; Interview with Dikran Kaligian.

20. American Embassy (Ankara) to George P. Shultz, June 17, 1981, Ankara 04525 180533Z; American Embassy (Ankara) to George P. Shultz, August 17, 1982, Ankara 06765 171512Z; American Embassy (Ankara) to George P. Shultz, September 2, 1982, Ankara 07219 020739Z; American Embassy (Ankara) to George P. Shultz, September 2, 1982, Ankara 07220 020743Z; American Embassy (Ankara) to George P. Shultz, September 10, 1982, Ankara 07508 101615Z; American Embassy (Ankara) to George P. Shultz, September 24, 1982, Ankara 08027 241517Z; American Embassy (Ankara) to George P. Shultz, January 24, 1983, Ankara 00707 241454Z; American Embassy (Ankara) to George P. Shultz, March 2, 1983, Ankara 01938 021437Z; American Embassy (Ankara) to George P. Shultz, July 18, 1983, Ankara 06192 190443Z; American Embassy (Ankara) to George P. Shultz, July 22, 1983, Ankara 06334 221524Z; American Embassy (Ankara) to George P. Shultz, July 22, 1983, Ankara 06318 221335Z; American Embassy (Ankara) to George P. Shultz, March 30, 1984, Ankara 03187 301431Z.

21. Administration position on H.J. Res. 192 and similar resolutions (undated), Armenian Genocide Files, HU030 301529, RWR; George Deukmejian to Ronald W. Reagan, April 13, 1984, James W. Cicconi Files, Series II, Box 6, Armenian-Americans (1), RWR; Memorandum from Robert C. McFarlane to Lee L. Verstandig, April 18, 1984, James W. Cicconi Files, Series II, Box 6, Armenian-Americans (2), RWR; Memorandum from Andrew H. Card, Jr., to Peter R. Sommer, April 18, 1984, Armenian Genocide Files, HO 213428, RWR; Memorandum from Lee L. Verstandig to Michael Deaver, April 20, 1984, James W. Cicconi Files, Series II, Box 6, Armenian-Americans (2), RWR; Memorandum from Lee L. Verstandig to James A. Baker III, May 31, 1984, Armenian Genocide Files, HO 213428, RWR; Memorandum from Robert C. McFarlane to James A. Baker III, June 9, 1984, James W. Cicconi Files, Series II, Box 6, Armenian-Americans (2), RWR; Memorandum from Robert C. McFarlane to James A. Baker III, June 30, 1984, James W. Cicconi Files, Series II, Box 6, Armenian-Americans (1), RWR; Memorandum from James W. Cicconi to James A. Baker III, August 20, 1984,

James W. Cicconi Files, Series II, Box 6, Armenian-Americans (1), RWR; Un-
dated memorandum from Peter R. Sommer to Robert C. McFarlane, Armenian
Genocide Files, HO 213428, RWR; George Deukmejian to Ronald W. Reagan,
April 22, 1985, Christopher Lehman Files, Armenian Resolution File, Box 90513,
RWR.

22. Memorandum from Ed Derwinski to James A. Baker III, September 17, 1984,
James W. Cicconi Files, Series II, Box 6, Armenians (2), RWR.

23. George P. Shultz to Thomas P. O'Neill, Jr., March 4, 1985, Armenian Genocide Files, HU030 292306, RWR; George P. Shultz to Thomas P. O'Neill, Jr.,
November 25, 1985, Armenian Genocide, 1990–1995 Files, 329–96–336, Box
127, Folder 5, RJD; American Embassy (Ankara) to George P. Shultz, December
6, 1985, Ankara 12201 061709Z; Memorandum from Alison B. Fortier to
Frank C. Carlucci, July 31, 1987, Armenian Genocide Files, HO 528887, RWR;
George P. Shultz to all members of the U.S. House of Representatives, August
4, 1987, John H. Sununu Files, Armenian Joint Resolution (1990)[1], OA11D
29135–007, GHWB; Vigen Guroian, "The politics and morality of genocide," in
The Armenian Genocide: History, politics, ethics, ed. Hovannisian, 316–17.

24. "Advertisement—Attention members of the U.S. House of Representatives,"
Washington Post, May 19, 1985; "Advertisement—Attention members of the U.S.
House of Representatives," *New York Times*, May 19, 1985.

25. Kaiser, "Continuities of Turkish denial," 3–15; Vigen Guroian, "Collective re-
sponsibility and official excuse making: the case of the Turkish Genocide of the
Armenians," in *The Armenian Genocide in perspective*, ed. Hovannisian, 141;
Hovannisian, "Patterns of denial," 117; "Turkey's case given away," *New York
Times*, December 17, 1922.

26. Kaiser, "Continuities of Turkish denial," 12–15; Foss, "Turkish view," 258, 270.

27. Hovannisian, "Patterns of denial," 113, 122–25; Rouben P. Adalian, "The ramifications in the United States of the 1995 French court decision on the denial of
the Armenian Genocide and Princeton University," *Revue du monde arménien
moderne et contemporain* 3 (1997): 101n14. Shaw was a student of an earlier
revisionist, Lewis Thomas, see Bloxham, *Great game*, 213–14.

28. "Terrence Des Pres, "Introduction: remembering Armenia," in *The Armenian
Genocide in perspective*, ed. Hovannisian, 10–11; Terrence Des Pres, "On governing narratives: the Turkish-Armenian case," *Yale Review* 75, no. 4 (1986): 518. For
more on Turkey's tactics, see Henry C. Theriault, "Denial and free speech: the case
of the Armenian Genocide," in *Looking backward, moving forward: Confronting the
Armenian Genocide*, ed. Hovannisian, 235–36.

29. Judith Lewis Herman, *Trauma and recovery* (New York: Basic Books, 1997), 7–8;
James Ring Adams, "Facing up to an Armenian Genocide," *Wall Street Journal*,
August 12, 1983.

30. Theriault, "Denial and free speech," 242–46; Staub, "Healing and reconciliation,"
270; Roger W. Smith, "The Armenian Genocide: memory, politics, and the
future," in *The Armenian Genocide: History, politics, ethics*, ed. Hovannisian, 4.

31. George P. Shultz to Thomas P. O'Neill, Jr., November 25, 1985, Armenian
Genocide, 1990–1995 Files, 329-96-336, Box 127, Folder 5, RJD; Mark C.
Lissfelt to John S. Schmotzer, July 13, 1987, Armenian Genocide Files, HO
505420, RWR; Hovannisian, "Etiology and sequelae," 131; Israel W. Charny
and Daphna Fromer, "Denying the Armenian Genocide: patterns of thinking as
defence-mechanisms," *Patterns of prejudice* 32, no. 1 (1998): 40; Talking points to
oppose Armenian resolution (undated), Armenian Genocide Files, HO 528887,
RWR.

32. VZK; *The Hidden Holocaust*, directed by Michael Jones (Panoptic Productions, 1992).

33. Isabel Kaprielian-Churchill, "Armenian refugee women: The picture brides, 1920–1930," *Journal of American Ethnic History* 12, no. 3 (1993); Alexander, "Armenian and American," 91–93; Suny, *Looking toward Ararat*, 218; "200 picture brides come here to wed," *New York Times*, August 3, 1922.

34. VZK.

35. Ibid.; *The Hidden Holocaust*.

36. http://www.armenian-genocide.org/Affirmation.152/current_category.7/affirmation_detail.html; Interview with Harut Sassounian; American Embassy (Ankara) to Henry A. Kissinger, March 5, 1974, Ankara 01623 061801Z, SD-ER; U.S. Mission (New York) to Henry A. Kissinger, March 7, 1974, USUN N 00794 072014Z, SD-ER; Henry A. Kissinger to U.S. Mission (Geneva), August 21, 1975, State 199560, SD-ER; Henry A. Kissinger to U.S. Mission (Geneva), August 25, 1975, State 201928, SD-ER. The American delegation agreed to push for an "even-handed approach" but declined to delete the Armenian Genocide in its entirety unless other participants in the subcommission went along. See U.S. Mission (New York) to Henry A. Kissinger, March 4, 1974, USUN N 00738 042255Z, SD-ER; Henry A. Kissinger to U.S. Mission (New York), March 5, 1974, State 043578, SD-ER.

37. U.S. Delegation Secretary in Athens to George P. Shultz, May 16, 1982, SECTO 07049 161033Z; American Embassy (Ankara) to George P. Shultz, November 6, 1982, Ankara 09172 060749Z.

38. Simon Payaslian, *U.S. foreign economic and military aid: The Reagan and Bush administrations* (Lanham, MD: University Press of America, 1996), xvi, 120–29.

39. Interview with Robert J. Dole; VZK; Interview with Alice A. Kelikian; Memorandum from Barbara Bodine to Robert J. Dole, February 10, 1984, 329-91-263, Box 26, RJD; *AIM*, "A friend indeed," September–October 1996, 43; Giovanna Breu, "Dr. Hampar Kelikian is a dear and glorious surgeon and, at 80, still among the best," *People Weekly*, October 8, 1979, 114; *Armenian Genocide Day of Remembrance*, SJR 212, 101st Cong., 2d sess., *Cong. Rec.* (February 21, 1990): S 1333 (hereafter cited as *AGDR*; February 21, 1990).

40. Hedrick Smith, *The power game: How Washington works* (New York: Random House, 1988), 488–89, 492.

41. RPA; VZK; RV.

42. Presidential candidate questionnaire, June 1988, John H. Sununu Files, Armenian Joint Resolution (1990)[1], OA11D 29135-007, GHWB.

43. Interview with Kenneth Khachigian.

44. RV.

45. Ibid.; Interview with Sheila Burke.

46. Susan Bennett, "Recalling massacre of Armenians tribute turns into hot potato," *Bergen Record*, November 5, 1989; *Armenian Genocide Day of Remembrance*, SJR 212, 101st Cong., 1st sess., *Cong. Rec.* (October 18, 1989): S 13653; *Armenian Genocide Day of Remembrance*, SJR 212, 101st Cong., 1st sess., *Cong. Rec.* (November 3, 1989): S 14647.

47. Memorandum from George H. W. Bush to James A. Baker III, Robert C. McFarlane, Ed Derwinski, August 13, 1984, James W. Cicconi Files, Series II, Box 6, Armenian-Americans (1), RWR.

48. George H. W. Bush to Robert J. Dole, October 13, 1989, HU030, GHWB; George H. W. Bush to George J. Mitchell, November 2, 1989, HU030, GHWB; George H. W. Bush to Thomas S. Foley, November 2, 1989, HU030, GHWB; George H.

W. Bush to Robert H. Michel, November 2, 1989, HU030, GHWB; George H. W. Bush to Richard A. Gephardt, November 2, 1989, HU030, GHWB; Janet G. Mullins to Richard H. Lehman, December 11, 1989, HU030, GHWB. The 1987 Letter Agreement supplemented a more comprehensive agreement on defense and economic cooperation dating back to 1980.

49. State Department briefing, October 18, 1989.

50. Scowcroft was familiar with the Armenian issue. He had taken an identical position on the 1975 resolution while serving in the same post in President Ford's administration. See Memorandum from George S. Springsteen to Brent Scowcroft, October 25, 1974, White House Central Files: Subject Files, Box IT 10, Folder IT 64-13, United Nations Commission on Human Rights, GRF; Memorandum from A. Denis Clift to Brent Scowcroft, November 1, 1974, White House Central Files: Subject Files, Box IT 10, Folder IT 64-13, United Nations Commission on Human Rights, GRF; Memorandum from Brent Scowcroft to Ron Nessen, November 11, 1974, White House Central Files: Subject Files, Box IT 10, Folder IT 64-13, United Nations Commission on Human Rights, GRF; Memorandum from Jeanne W. Davis to John W. Hushen, December 12, 1974, White House Central Files: Subject Files, Box IT 10, Folder IT 64-13, United Nations Commission on Human Rights, GRF; Memorandum from George S. Springsteen to Brent Scowcroft, May 23, 1975, White House Central Files: Subject Files, Box HU-12, Folder HU 4 Genocide, GRF.

51. *Armenian Genocide Day of Remembrance*, SJR 212, 101st Cong., 2d sess., *Cong. Rec.* (February 20, 1990): S 1215 (hereafter cited as *AGDR*, February 20, 1990); *AGDR*, February 21, 1990, S 1349; State Department briefing, October 3, 1989; House Subcommittee on Europe and the Middle East, *Hearings on Developments in Europe, October 1989*, 101st Cong., 1st sess., October 31, 1989, 2; Senate Foreign Relations Committee, *Hearings on foreign policy priorities*, 101st Cong., 2d sess., February 2, 1990; Janet G. Mullins to Richard H. Lehman, December 11, 1989, HU030, GHWB; "Ambassador recalled from Ankara to lobby against Genocide resolution," *Greek American*, October 14, 1989; "Q&A with Ambassador Morton Abramowitz," *Turkish Daily News*, December 14, 1989.

52. *CC*, October 12, 1989; *AR*, October 12, 1989; *AMS*, October 14, 1989; "Parliament asks US Congress to stop Armenian resolution," *Greek American*, October 14, 1989; *AMS*, December 16, 1989; *AMS*, January 20, 1990; David Rogers, "Senate may block call to remember Armenian deaths," *Wall Street Journal*, February 23, 1990; *The Hidden Holocaust*.

53. Speros Vryonis, Jr., *The Turkish state and history: Clio meets the grey wolf* (Thessaloniki, Greece: Institute for Balkan Studies, 1991), 97–98; R. Hrair Dekmejian and Angelos Themelis, *Ethnic lobbies in U.S. foreign policy: A comparative analysis of the Jewish, Greek, Armenian & Turkish lobbies*, Occasional Research Paper No. 13 (Athens: Institute of International Relations, 1997), 40; Morton Abramowitz, "The complexities of American policymaking on Turkey," in *Turkey's transformation and American policy*, ed. Morton Abramowitz (New York: Century Foundation, 2000), 169.

54. *AGDR*, February 21, 1990, S 1349-51; David Rogers, "Senate may block call to remember Armenian deaths," *Wall Street Journal*, February 23, 1990; *AMS*, February 24, 1990; Shawn Pogatchnik, "Armenian remembrance day bid fails Congress," *Los Angeles Times*, February 28, 1990; Larry G. Bowles to Roger B. Porter, October 4, 1989, HU030, GHWB.

55. Alan Weisman, *Prince of darkness: Richard Perle: The kingdom, the power, and the end of empire in America* (New York: Union Square Press, 2007), 65, 116, 118.

56. Exhibit B to Registration statement of Gray & Company Public Communications International, Inc., for representation of Turkey, August 14, 1985, DOJ-FARU; Exhibit B to Registration statement of Gray & Company Public Communications International, Inc., for representation of Turkey, August 4, 1986, DOJ-FARU; Exhibit B to Registration statement of Hill & Knowlton, Inc., for representation of Turkey, September 28, 1987, DOJ-FARU; Exhibit A to Registration Statement of Dewey, Ballantine, Bushby, Palmer & Wood for representation of Turkey Embassy, July 28, 1988, DOJ-FARU; Exhibit B to Registration statement of Hill & Knowlton, Inc., for representation of Turkey, November 18, 1988, DOJ-FARU; Exhibit B to Registration statement of Hill & Knowlton, Inc., for representation of Turkey, July 19, 1989, DOJ-FARU.
57. Exhibit A to Registration Statement of International Advisers, Inc., for representation of Turkish Embassy, January 11, 1989, DOJ-FARU; Weisman, *Prince of darkness*, 118; Yo'av Karny, "Jews and Israeli diplomats try to block a commemoration of the Armenian Holocaust in the U.S.," *Ha'aretz*, October 17, 1989; CNN's Evans and Novak, January 20, 1990.
58. Exhibit A to Registration Statement of McAuliffe, Kelly, Raffaelli, and Siemens for representation of Turkish Embassy, January 18, 1990, DOJ-FARU; Exhibit A to Registration Statement of Thompson & Company for representation of Turkish Embassy, January 18, 1990, DOJ-FARU; Vryonis, *Turkish state*, 98; Yo'av Karny, "Jews and Israeli diplomats try to block a commemoration of the Armenian Holocaust in the U.S.," *Ha'aretz*, October 17, 1989; Wolf Blitzer, "Turkey seeks help of Israel and U.S. Jews to fight U.S. Senate resolution marking Armenian genocide," *Jerusalem Post*, October 24, 1989; "Foreign relations and forgetting," *Nation*, Beltway Bandits, November 27, 1989; David Rogers, "Greek, Turkish lobbyists fear the new winds in east bloc may dry up U.S. military-aid pool," *Wall Street Journal*, January 10, 1990; David Judson, "Armenian lobby flexes muscle," *Gannett News Service*, January 10, 1990.
59. Yo'av Karny, "Jews and Israeli diplomats try to block a commemoration of the Armenian Holocaust in the U.S.," *Ha'aretz*, October 17, 1989.
60. "Israelis said to oppose parley after threat to Turkish Jews," *New York Times*, June 3, 1982; "Armenians to take part in Tel Aviv seminar," *New York Times*, June 16, 1982; "Genocide seminar, opposed by Israel, opens," *New York Times*, June 22, 1982; *CC*, July 8, 1982; Israel W. Charny, ed., *Toward the understanding and prevention of genocide: Proceedings of the International Conference on the Holocaust and Genocide* (Boulder, CO: Westview Press, 1984), 270, 275, 278, 281–92; Ofra Bengio, *The Turkish-Israeli relationship: Changing ties of Middle Eastern outsiders* (New York: Palgrave Macmillan, 2004), 2–3, 45; Abramowitz, "Complexities of American policymaking," 167; http://www.anca.org/action_alerts/action_docs .php?docsid=30.
61. Mark Arax, "Target of Turkish campaign," *Los Angeles Times*, April 22, 1985; Yo'av Karny, "Jews and Israeli diplomats try to block a commemoration of the Armenian Holocaust in the U.S.," *Ha'aretz*, October 17, 1989; Alan Elsner, "Israel seeks to stifle Armenian genocide day," *Fresno Bee*, October 23, 1989; "Armenian bill draws Jewish fire," *Washington Times*, October 23, 1989; Wolf Blitzer, "Turkey seeks help of Israel and U.S. Jews to fight U.S. Senate resolution marking Armenian genocide," *Jerusalem Post*, October 24, 1989; Yair Auron, *The banality of denial: Israel and the Armenian Genocide* (New Brunswick, NJ: Transaction Publishers, 2005), 109.
62. Robert J. Dole to Moshe Arad, October 23, 1989, Armenian Genocide, 1990–1995 Files, 329-96-336, Box 127, Folder 5, RJD; Embassy of Israel to Robert J.

Dole, October 25, 1989, Armenian Genocide, 1990–1995 Files, 329-96-336, Box 127, Folder 5, RJD; Yosef Goell, "The tragedies of other people," *Jerusalem Post*, October 26, 1989; Editorial, *Washington Jewish Week*, November 2, 1989; Moshe Arad to Robert J. Dole, November 9, 1989, Armenian Genocide, 1990–1995 Files, 329-96-336, Box 127, Folder 5, RJD.

63. Akiva Eldar, "MK Sarid denounces Foreign Ministry's attempt to block an Armenian 'Holocaust Day' in the US," *Ha'aretz*, October 19, 1989; Wolf Blitzer, "Turkey seeks help of Israel and U.S. Jews to fight U.S. Senate resolution marking Armenian genocide," *Jerusalem Post*, October 24, 1989; Yosef Goell, "The tragedies of other people," *Jerusalem Post*, October 26, 1989; Gershom Gorenberg, "Israel demeans itself in an affront to Armenians," *Los Angeles Times*, October 30, 1989; Editorial, *Washington Jewish Week*, November 2, 1989; Claudia Wright, "Israel lobby joins Turks to oppose Armenian remembrance resolution," *Washington report on Middle East affairs* (December 1989): 17; Auron, *Banality of denial*, 107–9.

64. Jerry Bier, "Rabbi decries intimidation," *Fresno Bee*, October 24, 1989; John G. Taylor, "Genocide resolution near approval," *Fresno Bee*, November 6, 1989; John G. Taylor, "How Fresno genocide resolution won the day," *Fresno Bee*, November 11, 1989; "Armenians hail Jewish resolution," *Hellenic Journal*, November 23, 1989. Other Jewish institutions also joined in support of the Armenians.

65. *Armenian Assembly of America Information Service Bulletin*, October 18, 1989 (hereafter cited as *Service Bulletin*); AR, October 19, 1989; AGDR, February 21, 1990, S 1328–29.

66. *Service Bulletin*; *Designating April 24, 1975, as "National day of remembrance of man's inhumanity to man"*, HJR 148, 94th Cong., 1st sess., *Cong. Rec.* 121 (April 8, 1975): H 9252; AR, January 4, 1990; AMS, February 10, 1990; CC, February 22, 1990; CC, March 15, 1990; Interview with Dr. Raffy Hovanissian; *The Hidden Holocaust*.

67. 98th Cong., 1st sess., *Cong. Rec.* 129 (April 27, 1983): S 9891–92; AGDR, February 21, 1990, S 1328; *Service Bulletin*.

68. VZK.

69. *Service Bulletin*.

70. Alan K. Simpson to Robert J. Dole, October 30, 1989, Armenian Genocide, 1990–1995 Files, 329-96-336, Box 127, Folder 5, RJD; Exhibit B to Registration statement of Hill & Knowlton, Inc., for representation of Turkey, July 19, 1989, DOJ-FARU; Susan Bennett, "Recalling massacre of Armenians tribute turns into hot potato," *Bergen Record*, November 5, 1989.

71. VZK; Joan Mower, "White House summons Dole over Armenian resolution," *Associated Press*, October 16, 1989; *Service Bulletin*. Days before the committee session, Harut Sassounian, who helped place the Genocide in the 1985 UN report, had asked Carl Terzian, a political public relations expert with ties to Thurmond, for help. Thurmond told Terzian that the administration's pressure led to his about-face and that he would support the Armenians; see CC, November 2, 1989; CC, December 21, 1989.

72. VZK; Robert J. Dole to John H. Sununu, November 20, 1989, John H. Sununu Files, Armenian Joint Resolution (1990)[1], OA11D 29135-007, GHWB; "Turkey acts against U.S. over pro-Armenian bill," *Reuters*, October 18, 1989; State Department briefing, October 26, 1989; Kate McKenna, "Account of Armenian massacre provokes diplomatic storm," *New York Times*, December 3, 1989.

73. At one point, a delegation of Turkish-Armenians arrived claiming the tiny Armenian community in Istanbul would be endangered should the resolution pass, see

Note from Al Lehn to Robert J. Dole (undated), Armenian Genocide, 1990–1995 Files, 329-96-336, Box 127, Folder 5, RJD.

74. *CC*, November 23, 1989; *AMS*, November 25, 1989; *AR*, February 15, 1990; Claudia Wright, "Israel lobby joins Turks to oppose Armenian remembrance resolution," *Washington report on Middle East affairs* (December 1989): 17; "Founder of Maine's Barber Foods dead at 87," *Boston Globe*, November 22, 2008; VZK.

75. VZK; RPA; Office of the Senate Curator, *The U.S. Senate Republican Leader's suite*, S. Pub. 110-6; Richard L. Berke, "The nation; it's hard, learning to be an ex-Majority Leader," *New York Times*, June 9, 1996; Martin Tolchin and Jeff Gerth, "The contradictions of Bob Dole," *New York Times*, November 8, 1987.

76. Rouben P. Adalian, "Finding the words," in *Pioneers of Genocide studies*, eds. Samuel Totten and Steven L. Jacobs (New Brunswick, NJ: Transaction Publishers, 2002), 3–26; RPA.

77. In the 1980s and 1990s, Vahakn N. Dadrian and Richard G. Hovannisian were the most prominent academicians (along with various Holocaust scholars) to produce works on the Genocide.

78. Rouben P. Adalian, "Father Krikor Guerguerian: The scribe of the Armenian Genocide," *Armenia Assembly of America Journal* 16, no. 1 (1989): 5, 10, 16; Adalian, "Finding the words," 16.

79. Adalian, "Father Krikor Guerguerian," 5, 10, 16; Adalian, "Finding the words," 14–19, 25; Rouben P. Adalian, "American diplomatic correspondence in the age of mass murder: The Armenian Genocide in the US archives," in *America and the Armenian Genocide of 1915*, ed. Winter, 148n6; RPA.

80. "Dear Colleague" letter from Robert J. Dole, September 28, 1989, Armenian Genocide, 1990–1995 Files, 329-96-336, Box 127, Folder 5, RJD; *AGDR*, February 20, 1990, S 1209–11. Dole placed blowups of newspaper headlines in the back of the chamber to visually portray the loss suffered by the Armenians, see *Armenian Genocide Day of Remembrance*, SJR 212, 101st Cong., 2d sess., *Cong. Rec.* (February 22, 1990): S 1445 (hereafter cited as *AGDR*, February 22, 1990); RPA.

81. 96th Cong., 1st sess., *Cong. Rec.* 125 (February 1, 1979): S 1683; *AGDR*, February 20, 1990, S 1219–32; *AR*, March 1, 1979; RV.

82. Frank Ahrens, "The unyielding Robert Byrd," *Washington Post*, February 11, 1999; Interview with Sheila Burke; http://www.senate.gov/artandhistory/history/minute/Civil_Rights_Filibuster_Ended.htm.

83. *AGDR*, February 21, 1990, S 1316; Interview with Robert J. Dole.

84. Ahrens, "The unyielding Robert Byrd," *Washington Post*, February 11, 1999.

85. *AGDR*, February 20, 1990, S 1215, 1235.

86. RPA; VZK. For an example of the legislative assistance provided to Dole, see Note and enclosed speech for February 27, 1990, Armenian Genocide, 1990–1995, 329-96-336, Box 127, Folder 5, RJD.

87. *Armenian Genocide Day of Remembrance*, SJR 212, 101st Cong., 2d sess., *Cong. Rec.* (February 27, 1990): S 1692–95, 1705 (hereafter cited as *AGDR*, February 27, 1990).

88. As an example of the preparation, Krikorian sent another Dulles letter to Dole a fortnight earlier, see Van Z. Krikorian to Robert J. Dole, February 12, 1990, Armenian Genocide, 1990–1995, 329-96-336, Box 127, Folder 5, RJD.

89. RPA; VZK.

90. Ibid.

91. *AGDR*, February 21, 1990, S 1319–21.

92. *AGDR*, February 21, 1990, S 1323–27; Israel W. Charny, "The psychological satisfaction of denials of the Holocaust or other genocides by non-extremists

or bigots, and even by known scholars," *IDEA* 6, no. 1 (2001), http://www
.ideajournal.com/articles.php?id=27; Vahakn N. Dadrian, *The key elements in the
Turkish denial of the Armenian genocide: A case study of distortion and falsification*
(Toronto: Zoryan Institute, 1999), 9–10; Adalian, "Ramifications," 114.

93. Scott Jaschik, "Is Turkey muzzling U.S. scholars?", *Inside Higher Ed*, July 1, 2008,
http://www.insidehighered.com/news/2008/07/01/turkey; *AR*, May 31, 2008;
Interview with Donald Quataert; Donald Quataert, "The massacres of Ottoman
Armenians and the writing of Ottoman history," *Journal of Interdisciplinary History* 37, no. 2 (2006): 249, 251–52.

94. Richard G. Hovannisian, "Denial of the Armenian Genocide in comparison with
Holocaust denial," in *Remembrance and denial: The case of the Armenian Genocide*,
ed. Hovannisian, 224; Roger W. Smith, Eric Markusen, and Robert Jay Lifton,
"Professional ethics and the denial of the Armenian Genocide," in ibid., 274–75;
Vryonis, *Turkish state*, 105.

95. Smith, Markusen, and Lifton, "Professional ethics," 278, 280–81.

96. Ibid., 282–83.

97. *AGDR*, February 22, 1990, S 1414, 1428.

98. Adalian, "Ramifications," 112.

99. S.J. Res. 359, May 11, 1920, 66th Congress, 2d Sess.; House Committee on
Un-American Activities, *Soviet Total War: "Historic mission" of violence and deceit.
Vol. 2*, 84th Congress, 2d sess., 1956, 714; http://www.armenian-genocide.org/
Affirmation.388/current_category.6/affirmation_detail.html; House Select Committee to investigate communist aggression and the forced incorporation of the
Baltic states into the U.S.S.R., 83rd Congress, Special Report No. 5, 3.

100. *AGDR*, February 22, 1990, S 1440.

101. *AGDR*, February 21, 1990, S 1326–34, 1338–45, 1402–07; Tony Halpin and
Vartan Oskanian, "Voices on the hill," *AIM*, April 30, 1991.

102. *AGDR*, February 22, 1990, S 1446.

103. Robert J. Dole to George H. W. Bush, June 28, 1989, HU030, GHWB; NSC
profile of September 20, 1989, meeting between Robert J. Dole and Brent Scowcroft, HU030, GHWB; Van Z. Krikorian, "Senate debates, sidesteps action on
Genocide resolution," *Armenia Assembly of America Journal* 17, no. 1 (1990):
13; Michael Kranish, "Dole, Bush clash in Senate debate on Armenia massacre,"
Boston Globe, February 23, 1990.

104. Joan Mower, "White House summons Dole over Armenian resolution," *Associated
Press*, October 16, 1989.

105. Compromise draft of House Resolution 171, April 21, 1983, James W. Cicconi
Files, Series II, Box 6, Armenians (2), RWR; Compromise draft of Senate Resolution 241, October 7, 1983, James W. Cicconi Files, Series II, Box 6, Armenians
(2), RWR; Memorandum from James W. Cicconi to John M. Poindexter, September 17, 1984, James W. Cicconi Files, Series II, Box 6, Armenians (2), RWR;
Memorandum from Peter R. Sommer to John M. Poindexter, December 5, 1985,
Armenian Genocide Files, HO 321111, HO 354734, RWR.

106. RV; VZK; Statement by press secretary Marlin Fitzwater on Armenia's expression
of appreciation to Jeb and George P. Bush for their earthquake relief efforts, May
17, 1990, Public Papers, GHWB.

107. RV; VZK.

108. George Deukmejian to Ronald W. Reagan, April 13, 1984, James W. Cicconi
Files, Series II, Box 6, Armenian-Americans (1), RWR; Memorandum from Robert C. McFarlane to Lee L. Verstandig, April 18, 1984, James W. Cicconi Files,
Series II, Box 6, Armenian-Americans (2), RWR; Memorandum from Andrew

H. Card, Jr., to Peter R. Sommer, April 18, 1984, Armenian Genocide Files, HO 213428, RWR; Memorandum from Lee L. Verstandig to Michael Deaver, April 20, 1984, James W. Cicconi Files, Series II, Box 6, Armenian-Americans (2), RWR; Memorandum from Lee L. Verstandig to James A. Baker III, May 31, 1984, Armenian Genocide Files, HO 213428, RWR; Memorandum from Robert C. McFarlane to James A. Baker III, June 9, 1984, James W. Cicconi Files, Series II, Box 6, Armenian-Americans (2), RWR; Memorandum from Robert C. McFarlane to James A. Baker III, June 30, 1984, James W. Cicconi Files, Series II, Box 6, Armenian-Americans (1), RWR; Memorandum from James W. Cicconi to James A. Baker III, August 20, 1984, James W. Cicconi Files, Series II, Box 6, Armenian-Americans (1), RWR; Undated memorandum from Peter R. Sommer to Robert C. McFarlane, Armenian Genocide Files, HO 213428, RWR; George Deukmejian to Ronald W. Reagan, April 22, 1985, Christopher Lehman Files, Armenian Resolution File, Box 90513, RWR; RV.

109. Richard C. Paddock, "Ignore Turks' pressure on Genocide, Deukmejian asks," *Los Angeles Times*, April 28, 1985.

110. Interview with George Deukmejian; *CC*, February 15, 1990; "Californian removes himself from running for No. 2 spot," *New York Times*, August 5, 1988.

111. Interview with Charles Pashayan, Jr.; National Security Council profile of October 24, 1989, meeting between Brent Scowcroft and Charles Pashayan, Jr., HU030, GHWB; Press Release of Charles Pashayan, Jr., January 11, 1990, John H. Sununu Files, Armenian Joint Resolution (1990)[1], OA11D 29135-007, GHWB; *CC*, February 15, 1990; *AR*, March 15, 1990; *CC*, March 22, 1990.

112. George H. W. Bush to Robert J. Dole, October 13, 1989, HU030, GHWB; George H. W. Bush to Robert J. Dole, November 2, 1989, Armenian Genocide, 1990–1995 Files, 329-96-336, Box 127, Folder 5, RJD; Undated draft of concurrent resolution, Armenian Genocide, 1990–1995 Files, 329-96-336, Box 127, Folder 5, RJD; Undated markup of resolution, John H. Sununu Files, Armenian Joint Resolution (1990)[1], OA11D 29135-007, GHWB; Draft of joint resolution, November 15, 1989, Armenian Genocide, 1990–1995 Files, 329-96-336, Box 127, Folder 5, RJD; Undated markup of joint resolution, Armenian Joint Resolution (1990)[1], OA11D 29135-007, GHWB; Draft of joint resolution, November 14, 1989, John H. Sununu Files, Armenian Joint Resolution (1990) [1], OA11D 29135-007, GHWB; Draft of joint resolution, December 20, 1989, John H. Sununu Files, Armenian Joint Resolution (1990)[1], OA11D 29135-007, GHWB; Charles Pashayan, Jr., to John Sununu, December 14, 1989, John H. Sununu Files, Armenian Joint Resolution (1990)[1], OA11D 29135-007, GHWB; Markup of Karl Samuelian draft of joint resolution, February 6, 1990, John H. Sununu Files, Armenian Joint Resolution (1990)[1], OA11D 29135-007, GHWB; Draft of concurrent resolution, February 15, 1990, John H. Sununu Files, Armenian Joint Resolution (1990)[1], OA11D 29135-007, GHWB; Undated draft of resolution, John H. Sununu Files, Armenian Joint Resolution (1990)[1], OA11D 29135-007, GHWB; Undated draft of resolution, John H. Sununu Files, Armenian Joint Resolution (1990)[1], OA11D 29135-007, GHWB.

113. James S. Roy to Brent Scowcroft, November 7, 1989, John H. Sununu Files, Armenian Joint Resolution (1990)[1], OA11D 29135-007, GHWB.

114. Charles Pashayan, Jr., to John H. Sununu and Andrew Card, Jr., November 1, 1989, John H. Sununu Files, Armenian Joint Resolution (1990)[2], OA11D 29137-008, GHWB; Charles Pashayan, Jr., to John H. Sununu, December 14, 1989, John H. Sununu Files, Armenian Joint Resolution (1990)[1], OA11D 29135-007, GHWB.

115. Markup of Karl Samuelian draft of joint resolution, February 6, 1990, John H. Su-

nunu Files, Armenian Joint Resolution (1990)[1], OA11D 29135-007, GHWB; Undated draft of joint resolution from Barry Zorthian, John H. Sununu Files, Armenian Joint Resolution (1990)[2], OA11D 29137-008, GHWB; George H. W. Bush to Robert J. Dole, February 21, 1990, John H. Sununu Files, Armenian Joint Resolution (1990)[2], OA11D 29137-008, GHWB; George H. W. Bush to Robert J. Dole, February 22, 1990, Armenian Genocide, 1990–1995 Files, 329-96-336, Box 127, Folder 5, RJD; George H. W. Bush to Robert J. Dole, February 22, 1990, John H. Sununu Files, Armenian Joint Resolution (1990)[2], OA11D 29137-008, GHWB.

116. *AGDR*, February 20, 1990, S 1215; *AGDR*, February 22, 1990, S 1447; VZK; Interview with Robert J. Dole.
117. *AGDR*, February 22, 1990, S 1447.
118. RPA; VZK.
119. *AGDR*, February 21, 1990, S 1344.
120. RPA.
121. *AGDR*, February 21, 1990, S 1353; Beth Pechta, "Armenians: Once-bland commemorative proves to be hot potato," *Congr. Quarterly Weekly Report*, February 24, 1990.
122. VZK.
123. *AGDR*, February 21, 1990, S 1328.
124. Dole, *One soldier's story*, 152, 214–16.
125. *AW*, December 30, 1989; *AMS*, January 6, 1990; *CC*, January 11, 1990.
126. 89th Cong., 1st sess., *Cong. Rec.* 111 (April 26, 1965): S 8420.
127. "About face," *Vanguard Press*, March 22–29, 1990.
128. *AGDR*, February 21, 1990, S 1356.
129. *AGDR*, February 22, 1990, S 1431.
130. *AR*, June 16, 1988; Senate Foreign Relations Committee, *Hearings on State Department nominations*, 101st Cong., 1st sess., June 8, 1989.
131. *AR*, November 2, 1989; *AMS*, January 20, 1990; Tony Halpin and Vartan Oskanian, "Voices on the hill," *AIM*, April 30, 1991; VZK.
132. *AMS*, February 3, 1990; *AGDR*, February 22, 1990, S 1419–21, 1425–27.
133. *AGDR*, February 22, 1990, S 1427.
134. VZK.
135. Ibid.; Memorandum from Frederick D. McClure to George H. W. Bush, February 22, 1990, HU030, GHWB.
136. *AGDR*, February 27, 1990, S 1693, 1731.
137. VZK.
138. RPA; VZK.
139. Abramowitz, "Complexities of American policymaking," 165.
140. Michael K. Frisby, "Congress, after emotional debate, authorizes use of force in the gulf," *Boston Globe*, January 13, 1991.
141. Statement on the observance of the 75th anniversary of the Armenian massacres, April 20, 1990, Public Papers, GHWB.
142. Alice A. Kelikian to Robert J. Dole, February 28, 1990, Armenian Genocide, 1990–1995 Files, 329-96-336, Box 127, Folder 5, RJD.

"The past is not dead"

1. VY; *AR*, February 12, 1976.
2. VY.
3. Balakian, *Burning Tigris*, 219–24.

4. Morgenthau, *Ambassador Morgenthau's Story*, 339.
5. Interview with William Werfelman; VY.
6. New York Life Insurance Company to Charles Evans Hughes, November 20, 1922, MM-CM; Sullivan & Cromwell to Charles Evans Hughes, December 12, 1922, MM-CM. For additional correspondence regarding New York Life's claims against Turkey, see Department of State, Office of the Solicitor to Division of Near Eastern Affairs, December 29, 1922, MM-CM; Memorandum by Allen Dulles, January 2, 1923, MM-CM; William Phillips to Sullivan & Cromwell, January 16, 1923, MM-CM; Charles Evans Hughes to American Mission in Lausanne, January 16, 1923, MM-CM; Joseph C. Grew to Charles Evans Hughes, January 29, 1923, MM-CM; and American Foreign Insurance Association to Charles Evans Hughes, June 1, 1923, MM-CM. The Dulles brothers joined Eisenhower's cabinet in the 1950s where they oversaw America's growing military ties with Turkey.
7. VY.
8. Ibid.
9. Balakian, *Burning Tigris*, 226; SMM.
10. Setrak Cheytanian insurance policy, MM-CM; SMM; California Senate Judiciary Committee, *Hearings on S.B. 1915*, May 9, 2000.
11. Balakian, *Burning Tigris*, 232; SMM; Complaint, November 22, 1999, MM-CM; Declaration of Martin Marootian, September 29, 2000, MM-CM.
12. SMM; Complaint, November 22, 1999, MM-CM; Zaven Der Yeghiayan, *My Patriarchal memoirs* (Barrington, RI: Mayreni Publishing, 2002), 199.
13. VY; *CC*, January 18, 1990; Amy K. Spees, "Paper trail," *Daily Journal*, November 8, 2004.
14. SMM; Steve Wasserman, "Author Susan Sontag Dies," *Los Angeles Times*, December 28, 2004. After Seda passed away, Martin moved to San Diego.
15. SMM; VY.
16. "LA lawyer battles giants for Armenian 'genocide' heirs," *AFP*, February 6, 2008.
17. VY.
18. Interview with Eugene R. Anderson.
19. VY; Interview with Brian Kabateck; Laurence Darmiento, "Garamendi appeals approval of quake deals; up front," *Los Angeles Business Journal*, January 27, 2003; http://transcripts.cnn.com/TRANSCRIPTS/0311/25/lkl.00.html; Amy K. Spees, "Paper trail," *Daily Journal*, November 8, 2004.
20. Spees, "Paper trail," *Daily Journal*, November 8, 2004; Interview with William Shernoff; Interview with Brian Kabateck; VY. Kabateck later moved to another building in downtown Los Angeles.
21. *Bodner v. Banque Paribas*, 114 F. Supp.2d 117 (E.D.N.Y 2000).
22. Stuart E. Eizenstat, *Imperfect justice: Looted assets, slave labor, and the unfinished business of World War II* (New York: Public Affairs, 2004), 83, 320–21; "Transcript: the strategies used to achieve non-monetary goals," 25 *Fordham International Law Journal* 177, 202–3 (2001); Michael J. Bazyler, *Holocaust justice: The battle for restitution in America's courts* (New York: NYU Press, 2005), 312, 315, 323; Michael J. Bazyler and Adrienne Scholz, "Holocaust restitution in the United States and other claims for historical wrongs—an update," *ACLU International Civil Liberties Report* (2002), 101–17. Other Holocaust-era cases not of the class action variety also survived dismissal motions, see Bazyler, *Holocaust justice*, 126–27, 245.
23. VY; Interview with William Shernoff; Interview with Frank Kaplan.
24. VY; Interview with William Shernoff; Interview with Brian Kabateck; Interview with Mark J. Geragos; Beverly Beyette, "He stands up in the name of Armenians,"

Los Angeles Times, April 27, 2001; *Marootian, et al., v. New York Life Insurance Company*, 2001 U.S. Dist. Lexis 22274 (C.D. Ca. 2001).

25. VY; Interview with Robert Yousefian; Hrag Vartanian, "New York Life recognizes Genocide era insurance claims," *AGBU News*, April 2004; Declaration of Charles S. Poochigian, October 2, 2000, MM-CM. Reliable population figures of Armenian-Americans in California are hard to come by as many Armenians have changed their names or include parentage of non-Armenian descent.

26. California Senate Judiciary Committee, *Hearings on S.B. 1915*, May 9, 2000.

27. Interview with William Shernoff; Declaration of Charles S. Poochigian, October 2, 2000, MM-CM. Schiff moved on to Congress, where he became a major supporter of Armenian causes.

28. Interview with William Shernoff.

29. New York Life Insurance Company, Press Release: "Agreement in principle reached to settle Armenian claims," April 11, 2001; Quisenberry & Kabateck, Press Release: "Armenian Genocide heirs settle New York Life class-action lawsuit," April 11, 2001; Shernoff Bidart & Darras, Press Release: "Armenian Genocide heirs settle in New York Life class-action lawsuit," April 11, 2001.

30. Joseph B. Treaster, "Insurer to pay Armenian massacre claims," *New York Times*, April 12, 2001.

31. SMM; VY; Interview with William Shernoff; Interview with Brian Kabateck; Beverly Beyette, "He stands up in the name of Armenians," *Los Angeles Times*, April 27, 2001; Zev Chafets, "The ghosts of Armenia," *Daily News*, February 17, 2002; Kristen Kidd, "The lives they kept," *AIM*, April 2002, 25.

32. Memorandum from George J. Trapp to All Home Office Employees, April 23, 2002, Armenian Bar Association; VY; Interview with William Shernoff.

33. VY; Interview with Mark J. Geragos; Beyette, "He stands up in the name of Armenians," *Los Angeles Times*, April 27, 2001.

34. VY; Interview with William Shernoff; Interview with Brian Kabateck; Interview with Mark J. Geragos; http://transcripts.cnn.com/TRANSCRIPTS/0311/25/lkl.00.html.

35. VY; http://www.gsa.gov/Portal/gsa/ep/contentView.do?contentType=GSA_BASIC&contentId=20284&noc=T; http://www.nps.gov/history/history/online_books/sontag/underwood.htm.

36. The account that follows is based on an interview with VY.

37. Ibid.; SMM; *Marootian, et al., v. New York Life Insurance Company*, 2001 U.S. Dist. Lexis 22274 (C.D. Ca. 2001). Poochigian's removal of troublesome provisions miring a previous Holocaust insurance statute allowed the Armenian bill to pass constitutional muster.

38. Memorandum from George J. Trapp to All Home Office Employees, April 23, 2002, Armenian Bar Association; Karen J. Lamp to John V. Pridjian, July 23, 2002, Armenian Bar Association; VY; Interview with William Shernoff.

39. Eizenstat, *Imperfect justice*, 67–69, 123–25, 144, 158–61; "Strategies used to achieve non-monetary goals," *Fordham International Law Journal*, 194; Michael J. Bazyler, "The legality and morality of the Holocaust-era settlement with the Swiss banks," 25 *Fordham International Law Journal* 64, 90–91 (2001).

40. VY; Interview with Mark J. Geragos; Interview with William Werfelman; Interview with William Shernoff; California Department of Insurance, Press Release: "Insurance Commissioner John Garamendi announces settlement on behalf of survivors of victims of the Armenian Holocaust," January 28, 2004; Spees, "Paper trail," *Daily Journal*, November 8, 2004.

41. VY; *AR*, January 31, 2004.

Epilogue

1. Maya Angelou, *On the pulse of morning* (New York: Random House, 1993), n.p.
2. VZK.
3. David L. Phillips, *Unsilencing the past: Track two diplomacy and Turkish-Armenian reconciliation* (New York: Berghahn Books, 2005), 59.
4. Ibid., 53, 85.
5. Ibid., 91–100.
6. VZK; Phillips, *Unsilencing the past,* 109.
7. The ICTJ's report can be found on the organization's Web site, http://www.ictj .org/en/index.html. The ruling also stated that the governing 1948 Convention on the Prevention and Punishment of the Crime of Genocide cannot be applied retroactively to events taking place in 1915.
8. Christine Chinlund, "Should we call it a massacre or a genocide?" *Boston Globe,* May 5, 2003; Gary Bass, Department of Style, "Word problem," *New Yorker,* May 3, 2004.
9. After a committee voted to pass the resolution, it did not make it to the House floor.
10. The letter to Speaker Nancy Pelosi can be found on the ANCA Web site, http:// www.anca.org/; Steven Lee Myers and Carl Hulse, "House panel votes to condemn Armenian killings as genocide," *New York Times,* October 10, 2007.
11. Keith O'Brien, "ADL local leader fired on Armenian issue," *Boston Globe,* August 18, 2007; Keith O'Brien and Matt Viser, "2 members of regional ADL board quit," *Boston Globe,* August 19, 2007; Calev Ben-David, "Inside story: Caught between an Armenian anvil and Turkish hammer," *Jerusalem Post,* October 14, 2007.
12. Response from Ambassador-Designate Marie L. Yovanovitch to Senator Barbara Boxer, http://www.anca.org/.
13. Response from Ambassador-Designate James Jeffrey to questions submitted by Senator Joseph R. Biden, Jr., http://www.anca.org/.
14. Armenians in past generations called the risk of assimilation the "White Massacre."
15. Interview with Brian Kabateck; Nabi Şensoy to Margaret M. Morrow, February 23, 2007 (courtesy of Mark J. Geragos).
16. VY.

Acknowledgments

For a project years in the making, the number of people I need to thank is innumerable. A few individuals deserve special mention.

This book was born in a classroom at the Columbia University Graduate School of Journalism in 2003, so I shall begin there. My classmates prodded and supported me at a time when the book was nothing more than an idea. As for my professor, Samuel G. Freedman, no teacher has ever demanded so much of me and given so much more in return. I am appreciative of his continuing mentorship.

A number of friends and colleagues provided encouragement, advice, and assistance along the way. They include Alice Sparberg Alexiou, Amy Alfano, David Biello, Shira Boss, Harry Bruinius, Lincoln Caplan, Jonathan Englert, Kris Fischer, Haik Hakobian, Susan Harper, Reynolds Holding, Kris Fischer, Dickran Kouymjian, Dana Mackey, Vartan Matiossian, Bedross Der Matossian, Neery Melkonian, the Mesrobian family, Michael Nahabet and family, Garnik A. Nanagoulian, Lindsay Pollock, Sarah Richards, Arto Vorperian, and Phyllis Vine. Vikram Reddy, an endless source of humor throughout the rough patches, put aside his childhood fear of microfiche and retrieved some obscure court records for me. Sophy Chen and Patrick Landers provided me with lodging and home-cooked meals on multiple occasions. Patrick, an undying voice of encouragement, dug up some government archives. Eric Ward also opened the doors to his home. Mark Arax's encouragement meant a great deal to me, as did his willingness to share sources and provide a place for me to stay in Fresno. Finally, Sidney Fine infused in me a passion for history more than a decade ago. That passion never waned and served me well during the preparation of this book.

I interviewed more than sixty-five people in conducting my research. A few of them were particularly helpful and forthcoming, including: Ben Alexander, Bryan D. Ardouny, Michael Berenbaum, George Deukmejian, Robert J. Dole, Mark J. Geragos, J. Michael Hagopian, Missak Haigentz, Aram Hamparian, Paruyr Hayrikyan, David Hovhanissian, Bruce Janigian, Brian Kabateck, Dikran Kaligian, Parsegh Kartalian, Alice A. Kelikian, Osheen Keshishian, Levon Kirakosian, Gerard Libaridian, George K. Mandossian, Linda J. Melconian, Charles Metjian, Jr., Michael Minasian, Set Momjian, Patricia Montemayor, Barlow Der Mugrdechian, Charles Pashayan, Jr., Helene Pilibosian, Hagop Sarkissian, Harut Sassounian, and Manoog S. Young. I gratefully acknowledge Rouben P. Adalian, Robert A. Kaloosdian, Van Z. Krikorian, Seda and Martin Marootian, Ross Vartian, and Vartkes Yeghiayan for spending countless hours answering my questions and opening up their memories and lives to me.

Sam Azadian, Richard H. Dekmejian, Sarkis Keochekian, Razmik Panossian, Ara Sanjian, and most notably David D. Minier shared indispensable materials with me. Walter Karabian was generous enough to arrange for several interviews that opened up many avenues of research.

I also want to acknowledge my research assistants, Taralee Kemp, Rachel Rawlings, Dennis Whitehead, and especially Billy Goldstein, a whiz kid who chased down every request, no matter how obscure.

The librarians and staff of Columbia University were always helpful in responding to my questions. Elsewhere, Diane Barrie at the Ronald W. Reagan Presidential Library, Jirayr Beugekian at *Hairenik*, Jean B. Bischoff and Judith Sweets at the Robert J. Dole Institute of Politics, Bob Bruns at Boston College, Ara Ghazarians at Clark University, Geir Gundersen at the Gerald R. Ford Presidential Library, Beth Hahn at the Senate Historical Office, Zachary Roberts at the George H. W. Bush Presidential Library, Dace Taube at the University of Southern California, and the archivists at the National Archives provided valuable assistance. The staff at the Zohrab Center, including Taleen Babayan, Lucia Vorperian, and its director Rachel Goshgarian, tracked down many sources for me and helped me in countless other ways, as did Sandra Jurigian, Cathy Minassian, and Hripsime Mkrtchyan of the National Association for Armenian Studies and Research. NAASR's director Marc A. Mamigonian deserves immense praise for maintaining a robust collection of Armenian materials that proved indispensable. His ability to track down rare items for me and put me in touch with important sources saved me weeks if not months of time. His bonhomie and interest in this book made my visits to Massachusetts not only productive but enjoyable.

My efforts would have been severely handicapped without Aris Sevag's translations. Aris has a unique talent for language and a professional's eye for detail. Aram Arkun was generous enough to review some chapters, as did Dennis R. Papazian, who also pointed out some critical themes early on in the process. Richard G. Hovannisian shared with me valuable insights and directed me to various important sources. The early chapters of this book would have been impossible to compose without his scholarship.

I am thankful that my agent Jennifer Carlson believed in second chances. Her sincere interest in the subject as well as her guidance and support throughout the process were indispensable.

The improvements made to this book by my editor Dedi Felman are immeasurable. I will be eternally grateful for her belief in me and this project from the beginning to the end. Writing a book is a collaborative effort and I could not have found a better partner than Dedi. The lessons I learned from her will serve me for a lifetime. I also want to thank Michele Bové at Simon & Schuster for navigating the book through its final stages, as well as Elisa Rivlin and Edith Lewis.

Last of all, I want to thank my family. The debates I engaged in with my in-laws, Hampartsum and Marie Ghazarossian, helped me sharpen the themes of this book. This work is a testament to my parents, Antranik and Sheny, and the sacrifices they have made on my behalf. Most of all, my wife Edina stood by me through years of setbacks and triumphs with unwavering love. Her belief in me never diminished and her sacrifices for me never faltered. To her, I owe a debt of gratitude that words cannot communicate. And finally, I am grateful to my daughter Zabelle, whose birth came a few months before I started writing this book. Her joyfulness and affection helped me endure countless stories of death and despair. I hope that by the time she and her generation reach my age, they—the future children of Armenia—will no longer be haunted by the ghosts of the past.

Index

Page numbers in *italics* refer to maps.

Printed in the United States
By Bookmasters